The ACE of Soft Skills

The ACE of Soft Skills

Attitude, Communication and Etiquette for Success

Gopalaswamy Ramesh
Mahadevan Ramesh

Pearson

Original edition, entitled *The ACE of Soft Skills*, 6thedition by Gopalaswamy/Mahadevan, published by Pearson Education Ltd., Copyright © 2010.

Indian Subcontinent Reprint

ISBN 978-8131-732-85-4

First Impression, 2010
Current Impression, 2026

Published by Pearson India Education Services Pvt. Ltd, CIN: U72200TN2005PTC057128.

Head Office: 1st Floor, Berger Tower, Plot No. C-001A/2, Sector 16B, Noida - 201 301, Uttar Pradesh, India.

Registered Office: 6th Floor, Tower A, Unit A and B, International Tech Park, CapitaLand Chennai, 200 Feet Radial Road,Zamin Pallavaram, Old Pallavaram Chennai – 600117, Tamil Nadu, India

Website: in.pearson.com; Email: companysecretary.india@pearson.com

Digitally printed in India by Trinity Academy for Corporate Training Ltd, New Delhi in the year of 2026.

In fond memory of 'Appi' who epitomized lifelong learning,
a cheerful attitude and endeared himself
to people in diverse cultures and age groups

—Gopalaswamy Ramesh

To my mother and to the memory of my father

—Mahadevan Ramesh

Contents

Foreword

Foreword from Industry

A recent report by a global research firm has indicated that the Indian IT industry is targeting multifold growth in exports in the next couple of years. This directly translates to an estimated demand of 850,000 IT professionals and 1.4 million ITeS-BPO personnel. Since Indian academia adds close to 3.5 million graduates and postgraduates every year, on the face of it, this does not seem to be a major challenge. But a large number of these young professionals are not adequately equipped to face the highly competitive and very demanding corporate world of today. Most of their focus in the technology domain remains limited to working as a one-man army reproducing what they read, with little emphasis on application and creativity. This makes it very difficult for them to work in teams. There is a need to polish their skills with respect to disciplines like documentation, systematic processes and all-round excellence.

In my view, the above problem of people not being able to work in teams and not being able to write or follow documentation is a symptom of a more deep-rooted problem—that of a lack of proper imparting of soft skills in aspiring students. We in the corporate sector want the students to be 'industry ready'. By that I mean that they should be able to get into a job and be able to contribute right from day one—they should hit the road running. That is not happening today. The main ingredient missing in the making of a perfect professional is that of non-existence of what goes by the generic term 'soft skills'.

It is in this context that this book *The ACE of Soft Skills* is very relevant, and addresses some of the core issues we need to retrain our students and professionals in. It is rare to find a book that provides in one place a compendium of all relevant skills, starting ground up from the basic attitude and going through the layers of communication and etiquette. From the industry perspective, I think some of the most relevant aspects that caught my eye in this book are the following:

- As we move towards globally distributed teams, which is more a norm than an exception in the IT and BPO sectors, it is essential that the Indian employees should know how to cope with and appreciate *diversity.*
- As India makes more advances in the BPO space, it is likely that the Indian professionals may be performing activities that are essential for business success, but may not be considered glamorous. This calls for the Indian employees to get a panoramic 'big picture', understand and value their contribution to the bigger cause and *take pride* in their contribution.

- Yet another demand placed by the geographic distribution of teams is that the team members must be able to communicate using multiple media like the *phone, e-mail, blogs and tweets*. For a country in which telephones have become mainstream only in the last decade or less, and Internet penetration is still not comparable to other industrialized countries, these are not skills that are very familiar and seldom taught in colleges.
- The Indian IT industry has moved from a pure resource model to a highly respected integrated team model, where the Indian engineers today work shoulder-to-shoulder with their counterparts from the USA and other countries. This requires them to interact in a sense of mutual respect, rather than act in a subservient, subordinate mode. This requires the soft skills of *effective communication* and embellishing with polished *etiquette*.
- As Indian professionals work with the more demanding and highly empowered professionals from other cultures like the ones from the USA, they should learn to be more assertive and know how to *make meaningful commitments and be able to say 'no'* when necessary.
- Finally, if you think I am being too narrowly focused on the IT and BPO segments, consider this: With its growing domestic market and increased wealth building of the middle class, international business houses like manufacturing companies, airlines, retail stores, fast-food chains and financial services companies are increasing and widening their presence in India. Employees in these segments are also going through the same effects of globalization and require the same skills to be able to communicate with, visit and to gel with people from other cultures. It is fair to say that these skills are very unique in that these are absolutely essential irrespective of which profession they are in.

The HCL Enterprise has always been contributing to improving skills of students as well as its employees. We have launched the HCL Career Development Centers (HCL CDC), where we place a significant emphasis on making the aspirants 'industry ready', employable professionals of which imparting the necessary soft skills is an essential part. Our efforts in helping career development would not bear full fruit unless people who have rich practical experience come forward to share their experiences with the community. It is indeed fitting that two seasoned professionals who come from very strong multicultural and multidisciplinary industry backgrounds are writing this book. What is more, their simple, easy-to-read style, adorned by practical examples brings to life realistic scenarios that one faces.

I am sure this book will be an indispensable addition to anyone who wants to get a real perspective on soft skills and aims to go further in his or her career. I wish the authors all the best in repeating and exceeding the success of their earlier books.

Ajai Chowdhry
Founder-HCL
Chairman & CEO-HCL Infosystems Ltd

Foreword from Academia

Over the past four decades, I have been privileged to be associated with such institutions as Carnegie Mellon University, Kellog School of Management, Bauer College of Business in University of Houston, in the USA. In India, too, I have been involved, over the last 20 years, in founding the PGPM programme at MDI, Gurgaon; as the founding faculty and chairman of the faculty of the Indian School of Business (ISB); and, as the Dean, in founding Great Lakes Institute of Management, a reputed and successful institution in India. During this exciting journey, I have had the opportunity to work with and mentor literally hundreds of students from India, who are highly successful in their chosen careers. All these great men and women have a few things in common—that they are not only experts in their chosen fields, but are also the most articulate; their power of compelling communication match their high level of intellect; their strong conviction and pride in what they believe in fuel this intense drive and conviction; their adaptability to multiple cultures and environments make them successful in the global arena. In short, I believe that the success is directly attributable to the appropriate mix of the so-called soft skills in their persona. I have seen this belief reinforced in my association as a board member in Personalitree, which inculcated soft skills in the Indian college students of engineering and management, by making them cultivate the right-brain functions that are so essential for soft skills.

When one of our adjunct faculties, Gopalaswamy Ramesh, approached me with a request for a foreword for a book on soft skills, I was intrigued and had several questions—what new things can be written about soft skills? In what new ways can these be said to create a lasting impression? Upon closer look, I found several things unique about this book:

- By defining soft skills as those skills that are required to succeed in one's environment, the authors have given the most broad-based, appropriate and results-oriented definition of soft skills that I have seen.
- By covering a broad spectrum of topics relating to soft skills—a positive attitude towards oneself and towards the group, taking ownership, dealing with tough situations and so on—this book is significantly more than a quick-fix, spoken-English communication guide.
- This book includes the full range of communication scenarios in a business environment—starting from resumé-writing to interviews to meeting management and proposal-writing—and, hence, would be useful to everyone, regardless of which stage of their career they are in.
- The authors have brought in challenges and solutions relating to the use of modern-era-communication vehicles such as e-mail, phone and text messaging, thus increasing the direct practical relevance of the book. Most of the earlier business communication text books sidestep this important aspect of adapting to these new media.

- The authors have followed a novel approach of using typical work scenarios (which they have called 'Snapshots') to illustrate the concepts and approaches, making the learning highly experiential. The presence of cartoons lightens the reading, without reducing the quality of content.
- A number of graduates from successful academic institutions like the Great Lakes get placed in MNCs. It is essential for these students to get sensitized to the realities of working in multicultural, trans-border, multifunctional teams. This book amply highlights this important area. The authors have also shown that they have a clear pulse of the sensitive areas by covering topics dealing with diversity awareness and how to say 'no'.

I strongly believe that we should ingrain soft skills into our professionals by catching them young. As a part of our social responsibility, Great Lakes is working with a few schools in Chennai and providing exposure and experience to school students to inculcate effective soft skills. This will enable them to hit the road running when they get into college. And we should continually reinforce these skills at all levels, till they become a habit for them.

I am delighted that Professor Gopalaswamy Ramesh, who teaches in the MBA programme at Great Lakes, which nurtures all the values, has put in this effort in co-authoring this book. I would like to suggest that this book and the principles and practices discussed here should be covered at the school level itself and re-emphasized at the college level.

The most important attribute for a student to succeed in soft skills is attitude, if they want to compete with the best of class from the USA and the rest of the world. I am confident that this book will enhance this recognition and make the students and professionals, at all levels, master this aspect. It is certain that all of them will immensely benefit from this book. I wish the authors and the book all the very best in this endeavour.

Bala Balachandran

J. L. Kellogg Distinguished Professor Emeritus of Accounting and Information Management
Northwestern University, Evanston, IL, USA;
Founder and Dean, Great Lakes Institute of Management, Chennai, India;
Executive Professor and Strategy Advisor to the Dean,
Bauer College of Business, University of Houston, TX, USA

Preface

The past decade or so has been an exciting time in India. The behemoth, India Inc. not only woke up, but also has been on a relentless march towards a dominant position in the international business arena. And this is happening against the backdrop of an increasingly globalized world economic order and to the sounds of revolutions in telecommunication and information technologies. The growth hormone that is driving this process is the millions of young men and women professionals of India who design electronic chips, develop software, manage off-shored infrastructure remotely and answer phone calls in BPO call centres. As the world gets even more globalized and as India's competition is trying to chip away at its advantages, it is crucial that India's workforce remains world-class, through re-training and continued improvement and that a steady stream of fresh men and women are groomed in the art and science of being professionals. We believe, based on our personal experience in various capacities, that to create and nurture successful professionals, one needs to instil in them a strong measure of the so-called soft skills. It is our opinion that to succeed in today's—and tomorrow's—competitive environment the acquisition, cultivation and fine-tuning of soft skills is highly essential. This book is born out of our desire to articulate this point of view, and be a part of this educational process that produces top-notch professionals.

'Soft skills' is an abstract (and somewhat nebulous) concept, which is, in fact, a compendium of several components like attitude, abilities, habits and practices that are combined adeptly to maximize one's work effectiveness. They are much more than just a set of good habits or key abilities. Soft skills are about integrating the right proportion of these components into formidable skills and eventually transforming those skills into competencies. Our first task in this book is to demystify what one means by soft skills, and then, to provide a fairly comprehensive list of such skills in an organized and systematic manner. We then proceed to examine and analyse each of these skills in detail.

We believe that soft skills are not just the icing on the cake, but part of the dough itself. Good soft skills have their roots in a strong and healthy attitude, of feeling good about oneself and being able to relate to the environment better. This attitude will be reflected in effective communication, polished by proper application of etiquette appropriate to a given situation. It is, in our view, essential that all the three components—attitude, communication and etiquette—get their due importance and attention, and in that order. You cannot have good communication gushing out of a poor attitude, nor can you sugar-coat poor communication with etiquette that is superficial. That is why we have organized this book into the three parts—Attitude, Communication and Etiquette (ACE), in that sequence. The unique approach we have tried in this book is to get a *holistic* coverage of the attitude, communication and etiquette dimensions, focusing attention on basics (not complicated theories), detail-orientation through examples and emphasizing ethics and flexibility. Perhaps, a more complete title for this book could be the ABCDEF (Attitude, Basics, Communication, Detail-orientation, Etiquette and Ethics, and Flexibility) of soft skills, but for reasons of brevity and sharper focus, we stay with the ACE of soft skills.

Our effort is mainly aimed to help those young professionals who are just starting out their corporate careers. This book should be an ideal companion to company-sponsored orientation programmes for new employees. Undergraduate students nearing graduation would also find this text useful and may want to incorporate this in their preparation for campus interviews and so on. This can be used as an ideal textbook for a one- or two-semester, non-credit or informal course during the final year of engineering or MBA/MCA courses. Even experienced employees and managers will find this book useful and HR departments should be able to design short courses and workshops based on the material covered in this book. This is a values-based book and, therefore, one can view this book as a general book on work ethics and organizational behaviour, whether you work in the corporate sector or not.

We have designed this book to mean different things at different levels. At one level, this is a self-help book to be read and discovered by a reader at his or her own pace and in his or her own sequence of topics. To facilitate the non-linear reading of this book, we have included a lot of hypothetical case studies ('snapshots'), boxed examples, tables, diagrams and detailed cross-references to related topics elsewhere in the book. We would like this book to be a comprehensive tool in one's career growth plans and be an effective handbook, to be referenced again and again. We don't aim to be an encyclopaedia of soft skills, but we have tried to capture the essence.

This is the culmination of nearly sixty person-years of combined experience the authors have between them—years spent working in international teams in multinational corporations, universities and research establishments—an experience that spans not only India and the USA, but also other countries such as Singapore and the UK. Our book is based on our collective work experience and on the best practices of corporate houses and other organizations, as we inferred them.

We owe a tremendous measure of gratitude to all our present and former colleagues from whom we learnt many things. Some of them were amazing corporate citizens who embodied not only the best in soft skills, but also set themselves as examples for others to follow. We are also grateful to the editorial staff of Pearson Education, especially Ms Anindita Pandey and Ms Sukanya Chakrabarti, for their detail-orientation in the editing process as well as during the final production. We would also like to thank our artist Mr Laxmi Pillai for his lively drawings. And finally, we would like to thank our respective families for their unflinching support during the long days of writing this book.

We hope this book proves to be a veritable source on soft skills.

Gopalaswamy Ramesh (gopalaswamy_ramesh@yahoo.com)

Mahadevan Ramesh (mahadevan_ramesh@hotmail.com)

Acknowledgements

I would like to express my sincere thanks to Prof. H. N. Mahabala, who has been a source of inspiration and guidance to me throughout my life. My desire to write a book on soft skills stemmed from a course on ethics that I co-offered with Prof. Prabhu of IIIT, Bangalore. Prof. Prabhu's inspiring lectures and the long hours of discussion we have had made a deep impression on me and some of these are captured in this book. I also owe a debt of gratitude to Mr R. Vidyasagar, Senior Director, Human Resources in EMC^2 India, Bangalore, with whom I have bounced off various ideas during the early stages of conceptualization of this book. I also want to thank my daughter, Vyshnavi, and son-in-law, Ashish, and my son, Venkatesh, for being my 'beta test' audience and giving me the 'next generation feedback'. I want to thank my wife, Lakshmi, for her patience and understanding in my spending countless hours in this as well as my earlier books.

—Gopalaswamy Ramesh

I would like to thank Mr Pradeep Ravi of IBM (USA) for sharing a lot of his international experience and insights with me. Thanks are also due to Mr A. Ganesh, Avaya (USA), for his useful inputs.

—Mahadevan Ramesh

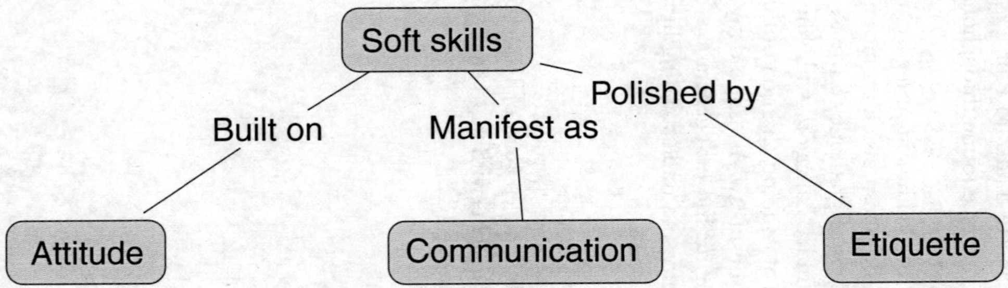
Soft skills
Built on
Manifest as
Polished by
Attitude
Communication
Etiquette

1

Let Us Get Started!

"Bigness comes from doing many small things well. Individually, they are not very dramatic transactions. Together, though, they add up."
–Edward S. Finkelstein

The corporate world has always been the preferred career destination of many young men and women; not merely because corporations are perceived to be good paymasters, but also because they are thought of as very fair places, which recognize and reward employee excellence. Competition to get a job in these corporations, especially in some prestigious multi-national corporations (MNCs), is so severe that these companies resort to a long and arduous recruitment process punctuated by resumé-screening, aptitude tests and multiple levels of interviews. Their HR departments are fine-tuned not only to filter out inappropriate candidates, but also to spot talent and pick out those who have that 'certain something' in them that will make them highly effective and special.

Once the best and the brightest are recruited, corporations always tend to nurture their employees throughout their careers and actively encourage them to reach newer and newer levels of personal excellence. They know that employees are their biggest asset and that a high-quality workforce makes a direct difference to the company's growth, finances and competitive advantage. For their part, employees with the 'right stuff' would often take advantage of the system and grab the career growth opportunities offered to them by their employers. They would try all avenues like self-improvement, learning new tools and technologies and impeccable execution to distinguish themselves from the crowd and go on to have glorious careers. History is full of examples of people with phenomenal corporate careers and personal excellence, and corporate superstars like Jack Welch, Indra Nooyi and Narayana Murthy are such well-known names that they have become role models for thousands of young men and women who are just starting their careers.

But what do we mean by this 'certain something' or the 'right stuff'? What goes into someone getting sought after by top corporations and eventually having a successful career? How come some people manage to rise from the lowest rungs of the corporate ladder to become the CEO of their company? How is it that some of the most successful people in the corporate world were often not class toppers in college? Can it be that some men and women are predestined for success? Even a cursory look at the lives of successful people in a corporate setting reveals that they set themselves apart through their vision, hard work and by being skilled, among other things. While hard work and vision are reasonably easy concepts to comprehend, the term 'skills' is more general and complex and needs to be understood more carefully. It is a term encompassing a whole range of abilities, right from technical skills to emotional intelligence to how to manage one's time. But we can broadly divide them into two categories—the technical or 'hard' skills and a whole bag of non-technical skills classified as 'soft' skills. Soft skills complement hard skills and make one's efforts much more effective. But, unlike hard skills on which one can put a finger, there is an air of mystery to soft skills and what it includes. As important as hard or technical skills are, the corporate world also puts tremendous emphasis on soft skills. Not just that, it looks out and recruits people with exceptional soft skills from among the pool of technically skilled people. Within its own workforce, an organization always gives importance to employees with great soft skills.

In the last few decades in India, there has been a mushrooming of demand for well-rounded employees—people who are not only technically savvy, but also have the complementary soft skills. This spurt in demand is essentially due to a large increase in corporate employment opportunities. These increased opportunities arise due to new foreign-based multi-national corporations setting up shop in India, existing multinational companies that are expanding their operations in India and the emergence of modern Indian companies, especially in the information technology (IT) and IT-enabled Services (ITeS) sectors. India's splash entry into an increasingly globalized world commerce meant that for continued growth, there must be a steady supply of highly skilled workers to satisfy the needs of industries. While India's technical schools and colleges have done a great job of imparting world-class technical training, concepts like soft-skills training are only now beginning to take root. For 'Advantage India' to work, and for India to be competitive in the world arena, several educators and employment consultants have suggested that we re-double our efforts in educating our college students and young professionals in the virtues and basics of soft skills. We believe that already giant steps are being taken to achieve a high degree of 'soft-skills literacy' through formal and informal channels and we see our book as just a part of these efforts.

Now, the concepts of soft skills and professionalism have percolated down to other spheres as well—beyond the campuses of the corporate world. It is now considered generally a good idea to inculcate a measure of soft skills into anyone's skill-set, as a way of charging him or her with skills for life and as a lesson in civics.

So what are soft skills anyway? The best way to answer this question is to actually examine some of the popular notions about soft skills.

1.1 Characteristics of Soft Skills

While there is no formal definition of the term, we would like to define soft skills *as those skills—over and above the technical knowledge and expertise in the chosen field—required for an individual to relate to and survive and succeed in his or her environment.* This definition—just like soft skills itself—is very open-ended and subjective. But that is how it is! 'Soft skills' is an oft-used term in hiring parlance, but is perhaps the most maligned, often misunderstood and misinterpreted term. We will now characterize what we mean by this term and also highlight what we strongly believe soft skills are not.

Soft skills is that 'touchy-feely stuff': It is not pure technical wizardry; it is not just 'pleasing personality'; it is not just 'smooth talking'; it is not just 'command over language'; it is a combination of all these things and many more attributes that are difficult to lay your hands on. This combination varies from time to time, culture to culture and situation to situation to be successful.

Soft skills are conspicuous by their absence in an individual: Well, if it is possible to recognize the presence of soft skills in an individual, it is most certainly possible to detect the absence of soft skills in an individual. In fact, soft skills tend to be more conspicuous by their absence than by their presence! This is somewhat like the view of a cynic who knows that 'something is wrong' in a thing without being able to tell what to do to make it right or what constitutes the right thing.

Soft Skills apply across the board to any industry: Whether you work in the IT industry or manufacturing industry, whether you work in a family business or a multi national corporation, soft skills are those skills that are absolutely essential for success. Since we have defined soft skills to be those needed to survive in the environment and since any profession has to exist in the context of the environment, it makes sense that soft skills apply across the board to all human endeavours and to all industries.

Soft Skills are not 'quantifiable' and tend to be subjective: One can never assign an undisputed numeric Soft Skills Quotient or 'SSQ' to an individual as one can assign a numerical Intelligence Quotient or 'IQ' (of course, even IQ numbers have always been questioned by various people). This makes it very difficult to 'measure' soft skills. This is so because the specific soft skills required vary from person to person, and as stated, from culture to culture and even from situation to situation.

Soft Skills are seldom taught, but often caught: We believe that practical soft skills cannot be formally taught in the same way as you can teach engineering principles or mathematics but people learn more by observation and example setting. Soft skills are somewhat like survival instincts wherein people get fine-tuned and adapt to their environment. The approach to be followed to inculcate better application of soft skills in people is to tune their antennae to catch the soft skills.

Defining how good a person's soft skills are is somewhat culture dependent: For example, in the Indian context, being assertive and vocal may be considered 'poor soft skills' while in the US context, the lack of these attributes may be termed a weakness.

1.2 Misconceptions About Soft Skills

Let us also highlight some of the misconceptions that we have heard people have about soft skills:

'Soft skills' equals good language command and vocabulary: Words and language are important alright, but being able to use mere empty poetic words or big fourteen-letter words (that seldom find any use outside the GRE!) is no measure of possession of soft skills. It is just like a programmer saying 'I know the complete syntax of Java and hence I can program well in Java!' We hear of people, who to become better soft-skilled, try hard to improve their vocabulary of complicated English words! We have also seen quite a few training institutes claiming to offer 'soft-skills training', but all they do is to teach (what they think is) 'good English' by teaching what is meant by synonyms, antonyms, propositions, articles and other elements of English grammar. Sure, soft skills are about being able to apply the right language at the right time and at the right place. But, there is much, much more to them.

'Soft skills' equals good talking: Soft skills are often equated to communication and more specifically to spoken communication. While these are no doubt essential aspects of soft skills, we believe that there are more fundamental aspects we need to address for acquiring strong soft skills. If indeed soft skills are the same as good talking, then it follows that the people with the best soft skills are theatrical nimble-tongued politicians! That is why we believe that focusing excessively on oral communication is not a panacea to better soft skills.

'Soft skills' is essential to management jobs but not for 'technical' jobs: You will find this very often when you are discussing promotions and career paths. 'Oh, this guy is not fit to be a manager because he lacks soft skills, so let him remain a technical person.' While the first half of the argument, that he can't become a manager because he lacks soft skills is true, the second part—that he can remain a technical person because he lacks soft skills—is absolutely baseless. Whatever be the nature of the job you are in—technical , managerial, administrative, etc.—soft skills are absolutely essential. Don't try to 'develop' soft skills in an individual 'just in time' before taking on a management role. It simply won't work.

Soft skills eliminate the need for 'hard skills': If the previous fallacy was that 'techy skills' or 'hard skills' obviate the need for soft skills, there are also people who think they can succeed just because they are highly social and can talk about any topic with apparent conviction, i.e., they believe that one can succeed with just 'soft skills' and no 'hard skills'. One of the main messages we want to convey in this book is that soft skills are not the same as being able to talk to everyone with flowery language and conning everyone without knowing the details. Soft skills are not a camouflage for the lack of basic 'hard skills'.

People with soft skills are born, not made: This is probably one of the most widely held misconceptions about soft skills. Most people make excuses like 'I am a very shy individual' or 'I am not a politician to keep talking' or 'Well, this is not like programming or riding a bike that I can learn—this is more like my appearance, which cannot be changed easily'. All these arguments (which are misconceptions) presuppose that soft skills run in the blood and cannot be changed unless you transfuse new blood! Soft skills, like any other skills, can be honed by an individual just as he or she can hone programming skills or bike-riding skills or cooking skills. We may not be able to fully 'teach' soft skills (as we could teach say a programming language), but we can certainly awaken the sleeping giant in each individual to be better equipped in soft skills. We talk about soft skills so that you can ponder over it and discover its aspects rather than 'teach' you per se.

1.3 Dimensions of Soft Skills

We believe that soft skills essentially comprise three dimensions: what we call 'ACE' - ***A***ttitude, ***C***ommunication and ***E***tiquette. *Attitude* is about having the right mental make-up and a desire to interact with the people and environment. This also requires willingness and ability to fine-tune and blend oneself with the environment. *Communication* is the ability to express that attitude, conviction and technical skills in a form that can effectively reach the intended audience and persuade them to take the actions that one desires them to take. *Etiquette* are those commonly accepted protocols, norms and conventions that are needed to be followed to achieve effective communication (see Figure 1.1).

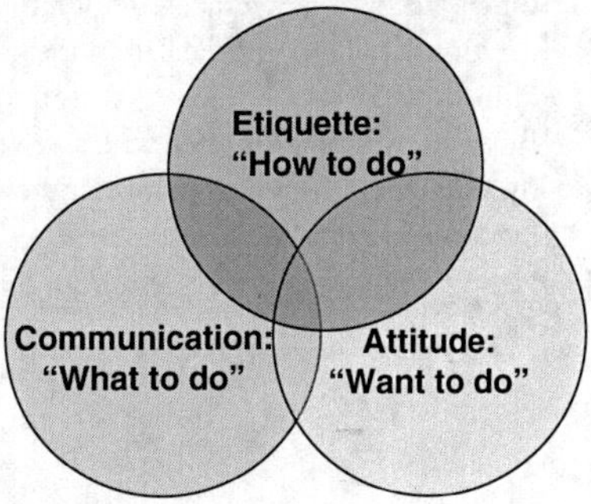

Fig. 1.1 *ACE dimensions of soft skills*

'ACE' is not unique to just soft skills—these are applicable across the board to any human endeavour. To succeed in any chosen profession or activity, one must '*want to do*' that profession or activity. Engaging in something that one is not passionate about will not bring success. The 'attitude' component is nothing but this 'want to do'. Building on this strong foundation of 'want to do' is gaining the basic knowledge of '*what to do*'. If the chosen field was, say, software, then the knowledge component would map to knowing about programming languages, development tools and databases. Knowledge for soft skills maps to 'communication'. By and large, as strong basic knowledge is essential for success in a chosen field, so also communication is essential for success in soft skills. Raw knowledge, by itself, would not be sufficient to succeed. A practitioner should be able to adapt, fine tune and apply the knowledge gained to different scenarios and situations. This '*how to do*' builds upon knowledge and graduates to 'skills'. For soft skills, this 'how to do' part corresponds to etiquette—how you adapt your communication styles and methods to suit different cultures, conventions, protocols and media.

An effective 'soft-skilled' person has a good mix of all these three dimensions of ACE. It is impossible for any one book or individual to address all the aspects of these

Snapshot 1.1

Assume that you are walking into someone's house. What catches your eyes? Perhaps the pleasing colours of the interior, perhaps the artistic paintings hung up on the wall and perhaps the neat manner in which the house is maintained. This is what immediately grabs your attention. You may also notice the well planned, airy, rectangular rooms. What you most likely do *not* notice is the strong foundation of the building. You almost take it for granted. Without the strong foundation, the physical structure would not be strong. If the physical structure was weak, no amount of flashy wall colours or pleasing pictures will serve any purpose.

Attitude is like that foundation. This is the very basis for the entire building called soft skills. Without strong attitude and a basic system of beliefs, soft skill cannot blossom. Often, we don't pay much attention to attitude, much as we don't ever get to look at the foundation. Communication is the strong physical structure which is built on top of the foundation. We do see parts of this in individuals when we interact with them. But what we see most often when we work with people is their external manifestation—the etiquette. It is hoped that by addressing all the three dimensions—of attitude, communication and etiquette—the reader gets a holistic picture, both from the point of view of developing oneself and from the point of view of interacting with others.

Fig. 1.2 *The analogy of foundation—physical structure—external appearance of a house for the ACE dimensions*

dimensions, because not only are there a huge number of aspects but these aspects also span multiple and diverse subjects like psychology, human behaviour, language skills, etc. We don't profess to be experts in all these fields. The purpose of this book is to cover those aspects of each of these dimensions which we believe are very important from the point of view of working in trans-cultural, geographically distributed teams, with a distinct focus on working with US teams and teams in India. We believe that the aspects we have discussed in this book are necessary and essential but they are by no means exhaustive or sufficient for success of such teams.

1.4 The Changing Business Environment and Its Impact on Soft Skills

The business environment has changed significantly over the past decade or so largely due to the advent of the Internet and the convergence of computing and communication. As in the ex-US President, Ronald Reagan's call, 'Tear Down That Wall', technology has changed business dramatically, changing the world to be a global village, or as Thomas Friedman said where geography is history, where boundaries are shrinking (or even vanishing) and cross-cultural interaction is more a norm than an exception.

In most businesses today, work almost seamlessly flows across geographies. If you take the example of the manufacturing industry, raw materials may come from India, assembling can take place in Taiwan, the finished goods may be transported to and sold in the US. An employee in Australia may enter his expense report into a central system, this may get processed by a BPO outfit in India and the payment may be made through an American bank.

This cross-border workflow has necessitated increased communication and has placed additional demands on soft skills. One may have to interact with many, many people from different cultures. Both the quantity and diversity of interactions have increased substantially. This brings about several additional challenges.

First is the *linguistic* challenge. An individual should be able to articulate his or her thoughts so as to cross the language barrier. Even between India and the USA where one can argue that English is the common language, the usage and conventions used are different. We have dedicated one full chapter to typical differences in the way English is used in the USA vs the way it is used in India (Chapter 39).

A second challenge is the *cultural* challenge. As we have said earlier, soft skills transcends communication. The diversity of cultures in different countries has necessitated that people adapt themselves to the cultures of each of these countries. When interacting with people from more than one country (as is typical with trans-national teams), this quick adaptation becomes a serious challenge.

A third challenge—perhaps where the effect of technology is highest—is the proliferation of the different *media of communication and collaboration.* Communication and collaboration today has to be effective through various means like e-mail, chat[1], video conference, phone calls as well as face-to-face meetings.

---

[1] By chat we mean computer chat or instant messaging.

The ACE dimensions acquire additional hues because of these challenges. For example, the attitude part must now address the linguistic and cultural aspects of having to work in environments completely different from what one is used to. This leads to topics like diversity awareness, which otherwise would not be discussed. The new media of communication require a person to adapt himself or herself to them. For example, a person may have to get used to the SMS culture of sending messages vis-à-vis the traditional (perhaps easier and more expensive) route of talking on the phone. In this book, we would be covering some of these complex dynamics of interaction between the ACE dimensions and the emerging global business environment.

1.5 What (and What Not) Is This Book About?

This book is for the modern Indian professionals, to make them more effective in their interactions with their international business partners. Being from India provides one with several unique advantages in terms of soft skills, which can be leveraged effectively. For example, most Indian professionals pick up sufficient knowledge of English grammar and usage in their college years. They may only need to 'tweak' it a bit to reach the next level of competence. No wonder we have a proliferation of call centres that are able to train a large number of people in a short time to meet the international standards in spoken English. Indians generally know several languages and this gives Indians a big advantage over mono-linguistic cultures in terms of the ability and ease to learn a new language. India is also a pluralistic society with various ethnic, religious and social groups and this gives an awareness and insight into other belief systems, cultures and values. This sensitivity will be definitely useful when interacting with an ever-shrinking world, populated by many unfamiliar cultures. Above all, India has a rich history of democracy and freedom, which has empowered the people in ways that people in some other countries can only envy. In this book, where appropriate and possible, we have tried to highlight such strengths that come inherently from the Indian ethos that can be leveraged upon to build effective soft skills.

The same factors above can also act as negatives. Even though most educated people speak reasonably good English in India, Indians sometimes do not adapt and change with the times. English in India tends to be archaic and a remnant of the British Raj. Added to this is a modern generation growing up on Internet chats and SMS messaging. There is a danger of Indians using a peculiar brand of English that may help to communicate with immediate friends, but will not be understandable to an American colleague at the other end of a telephone. Also, we may be language experts, but very few of us have enough knowledge of international languages like Japanese, French or Spanish. Our pluralistic society can sometimes give rise to tensions and irrational fears and some of us can be very parochial, resorting to stereotyping. Years of endemic feudalism is the reason why we tend to punctuate our sentences with 'sir' when we talk to our immediate bosses, while our American counterpart doesn't think twice about addressing his manager by his first name. Finally, our sense of unlimited freedom of expression may cause an occasional Indian professional to become an office 'loose cannon' that might be detrimental to any corporation.

This book attempts to look at some of the above Indian aspects of how to acquire soft skills that are relevant to the global marketplace, specifically addressing the USA. As people from India, what are the skills we must hang on to and further develop? What are the skills that we need to polish and hone or merely tweak? What are the skills that we need to acquire through proper training? And what are the traits that we need to completely get rid of? Should we make wholesale changes in our skill-set and mindset? What kind of introspection is needed to make this process easy? What are the soft skills elements that the international business community worships and how does an Indian professional glean such things? These are some of the difficult questions that we have strived to find an answer to in this book.

There is another side to this book too. This book can be equally useful to that international business-person who hopes to do business in India. This book, in its own way, will sensitize them to the Indian professional and their paradigm. If an American customer addresses his Indian software developer as Gupta-*ji* or talks about four *lakhs* of rupees, it will go a long way in fostering better business relationships across the borders.

This is not a simple 'how-to' book. When we talk about e-mail etiquette and resumé writing, we don't intend to offer you a ready template to send your next e-mail or resumé. Rather, we point out those ingredients embedded in what is considered a good resumé or an appropriate e-mail. Our intention is to take you outside the world we are in and look at ourselves from the outside through a window. Simultaneously, we are also going to let you have a peek through another window, at the standard international business practices.

We also don't delve into the psychological and sociological factors that go into the making or acquiring of soft skills. There are many books written about the nature-vs-nurture debate, cross-cultural studies and theoretical frameworks. We merely present our observations and remarks based on our years of experience in the international corporate setting and classroom teaching. We avoid passing judgement on whether the business world is right or wrong in its insistence of a particular set of skills.

1.6 Organization of Rest of the Book

This book is organized into three parts—along the three dimensions of attitude, communication and etiquette.

Attitude is the foundational aspect of soft skills and is further divided into attitude about self and attitude towards others. Oftentimes, lack of the attitudinal component is the root cause for poor communication and ensuing soft skills. We believe that a more conscious awakening of setting the right internal attitude is the first step towards better fitting into the environment. Hence, the first part is dedicated to attitude.

The second aspect of soft skills that we cover—and put most extensive focus on—is the area of communication. Indian professionals need to cut to the chase and communicate with the world effectively. This would surely improve our stakeholders' value. The communication section has three parts—the first part covers the basics of communication, the second part covers the elements of communication and the third part covers the different communication scenarios.

We would caution our readers that even though communication forms the bulk of the chapters in this book, it is not the be-all and end-all of effective soft skills—it has to exist in the context of attitude and etiquette.

The etiquette section is divided into three parts for media etiquette, travel etiquette and miscellaneous (or other) etiquette. We don't claim our treatise to be one that covers all aspects of a cross-cultural environment; for example, how you shake hands or how you bow down to greet someone. Rather, we focus on those aspects of etiquette that we consider are significant for effective communication, with a special emphasis on some of the common pitfalls we have seen on this front and specifically in the context of Indo-US scenarios.

As we move from the attitude section through the communications section to the etiquette section in the text, you will find a few transitions:

- There is a move from covering views, philosophies and generalities in the attitude part to more specific guidelines in the communications part to extremely specific dictums in the etiquette part. Thus, there will be a steady but marked progression from being generic to being specific. This is intentional, given the increasing specificity of communication and etiquette compared to attitude.
- The chapters have a number of gray box insets (called 'snapshots') which describe typical scenarios and characters we find in business environments to illustrate the concepts discussed in the chapter. These insets are designed to provide some concrete examples to the somewhat abstract concepts that constitute attitude. As you move to communication and etiquette, these examples reduce as the chapters are dealing with less abstract and more concrete concepts that do not warrant more specific examples.
- The communication and etiquette sections contain a number of do's and don'ts that are absent in the attitude section. This is again due to the increasingly prescriptive nature of the communication and etiquette sections. Where appropriate, we have also included templates that can act as the starting point for certain artifacts (e.g., minutes of meeting)

With that said, let us move on to the Attitude part.

Part I: Attitude

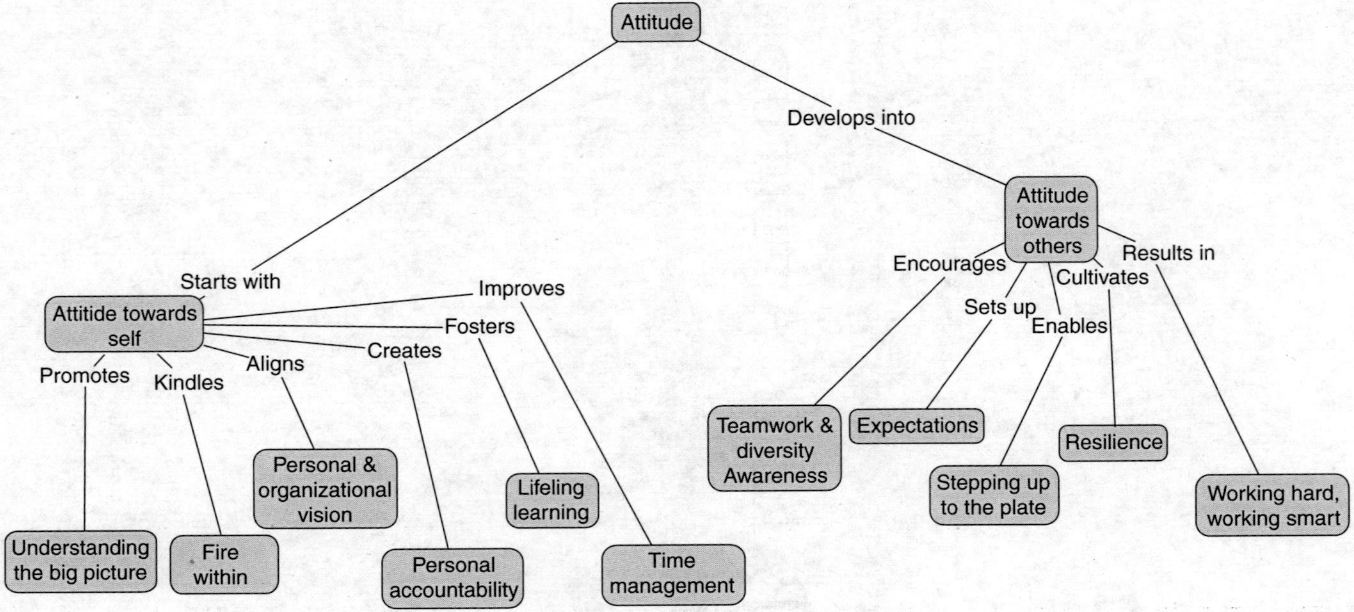
Attitude
Starts with
Develops into
Attitide towards self
Promotes
Kindles
Aligns
Creates
Fosters
Improves
Understanding the big picture
Fire within
Personal & organizational vision
Personal accountability
Lifeling learning
Time management
Attitude towards others
Encourages
Sets up
Enables
Cultivates
Results in
Teamwork & diversity Awareness
Expectations
Stepping up to the plate
Resilience
Working hard, working smart

2

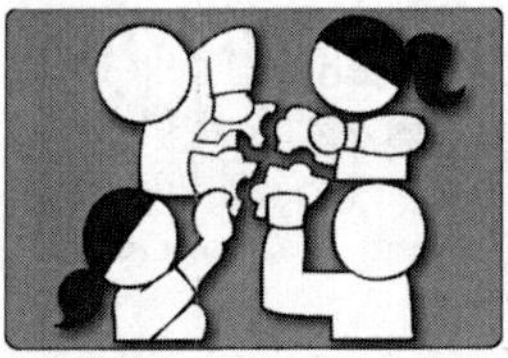

Big Picture, Pride, Passion and Process

"If you want to be happy for a year, win the lottery. If you want to be happy for a lifetime, love what you do."

–Unknown

Snapshot 2.1

First Things First

Ashok Shukla is still in a dream-like state. He cannot believe that he is actually in the campus of MNO Software Solutions as a new employee. He has even got his own employee number and a badge. He looks back on his years of training in various aspects of information technology and software, months spent as a summer-intern, the gruelling recruitment process to get into MNO Software, the tense wait to get his call letter, and now finally, everything has fallen into its place and he is in a posh conference room in the HR department of MNO, getting 'oriented'. Some HR bigwig has just now finished a session on insurance, provident fund, company policy and the likes and now they are waiting to have lunch with the CEO of the company himself! Shukla's adrenalin level is shooting up. All kinds of thoughts criss-cross his mind.

'I am going to be the best employee they have ever recruited' he resolves. 'And I am going to do whatever it takes.'

And after a couple of minutes of pondering, it becomes clear to him that the 'whatever' is actually a long list of soft skills and hard skills. Although he has some grounding in hard skills, he realizes that he has barely had the time or the opportunity to pick up soft skills while in college. 'Mastering soft skills should be my goal now,' he tells himself.

At the very top of Shukla's list comes 'understanding the big picture'. He reckons that even before the first ball is bowled—even before he writes a single line of code or gets into his first training session or acquires a milligramme of any other soft skill—he needs to get a grip on the new environment he is now in. Where is he? Why is he here? What should he do here? And how should he do what he should do? When he does such an analysis, he hopes he will not only figure out his whereabouts in the jungle called MNO Software, but also stumble upon concepts closely related to that 'big picture', like passion for his work in MNO Software (we have also called it the 'fire within'), and the link between the two—the pride/modesty factor, the process and so on. Once these initial concepts are established and they become his second nature and a big part of his attitude, he figures that he can move on and pick up other soft skills systematically.

Throughout the rest of the orientation programme, Shukla throws up his hand and asks a lot of questions. He even buttonholes the CEO during lunch and bombards him (and impresses him) with a lot of interesting questions that help him frame an understanding of the 'big picture'. He knows that his present idea of the 'big picture' is still rough and a bit fuzzy and that he has to refine it in the months to come. But he has made a good beginning and the stage is already being set for a fabulous career in MNO Software.

So, let us help Shukla—and you—understand this very first soft skill some more. In the previous chapter, we have defined soft skills as the skills you need to succeed in your environment. For this, you must first be able to be cognizant of and relate to the environment. An essential ingredient of this is to know the ecosystem you are in, the big picture of which you are a part and your role and contribution to this big picture. In this chapter, we first discuss what is meant by 'the big picture' and how this would enable you to relate to the environment better. We follow this up with a discussion of pride in your work and how the right level of pride is closely tied to seeing the big picture. This right level of pride would automatically create a 'fire within'—a burning desire and a passion in you to do your best, resulting in your success and that of the organization as well. This fire within, along with the vital glue of systematic processes, will enable you to have a vision and align that vision to that of the organization and thus, relate to the environment even better. This will naturally lead us into the next chapter on vision.

The elements described in this chapter, right from the 'big picture' to the 'fire within', are such basic blocks in soft skills-building that we will keep returning to them in future chapters.

2.1 What Is the 'Big Picture'?

Let us take a simple example of putting together a jigsaw puzzle. Also let us assume that it is a fairly large puzzle that several of you are putting together (Figure 2.1).

Fig. 2.1 *Knowing the big picture*

The first step would be to *know the final picture your entire team or organization is aiming for.* You will probably look at the picture on the cover of the puzzle box. That will give you important information as to what type of picture it is (natural scenery, people, vehicle parts, etc.). You will also assimilate other facts about the picture like the different shades of colours in the different parts of the picture (like the sky, trees, major characters, etc.). You will then use these facts to arrive at a *plan* of how you will distribute the work (and the pieces) among the team members. For example, you can distribute the jigsaw pieces amongst all of you by handing out the pieces that look like those corresponding to the sky (blue colour) and the clouds (white/grey colour) to one person, those that look like the pieces corresponding to a tree (brown/green colour) to another person and the other pieces to a third person. Thus, you have arrived at a plan to divide the work amongst all of you, with a clear understanding of the roles to be played by each. *Each of you work in a focused manner attempting to solve a narrower problem* than the original jigsaw puzzle. All of you are *working towards a common goal.* While doing so, if you do find pieces of the puzzle that you cannot use, you will not have any hesitation in passing on the pieces to the other team members. Likewise, other team members would not hesitate to pass the pieces that you need on to you that they have. There are no territorial fights like 'these are my pieces' or 'these are your pieces, get them out of here!'

Since we defined soft skills as what is needed to relate to and succeed in the environment, is it not obvious that knowing the big picture is indeed the first step in effective soft skills? Most people fail in relating to their environment because they simply don't see the big picture and become extremely self-centred (see Box 2.1).

Box 2.1

What is the 'Big Picture'?

Summarizing the question of 'what is the big picture?' one can conclude that knowing the big picture is made up of the following steps:

- Knowing the end goal
- Having a plan to get to the end goal
- Knowing your role in getting to the end goal
- Knowing how your role complements and supplements the roles played by others
- Making necessary mid-course corrections to make sure you reach your end goal quickly

2.2 Why Should You See the Big Picture?

Makes you share a common vision with other members of the group: When everyone sees the same big picture, there is a shared vision, a common goal that everyone aims for. The barriers of communication reduce and there is likely to be a better receptiveness for your views and perhaps of the way you express your views.

Makes you less self-centred: Again, taking the jigsaw example, once you know the big picture, there is no longer the 'hoarding' of pieces or information. When you find a piece that does not belong to the part you are solving, there is no hesitation in giving the piece away to others.

Helps articulate 'your' requirements to elicit better co-operation from the team: Taking the analogy further, you would be in a better position to tell your team-mates 'Hey, if you find any light blue colour pieces, please give them to me.'

An obvious by-product of all the above points is that the team, as a whole, becomes more effective and efficient. There is very little reinventing the wheel, very high shared vision and, thus, the entire team is acting as a laser beam targeted on the ultimate goal without any territorial fights. Everyone relates to the environment, succeeds in the environment and helps others succeed in the environment.

2.3 What Happens When You Don't See the Big Picture?

We will continue to use the example of the jigsaw puzzle. We did a small experiment that made people put together jigsaw puzzles individually but with the pieces face down (i.e., not seeing the full picture). As you can guess, it took several times longer for an individual to put together the jigsaw. The trying of pieces was no longer based on natural factors like colour that relate directly to the final picture. Rather, the pieces were tried based on the shapes of the contours and whether one side of the piece was straight or not. Such parameters that do not link directly to the final picture are not only unnatural but are also error-prone. Furthermore, when you are solving the puzzle in a team, this approach will lead to a conflict of several team members trying to grab the same piece saying 'Hey, I need a piece rounded on the left and straight on the right—who has it now?!'. Of course, the others are not interested in taking an inventory of their pieces to see whether they have that piece that is rounded on the left and straight on the right. Even if they did have such a piece, since they don't know they don't need the piece, they are likely to hold it back 'Just in case I need it for *my own* part of the puzzle.'

There will be an increased communication overhead: When the team members don't see the big picture, there is no clear division of labour. Hence, communication overheads increase substantially. You will be digging into the pile of pieces 'owned' by somebody else very often.

You may be perceived as too myopic and egoistic: When your team members want to get important information from you, you may not be able (or willing) to give it to them as you may be more engrossed in solving 'your problem'.

You may win the battle but lose the war: Since you are busy solving 'your problem', you often lose track of the bigger problem of which your problem is a smaller part. This may result in a lot of effort focused towards 'local optimization' (i.e. solving your problem faster), while compromising a 'global optimization' (i.e. achieving the overall objective in a more efficient way).

You may get into a 'not invented here' ('NIH') syndrome: Since there is no shared common vision, each person ends up reinventing the wheel for every little component. Each person's style is unique and after some time it becomes a battle of politics as to whose approach or style is better. In the process, the over-reaching goal gets compromised.

2.4 Pride in Work

Closely coupled with seeing the big picture is taking pride in your work, in your contribution to the big picture. In every organization and in every project, there are different types of activities that need to be carried out. Not all are equally 'glamorous' or considered prestigious. But it is required that all the jobs be done and the glamorous parts will not receive their sheen unless the not-so-glamorous ones are also completed.

In order for a person to stand up and communicate effectively with the team, he should feel good about what he is doing and carry a sense of pride about it. This sense of pride will come only if he can see how his contribution completes the big picture.

In a globally distributed team, this sense of pride is even more important. In these days of BPOs and outsourcing, there is a common perception that the outsourced activities are all 'low-tech'. If this perception is allowed to continue, it is not good either for the people working in the outsourcing location or for the people in the outsourced location. For the people in the outsourced location, this perception will lead to de-motivation and as a self-fulfilling prophecy that makes them believe that their work is not useful. Thus, the work quality is likely to suffer. They can never really further the cause of healthy respect from the outsourcing location. This in turn can make the outsourcing location give less strategic work to the outsourced team, widening the gap even further.

In Figure 2.2(a), at one end was the first person who saw nothing but his immediate and self-centred wants. Obviously, he was neither enjoying his job nor relishing his contribution to the final goal. The second person, in Figure 2.2(b), had a clearer perspective of what he was doing and perhaps derived better satisfaction from his job, albeit doing his job mechanically and being narrowly task oriented. Still, he would

Fig. 2.2

not have been able to articulate his contribution and hence would not have been very successful in relating to his environment. The third person, in Figure 2.2(c) not only saw the big picture, but was also able to visualize his role and contribution to the big picture. This made him see the factory being built and he started feeling proud of the fact that the factory would outlive him and that he had been part of leaving something behind for the society. This would certainly make him a more satisfied individual who would relish his contributions and hence, be able to communicate with the rest of the team in a non-threatening and enjoyable way.

This sense of pride leads to a fire within that will propel one's contribution much further. We discuss this in the next section.

2.5 Passion—The Fire Within

The sense of pride discussed above is closely linked to passion or the 'fire within'. When you see the big picture and understand your role in creating the big picture and take pride in it, you will be automatically filled with a lot of passion and motivation. This motivation will surely light a fire within that will act as fuel for you to feel good about yourself and you will be able to display better self-confidence and thus relate to the environment better.

How do you identify such a passion or 'fire within'? You will feel, see and display a visible excitement for your work. Whatever you do, you will no longer consider it drudgery; you will no longer consider yourself a mere cog in the wheel, someone who moves files around. You will realize that everything you do has a purpose and that this overarching purpose will propel you forward. No doubt, in any job you will see challenges, obstacles that look insurmountable. But, with this passion, with the fire within glowing brightly, you will see every challenge as an opportunity. You will not get disheartened by obstacles, but at the same time, you will not be foolhardy to ignore the perils of the challenges. Your clear sense of direction towards the big picture will lead you to identify alternative strategies to overcome the obstacles. The most important result of this passion is that you will always strive for excellence and nothing but the very best. You will never get satisfied with work of average quality; you will never make do with 'just-sufficient quality'; you will never resort to compromises because good is the opposite of best and best is your benchmark. You will also be able to identify 'the best' as what is best for the bigger cause, rather than what is best to achieve narrow goals of self-interest. In short, your passion is one for results, results of the team. It unleashes a totally positive attitude towards your work, your career and your workplace.

2.6 A Delicate Balancing Act

We have been discussing pride in work, fire within and passion. This chapter would not be complete if we do not mention a couple of possible dangers in these attitudes, especially in the context of multi-location teams that is typical of the IT / ITeS arena.

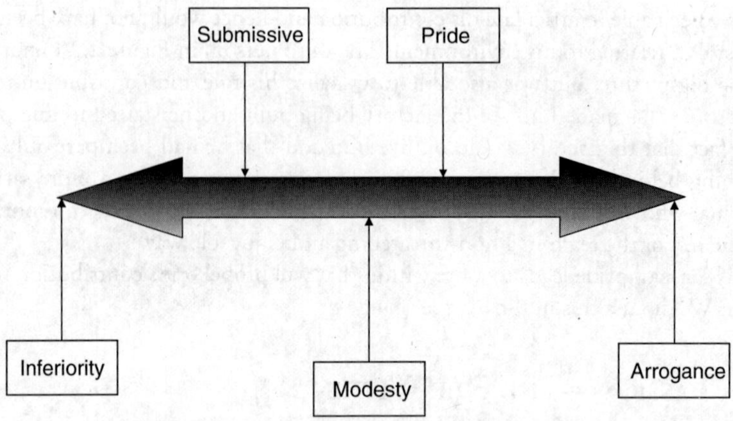

Fig. 2.3 *The continuum of inferiority to arrogance*

Rather than treating pride as a one-off attitude, it is important to realize that there is a spectrum or continuum of attitudes about your work and where you stand in this continuum.

A typical multi-location IT team has many diverse functions, like software development, testing, maintenance, documentation and so on. Some of these jobs are considered more glamorous than others. For example, software development is considered 'more cool' than say, maintenance. Obviously, this is a misconception; a successful product requires good developers, good testers and people who are good at all the other aspects like maintenance and documentation. The chain is only as strong as its weakest link. At the end of the day if a product fails, for whatever reason, the entire team suffers.

A second fuel to this fire of 'cool work' vs 'grunt work' is that different jobs demand different backgrounds. For example, a person doing software development may come from a prestigious college with a flashy computer science degree, whereas a person doing documentation may come from an arts background. There may be huge disparity between the pay scales of the two jobs, the perceived background reputation of the people doing the two jobs and the levels of visibility for the two job functions. For example, while the software developer may have visibility to the customers and the senior management, the person doing the documentation may not be in the forefront or limelight. This can lead to a perception of one job being more important than the other and thus, undermining the less visible job function. If the people performing such less visible—but by no means less important—functions *themselves* feel that their work is indeed less important and inferior, they are setting themselves up for failure. This is the inferiority end of the continuum in Figure 2.3.

The people performing the more 'cool' job function may tend to dominate the others and this is certainly not going to foster good teamwork. One possible reaction of the affected party would be to say, 'Okay, I *think* my job is good and I am proud of it, but you are more powerful and I guess I will accept what you say—maybe I don't have a choice.' This part of the continuum, being *submissive*, is slightly better than the inferiority end. Another possible reaction, without being offensive could be 'I know my job is good and I am proud of it, but I don't have to waste my energy in trying to convince you nor am I forced to agree with you'. This is the *modesty* part of the continuum.

What we have been advocating in this chapter is *pride and passion,* that come after modesty in the continuum. The line between pride and modesty is sometimes very blurred, especially for the Indian culture. There is a certain philosophical modesty that is ingrained in traditional Indian culture. It is sometimes considered blasphemous and impolite to take credit for anything. While continuous bragging about what one has achieved is obviously painfully boring and not well appreciated, it is equally inappropriate *not* to take credit for something that one has actually earned and deserved. For example, if you have gone beyond the call of duty and covered extra ground to achieve something, you should not simply keep quiet and assume (or hope) that someone will take note on their own. No one really will, at least not immediately. Given the pace at which things happen, either someone else will accomplish what you did a little later and take credit for it promptly, making your work and effort redundant, or worse, someone will take credit for what *you* did, making you a loser.

As Agatha Christie said in her famous thriller *Witness for the Prosecution,* 'Justice must not only be done, but also *seen* to be done'. You should not feel that pride and modesty are the opposite of each other. Some amount of modesty is required, but that need not be at the cost of someone else taking the credit for what you have done.

The line between pride and modesty is not the only thin line. The pride that one has and the passion and the fire that it stirs within should not be at the cost of pooh-poohing the other members of the team. Perhaps they come from a different background and perhaps they perform a different job function, but they are by no means unimportant for the final product. The pride in performing one's job should not be assumed to be a license to trample over and hurt other job functions and be *arrogant,* nor should any one job function be glorified at the expense of any other job function. Once a person truly knows the big picture and realizes his contribution to the big picture, he would be able to get a better appreciation of the contribution made by the other people as well. The pride will not just be in his work, but in the final outcome; he would see his job as building the factory and not breaking stones; he would see his job not as being a show of independent strength, but as a cohesive force to inter-dependently lead to the final factory. There is a thin line between pride and arrogance and the real winners will know where the line is.

One way to achieve a good balance in the pride continuum is to celebrate the achievements of the team. Even if the achievement is yours personally, surely others would have contributed to it in some way. By announcing the achievement and by acknowledging the contributions of others in the accomplishments, you will not only be able to make people take notice of your work, but they will also appreciate your being a team player.

2.7 The Glue that Holds All these Together: Process

In this chapter, we have discussed three related concepts that are the vital starting point for soft skills—seeing the big picture, pride in work and the fire within. We would like to conclude this chapter by pointing out the interesting inter-dependency of these factors and the important glue that holds these three factors together.

Knowing the big picture makes sure that there is clear results-orientation. If you don't know the big picture, but are extremely passionate about what you do, then the situation is one of:

> 'Think of the chaos that would be created if everyone did their best, not knowing what to do.'
>
> – Edward Deming

You not only need to know what the big picture is, but you also need some discipline and ***process*** to get there. Process is another word for the method, the procedure, the practical routine that you evolve by suitably combining these three elements. A good process not only connects you to the big picture at all times, it also regulates and makes use of your pride and passion in a synergetic manner, to achieve the end goals. Sometimes in large corporations like MNO (Snapshot 2.1) some steps in the process are defined and 'operationalized' by the company itself, based on its policies and you will have to abide by them. Process is the essential glue that interprets and connects the destination to a route. While passion and pride are essential for innovation and better self-expression, undirected (and uncontrolled) passion and pride without a proper process will just lead to a Tower of Babel syndrome.

> Passion without process is anarchy.

Sometimes, people go to the extremes of following the laid-down process, without understanding the rationale behind the process. Then, it is likely that decisions and actions don't have a worthwhile contribution to the big picture.

> Process without passion is bureaucracy.

Hence, all the elements we have discussed in this chapter have to be combined and shaped together.

> Big picture + Process + Pride + Passion = Quality

A key part of this glue—process—is to ensure there is

> Appreciation of the inter-dependence on one another.

When this interdependence is appreciated, people find the right place to be in on the pride continuum and this develops a healthy relationship among the team members. This will lead you into developing a common shared vision. That is the topic for the next chapter.

Fig. 2.4(a) *Attitude without knowing the Big Picture and roles*

Fig. 2.4(b) *Attitude knowing the Big Picture and roles*

3

Vision

"If you don't know where you are going, no map would help you."
–Chinese Proverb

Snapshot 3.1

We are at the Phone Circuits Inc., a large designer and manufacturer of cell phone equipment and components. The CEO, Mr Rao, is presenting the technological and financial roadmap of his company to his top investors. He says that by mid next year, his company will have three products in the 3G technology space and hopes to derive nearly 60 per cent of its revenue through this line of products. Although the initial margins will be in the range of 20 to 25 per cent, he expects competition to be severe in the fourth quarter and erode the margin to about 15 per cent. In two years' time, he expects nearly 85 per cent of the revenue to come from 3G products. He also expects to go into production with a new Femtocell technology product in 10 quarters.

In another conference room, the VP of marketing, Ms Kelkar, is elaborating the marketing vision of the company to her crew. Among other things, she says that the market penetration of 3G in India will be easier in the North and the South, whereas in the East, it will be slow. The rural market will pick up once all three of their products hit the market. She also projects that her entry-level product will capture about 25 per cent of the Malaysian and Thai markets.

Half a campus away, Mr Banerjee, the Production Manager is sitting in his office, diligently working on his raw material and labour requirement for the next few weeks. He has the master production schedule laid out on his desk. He is trying to see what the suppliers have in their pipeline and how much to order from whom. He also knows that the schedule is not etched in stone and can change abruptly to accommodate orders from his top customers. He pictures various production scenarios in his mind and comes up with what he considers the best set of purchase orders for the raw materials and the best possible labour schedule.

Meanwhile, in the swank main building of the campus, Mr Lal, a prospective entry level process engineer is being interviewed. The HR interviewer asks him, 'Mr Lal, where do you *envision* yourself five years from now?' Mr Lal ponders for a few moments and then answers with confidence that given his engineering background and a penchant for management, he expects to be a process manager, leading a team of engineers and technicians. And in 10 years, he says he hopes to lead the entire Research and Development organization and productize several new and exciting technologies. In 10 years, he says, Phone Circuits will be the global leader in its industry.

3.1 Vision, Vision Everywhere

Snapshot 3.1 illustrates how pervasive and important vision is in the corporate world. Whether you are the CEO, pumping your company, or simply a potential recruit, you will be asked to generate your vision and often, you will be judged on it. Regardless of your experience level or seniority, your vision is an essential soft skill and helps in your ability to relate to your environment (see Table 3.1 at the end of the chapter). So, it is absolutely important that you develop this capacity to come up with corporate prophecies.

The picture gets somewhat muddled once you realize that the term 'vision' can mean different things depending on the subject matter of the vision and who is conjuring it. For example, the CEO's vision in Snapshot 3.1, (which is probably recorded as the corporation's 'Vision Statement') is essentially about *seeing far into the future* and how (and in what sequence) events might unfold. It has elements of forecasting in it. The marketing VP's vision is about the *scope* of things. What the ramifications are and how broad and deep will the impact be. The production manager, on the other hand, is simply *visualizing* his world next week and the action–reaction scenarios, paying attention to all the relevant variables and other details. And finally, the interview candidate's vision is about *himself and his role* in the bigger organization. Initially, he plays a part in his vision, but as his vision wanders further into the future, the 'first person singular' gets de-coupled from the equation and his picture of things to come turns into a 'managerial and leadership' kind of vision that helps him to relate better to the environment around him. In short, vision is anything but a monolithic, simple-minded entity, even though most of us feel that it is an obvious concept that we already know a lot about.

That is fine. But how can we crank it up and turn into 'visionaries'? Some of these visionaries seem to be standing on the world's tallest watchtowers, with the most powerful binoculars. These nearly clairvoyant people can visualize complex and abstract things effortlessly and help usher in successful businesses, technological changes and even revolutions. They make stunning master plans using their perception and effectively navigate into the future with incredible results. Won't it be nice to have at least a fraction of the vision of a Bill Gates or Jamshed Tata? How can we generate such eagle vision and how did the CEO and the marketing VP in the example in Snapshot 3.1 get such powerful insights?

At the outset, we would like to plead ignorant of how one develops a great vision. In our opinion, there are no step-by-step instructions or secret recipes that would lead us from being gazers to seers. We don't know of any miracle laser surgeries. The only way to gain good vision is by poring over the biographies of famous visionaries and adapting some of their techniques—and hoping that they work for us. Toward the end of this chapter, we do go into some speculation on why some people have this superior gift of a third eye. Interested readers can refer to any number of books on vision to go deeper into such things.

Our goal in this chapter is more modest—to examine the various characteristics of vision and glean what it is, what it is not, what benefits we can accrue from it and how it helps you relate better to your environment and thus, how it is a determinant of your soft skills. You can check your own visioning process against our analysis and make the appropriate tweaks, augmenting your strengths and reducing your weaknesses.

3.2 Characteristics of Vision

The following are some of the characteristics of vision.

Vision is the ability to project into the future: Vision is your perception of the future. It is a careful projection of today's world into tomorrow. Like the CEO's technology plan, it has the time progression of events spelt out unambiguously. It lists important dates, epochs and deadlines. It tells you when you can expect specific things to happen. Any cause–effect relationship between events will be maintained accurately.

Visions also have time horizons—long-term (strategic), intermediate-term and near-term. Extremely short-term visions are more or less 'plans' and 'things to do', whereas the longer-ranged visions, such as the CEO's or the candidate's 10-year vision are less clear-cut. Near-term vision has the highest probability of being accurate.

Time also gives your vision a sense of 'pace', urgency and timing. It compels you to periodically ask questions like 'Is our present vision okay or should we modify it? Or should we abandon it and pick an entirely new one?'

Vision has a firm subject matter, end goals and intermediate milestones: You can imagine vision to be a two-dimensional xy graph. The horizontal axis or the x-axis is the time axis, and the vertical axis is the specific subject matter of the vision—the domain where events unfold, such as the finance of the company, product line or the number of units produced.

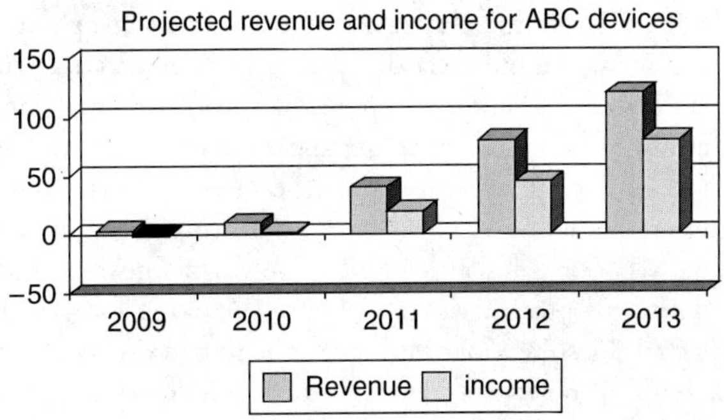

Fig. 3.1 *A time–target graph*

Vision starts with today and sequentially progresses to the final, 'target' scene in the future. The final scene can be the financial health of the corporation in two quarters or the market situation in three years. These can also be the 'goals' of the company. The transition to the future does not occur in one giant leap, but goes through a series of clearly spelt out intermediate milestones—such as the market situation next year, or six quarters from now. These intermediate montages and checkpoints are very important to vision.

You can also add your own directorial touches to your vision. For example, the vision of Mr Banerjee, the production manager, can be a 'snapshot' of the factory next Monday, or he can 'zoom in' on the second shift in mass production line 2. Or he can 'watch' products streaming out of the production line into his finished-goods warehouse. You can invoke it any way you choose. You can serve your vision in different bottles for different audiences—if you are Mr Rao, the CEO, you can have a predominantly technology-oriented vision statement for one set of audience and for another bunch of people, you can focus on the financials of the company. Note that such an articulation of vision to different people cultivates a shared vision, which leads to better communication and coordination and thus, to conditions of better harmony in the work environment.

Vision is about understanding the big picture: Your vision or visualization will have to be in conjunction with the larger environment you operate in. You may be the production manager planning next week's production. But the parameters you are manipulating are all probably set by the big picture. There should be a reasonable overlap between your vision and the vision of the organization. So, understand the big picture for all its worth and derive your vision from the strategic vision of the corporation or what are known as the *aggregate plans*. Your vision does not work in isolation. To reiterate what we saw in the last chapter, understanding the big picture and having a shared vision go hand in hand.

Vision gives clarity: Despite the clutter of things around us, a good vision focuses clearly on things that matter and filter out the noise. It enhances clarity of thought which in turn could lead to clarity of expression and communication. It sticks to its subject matter and does not confuse the audience with side stories or irrelevant excursions. In case of Mr Lal, the candidate, he doesn't obfuscate his vision with possibilities of other conflicting visions—such as quitting the job in three years and going off to do an MBA or going abroad after five years. Those are possibilities, but they are tangential to his present vision of himself working for the Phone Circuits organization. Similarly, despite a lot of things happening in the background, Mr Rao, the CEO, locks in on his objects of interest—the technology direction and financial performance—and follows them for a long period of time.

Vision is about paying attention to details: As clichéd as it may sound, the devil is in the details. Mr Rao would have paid perfect attention to all the details, all the important variables and factors, all the trends, etc. to come up with his numbers. Otherwise, his vision statement is meaningless. He may not outline every single step of his analysis to his audience for the sake of brevity and clarity, but be assured that he would have considered every little thing and would leave nothing hanging. A big differentiator between a good vision and bad vision is how much detail went into generating them.

Vision should be 'on-demand': In our Phone Circuits example above, the visions were generated by our protagonists 'on demand'. They were not a result of sitting under a *Bodhi* tree and attaining enlightenment. So, you should be ready to routinely churn out your visions time after time—and at somebody else's behest. Ask Mr Banerjee, the factory manager. He is tasked by his boss to generate his production 'vision', week after week.

The hallmark of good visionaries is that they can turn on their vision as needed. New situations, new paradigms, won't faze them. They may face a different client and a different situation each day. But they always deliver on their vision. These visionaries quickly get into the battle, survey the scene, comprehend the situation, figure out why their side is winning or losing and make appropriate adjustments. And they eventually win the battle. They go on to become successful consultants, doctors, technologists and so on.

Snapshot 3.2

A truly great visionary like Steve Jobs, rarely stops at just one grand vision in a lifetime. He headed Apple Computers in the eighties, where he galvanized the industry with his brand of computers. He then started Pixar, where he dreamed up a vision of Computer Graphics and Animation in popular entertainment. And then, again, he returned to Apple and launched the iPod and the iPhone revolution. This is a great example of visions being conjured and realized again and again.

Vision is about the fire within: We saw about the power of the 'fire within' or pride, in the previous chapter. Personal visions, such as the one of the interview candidate, have a few extra characteristics—you are now a part of the vision itself. Not just that, you are also its hero (or at least one of its heroes). You are actually influencing the environment and changing it. You are the enabler of all kinds of activities listed out in the vision. It then becomes a projection of your desires, hopes and ideals. There is a component of wish and a component of making it happen.

What is fuelling that fire within and how does it relate to the vision? How do you know where you would want to go? To a large extent, it is dictated by your inherent desires. Each of us can get motivated and excited by certain things. Ask yourself the following questions:

- Are you passionate about what you want to do?
- Does what you do excite you?
- Do you strive for the 'best', instead of being satisfied with the 'good'?
- Do you cherish the challenges on your way and view them as opportunities for learning?

If you answered 'no' to any of these questions, chances are that the 'fire within' is not glowing well enough and hence your 'vision' is somewhat blurred.

Vision is tailored to one's strengths and weaknesses: This is an extension of the previous point. Effective people custom-design their vision and maximize their advantage. If you are Mr Lal, the candidate, you will play on your strengths—such as your leadership quality in a research environment. Ask yourself the following:

- What are my core competencies?
- How can I acquire some more skills?
- How can I hone some existing ones?
- What resources will it take and in what time-frame?
- Can I turn some of my 'weaknesses' to my advantage?
- How can I compensate for some of my weaknesses?

A careful assessment of all these will make sure that your visions are more reality-based and your expectations are set to achievable levels. This will enable you to position yourself most appropriately for the given environment.

Fig. 3.2 *Vision should be tailored to one's strengths and weaknesses*

3.3 What Is NOT Vision

Vision is not a fantasy: Vision is not a pipe dream. It is not a delusion nor is it fortune telling. It is a reality-based strategy statement with utility, as well as limitations. The idea is not to come up with outrageous statements about the future, as much as to have a basis for a future situation. Mr Rao, the CEO, doesn't have visions of quadrupling his revenues in one quarter because given the ground reality, that simply will not happen—he sometimes dreams of such things, though.

Vision is not just a simple plan: Vision is much more than a simple Gantt chart or a timeline. It is a compendium of timelines, contingency plans, workarounds, strategies and desires. Mr Banerjee's vision of production each week will include alternative plans if vendors default on their delivery dates or if customers demand a different model to be manufactured. It will have ways of handling potential quality problems on the line.

A vision is not just about today's reality, but is about tomorrow's possibilities: Even though good visions are anchored in reality, history is full of examples of 'crazy' people who dared to cook up (almost) impossible visions. Ms Kelkar, the marketing VP may have sounded crazy when she said that she hopes to capture 25 per cent of the Malaysian and Thai markets in the next two years. But obviously, her vision is backed up by her (and her organization's) strengths and passion. E. Sreedharan's vision translated into Delhi Metro Rail, Steve Jobs' vision of a computer at every desk now seems like a prophecy come true. And Shah Jahan did build a Taj Mahal against all odds. Every good vision has that beating the odds or the 'stretch' element in it. Vision or daydream—who decides on the calibre? Who is to say that Mr Lal's wanting to become the head of the R and D of Phone Circuits is a fantasy and not an achievable vision?

A good vision is not dogmatic or fixed: Vision is like shooting at a moving target. Plenty of things can go wrong in the future and plenty more can change in unpredictable ways. When such things happen, you should be prepared to tinker with your vision as necessary and make it conform to the new reality.

Mr Rao's optimistic forecast can be blown away by a cruel recession or by aggressive competition in ways he could not have foreseen. Or in another scenario, his sales can skyrocket and his numbers can get even better. In any event, he will be foolish to stick to his old vision in the face of new data. There is nothing wrong in modifying your vision or even abandoning it, as necessary. You should not irrationally cling to your initial vision and untenable positions.

Vision is not empty words: Politicians can make statements like 'We will abolish social inequality' and get away with it. But in business organizations, you cannot make vague and generic pseudo-vision statements like 'we will improve quality' or 'we will have the best customer service in the industry'. Such utterances are more like optical illusions than embodiment of vision, unless backed by suitable quantitative metrics, which will help measure the 'improvement' and 'level of customer service', along with a reasonably tangible roadmap of how to accomplish such end goals. Vision is not an empty rhetoric. It is something that can be implemented. It is not just a wish. It is an action plan.

Fig. 3.3 *Vision is not empty words, it is paying attention to detail*

3.4 What Are the Benefits of Vision?

Once you develop an ability to formulate vision, especially 'on-demand', several benefits will flow to you. Some of these are:

Instills a sense of confidence: First and foremost, you will develop a strong sense of poise and confidence. The unknown will no longer scare you, because you will be able to 'picture' it. You will work with an American client this year and then smoothly transition to a Brazilian client a year later. You will move from situation to situation with ease. This will help you to adapt yourself to changing environments and scenarios.

Keeps you pressing forward: Your vision gives you that forward momentum that drives you enthusiastically toward your goal—unlike some other people who would rather follow instructions and set themselves up to be micromanaged. With a clear vision in your mind, you will not wander into your office wondering how to start your day's work. Instead of looking at your job as disjointed activities, you will perceive it as an integrated story that is unfolding. You will keep forging ahead through challenges and problems. There will be a sense of self-actualization in everything you do. This enthusiastic self-actualization can make you a popular person in your environment.

Makes you pro-active: Since you have a sense of the future, you will also tend to be pro-active. You will be more battle-ready for the coming challenges, mobilize resources well in advance and have a head-start in executing your plans. For example, your vision of your retirement years might involve living in a nice house in your home town. And this in turn might prompt you to forego some of today's luxuries and instead save up money for a house. With such a proactive lifestyle, there will be fewer surprises and even fewer regrets.

Gives you a sense of direction and a sense of purpose: There is a sense of idealism that is advocated in your vision and that will give you something to live for. Once you know where you want to go, it will be easy for you to identify the right environment for you to be in and that will motivate you to get there and thrive. Since a good vision helps you choose the right environment to work in, it increases the probability of your succeeding in that environment.

Enables you to communicate better through vision-sharing: Your vision provides you with enthusiasm, idealism and purpose. Once you give shape to your vision, it is natural that you should articulate its features to your peers and managers and to anyone else who may have a stake in it. In turn, they might give you their feedback and perhaps a dose of their own vision of things. This kind of 'vision-sharing' should improve the level of interpersonal communication all around. Sometimes you may have to 'hard-sell' your vision because it may be unconventional or may not seem plausible. This again should lead you to become better communicators if you want to convince the skeptics of your points of view.

Can help to be a part of the strategy team: As you establish a track record of good vision, you get more credibility and your voice is heard more. Your boss might actually solicit your opinion and insights about things, instead of dismissing your pronouncements as naïve, tail-wagging-the-dog-type remarks. In future projects, you may be recognized as a natural leader and be asked to chalk up the entire strategy.

Provides better managerial and leadership vision: Once you become a master at coming up with successful visions, it is natural that you will be called upon by your organization, your industry and perhaps even by your government, to provide vision for a larger group. You will be recognized as the leader and spokesperson who set the tone and came up with ideals for others to live by. Your responsibilities will no doubt multiply, your time and presence will be in high demand and your vision will acquire a touch of magic.

Improves risk management: Good vision automatically leads to better risk management. In personal life, one may take a lot of risks, but in your professional life and in businesses, where you are responsible for several people and things, you may have to be conservative, manage your risks and see if the risk-to-reward ratio is acceptable and is consistent with the policies and risk appetite of the organization. You need to have good intuition – arising from a focused vision -- and you need to back it up with a sophisticated, quantitative analysis to establish the details of all the risk factors. Better risk management is a natural by-product of generating good vision.

3.5 What Makes Great Visionaries?

How did the CEO, Mr Rao, come up with his numbers? He probably used standard forecasting techniques like the Delphi Method or econometric modelling or exponential smoothing, with an army of marketing people working the computers. The VP Ms Kelkar probably used anecdotal or empirical evidence in figuring out her vision. Mr Banerjee, the production manager probably used his hunches—and he has a whole bagful of them. He knows that when a new cell phone model comes into production, there will be quality problems in the first month. The next month, most of the quality problems will be solved, production volumes will go up and there will be raw-material-supply-related problems instead. His production plan evolved out of such observations. All three prognosticators above used what are called *heuristics*, to come up with their visions. Heuristics is just the generic name given to all the thumb rules, theories, scientific and non-scientific hypotheses, folk wisdom, statistical correlations, empirical and anecdotal observations, social norms—just about anything that can help people make sense of complex things, such as the future. The heuristics you employ form the basis of your vision and the more sound the heuristics you use, the better your chances are of coming with a good vision. If you have a failed vision, you must examine the heuristics that went into it and replace them with better ones, by learning from what went wrong and what went right. Your vision is only as good as the heuristics you used and heuristics can be a major differentiator between a good vision and a fuzzy one.

"Wonder what management technique our boss uses to come up with his amazing corporate vision"

Fig. 3.4

Your heuristics are derived from your domain knowledge, personal experience and the tools of inference you have available to you. The quality of heuristics will improve with better and more interaction with your colleagues and professional contacts. Some of the best employees who have this ability to interact and derive heuristics are usually put to work to come up with the task of formulating the heuristics. However, in spite of all this, there is no guarantee that your heuristics will be effective or infallible. Inasmuch as your vision is about the future, there will always be a fuzzy component to it. (We firmly believe that predicting or accurate forecasting of the future is almost impossible). It gets worse if your time horizons are farther and farther out. Our CEO, Mr Rao, for all his cleverness and his army of brains in his marketing department, will still be very iffy when he tries to generate sales numbers five years out. Why, there is no guarantee that he will hit his one-year-forecast numbers even under calm, steady market conditions. So much for good heuristics and good vision.

Some of the greatest visionaries who ushered in great innovations—thanks to their amazing heuristics—have also had their share of failures. Steve Jobs, for all his vision, wasn't much successful in his business venture, Next Computers.

The Book of Predictions[1], published in 1981, lists a number of futuristic 'visions' by several people ranging from Nostradamus and Jules Verne, to the so-called futurologists of those days. When you examine their vision for the year 2000 (a mere generation into the future from when the book was published first), you see that not one person had envisioned a product called the cell phone (the closest anyone comes in making predictions about future telephony was someone predicting that by 2000, phone callers may have distinctive, signature ringtones). Instead, there are visions of people living in colonies on the moon! It may be comforting for you to know that as far as making long-term projections go, you and Nostradamus are on a level playing field.

So, given all this and how inaccurate heuristics (and the resulting long-term visions) can be, should you then even formulate a long-term vision for yourself or for your organization? Our answer is an unequivocal 'yes', because however flawed it may be, you must still have a personal vision of where you will be five years or ten years down the road, as a guiding light for your journey ahead—and for all the good it does to your psyche. This vision will be the roadmap against which you will measure yourself. You will also use this roadmap to position yourself appropriately in your environment.

3.6 In Summary

One thing that has come out of our discussion thus far is that you stand a better chance of a good vision if you restrict yourself to the near-term and limit your sights to a specific domain—much like the production manager, Mr Banerjee. In fact, this is the area where most of us will be operating in our workplaces. Very seldom will you be called upon to offer your views on corporate profits two years from now or the anticipated technological changes in the next five years, unless you are at a very senior level within an organization.

Now your prophecies no longer have the veneer of being generated by a crystal ball. They will be more useful and will go into standard day-to-day activities such as project planning, budgeting, costing and quality improvement. In this restricted space, vision now is thoroughly demystified and becomes just another soft skill—to be cultivated, honed and unleashed in your organization. You may not develop a reputation for being the next Nostradamus, but then, you will be quite a bit in demand for your prowess in planning and visualizing no matter what your role is (see Table 3.1).

---

1 David Wallechinsky, Amy Wallace and Irving Wallace, *The Book of Predictions* (New York: Bantam Books, 1981).

Table 3.1 ***Every role needs and has a vision***

Role	What the Vision Pertains To	Range of Vision	Comments
CEO	▶ Where the company should be three or five or ten years from now ▶ Product or market penetration targeted	Long-term; strategic	Full of uncertainties; needs to get buy in from the entire organization; Spans multiple job functions.
VP, marketing	▶ Specific market share numbers for coming several quarters ▶ Winning over some specific targeted accounts	Medium-to-long-term	More specific vision than the CEO's; needs to be committed to more specific numerical targets to be achieved in the medium-term; would still be quite broad based, spanning a large part of the organization.
Production manager	▶ Meeting production targets for the week ▶ Achieving quality targets for the batches produced	Usually very short-term	The vision is quite specific and deterministic; less uncertainties; vision confined to a smaller set of people.
Individual contributors	▶ Individual career paths ▶ Personal financial goals ▶ Leadership vision	Short-to-medium-term	The vision is centered on the person; very little relationship to the rest of the team to start with, but can eventually encompass a larger group.

So, from the point of view of soft skills as a means of succeeding in the work environment, let us summarize what constitutes vision.

- It is an ability to put together a detailed and complex plan using your experience and ideals, by leveraging your strengths, building on your passion, and carefully avoiding your weaknesses.
- It is about being a player in the above plan by enabling relevant activities during its execution stage, by paying attention to detail and by intelligent use of heuristics.
- It is about being constantly aware of the end goals and being able to embed potential course-correction mechanisms into the plan.
- Finally, it is about being able to visualize scenarios at any point in the future, more often in the short-to-medium term and on occasion in the long term.

Let us also quickly summarize what vision is not about:

- Vision is not daydreaming.
- Vision is not hazy, but has a focused and clear target (albeit a moving target).
- Vision is not cast in stone—you have to be able to adjust your vision based on how events unfold.
- Vision is not limited to a single situation. It should be truly on-demand.

Once you are part of this visualizing process, you will automatically begin to take ownership for fulfilling your commitment to realizing the vision. This leads us into the next related soft skill–personal accountability.

4

Personal Accountability

"We are accountable for our decisions in our personal life so why shouldn't we be just as accountable in our work life?"
–Catherine Pulsifer

Snapshot 4.1

Ajay Gupta is a quality test engineer in CBA Electronics Enterprises. His official job description states that his 'responsibilities' include 'testing several kinds of circuit boards for his customers'—but the same job description does not provide him with any algorithm or guideline on how exactly to do that. Nor does it suggest what kind of technical expertise he should apply to his job or how he should resolve engineering problems. His job description further says that he is 'required' to lead technical teams and 'design new quality tests', but it does not tell him what specific quality metric he should go after or what his technical philosophy should be. Gupta is 'personally accountable' for all these unsaid things and for bringing in all the technical knowledge and tricks needed to do his job.

Gupta's role in his organization is a privilege bestowed upon him by his employer. When he joined CBA, he was automatically married to the goals and policies of CBA and it became his *responsibility* to abide by them. But, when he made the quantum leap and started sharing CBA's vision, he became *accountable* to live up to those ideals. The tremendous bonding and the loyalty he feels toward CBA, which goes beyond any role playing—or job description—is a part of that accountability.

While vision is about things that are fuzzy, distant and often pertaining to the 'big picture', a soft skill called 'personal accountability' deals with issues that are more transparent and immediate. This soft skill is about being an enabler of things and having the will to do anything in your power—technical and otherwise—to make things happen instead of passively spinning around as a cog in the wheel. Personal accountability is about how deeply you are committed to your job. It is about being thoroughly knowledgeable in all aspects of your domain, so that you can solve problems expertly, without twiddling your thumb or expecting someone else to do it for you. It is about how much you love your job and enjoy doing it. It is about how much you identify with your team and look out for it, instead of quickly blaming others for things going wrong. It is about accepting your role and responsibilities at work, without making any excuses. It is about looking inwards for directions, rather than waiting for your manager's instructions on everything. It is about completing a job perfectly, without any loose ends. Given that so much excellence is expected out of all of us these days, this is indeed a very vital soft skill that you will need to excel in your job and become a shining star of your organization.

At first glance, personal accountability doesn't even have the feel of a soft skill, let alone be considered in the same league as other seemingly interesting and apparently important soft skills like time management or presentation skills. If anything, it has an accusatory and negative ring to it, almost as if it is a whip that the management can crack on you, if they find something going wrong in your vicinity at work. So, to better understand what personal accountability means, you need to go beyond the touch and feel of this phrase and look at it deeply from various angles.

4.1 What Is Personal Accountability?

Personal accountability is much more than personal responsibility: Although personal responsibility sounds like personal accountability, we would like to distinguish between the two (some other authors may not share our views on this). In the context of business management, personal responsibility is more or less a synonym for job description—that verbose and almost legal-sounding statement, spelling out the requirements of your job. (Your HR department routinely comes up with such things, based on the division of labour in your organization.) After you joined your job, your boss probably added his own expectations—or responsibilities—to your job description and fattened it a bit. But still, it is only an approximation of what you actually do in your job and what your function and role in the organization really are. Personal responsibility may be a good starting point, but it definitely does not capture the spirit of your job. Neither can it alone be an inspiration for your career.

Personal accountability, on the other hand, is a much larger concept. It is an implicit collection of a lot of things like goal-setting and execution based on your stakeholders' expectations, your own vision of your job, responsiveness to customers, the fire within you, your views and ideals—just about anything *that will make you a self-starter and a clean-finisher of things* in your area of expertise. While personal responsibility stopped after a few highlights, personal accountability is almost open-ended about what it includes.

And finally, personal responsibility doesn't make any demands on your passion for your job. But a big part of personal accountability is your sense of commitment, pride in your workmanship, your own values and your quest for self-actualization. It makes your job a lively, interesting activity and puts you in the driver's seat. *Personal accountability is the difference between someone who just exists as a worker in the payrolls and that Mr Dependable, who moves and shakes an organization.* Obviously, this makes the difference between someone who is successful in relating to the environment and someone who is not.

Personal accountability implies accepting ownership: Let us suppose that CBA's customer, YZYZ Computers Corp., needs to have a new quality test developed. CBA may task Gupta with designing and implementing this new test procedure. In that case, it is not as if Gupta's manager will tell him what exactly to do and Gupta will blindly do it. Most likely, his boss will give him a free hand (well, almost) and leave him alone to figure out what needs to be done—right from the technical aspects to things like tapping into the required resources, planning the schedule, communicating with the customer (and also with CBA management) and delivering the proper deliverable by the desired deadline. In effect, Gupta assumes *ownership* of this particular activity and is completely *accountable* for its perfect execution. Putting it another way, personal accountability implies that you assume complete ownership of your activities and it is almost as if you tell the stakeholders '*Don't worry, I will take care of everything.*' You are up and running and not meekly pushing some buttons, thinking your job ends by sending a few emails here and there.

Gupta in essence 'owns' his testing machine and is the king of his quality test work area. This new quality test he is trying to develop will be one more thing he will own—right from its conception to inception. He will be the *single point of contact* (SPOC) for his customer and other stakeholders on *all* aspects of this task. Ownership will no doubt give Gupta some leeway in planning and execution, but it will also add pressure on him. Call it ownership, call it accountability, Gupta is the point man for this new quality test.

Accountability is much more important when you interface with customers: If you interface with customers at work (such as Gupta of CBA), then personal accountability takes on a much larger meaning. Responding to customers effectively will be a big part of your personal accountability. You must remember that your customers are the reason why you even have a job. And you have to not just serve them, but 'wow' them.

And customers are usually the biggest stakeholders—at least the most vociferous—and they can be a very finicky lot. They don't care for CBA's internal workings or its organizational structure or how complicated Gupta's testing can be. They are only interested in getting their job done, which is getting a new quality test in place and using it to test their merchandise. They will see Gupta as a gateway to CBA and will streamline their communication and dealings with CBA through him. Gupta now embodies complete CBA for his customer and may even be called to answer questions on say, billing. Even if he doesn't know the answers right away, the onus is on him to get them from wherever. Thus Gupta now takes on additional 'responsibilities', thanks to his customers.

Personal accountability is a soft skill: Taking initiative at work, pushing for a solution and achieving complete closure is the essence of personal accountability. Several elements come together to make up this soft skill. It is something that you acquire out of your own choice and is not something thrust on you by your management. Nor is it something you are born with. Like all other soft skills, you can learn it, cultivate it and be good at it. It too, is part attitude and part techniques. Aspects of personal accountability like dedication to one's job, loyalty toward one's organization and so on basically belong to the attitude part of this skill and facets like problem solving and communication skills are more in the category of practical techniques. In this chapter, we will take a detailed look at some of these major attitudinal elements of personal accountability.

In today's fast paced environment of high-tech global corporations, it is not unusual for employees to have to think on their feet and take some decisions on their own, instead of waiting to receive specific and detailed instructions on everything. In this sink or swim environment, an obvious ingredient to success is the ability to take ownership and be accountable (in the above sense of the word) to the (sometimes implicit) tasks assigned to you.

4.2 Components of Accountability

Let us look at some components of accountability in this section. We will do so through the example of Ajay Gupta, our test engineer and nominate him as the spokesman for the cause of personal accountability.

Taking initiative and boldness: The biggest component of personal accountability is the ability and the desire to take initiative to solve problems. It calls for a certain amount of boldness, a tremendous knowledge of the subject matter and a huge confidence in one's skills. Gupta therefore, doesn't need external pressures (such as his manager's prodding) to get going on the activity.

A person like Gupta, designing a new quality test, may have to get into uncharted territories to invent such a test. Yet he is not daunted by the unknown. He is not lost or panicky or lazy about making a start. The quick start he gives to the problem he is dealing with, gives him a solid edge at the finish line. Also, he is not opposed to completely abandoning his first attempt if it doesn't pan out and trying another approach. Gupta might consult with people who have more expertise than him on the subject or flip through technical manuals and books-but, that is just to complement his knowledge and not because he has trouble starting. This initiative stays with him every step of the way, as he arrives at the 'best solution' for the problem. Along the way, wherever necessary, he takes quick decisions and appropriate next steps.

The idea is to not let the complexity of the problem flummox and stall him. The net result of all this is that he does *whatever it takes* to get a job done.

Sometimes, Gupta may land a simple problem. Even here, he doesn't snicker at the simplicity of the problem, but instead goes methodically through with the solution.

Gupta's initiatives may not be limited to just his customer's problems. People like him with a good sense of accountability are in general also often volunteers. They take it upon themselves to solve any problem around them that they happen to notice (within limits of their bandwidth, of course)—rather than assuming that somebody else will take care of it.

Problem-solving: People with a vast reservoir of personal accountability are also good problem solvers. The ability to grasp the given data, the clarity they have about the end goals, their familiarity with a variety of problem-solving techniques and finally the methodical way in which they actually solve the problem and implement the solution—are all hallmarks of such people.

Gupta might have considered several alternative approaches. He would have indulged in various problem-solving techniques like thinking outside the box, lateral thinking, brainstorming with others, making a decision-tree and design of experiments and so forth, on his way to arriving at the best design for his test.

There is also a time factor associated with Gupta's activity—he needs to come up with a design by a specific deadline—and so, he will choose the appropriate problem-solving technique to meet the time constraints. If there are going to be delays, he will first get a 'buy-in' from his stakeholders and proceed accordingly.

Accuracy and perfection: As a professional, Gupta is also accountable for his test to be accurate and perfect—even if perfection is a loosely defined word here. His test should be thoroughly debugged by him and by his customer so that it runs mistake-free and remains the best solution. If there are things that can be tweaked to bring it to even greater perfection, Gupta will make those changes. Gupta will be graded on a number of sometimes very subjective parameters on the 'perfection' of his test like ease of use, consistency, robustness, accuracy, repeatability and so on, and he will have to come through clean on all these. What is more, Gupta's own yardstick for grading will usually be far tougher than what others will grade him on. This naturally makes him 'wow' others in the environment.

If you are working with end customers, in spite of your best efforts to be perfect, mistakes may creep in for various reasons. In which case, readily and genuinely apologize even for minor infractions—even if your gut tells you to protest and argue your case. Try to recover from the situation quickly and make sure that your customers have only a minimal impact and inconvenience. Remember that often you will be the sole representative of your organization to your customers and should there be serious flaws in your product or service, you will have to bear the brunt of their wrath.

Exceeding expectations or wowing the customers: Given the highly competitive nature of today's business world and how companies jump over each other to attract and retain customers, many customers now 'routinely expect their expectations to be exceeded'. They expect to be positively surprised and awed and get a thing or two extra that they had not bargained for. So, it is not enough if you merely get a passing grade in responding to customers. You also have to show them finesse and impress them deeply. A high level of customer service calls for innovation, diligence and understanding your customers and is a part of personal accountability.

In Gupta's case, maybe he can add a new feature to his quality test—an 'automatic mode' that will collect test data automatically and feed them into a host computer, thus increasing productivity and reducing errors. Such bells and whistles are becoming standard give-aways these days in the war for customers.

Managing performance expectations is so crucial that we have devoted an entire chapter, (Chapter 8), to it. People with a stellar sense of personal accountability routinely exceed expectations and this results in more satisfied stakeholders.

Taking up slack for others—relationship with team: A person who feels accountable doesn't have the 'It is not my job' attitude. Nor does he ask questions like 'Why doesn't Misra do it? Why are they always sending them over to me?' He doesn't do any 'inverse volunteering' and try to get out of the assignment and pass it on to someone else. Instead, he gladly accepts his responsibilities and sometimes takes up the slack for someone else. He jumps in and helps the bigger team when it needs extra help—especially when the team is shorthanded because of some members' non-availability. (We will deal with this in depth in chapter 10 on 'Stepping Up to the Plate'.) Ultimately, the team's success is his success and he doesn't think anything of doing that extra bit of work. In fact, some people invoke concepts like ***team accountability*** and ***shared accountability*** to look at this spirit of helping out one's team.

Resourcefulness: Gupta is resourceful—which means he knows where to get what and who to approach for what kind of help. He knows he can use a couple of old electrical parts he had put away in a back drawer to quickly rig up a fixture and check out some concepts he plans to use in his new quality test instead of waiting for newly-ordered parts to arrive from Hong Kong next week. Although he owns the problem of designing a new quality test and has to find a 'solution' for it, he knows that he doesn't have to do every bit of it all by himself. For the best solution, he knows he should tap into Sharma's mechanical skills and Srivastav's computer wizardry. He is also constantly trying to invent the *best* solution to the problem rather than just hit a *passable* one. He is resourceful enough to cut through bureaucratic hurdles of the company, get the requisite permissions and approvals and obtain all the information he needs to do his job. He never sits at his desk looking like he has reached the end of the road or looking confused and frightened by his assignment. In a nutshell, his resourcefulness helps him know exactly what he needs from the environment and that makes him a go-getter to get things done.

Open-mindedness: Personal accountability is characterized by open-mindedness about arriving at the most optimal solution to the problem on hand—which could sometimes mean abandoning some 'standard' ways of doing things and innovating. Gupta will also be open-minded about his customer's special needs and demands and will respond to them, instead of giving a 'No, cannot be done' kind of reply. He will also be open about correcting his mistakes, apologizing for flaws in service and be open-minded about how else to exceed expectations. He is smart enough to not repeat the same mistakes again. He doesn't have a cynical defeatist attitude. He will embrace others' good ideas if they can be used in his problem solving, but will not blame anyone if those ideas do not work. He will neither show a 'Not invented here (NIH)' syndrome nor take a high-pedestal attitude of 'I told you so' when things go wrong. This makes him endearing to the group.

Communication and follow-through: A big part of personal accountability is taking on all responsibilities for communication. This includes constantly keeping in touch with the customers and updating them on the progress, informing your management of what is going on (and quickly alerting them to any problems), putting in the right paperwork, talking to the vendors and suppliers and engaging in lateral communication with colleagues and so on. Gupta will also have to set up a communication loop of interested stakeholders and pass on packets of information to all concerned in a timely fashion. If meetings, conference calls and so forth need to be set up, Gupta will have to take care of those things as well. He will display the same initiative and enthusiasm for such communication as he showed for his technical work.

Professionalism: Personal accountability also reveals your professionalism. Being a professional means bringing commitment to your work—that extraordinary sincerity and competence. Being a professional means that the moment you enter the doors of your workplace, you are single-mindedly pursuing your work and related activities and not getting side-tracked by other things. Rain or shine, whether you have personal problems or bad days, you are going to give your best to the job on hand and manage to deliver a huge load of high-quality output. You will be the workhorse that even plays hurt. And you don't come up with lame excuses for not doing your job right.

A true professional is aware that his organization has many, many stakeholders (and perhaps some immediate customers) who crucially need his services. He also knows that he has to 'earn' his pay cheque and that it is not a gift cheque that is given to him no matter what. He has pride in being able to deliver high quality work and in making his stakeholders happy. He makes people count on him and puts them at ease with his dedication.

We discuss professionalism at several places in this book, with the intention of reinforcing these ideas in your mind. Often professionalism is so tightly interlinked with soft skills that it is difficult to say which the cause is and which the effect is.

4.3 Personal Accountability Vs Taking Matters into One's Own Hands

While personal accountability implies taking ownership and doing what it takes to get the job done, it does not give you an unlimited license to do what you want. We will now discuss the thin line that separates personal accountability from uncontrolled anarchy.

Know the limits of your job, what you can do: Even though accountability implies that you have a fair amount of latitude in getting things done, you have to be aware of your technical and territorial limits. Gupta may be an ace test engineer, but even he may not be able to build new test equipment in two days. Nor can he build a machine that does all kinds of impossible testing. So, occasionally, Gupta will have to summon more help and take the problem upwards. Personal accountability doesn't mean that you take on all kinds of unreasonable work and somehow get everything done without external help. An integral part of personal accountability is knowing when to seek external help, while trying to do as much as possible for whatever is within your capability.

Know the limits of your role in the organization: Personal accountability also means that you know your exact role in the organization and are aware of the limits of your authority. Respect your organizational structure. Don't unnecessarily do other people's jobs or overwhelm them and push them to the background in the name of taking initiative. In the 'single point of contact' customer-service model, you are supposed to provide all kinds of information to your customers—and do so as best as possible and by going through proper channels and interacting with the right people. Don't short-circuit this process.

If you are a technical person like Gupta, do not get into serious finance or marketing discussions with the customers unless you are authorized to do so. You can bend over backwards for your customers, but remember that you cannot do anything you want just to please them. Do not behave like you are the CEO of your company and negotiate all kinds of things with them. Understand what you can and cannot do for them. Knowing your limits is part of relating well with the environment.

Take the blame too, where appropriate; don't pass the buck: Sometimes, in spite of your best efforts, you may fail in the task you had set out to do—in which case, you graciously accept responsibility for not succeeding. It is not something to be ashamed of, but instead, it should lead to a detailed and objective failure analysis of how you and your organization can do better the next time. You don't make excuses or shift blame on others.

If Gupta failed or was only partially successful in his promise to deliver a new quality test, he would ask himself questions like,

- Why did I fail?
- Why did I take so long to come up with this test?
- Why isn't the test as elegant as I expected it to be?
- Why didn't I exceed the expectations of my customers?
- Were they demanding too much out of me?

Whether done in the privacy of his desk or done in his manager's office, failure analysis is a very important aspect of personal accountability.

4.4 Personal Accountability and You

Personal accountability benefits you in many ways. Not only does it give you a sense of fulfillment, but it also gives you tangible rewards and recognition. Let us look at a short list below.

You will be counted upon: You will find yourself included in important teams and assignments. You will be in demand. Sometimes it will overwhelm you that everyone wants you and includes you in their projects. (In which case, you have to make sure that you don't overbook your calendar.) You will also see that you will be given much more freedom to execute. You will be labelled the 'go to guy' and people will know that you *will* somehow get things done.

You will be considered a troubleshooter: You will be perceived as a special trouble-shooting ambassador—unravelling complicated problems, inking complex deals and completing impossible jobs. Your organization will have you represent it in meetings and negotiations. Even within the organization, you may be sent to trouble spots and tasked with fixing things.

You will not have the victim's mentality or put the blame on others: There are enough people in the workforce who would take the high road and blame everyone and everything, when things go wrong around them. They would surmise that they did their best but were helpless because of powerful extraneous circumstances. They have a long list of things to blame—their own bosses, the stifling company policies, crabby customers, family problems, their ill-health *ad infinitum*. 'It was Misra's idea in the first place' they would go on,' 'And I knew from day one that it would not work'. Although such self-pity may win them some support in the short run, it will not hold water in the long term. Here is where the personally accountable people differentiate themselves from the whiners and gallop forward. As someone famously said—*Don't complain. And don't explain.*

You will have the ability to learn lessons: You will see that you learn a lot of lessons on the job. Both from your successes and from your mistakes; by yourself and from the feedback you get. You will also see that you are constantly picking up cues on better time management, better communication and paying attention to details.

You will learn about what it means to raise your quality level even higher. Your experience-base will grow. You will discover new resources—even the remote ones. You will figure out people's mindsets and expectations. Every single day on the job affects you positively and you are better at the end of each day.

You will acquire the ability to 'close' issues: A lot of headaches at work occur because of imperfectly or partially 'closed' issues and projects. One of the hallmarks of a person with personal accountability is that he or she will completely finish off a project or activity with a touch of class—and no hanging threads.

You will be recognized: Personal accountability will earn you the label of a conscientious employee and may even put you in the elite 'top 10 per cent' category of your organization. You can imagine the kind of rewards and recognition that will follow, once you make the cut. But don't expect anything in a hurry—most managements will wait long enough to make sure that you are truly, personally accountable and not a one-timer.

Most importantly, people who take personal ownership and accountability do so not for any of the extrinsic rewards stated above, but simply because taking ownership and accountability is the right thing to do and they enjoy doing it for its own sake. Taking ownership and accountability then becomes a habit that more or less is in their blood.

4.5 In Summary

The success of an organization like CBA Enterprises is largely due to the performance of their key employees like Ajay Gupta—who are solution seekers and who will take it upon themselves to solve problems completely to the satisfaction of their customers and other stakeholders. And the primary soft skill that sets them apart is personal accountability. Even though it may seem like a difficult concept to relate to at first, it will give you the winning edge. We conclude this chapter by listing out the key attributes of personal accountability and some examples of the same (see Table 4.1). These attributes lead to teamwork, the topic for the next chapter.

Table 4.1 *Key attributes of personal accountability*

Attribute	Example
Initiative/boldness	Starting a project that could have long-term benefits despite initial challenges.
Problem-solving	Participating in brainstorming sessions to come up with good ideas.
Perfection	Striving towards zero defects.

(Continued)

Table 4.1 *(Continued)*

Attribute	Example
Exceeding expectations	Offering customers some extras that completely surprise them pleasantly and 'wows' them.
Teamwork	Giving a hand to a colleague when needed without compromising one's own work.
Resourcefulness	Knowing where to get a particular thing done or get the right kind of help.
Open-mindedness	Correcting one's errors when someone points them out-instead of taking a defensive approach
Communication	Arranging and conducting regular meetings and keeping stakeholders informed with the right level of detail.
Professionalism	Being known around work as Mr or Miss Reliable.
Knowing the limits	Knowing the limits of one's jurisdiction and authority and not trampling on others and taking on their roles.
Failure Analysis	Using techniques like Fish Bone analysis objectively and dispassionately and applying the corrections in future

5

Teamwork and You

"None of us is as smart as all of us."

–Ken Blanchard

If we start extolling the virtues of teamwork and the power of synergy, it would be like preaching to the choir. That is because our present day work culture is predicated upon working efficiently in groups and most of us have been indoctrinated into these concepts even before we started our careers. The conventional wisdom is that the group's well-being is far more important than your individual well-being and that you should surrender your individual identity at the gates of your organization and perform only as a member of your team. Your individual performance will be whitewashed by the larger performance of the group and in the end, you partake in the rewards doled out to the entire group. Even the standard exhortation to be a 'team player', can sometimes take on an ominous interpretation as 'either you or the team—but not both'.

However, in our discussion on teamwork here, we are going to take a different perspective and argue that individual excellence and group excellence need not be mutually exclusive, but they can rather complement and supplement each other quite well. At first glance, the above premise may seem like a contradiction in terms. But effective individual-group bonding is a two-way street, where the individual not only contributes immensely to the group's collective goals, but also derives an extra dose of strength and motivation from the group to achieve personal excellence. This ability to give to the group and enhance its cohesiveness and the reciprocal ability to receive from the group and improve one's individual performance is in our opinion yet another important soft skill and we would like to call it 'team intelligence'.

5.1 THE CHANGING NATURE OF TEAMS

In recent times, there has been a paradigm shift in the concept of group itself. The classical notion is that a group is a monolithic ensemble of drones, supervised by a queen bee, which does the ordering about. As a typical example of a group, we can point to a school of fish, which swims around in-sync as a well-oiled perpetual-motion machine, with every fish participating in the action and pulling the whole group. There is only a group identity and an observer will have to strain himself to follow an individual fish. If you are a researcher, you may argue that the fish sacrificed their individual needs so that they could optimize turbulence, shear, etc. for the entire group.

Now, if this school of fish were to swim up to the ZYX Corp., a cellular phone manufacturing company and take a peek through the door of a conference room in their facility, they would see another example of a team at work. A 'school' of six human beings synchronously discharging their duties—developing a new cell-phone product called Model M123. They match each other's schedules, meet each other often and virtually connect with each other via e-mails and phone communication. Our fish observers will even marvel at the idea of the group members sacrificing their individual identities for the good of the team.

But let us don the modern hat and zoom in on this M123 new product development group in ZYX Corp. Upon a closer look, we see that the six people involved actually have names and identities! And instead of being a homogeneous group, the members are from various departments of the organization, such as marketing, finance, engineering, etc. and they all have a stake in what kind of product this new Model M123 is. It is the responsibility of this team to bring out a consummate product with the best design, great features, world-class quality, at a reasonable price-point and to hit the market ahead of the competition. The marketing manager, Ms Mukherjee, is also the 'team-leader', although she is more like an enabler/facilitator, rather than a hierarchical leader.

The M123 group discussions can sometimes become acrimonious. Mr Singh, the quality engineer, may want a neat quality feature in the product, but the finance manager, Ms Reddy, would think that it would make the product more expensive. And Ms Mukherjee of marketing may want to accelerate the development of the product because she has reports that the competition is almost ready with its product. But, Mr Naik of engineering thinks that he may not be able to rush through the necessary engineering-development work. This is not a personal tug-of-war between egoistic individuals seemingly at cross-purposes. But it is more like thrashing out the details of orthogonal functions so that the best of all the worlds is incorporated into the product design. This kind of healthy conflict is even encouraged by the group, so as to look at things critically. This new product development group is in essence just an assembly of specialists, knit together by the need to develop a new product. This new face of a team (see Figure 5.1) is very different from say, a school of fish (although some fish might disagree with us!). The *group* of people is now gelling together to form a cohesive *team*.

Fig. 5.1 *A typical multi-functional team*

We can summarize our observations of the ZYX Corp. M123 new product development *team* as follows:

- Each person has a specific identity, role and responsibility.
- All roles are important; there is a clear division of labour.
- The role assignment is not random. It is based on expertise.
- Even though there is a 'leader of the team', the other members are very important as well.
- The team makes consensus decisions on many matters, moderated by the leader.
- It is not necessary that there be any shared history or geography among members.
- It can even be a virtual team, i.e., split among multiple locations.
- Synergy is demanded and obtained.
- Conflicts occur periodically, but are accepted as healthy.
- The team is highly democratic and everyone is free to voice his or her opinion. But once a group decision is arrived at, it is implemented by all members.
- The team is not necessarily permanent.

As the M123 project evolves, more and more people will be added to the team—sometimes on the order of hundreds of people—and the project meetings themselves will be attended by tens of people, zipping through the issues quickly, but methodically. On the one hand, the team will look like a multi-pronged behemoth, but on the other hand it will have the feel of a giant orchestra playing in harmony and delivering perfect music. This kind of smooth-functioning team does not develop by accident or magic. It calls for a solid team culture in ZYX Corp., with workers trained in team intelligence. Let us see what this concept team intelligence is in the rest of this chapter and how we can integrate ourselves into a modern group effectively. A number of the points discussed here are in line with knowing the big picture and understanding your contribution to it.

5.2 The Basics of Team Intelligence—Being a Part of the Team

We will present here some of the basic tenets of what we termed as team intelligence in the previous section.

Know the team goals: You must know the mission of your team in very clear terms. If you are a part of a new product-development team, then your goal is to develop a specific product with specific features, within a given deadline and of course, well within the budget. Be aware of all the 'specifics'. This goal is common to all team members and it is why the team is formed in the first place. These common goals should bind you with the other group members. This is the big picture that should hold the entire team together.

Understand the shared vision: Not only are the end goals of the team shared by the team members, but also, the path to achieve those end goals is common to all team members. It sets the tone for group action. Everyone has the same playbook, the same deadlines, the same project management Gantt charts and network diagrams.

Evince mutual trust: There must be trust among group members—that they can count on each other to deliver their own part of the activity in time and to the prescribed standards. There must be cooperation among immediate team members when they pass on responsibilities to one another. Especially these days when 'just in time' concepts are being used all over, trust is ever more important for things to run smoothly.

Display commitment: This is an extension of trust. A total commitment to the group's goals and vision and to the group members is essential to the group's ultimate success. If you are a part of the M123 team, you are committed to doing a few things for the group and you cannot later renege on those responsibilities. You cannot join a team to look important or because the group has a certain elite character to it. Team membership is a total commitment of a chunk of your time, energy and resources. Modern teams are so frugal in their size that they have just enough people to do the job. If any team member slacks off or does a poor job of his assignment, it can derail an entire project.

Know your role and others' roles: Find out the division of labour in your team. Find out not only your specific responsibilities, but also others' functions and responsibilities. This way, when there is an intersection between your role and some others' function, you can quickly discuss it with the right team member. Also, unless special situations warrant it, do not try to take on other people's roles. If you are a quality engineer, do not behave like a finance person just because you are privy to some financial information.

Team work–the wrong approach — Team work–the right approach

Fig. 5.2 *Know your role and others' roles*

Build relationships: You must actively cultivate relationships. It may be a bit tough if you are habitually a shy person. But remember that you don't have to be personal friends with every member of the group. You just need to develop a professional relationship—to the extent that you can interact smoothly with the other person. Exactly how one goes about building a relationship may vary from person to person. But if you have a common challenge or activity (projects are full of such things), that itself can nurture a basic relationship between two people. Most organizations conduct 'team-building' exercises often and these definitely aid in relationship-building.

Network: An extension of relationship-building is networking, where you have a vast web of interconnected contacts—some within your group and some even outside, which can prove to be useful resources in your group's mission. Given today's global reach of things, it is imperative that we develop our skills of rapport-development even if we are physically invisible to the person at the other end.

Be sensitive to international/distributed team issues: One of the new realities is the virtual team that dwells in different parts of the world or that is distributed across several locations. The cohesiveness of such a group will be hard to gauge and even more difficult to improve. This is where we need to pay special attention to phone and e-mail-communication skills to bond with the other members. Try to find details about your virtual partners the way you would if they were present right next to you. Don't let distance take anything away from getting to know the other person.

Be aware that you will be in a pen-friendship mode, and both you and the other person will be doing plenty of 'impression-management' and you will have to sort through a lot of details (as we will see in Chapter 6 on 'Diversity Awareness').

Communicate constantly: Staying in touch with the team members through extensive communication is absolutely vital for the group's performance. You must be in frequent communication with specific members with whom you have immediate interaction. A face-to-face meeting is the best mode of communication, although other relevant modes should also be pursued, given the realities of team distribution across geographic locations that have become common today. You must have a different line of communication with the team leader and the management. The conference calls and meetings are other places where you have to be an effective communicator to move the group's progress forward. No wonder we have devoted a good part of this entire book to communication!

Celebrate team-achievements: Any achievement of the team will have to be celebrated—appropriately and in a timely fashion. Participate in it graciously and enjoy the fruits of your labour and other people's. Whether you are singled out or not, remember it is a team win and act accordingly.

Fig. 5.3

Celebrations are also big team-building exercises. Even a simple, celebratory group lunch or outing should be used as an opportunity to liaison with your team members. A few moments with your colleagues outside work will reveal their personal sides, that can go a long way in improving your professional relationship with them.

The above list of the basics of team intelligence is by no means complete. Nor did we go into great details. Plenty of great tomes have been written about what makes a person a responsible, effective and efficient team member and what habits foster group spirit. We hope you will complement our presentation with material from such literature. Remember also that your main focus must be your job as an engineer or marketing professional or finance manager and don't let that be affected by your efforts to become a better team citizen.

5.3 Be the Glue That Binds the Team

While the above are the basic ingredients of team intelligence, some astute team members will bring much more to the team—such as adding value to it by improving team-cohesiveness. The mysterious glue they bring to the team is often referred to as 'team chemistry', one of those terms which doesn't have a precise definition. However, team chemistry is what characterizes any modern team like the M123 team (sports teams and political teams use this term extensively). In traditional teams, with conventional homogeneous group composition, team chemistry is not that much of an issue. The 'fish-ness' is enough of a gel for a school of fish to band together. At any rate, a traditional group will have a traditional leader at the helm who will take care of team-cohesiveness.

Team chemistry or group cohesiveness—whatever you want to call it—is not only a difficult thing to quantify and measure, but opinion is also divided on exactly how much of it is required to bring out the best performance from a group. Teams which are also socially cohesive (where team members not only work with each other but are also personally friends outside work) may seem ideal. But research has been inconclusive as to whether such high-chemistry groups have necessarily better work performance. There is, however, no denying that we need a certain bare minimum of chemistry to make the team functionally cohesive for it to perform efficiently. A modern team like the M123 development team counts on its team-savvy members to be the chemical agents and bring about this function or task of cohesiveness. This is where you too can be an important contributor.

And how exactly does one add chemistry to a group? By adding a different flavour to the team—like, by being:

- The team's *enabler*, who helps the entire team in starting new activities;
- The *technical wizard* of the team, who takes care of the team's needs in the technical front;
- That *Miss Dependable*
- The *Mr Conflict Resolver* who can resolve conflicts or by being the '*go-to guy*' for solving difficult problems;
- The *ice breaker* or team builder, by removing any misunderstandings;
- The *devil's advocate* by anticipating external problems and proposing solutions proactively.

It is important to appreciate that the roles we have discussed above are neither exhaustive nor mutually exclusive. You can even bring more than one of these attributes or roles to the table. In our M123 new product development team for example, D'Souza can not only be the team's enabler, but can also be its effective task finisher (besides, of course, being the representative of the manufacturing department). Similarly, the others can also bring in various elements of chemistry to make the team robust and perform at a high level. Some people, even if they are not the greatest experts in their field, may be highly sought-after by virtue of their ability to bring chemistry to the team. That is how important team intelligence is (see Figure 5.4).

Fig. 5.4 *Roles played in a multi-functional team*

However tempting it may be, it is difficult to itemize a master list of such elusive, group-binding 'chemical elements' or analyze your team's performance on the basis of such a list. That's why it is all the more critical for you to relate to your group in special ways and exude warmth towards everyone in the team.

5.4 What Can Destroy Team Intelligence?

A modern group, such as the M123 new product development team, is a creation of the parent organization. It is basically an assembly of individuals with none of the traditional structure and binding forces. For example, the members in an old-fashioned group, such as a battalion of soldiers, may have a shared past or common background, whereas an M123 group may have members who have not even seen each other. They will have to go on only on the basis of common goals. It is easy for centrifugal forces to weaken a modern group since loyalties do not have time to develop, unlike in traditional groups. Even one or two team members with poor attitude can greatly jeopardize a group's morale and performance in today's set up. So, we need to watch out for such things and nip them in the bud. Let us look at some examples of such low team-intelligence.

Fig. 5.5 *We don't find such examples in the world of ants*

'Win-lose' attitude: A very strong ego can kill all camaraderie and create a 'win-lose' attitude where as much as you want to win, you would want the other person to lose and look bad. Even though in the short term you may feel good, this is counter-productive and futile. If there are any personal differences with any group member, sit down with them and discuss the differences. In this highly competitive world, we cannot afford to self-destruct within the framework of our own group.

Individual opinion/interest domination: One variation of the high-ego situation is the 'my way or no way' attitude. You fall in love with your ideas so much that you are bull-headed about taking another look at things. 'I have done this so many times,' you might argue, trying to intimidate others in the group. Realize that if you give up your opinion in the interest of the goals of the team, it is no defeat. The idea is to reach a consensus opinion and push ahead with the project.

Poor inter-personal skills: Rudeness, discourtesy, bad-mouthing, hyper-sensitivity, social prejudices, etc. can all be rolled into the general poor inter-personal skills category and need to be remedied quickly. It may have something to do with the basic insecurity you may have. Get counselling if the problem persists even after discussing it with teammates. Leave office conflicts in the office. Taking them personally and feeling slighted or insulted at the flimsiest of circumstances is poor team-intelligence.

***Independence vs. interdependence*:** Some team members have a way of disconnecting from the group and doing their own things in the periphery no matter how much they are goaded into joining the mainstream. They are basically loners who have the 'leave me alone' attitude. These people view independence as a virtue and strength. This can kill team spirit. Good team chemistry thrives on, and builds upon, a strong sense of interdependence, where each member contributes to and enjoys the team's success as a whole without narrow territorial fights.

Confusion and flock mentality: Some people have no clue as to what the team is all about. They are excessively dependent on kind-hearted team members to pull them along. They are confused and overwhelmed by the task in front of them. They simply ride on other people's output and hope that nobody notices. They have minimal contribution to the group's performance. Such deadwood is best removed at the earliest for the benefit of the entire team.

5.5 The Other Face of Team Intelligence—Individual Development

Being a responsible team member and being able to add chemistry to the team is just one half of team intelligence. To be able to use the team as a platform to put on an impressive individual performance is the rest of the story. If you are Naik of engineering in the M123 team, left to yourself, you would probably invent several technologies. But with a Mukherjee pushing you toward a deadline and a Reddy limiting you on cost, you will innovate even more and come up with the perfect technological solution. Here are some ways in which your team can help improve your personal performance.

You manage risks and downturns better: A team is a great shock-absorber. Individual downturns and defeats may not stick out that prominently in the context of a team. Besides, the team also acts as extra sets of eyes and ears that will alert you ahead of time if you are heading in the wrong direction. Since other people's fortunes are tied to yours, you will tend to stay in the middle of the road than take extreme risks.

You learn something from others: Working in a cross-functional team, such as the M123 team, is a great learning experience. You learn a lot about other people's functions, roles and the big picture in general. Besides, you will see the many ramifications and perspectives of your own activities and how it rattles through the entire enterprise. Your knowledge will become well-rounded.

Better feeling of security, comfort level: Once you become comfortable with your team, you will be at peace with yourself. This sense of (job) security is an ideal atmosphere for personal growth. Instead of being complacent, use this positive ambience to perform better and further your career.

Your communication skills improve: Your communication skills will no doubt improve from what they were. Being a member of a project team like M123, you will hone your meeting, presentation and report-writing skills. Since you have to pitch to the upper management every once in a while, your skills in vertical communication will also improve. And if you are like Ms Reddy of finance, you have to constantly defend your position and articulate your viewpoint in all the group discussions and thus your verbal skills will also become stronger. There is nothing like 'immersion' to quickly pick up skills.

Feedback, help and encouragement motivate you: The biggest benefit you get out of teamwork is a fan club of several team members who will root for you in your endeavours. They will give valuable feedback, criticism and pointers to your performance. Some of them will actively help you. Some others will be a repository of great habits that you can emulate. The motivation and encouragement you derive from the team experience will be a major high that you can ride to the next level of personal excellence.

5.6 In Summary

Although this chapter is developed around a modern project team, team intelligence is a general enough soft skill that can be used in any group environment. Whether your group is modern or a traditional one depends on the composition and mission of your group and also on the nature and culture of your organization. So, a key success factor in teamwork is:

> Have a clear idea of the team's shared vision, mission and goals.

If you work on 'projects', and that too in a modern IT company, or any 'flat' organization, it is likely that your group is more along the lines of the M123 team, where responsibility is functional.

> Get a clear understanding of your role vis-à-vis others' roles and functions.

This produces 'team chemistry'. In order to achieve this team chemistry,

> Communicate, communicate and communicate—both within your team and with your network of professional contacts.

The team is greater than the sum of its parts. Make sure

> You all celebrate the team's achievements and take conscious part in team-building activities.

Instead of looking at teamwork as constraining, you ought to look at it as yet another avenue to discover yourself and enable significant self-improvement. Not only should you help your team to be the best that there is, but also you should personally aim to be the Most Valuable Player (MVP) of your team. To this end,

> Never lose an opportunity to learn from more experienced colleagues. It is your responsibility to seek feedback and work on improvement.

Once you start being an integral part of the team and start cherishing and living the team goals, your own stature and importance will grow in the organization. You will find that you will start enjoying being in the team and soon you will start appreciating the fact that it takes different types of people to achieve the shared team vision. This leads us to get better diversity awareness, which is the topic of the next chapter.

6

Diversity Awareness

"What counts in making a happy relationship is not so much how compatible you are, but how you deal with incompatibility."

–Daniel Goleman

Snapshot 6.1

A Day in the Life of LMN Corp

LMN Corp. is a thriving automobile components manufacturing company with huge factories in Pune and Chennai and operations in several countries. Their list of customers and suppliers covers over fifty countries. We are at their headquarters in Chennai.

- 6.30 A.M.: Bleary-eyed and with cups of strong coffee in their hands, Mr Hegde and his group are huddled around a telephone—they are on a conference call with their customers from an East-Asian country. But it is no walk in the park. The party at the other end is always tough as nails and demands an arm and a leg and slaps LMN Corp. with seemingly impossible deadlines. Hegde always feels flustered after each of these conference calls.
- 10.00 A.M.: An American delegation is here from Detroit to discuss the design of a component. A middle-aged white man in a suit is followed by a younger, elegantly dressed African-American lady and another person in T-shirt and jeans. You are the last minute substitute for your colleague who could not make

it due to some emergency. It is only after sitting down and exchanging business cards that you realize that the lady is the manager, the man in the T-shirt is a senior engineer and the middle-aged person is actually lower in hierarchy. Thank god, a *faux pas* is avoided.

- 1.00 P.M.: Ms Sultana of LMN Corp. is on her very first foreign business trip. She has just arrived in Amsterdam. She is amazed to see a canal-based boat transportation system, co-existing with trams and bicycles. Even though everyone speaks English, all the signs are in Dutch and she has no idea what any of them means. She has special diet restrictions and it is quite a task for her to find a restaurant that would serve her special food items.
- 3.00 P.M.: A Japanese delegation of suppliers is in a meeting with your team. The visitors speak very little English. No matter how hard you try, the delegation's leader, Tanaka-*san,* does not understand you at all. Finally, after two hours of forceful effort, everything is square and they take you out to a nice Japanese restaurant—but even though you are a meat-eater, *sushi* doesn't appeal to you.
- 6.30 P.M.: Half of Mr Krishnamurthy's team is in a conference call with the other half of the team, which is based in France. Ever since LMN Corp bought out a small French company, Krishnamurthy acts as the manager for even the French unit and he has been asked to integrate the two groups. It has been rough going for Krishnamurthy and he senses an undercurrent of hostility and suspicion from the French side. Or maybe he just feels that way. Now they tell him that entire Europe will be shut down for a month of vacation and he cannot expect anything to be done for a month. Krishnamurthy is flabbergasted.
- 12.00 Midnight: Third shift is over in the factory. All the factory production data of LMN Corp is uploaded from India to servers in the USA for later analysis. Another typical work day comes to an end in LMN Corp. Phew!!

As you can tell, LMN Corp. is a microcosm of today's globalized business world, where not only technical competence and business excellence matter, but also how effectively an organization interacts with its *international* stakeholders—for, it is the international customers, suppliers and colleagues who propel these organizations to even greater heights. Global partnerships and teams have become so pervasive that no modern organization can function without them any more.

But with global partnerships come globe-sized cross-cultural issues and problems. Situations such as the one faced by Krishnamurthy, the manager, are no longer just isolated, freak occurrences that make for dinner-time conversation, but are more routine and commonplace these days. Not just Krishnamurthy, given the enormous scope and reach of today's international operations, even little guys in the organization can find themselves in the middle of a culture clash. No wonder then that a modern, global organization like LMN Corp. would like its employees—managers and the little guys—to be part cultural anthropologists and part cultural ambassadors and display sensitivity and poise in dealing with their global partners. To facilitate this, LMN even organizes cross-cultural workshops for its employees every once in a while.

The smartness that LMN Corp. is looking for in its employees is technically known as *diversity awareness*. Although it is considered a core skill these days, diversity awareness is not an easy skill to acquire and hone. To begin with, you need to have an aptitude for cross-cultural experience and then, you should equip yourself with the mindset and the knowledge to pursue international dealings. You may be able to pick up part of this skill on the job, but supplementing it with self-learning and professional training can greatly enhance your job performance. In this chapter, we will break this soft skill into its components and discuss the various ways in which you can develop it. Diversity is not limited to cultural diversity alone, but can come about due to gender, differently abled workers and any other demographic factor. But, for reasons of brevity, we will only look at culture-induced diversity for most parts in this chapter (that too specifically US-India cultural issues), with short sections on gender issues and issues pertaining to the differently abled.

6.1 What Is Diversity Awareness and Why Is It a Good Thing?

What is diversity awareness? Is it like training in etiquette, where, if you want to know the right way of saying thanks in Germany, you just turn to Page 214 of a fat book on German culture and follow the instructions? Is it being familiar with a massive spreadsheet of 'us' vs 'them' cultural behaviour? Or could it be an expertise in 'if French…then' kind of rules-based algorithm? Or is it deep-rooted insights into their history? Or is it the National Geographic kind of getting a glimpse into an alien society? Is it more than just information?

We believe that diversity awareness is partly all of the above. And it is much more. We also believe that it is a fundamental attitude issue and not a sugar coated 'here is all that you want to know about diversity and presto…you now have diversity awareness!' pill. We would like to break it into what we consider to be its major components and examine it in some more detail.

Diversity awareness includes:

- ***Knowledge about other cultures:*** It is a bundle of facts and inferences about other cultures (subject to caveats, of course). If we have statistical or social-research basis for such inferences, all the better. Of course, one has to be careful about misinformation, out-dated information and plain ignorance masquerading as real information in popular media.
- ***Sensitivity toward other cultures:*** This 'live and let live' kind of attitude is a major aspect of awareness. You know that lifestyles can be quite different across cultures and that even if you don't personally do something, you respect

the others' right and desire to do it. You may not take a month-long summer vacation yourself, but you cannot resent people from another culture and society wanting to exercise what they consider almost their birthright.

- ***Knowledge about rules and restrictions in other cultures:*** At the very beginning you should develop an awareness for those inviolable rules and regulations of the other culture—because not knowing them cannot act as your defence, in case you get into trouble. For example, every country has its own maze of road rules, immigration laws, business restrictions and so on. Become familiar with at least the basics of these if you are going to do business with a country. As an example, when you drive on the roads, honking is almost mandatory in India, while it is simply a very discourteous act in the USA.
- ***Getting rid of cultural stereotyping:*** Diversity awareness is the realization that the world is neither simplistic nor is it governed by cultural stereotypes. 'The French love their coffee' is not an axiomatic truth, because there are many, many French who do not drink coffee. Diversity awareness is the ability to recognize individual situations and act accordingly.
- ***Ability to communicate your cultural coordinates to others:*** You should not just be able to understand the other culture, but you should also be able to sensitize others to your culture, special needs and situations. If you are a vegetarian, stick to your ground and make others aware of your requirement. Don't suffer in silence and end up eating two plates of lettuce.

Mastery over diversity issues is somewhat like mastery over engineering or law or accounting. Possessing fat books alone will not help you. You need to have a basic aptitude for the thing and solid analytical skills. Only then will you know which part of the book to turn to and how best to solve problems. Mastery in diversity awareness is like being a great car driver who has quickly figured out the alien terrain and topography and who is able to navigate through various alternative routes. It means knowing enough about the rules and laws to abide by them. And then being such a considerate driver that people of all cultures not only feel comfortable with you, but also enjoy their ride with you. It is not the same thing as knowing where the nearest Korean restaurant is; but it is *wanting to know* where the nearest Korean restaurant is. It is an attitude that sees the world as a limitless expanse of opportunities and not as a bunch of criss-crossing barbed wires.

No matter if it belongs to attitude or etiquette, and no matter how complex it is, diversity awareness is vital to modern businesses. As your employees become culturally sensitive, you will begin to notice some immediate, tangible benefits. Your conference calls and visitor pow-wows will no longer get out-of-control or confusing. There will be less frustration due to poor communication and even less misunderstanding. In fact, there will be more positive vibes and a sense of cooperation. Negotiations will go on smoothly and you will see that you avoid capitulation and surrendering, because there is less tension all around. International teambuilding will be like a sociology 101 class, fun and insightful, and the expected synergies will be realized very quickly. Conflicts will be solved easily.

As if these reasons are not enough, let us enumerate five near-philosophical reasons why diversity awareness is a good thing.

It is the right thing: With awareness comes sensitivity to the other person's specific viewpoints and at a fundamental level, it seems like a fair and courteous thing to do. It is not right to expect the other person to always switch over to our way of doing things and readily adopt our methods.

If our Japanese visitors falter in their English, decency demands that you help them understand better—perhaps by repeating and paraphrasing what you said and perhaps by talking slowly or by supplementing what you are saying with appropriate body language or even writing on a white board. Maybe our Indian accents confused them even more and we are equally to blame for causing this communication snafu.

It makes good business sense and makes it easier to do business: You know that if you take care of the non-business, cultural components, then the business side of things will automatically become easier. If her Dutch counterparts help Sultana find the food she was looking for, she would be in a much better frame of mind to conduct business.

It makes it easier to understand other systems: You can understand the other culture's 'system' better. You can get a feel for their business practices, broad social realities and government rules and regulations—basically, you can glean their business climate.

For example, by engaging closely with your Japanese partners, you may be able to learn about Japanese business systems, like their long term supplier-customer relationships or their *kanban* system of manufacturing. Your colleagues from Europe and the USA can help you understand their latest laws on outsourcing. And a person like Krishnamurthy will realize that people going on a month-long vacation is how the 'system' works in Europe.

It makes it easy to spot talent and harness it: One of the main reasons for forming international teams is to have a larger pool of ideas and solutions. In order to ferret out great ideas from across the globe, it is necessary to cut to the chase of non-business factors and go straight to the talent part. Don't let the poor English of your team-mate in Europe obfuscate her talent. Similarly, until you have absorbed diversity awareness and broken your habit of cultural stereotyping, you wouldn't have guessed that a person in a casual T-shirt is an engineer who can come up with great ideas. Diversity awareness takes you straight to the other person's perspective.

You will not have the victim mentality: In your international dealings, at a personal level, you may sometimes feel like you are victimized—victims of cultural misunderstanding, victims of cultural biases and so on. With better diversity awareness, you can actually pinpoint why there was a misunderstanding in the first place and then sort through the situation. It will make you more sensitive to the other person's situation, instead of building up your angst.

In the instance of LMN Corp.'s tough customer from the Far East, once Hegde realizes that the tough customer is simply playing his business role and not trying to pick on him, he and his team can be calmer during their early morning conference calls.

On the rare occasion when you actually experience any form of harassment or bias, report the matter to your superiors and let them take care of it through official channels. Don't lose your cool or try to fix the problem by yourself.

6.2 How Can We Cultivate Diversity Awareness?

The challenge then is to convert mere mortals into culturally aware, world citizens who can relate well to the pluralistic, multi-cultural business environments of today. The first part of this process is to tune one's attitude, such that it now has an international orientation. Our upbringing has a lot to do with this. Those of us growing up in multi-cultural environments are probably more open to other cultures. On the other hand, our upbringing can cut us the other way—we might have grown up with age old prejudices and ignorance about other people. Attitude-tuning here could mean our shedding these preconceived notions.

The other part of the process is to systematically instill knowledge about other cultures, diversity issues, etc. This can be quite daunting, given that there are vast cultural differences between one country and another (and even region to region) in almost anything we do—the food we eat, the way we communicate with each other, our body language, the way we relate to each other, how we view our jobs, etc. Even in the limited sphere of business activities, there can still be significant cultural overtones. So, any such knowledge-building will have to be done with great care and preferably cross-verified with several sources. Examples of such sources to pick up knowledge about other cultures are:

Seminars/workshops: Typically, corporations organize formal 'diversity training' programmes, where employees attend short seminars or workshops conducted by appropriate 'culture experts'. These training programmes vary in content, intensity, scope and sophistication. They can be narrowly-focused, intense courses, zooming in on just one culture or can be extensive treatments of multiple cultures. They are usually packed with examples, case studies and role-playing exercises to sensitize the participants to the other culture. At the end of the training, it is expected that the participants have developed some degree of understanding and appreciation for the other culture and see cultural diversity as a positive force. The main take away from such a training programme is to see things through other's eyes, respect cultural differences and come up with socially and politically correct international responses.

Large corporations in the USA often have orientation classes before sending their contingents to other countries such as India. Several 'India experts' will conduct the sessions and answer specific questions about India. 'What gifts are appropriate for your Indian hosts?' or 'What are the taboo topics that you will not discuss with your Indian colleagues?' and so on. Similarly, large corporations in India have cultural training for the employees being sent to other countries.

If you are going to host an international delegation, you must conduct mock-drills before they show up, with some of you playing the roles of your foreign counterparts. There is nothing like a dress rehearsal to put you in the groove. You must later review your mock-drill performance from several angles so that you do a perfect job in the real situation.

Books/articles: These are the traditional ways of getting information about other cultures and furthering one's awareness. Travel books, language phrase books, autobiographical accounts of cross-cultural experience—all have been the staple of international business folks for long. The biggest advantage of the print medium is that through it good writers can present deep and highly nuanced insights. Sometimes even fictional writing can be a good way to learn about other societies.

Given the proliferation of international business, an increasing number of culture-based articles like 'How to do business with Indians' or 'How to deal with the Chinese' are now appearing in business journals. Although they can give some important tips, be forewarned that they can be too simplistic and awash in generalizations.

TV/movies: Television and movies provide a wealth of diversity-oriented materials. There are now TV channels dedicated to showcasing other cultures. Also, a plethora of well-made documentaries and sensitive feature films are now available, that open up a whole new world for us. The biggest advantage of TV shows and movies is that the visual medium can offer a dramatic and powerful look into diversity issues. The disadvantage is that they too can have specific biases.

Internet/blogs: The Internet is a great source of information about other countries and cultures. Various Internet forums, blogs and even simple Google searches are very good tools in getting answers to your questions.

The Internet also offers several advantages. First of all, you can ask particular questions on specific topics like, 'What are the elementary schools like in Las Vegas, USA?' Secondly, you can go back and forth and have a follow-up discussion on the topic. Thirdly, you can get multiple answers from multiple people. And finally, the answers are likely to be from real people who went through a similar experience or from the natives. You may unearth a lot of inside information as well—like that as-yet-undiscovered restaurant in London whose bread pudding is out of the world.

With the ubiquitous presence of social networking, you can actually live in a virtual multi-cultural, diverse world today, without ever leaving home.

Talking to people: People who have had international experience are very good sources of information about diversity. This is especially so, if the person happens to be from your own workplace, and is just a few steps ahead of you in this matter. Such people will home in on the exact issues that have been bothering you and alert you on the pitfalls. They will share with you the lessons they learnt from their experience. They might even drop a name or two that may prove to be useful resources in your dealings over there.

Self-discovery: No matter how many external sources one refers to, there is nothing like self-discovery. One day spent in London or Paris can teach you much more than you can ever learn from any book or movie. Travel is just one example of how you can open your eyes to new things. Intense conversation with a person from another culture can be another avenue of self-discovery. Thanks to globalization, you now get a variety of international icons and products in your own backyard. It is now easier than ever to 'discover' and experience foreign things.

The 'India' advantage: India is a nation of many nations. Indians have their own cultural plurality, with numerous religions, regions and languages. Therefore, people in India in general have a natural tolerance and openness toward things that are different from their own. This nascent diversity awareness is a major positive for people from India.

Most Indians have a reasonable command of at least two languages—English being one of them. Hence language is usually not a major barrier for Indians. India has had a history of openness to foreign cultures and the long, democratic tradition has institutionalized the plurality of Indian culture. Creating solid cultural awareness should be easier from these building blocks. Unfortunately, we also have to watch out for some feudal and colonial era holdovers that are still vitiating the Indian socio-cultural landscape.

While these are steps you can take to improve your diversity awareness, we would like to touch upon two related, 'good-to-have-in-today's-world' kind of traits that go hand-in-hand with your efforts. These are as follows:

Developing a neutral profile: One of the trends these days is to develop a neutral profile, so that you don't stand out in a crowd and attract attention for all the wrong reasons. Your accent should be neutral, your food habits and clothes should be close to neutral and you should be flexible enough to choose from the available choices, instead of requesting special things. This kind of blending into the background—if you can pull it off—can be a valuable business-personality.

Being America-centric: The USA has always been the world business leader. Despite the dot-com bust, financial crisis, etc. American business practices and etiquette are still the *de facto* world standards. Whether it is the five day work-week, employee empowerment, casual business dressing or referring to each other by first names, American business culture continues to dominate the world. American values, such as rising up to a challenge and solving problems with fervor, dignity of labour and the likes, are worthy of being emulated by anyone. It is therefore important that we pick up as many of these essential 'Americanisms' as our bandwidth will allow.

The first Americanism that you pick up should be elements of American English, which is the unofficial business language of the world. Pay particular attention to American idioms, phrases and metaphors. Find out at least the major differences between the usage of Indian English and American English, so that things don't get lost in communication. For example, you may happen to mention that you *passed out* last year, meaning you *graduated* last year. But in American English, passing out means losing one's consciousness, such as due to heavy drinking, and your American friend might be shocked to hear this. We will discuss such language issues in Chapter 39.

6.3 Gender Issues

As important as cultural diversity awareness, is awareness toward women's rights and gender issues. These are not merely matters of propriety and manners, but have serious legal repercussions given today's zero tolerance policy toward most forms of sexist behaviour. Gender bias and sexism have still not been wiped out completely from the workplace and sometimes rear their ugly heads in subtle and covert ways.

Along the lines of diversity training, there should be periodic sensitivity workshops on gender issues for all employees—men and women. Such a workshop should include the latest legal aspects, complete with the latest definitions of what constitutes sexual harassment. Examples of appropriate and inappropriate behaviour with women colleagues should be given to highlight how things have changed since the early politically incorrect days. Male workers should understand that women don't need special treatment—only equal treatment. A workshop should teach them to be extra careful with visiting foreign women employees who can be ultra-sensitive to sexist or condescending remarks. Such a workshop should also attempt to break anti-social male behaviour like male 'clubbiness' or isolating and excluding women colleagues at work.

6.4 Sensitivity to Differently Abled People

Today's work environment is filled with diversity, not only of cultures or gender, but also of differently-abled people. In the less sensitive years gone by, some people were referred to by terms such as physically handicapped, mentally retarded and so on. These terms were later replaced with terms like 'physically challenged', 'mentally challenged' or 'people with special needs'. Even these terms were found to be condescending and negative and they completely ignored some of powerful and unique abilities that these people possessed. For example, Helen Keller scaled great heights even though she could not see, hear or speak. A number of people labelled as autistic have tremendous calendar and memory skills. Thus, recognizing their special strengths, these people are now referred to as *differently abled.*

Thanks to increased empathy for the differently-abled people and enhanced technology that offsets any disadvantages of any special need, today's workplace is full of people who are differently-abled. There is a software testing organization staffed by people with Aspergers Syndrome (a part of the autistic spectrum) employed because of the eye for detail that these people have. An organization in India has a policy to staff people who are differently-abled or who have special needs. In this section, we will quickly see what you should and should not do as a part of recognizing diversity of the differently abled people.

- When you choose people, do not give any consideration to any physical difficulties unless it pertains to the job. For example, if you are recruiting for a programming job, a person confined to a wheel chair should get the same chance as a person who is mobile by himself.
- Do not ask people about their physical difficulty or physical difference. For example, do not ask a person why he has a scar or why he limps (unless the job requires running around and the limp may prevent him from doing his job).
- Do not be condescending to these people; they don't look for your sympathy.
- Do make sure that the work environment does not hinder their access. For example, if it is within your power, do ensure that there are enough ramps and access paths.
- Do respect the ♿ sign in parking lots. Let the deserving people use these lots and don't let your unwillingness to walk a few steps extra come in way of parking your car in the right place and leaving these reserved lots for the people who really need them.
- Wherever possible, be considerate to the special needs. For example, if you can reduce the amount they need to commute across different floors, it would certainly help them.

6.5 In Summary

Diversity is the new energy that is lighting up today's businesses. It is the source of much-needed freshness, creativity and variety. But to rein it in and turn it into a useful force, you need well-orchestrated international hand-holding—or diversity awareness. Although it has an empire spread over several continents and cultures, LMN Corp. still needs its worldwide stakeholders to be on the same page of the book—except that the book now comes in several sizes, styles and languages and being on the same page can only come about through having diversity-sensitive employees with a global outlook.

Snapshot 6.2

- 6.30 A.M.: The next day, Hegde and his team are on the same conference call with the same client from the Far East. The clients are as forceful as always. From next week on, they want the conference call to be advanced to 5.30 A.M.! Hegde silently wonders who came up with the statement 'the customer is the king', as he reaches for his second cup of coffee.

  It is just another day in the office at LMN Corp.!

Unlearn a lot of wrong things and myths you learnt about other cultures somewhere along the way.

> Get rid of stereotypes.

Take the initiative and become friendly with your international partners. Usually, in business calls, a short, non-business preamble before the business part of the call is considered okay. Be aware that different people will respond at different levels and that you cannot impose yourself on others if they are not interested.

> Get to know your international colleagues better.

Each culture and nation is different. Seek out friendship with people from other religions and people of other backgrounds. Participate in their cultural events. This will broaden your horizon and increase cultural diversity awareness.

> Participate in cultural events of other cultures; try out new things from different cultures and geographies.

Different cultures will have different methods, lifestyles and customs. Don't try to be judgemental about different cultures.

> It is different strokes for different people.

Sexism has no place anywhere, much less in the office. Even though we have come a long way on this, the international standards are much more stringent.

> Get rid of gender biases.

Appreciating special needs, recognizing differently abled people is becoming extremely important in the global scenario.

> Cultivate sensitivity to the diversity of people with special needs and the differently abled.

Diversity appreciation requires being sensitive, patient and accommodating. You have to be sensitive about what humour or language is appropriate and accommodating to other people's customs. But, it does not mean that you have to subjugate your customs or lose your personal or organizational pride.

Always present a good image of yourself and your organization and culture—diversity awareness and your pride don't form a zero-sum game

As you go through a long career, you would get opportunities to work with multiple cultures, visit multiple countries. This will entail continuous honing of skills and awareness. This is just one of the aspects of lifelong learning – the topic for the next chapter.

Fig. 6.1

7

Lifelong Learning

"Those who will succeed in the 21st century are not those who can read and write, but those who can unlearn, learn and re-learn, again and again."

– *Alvin Toffler*

We live in times when breathtaking technological changes; dramatic business-paradigm shifts are occurring all around us. If you are out of touch with things for a week, you begin to feel like Rip van Winkle and seem several steps behind. In this super-charged climate, only the fittest survive and if you are not constantly aware of the changing environment around you—and able to adapt and change as necessary—you will find yourself slowly dropping out of the race.

It used to be that most people from the previous generation (at least in India) took up a job and stuck to it for their entire career. As a result, there was not much change in the environment and the people around them. But today, very rarely do you find that people stay in the same job for more than a few years (and sometimes, just a few *months*). Hence, the change in the people around you, exacerbated by the rapid changes in technology and business practices, makes it imperative that the information and skills needed to succeed in this changing environment be constantly honed. If we don't spend time sharpening the saw, then we will no longer be able to do our job.

This chapter is about *learnability* and the process of *lifelong learning* also called *continuous learning. Learnability* is another important soft skill and is the ability of an individual to continuously keep learning in the context of ever changing technology and environment. It comprises having a spirit of inquiry, an air of inquisitiveness and not having reservations about learning from any source. It transforms into a lifelong learning experience—unlearning and re-learning any shifting paradigm.

In Section 7.1, we outline the steps that you can practice to inculcate lifelong learning. We discuss some of the challenges in the quest for learning in Section 7.3. The chapter concludes with a set of tips for pursuing lifelong learning.

7.1 The Steps in Lifelong Learning

There are four essential steps you go through, as shown in Figure 7.1 below:

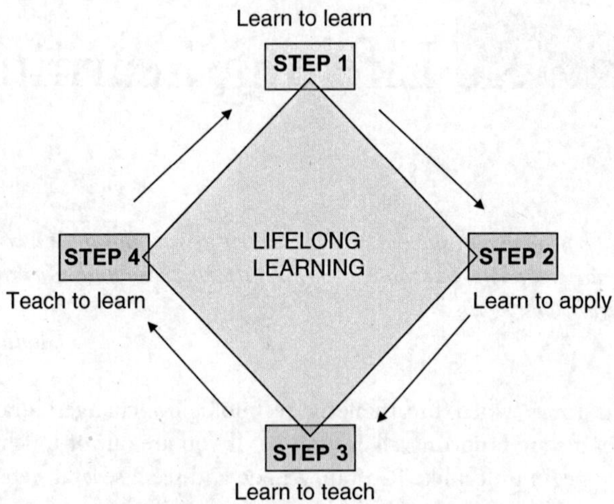

Fig. 7.1 *Steps in lifelong learning*

Learn to learn: Learning to learn is itself a challenging process. How you learn anything will depend on what you learn, your preferences, from whom you learn and finally, the learning environment. When you are working in an organization, you are already likely to be set in your ways and your learning preferences and styles are already well entrenched in you. Your learning preference and style (that has been built over the years) is like a tide or wave confronting you. You have to go with the tide for some distance and then, if necessary, turn against the tide. You have to learn to learn—learn how to go against the tide when required. This may first involve

- Unlearning some of what you have already learnt
- Unlearning some of your learning styles and methods
- Learning to adapt yourself to a new learning environment
- Learning the new content you have to learn.

Snapshot 7.1

Mukesh Sethi has moved from a large MNC, where he was a project manager leading a group of 20 people, to a start-up company where he is taking charge of product development of a new product. In his earlier role, there were strict procedures to be followed, everything had to get approved at multiple levels and Mukesh often had no clue as to when he would be able to carry out an activity. But, in his new job, he finds that he has to do everything himself—from liaisoning with multiple internal groups, collaborating with customers to find out their needs, essentially being in the mode of 'do what it takes'. In order to cope with the new environment, Mukesh has to change his learning style from 'awaiting instructions from the boss' to 'being a go-getter, able to chart his own destiny and how to get there'. He would also have to learn new tools and techniques for his new job. For example, he may have to get a crash course on finance and marketing to understand the nuances of these new facets of product development and get trained on how to interact with new types of stakeholders. He may have to attend workshops on communication to enable him to communicate better, as his new job has significantly more (and different types of) communication. Also, his learning may involve a variety of methods that include classroom training, observing others at work, participating in forums and learning from colleagues and case histories.

In essence he is learning to learn—learning *new learning styles*, learning *new methods of learning* and learning *new content.*

Learn to apply: All the learning to learn done in the previous phase will bear fruit only when you start applying what was learnt. Mere classroom training is not sufficient. Whether it is programming or making presentations, application of what was learnt is what makes the difference between success and failure. Most classroom learning materials are either theories of an idealized world or techniques, followed by illustrative examples of application of such theories and techniques. But real life situations are seldom cookie-cutter versions of these scenarios. They are combinations of the various basic scenarios you studied in the classroom. The ability to figure out which technique to use in what circumstance or scenario is what brings the learning to fruition.

Snapshot 7.2

As a part of his training for his new role, Mukesh was sent to a training programme on making presentations and using PowerPoint. The instructor discussed the role of graphs in effectively getting information across with the participants. He discussed when and where bar graphs, pie charts and line charts can be used. Each of them is effective for a particular type of presentation. For example, pie charts are useful for presenting the distribution of various types of categories, while bar charts enable better comparison of the same attribute over different time periods.

In real life, Mukesh may have a scenario where he would have to present a comparison of the various components of the total cost over the past three years. Should he use a bar chart or a pie chart? Should he use a combination of both? If so, how? Even though this example is one of using a tool, the same tough choices await on a bigger scale when trying to apply what is learnt to areas like negotiation, communication and such matters that are considered 'subjective'.

In essence Mukesh is learning to apply—learning *to categorize the learning to basic patterns*, learning *to identify the basic building blocks in a real-life scenario* and learning *to custom-make a solution for the new scenario.*

Learn to teach: In order to gain full conviction and appreciation of the new things you are learning, the next step is to be able to teach others what you have learnt. 'Teaching' in this context does not mean just taking classes of others. It could involve mentoring, the process by which you help another person to further his or her skills. It also involves management and leadership, by which you leverage another person's strength and competence for mutual benefit. Doing a thing or knowing a thing well does not always translate to being able to teach others how to gain mastery. But lifelong learning is not complete without learning to teach others. Unless your expertise is inculcated into others, you are going to be indispensable in your current job and thus, you will be expected to keep doing the current job forever. While this may give you a sense of job security, it will reduce your own learning and career opportunities. Further, from an organizational viewpoint, the expertise you have is not widespread enough, and so the organization becomes too dependent on your individual heroics. In order to increase the depth of your own knowledge and to enhance the collective learning of an organization, learning to teach is an important step in lifelong learning.

Snapshot 7.3

Ram Venkatesh was recruited from a leading Bangalore college into a medium-sized software product development company, two years ago. During his first two years on the job, Ram was a Java programmer in the Invoicing module of the company's ERP suite. The Invoicing module had several intricate discounting mechanisms. While being good at his Java programming, Ram also picked up the nuances of the invoicing and discounting domains. After two years, Ram's manager realized the potential that Ram had and assigned two fresh college graduates to Ram, to be trained on the programming aspects as well as some of the intricacies of the domain. As Ram brought the two fresh recruits up to speed in their work, he recognized new frontiers in his own ability and understanding of the subject. This increased his self confidence and propelled him to higher learning, creating opportunities for his career to reach new heights.

Ram has graduated to the state of *learning to teach*, increasing organizational learning and also setting himself free for and capable of more learning as he progresses through his career—he is well in the orbit for lifelong learning.

Teach to learn: When you teach or mentor someone else, first and foremost, you will want to have mastery over every aspect of the subject matter, so as to be prepared for any question from the audience. This will give you a depth of understanding that would be otherwise difficult to acquire. Further, when you teach or preach something, you will develop an internal conviction about what you teach and this will drive your understanding of the subject matter further. Finally, when you teach or mentor someone else on a subject, you will be surprised to find out how many new perspectives they can bring to the table. They can even surprise you by stretching your concept or idea to new dimensions that you did not even imagine possible. You will find *you* are actually learning new things about a topic that you thought you were an expert of. Realization of the fact that there is much more to learn is by itself a great learning experience that is central to the goal of lifelong learning.

Snapshot 7.4

Ram has now moved on to be a systems architect. As an architect, Ram is consulted for most technical decisions in his area. Ram also participates in reviewing a number of technical proposals made by people at various levels. When he does the reviews of proposals on new technologies, he is actually teaching the art of architecting to the people who are making those proposals. He is teaching what he has learnt from his past, diverse experiences and also how to apply these learnings to the new areas. At the same time, the people whom he is teaching have more in-depth knowledge of the new areas and Ram is himself learning the details about the new areas from them.

Thus Ram's review and teaching synthesize his *ability to learn* new technologies with his *ability to apply* his past experience along with his *ability to articulate* this past experience and knowledge in the form of teaching or reviewing.

7.2 Tips to Achieve Effective Learning

In order to go smoothly through the four stages described above, the following tips would be useful:

Listen to the appropriate stakeholders: Listening is the first step towards learning. How many times have we heard our teachers, right from kindergarten through college, ask us to keep quiet and listen attentively? As we will discuss in Chapter 17, listening is a whole body process. This includes observing what is happening around you and modifying your response by continuous learning. This also involves active participation with the environment. The net summary of this is to keep your mind open and free of distortion.

Question to remove any doubts: A questioning mind is often the one that learns best. Whenever a new concept or idea is to be learnt, it is very vital to internalize the concept or tool by removing any doubts you may have yourself. Blindly accepting anything will make you a less effective learner. When someone talks about a new technology and promises a two-fold increase in performance, ask yourself questions like: How can they achieve this improvement? If this improvement was possible, why was it not achieved earlier? At what cost is this improvement achieved? Are there any side effects? Is there anything in the fine print that is being missed? By this, we do not mean that you should be the permanent nay-sayer and get labelled as a pessimist. All this implies is that you be objective and meticulous and not be afraid to ask questions.

Apply and gain value by doing: As we saw in the previous section, you will gain value from any new learning only when you start applying your learning to your life. You can get that brand new leather-bound time management diary, but if you don't start using it properly, it is just as bad as the *ad-hoc* planning you used to do before.

Do not be afraid to make some mistakes: While today's environment does not allow you to make any errors, it is almost impossible to learn without making mistakes. So, the challenge is to make some mistakes to learn, but not serious ones that would endanger your job performance. One of the ways to achieve these seemingly conflicting objectives is to be able to get some of the learning you need *before* you actually need it in your job. Proactively picking up the skills you need by making mistakes in environments that are not 'live' would be one way to make mistakes that are not very expensive. Another way to minimize the impact of mistakes is through, what we call in project management parlance, 'project closure' as depicted in Figure 7.2. At the end of each project, the project team meets as a group and debriefs one another on mistakes that happened in the project and how to avert these in future, as well as things that went well that need to be institutionalized. This learning is captured in an organization-wide system and propagated to the entire organization by a 'quality group'.

Internalize and make it a habit: When you start applying something, it grows on you and slowly becomes a habit. For example, if you have chosen to learn about how to be punctual in meetings, you will find that this becomes almost irresistible and second nature to you. You will soon find that not only are you in time for your official meetings, but that you have also become more disciplined in your personal life. You will keep your commitments both at work and in your social groups. All this will definitely leave you with more time on your hands that you can utilize to learn new things which will in turn make you more effective. Once something becomes a habit, it comes more naturally and effortlessly. Good habits are natural by-products of effective learning.

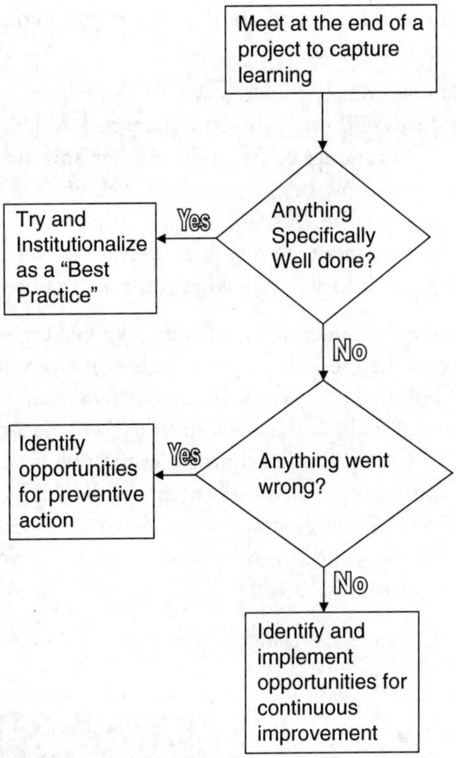

Fig. 7.2 *Using Project Closure to institutionalize the learnings*

Be a role model: This ties in with the last two stages of learning—learning to teach and teaching to learn. As you move up in your career, your success will depend on being a role model, a person who will be looked upon as a lifelong learner.

7.3 Some Challenges in Lifelong Learning

Much as we all know that it is essential to have this skill of learnability, let us not underestimate the substantial challenges that we are likely to encounter in this quest. In this section, we will highlight some of those challenges that you have to look out for and ways in which you can protect yourself against such challenges.

Making time to learn: 'I have already been hit with tough deadlines and am working eighteen hours a day to meet these deadlines. How do I make time to learn?' This is always given as a convenient excuse for not allocating time for any skill upgrading and learning. As you will see in the chapter on time management, you will always find that you will have time once you prioritize correctly. As someone said, 'Work expands to fill up all time.' Time is perhaps the most elastic, and at the same time the most rigid, of all things ever created.

Deciding what to learn: 'When I look at what I don't know and what I want to know, there are truck-loads of things. There are changes in technology; new processes have come in; new organizational certification mechanisms are becoming popular and this places demands on how I do my work. Which of these do I learn?' Merely jumping on the bandwagon of today's fads will not help you to be a lifelong learner. It is important that you consider the synergy between your competence, your desire and your organization's needs to ascertain what you need to learn.

Getting over personal ego: Sometimes challenges like making time, deciding what to learn and so on may be no more than camouflages or mere excuses to hide the true reason—the sense of personal ego. People become defensive and mistakenly assume that learning a new way of doing things is admitting that what you have been doing so far is sub-optimal or wrong. On the contrary, everything we do can be done better, more efficiently and more effectively. Further, this learning can come from any source—your bosses, your subordinates, your colleagues or even a book you read. You need to get over your personal ego, set aside the 'Not Invented Here (NIH)' syndrome and start the learning process.

Fig. 7.3

Not having inclusiveness: Closely related to the previous point is *inclusiveness*, which means an ability to listen to contrary points of view and being able to assimilate the best of all viewpoints, even if they don't agree with what your opinions are. One of the most common barriers for lifelong learning is the lack of inclusiveness. The first step in learning anything new is to accept the possibility that what you are going to learn may well contradict the beliefs you may have held so far. If this is not there, you will find excuses to reject the new learning experience.

Organizational or managerial blocks: Even if you are fully motivated and fired up to learn, it is quite possible that you will face a roadblock from your manager, who will force you to keep chugging along without giving you time to sharpen the saw. He may always swamp you with those ridiculous deadlines that don't make sense and keep you at work for eighteen hours. He may have some of the bad habits we discussed above, like not being open, and he may rub off these negatives on you. In these cases, it is better to have an open discussion with him or any other relevant authority to remove these blocks and make your learning aspirations clear. Have clearly spelt-out learning plans in your annual reviews—what workshops, seminars or courses you will participate in. If that does not work, you should seriously consider moving to a different job or role. Continuing in such an environment is like forgetting to do your exercises regularly—you may get through the short-term deadlines, but your long-term lifeline is dead!

7.4 Some Misconceptions About Lifelong Learning

Learning is optional and can be done only if one gets free time: Some of us seem to think that we are knowledgeable enough to carry on with our jobs perpetually and that we don't need to acquire any more knowledge. If time permits—after we finish the never-ending cycle of projects and activities—we might consider attending a workshop or a seminar. Giving learning such a low priority can come back to hurt us in the long run and we might find ourselves high and dry in our career ambitions, with obsolete and unmarketable skills. We should have the mindset that we have no choice but to keep learning for life and therefore, should make time for it. Even if formal learning opportunities conflict with our work schedules, workplaces offer enough informal and impromptu opportunities for learning and we should exploit them. Lifelong learning is an attitude and not something to be quickly rationalized as 'good to have, but not necessary' or something that can be delayed forever.

Learning means attending classes and getting a certificate of some sort: A lot of times learning is equated with attending classes and passing an examination to get a certificate. There are several modes of learning, each with their own advantages and disadvantages (see Table 7.1). Neither of these needs to be true in a business context. While formal classroom based training is preferable for certain areas, most of the learning you do in the business context is by observation and experience. In fact, 'On the Job Training' (OJT) is a euphemism for a person learning by being thrown in to the deep end of the pool. These learning avenues are usually far more productive than certificate-based or classroom-based training.

Unmonitored learning is not fruitful: The learning environment we are used to is always monitored, with a teacher looking over your shoulder and exams and tests galore. But today, the resources available over the Internet for self learning are enormous. E-learning, e-teaching and automatic evaluations are features of today's self-paced learning. In addition to the OJT mentioned in the previous paragraph, self-paced e-learning that goes on due to self-initiative without anyone monitoring or

Table 7.1 ***Various modes of learning***

Modes of Learning	Advantages	Disadvantages
Pursuing a formal degree/ diploma	Widely recognized	Big investment in time and money
Technical conference	Latest and advanced information provided	Expensive and often specialized
Short Courses/Workshops	Tutorial-type format suits easy learning	Can be expensive and too limited
Internal Training/Cross training	Easy to set up	Very limited in scope
Supplier/ Vendor demonstration and training	Very focused and methodical	Available only for limited subject matter
Mentor training	Very effective; getting feedback is easy	The effort to find mentors has to be made
Self learning via books, DVDs, etc.	Easily available, inexpensive	Testing, doubt-clearing not easy
E-learning via computer/ Internet	Done at one's pace and one's level	Needs discipline
Learning by teaching	Easy to set up	Should have the right motivation and interest
Looking and learning	Easy to do; no special preparation needed	Not systematic

Fig. 7.4

pushing you, is one of the most effective ways to keep your learning skills in top shape. This fuels initiative and kindles the fire within—one of the first soft skills we looked at!

Learning can be acquired only from professional teachers or people with a lot of experience: Somehow, we tend to accept to learn only from experienced people or people from outside the organization. Neither of these need be the case in the workplace. Given the fast pace at which technology changes around you, it is quite likely that the junior engineer in your organization probably has more technical knowledge than you do. You should not hesitate to learn even from juniors. Learning can come from any source. Keep your eyes, ears and mind open!

7.5 In Summary

The first step in lifelong learning—and this is a lifelong first step!—is

> Overcoming inertia to learn.

By consciously prioritizing learning and making time for it, you can overcome this first major obstacle.

Your learning will be continuous, lifelong and experiential. Experience will bring its share of 'failures' and rejections. Instead of getting disillusioned by such rejections, keep in mind that

> Defeat just tells you to take a different path; thus, you will know not just the paths to take but more importantly, the paths not to take.

Remember, your learning involves not just what you do, but how you take it and apply it to your life, how it changes your life and the lives of others.

> Experience is not what happens to a man, but what a man does with what happens to him.

Finally, the quality of your life depends directly on the quality of lifelong learning.

> It is not the years in life that count but the life (and the learning you get) in the years that count.

8

Performance-expectations Management

"Expecting the world to treat you fairly because you are a good person is a little like expecting the bull not to attack you because you are a vegetarian."

–Dennis Wholey

Snapshot 8.1

You are a junior sales manager in PQ Inc., an IT services company. Your team's function is to scout around the international scene and generate new business. One day, your boss tells you about a potential French customer, whose infrastructure service is in the market for off-shoring and he asks you to come up with a feasibility report on the bid. 'Do whatever needs to be done,' he instructs you tersely and disappears on an unrelated foreign trip.

This is the first time you have been tasked with such a major responsibility. So, you work day and night for a week, spending countless hours doing research, talking to several key sources and finally, writing what you consider to be one of the best reports you have ever written. Your boss returns after ten days, grabs the report with a surly 'This should have been in my hands four days ago.' As he flips through the report; his body language clearly indicates that he is not happy with it.

'Where is the section on LAN transition?' he demands to know. 'And your information on database administration is pathetic.' He then proceeds to point out ten more lapses. When you step in to explain what you meant, he will have none of it.

'You call this a report?' he finally explodes, tossing it back at you. 'And by the way, you must improve your written communication skills.'

As you exit your boss's office, you have this sinking 'what went wrong?' kind of feeling. Your report rests heavily in your hands. Goodbye, quarterly performance bonus.

Snapshot 8.1, albeit exaggerated, illustrates the brutal 'judgement by expectations' world we live in. Here, expectations others have of our performance matter as much as the performance itself. And whether we fail or succeed in our environment is determined by how well we live up to the expectations of our stakeholders. Remember that we all perform to satisfy our stakeholders, except that this satisfaction should now be recognized as a function of not only how we perform, but also on what the expectations are set to start with. We can say that the most fundamental tenet of any relationship (professional or otherwise) is

Satisfaction = Performance - Expectations.

Snapshot 8.2

Perhaps the best illustration of how satisfaction is governed as much by expectations as by performance is the behaviour of the stock market. If a company reports a loss, but the loss is less than what the analysts 'expected', its stock price may go up; on the other hand, if the company reports less-than-expected profits, its stock price may go down, even though it has made a profit.

Parties external to us—like the boss in Snapshot 8.1—put us under the scanner, impose their expectations on us and hold us accountable to their expectations. But, before we start blaming the boss in Snapshot 8.1 for being unreasonable, let us try to understand the performance-expectations dynamics and see how we can tame it—and perhaps even come out ahead.

The first thing to realize is that it is normal and natural for your boss (and your organization) to have 'expectations' about your job performance. After all, they do pay your salary and they are responsible to someone else for extracting a measure of work out of you. The boss in the story too had certain expectations about your report—expectations about the content, its quality, its schedule, style, etc.—and when he sensed a disconnect between those expectations and the actual report, he felt betrayed. Surely, he could have done things better. He could have had more *realistic* expectations of you, considering that you are a junior staff and this was your first time working alone. He should have *communicated* his expectations better, especially if he wanted particular topics covered in greater detail. 'Do whatever needs to be done,' is hardly a clear enunciation of his expectations. But then, bosses will always be bosses. And they speak in a language called 'expectationese'. We are the ones under scrutiny and we need to devise a work-around and build our defences.

In Snapshot 8.1, *you* should have *anticipated* most of your boss's expectations and should have *proactively* taken steps to *manage* them—by telling him upfront what you plan to include in the report (and what you don't). *You* should have found out when he needed the report, how much detail he wanted, etc. *You* should have stayed in touch with him several times during the report-writing phase so that you were in tune with his expectations. Instead, *you* bungled managing your boss's expectations.

If our repeated highlighting of the 'you' in the previous paragraph sounds intimidating, that is not the objective. The objective is to stress that each of us have to be proactive in managing expectations. You must remember that no matter how hard you work and how many times you jump through hoops, in the final analysis, your performance matters only in the eyes of a few beholders. You need to be alert about these beholders—and their eyes. You must develop this art of satisfying them, so that maximum impact of your hard work is felt around your organization. This takes us back to the equation we put forth at the beginning of the section.

8.1 THE BASICS OF PERFORMANCE-EXPECTATIONS MANAGEMENT

Expectations management basically involves the following steps, as identified by Figure 8.1 below:

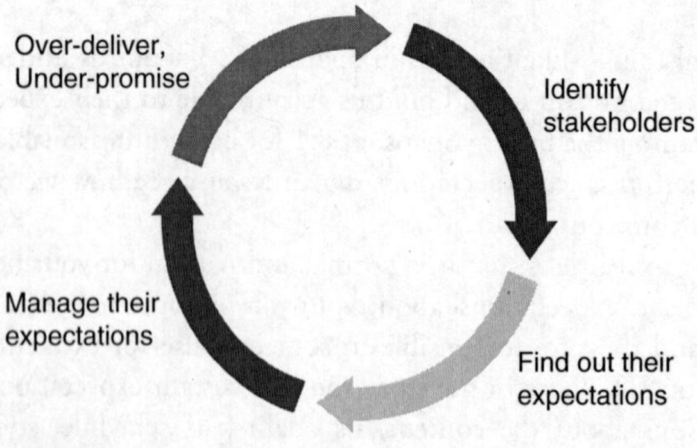

Fig 8.1 *Steps in performance-expectations management*

- First, *identify* the *stakeholders* are who are interested in your job performance and figure out which ones among them are really important.
- Next, you need to *find out what expectations* they have of your performance. Your stakeholders don't walk around wielding a comprehensive list of their expectations. It is up to you to use clever communication techniques and extract or surmise the expectations out of them. Some of the expectations will be nebulous and even implicit and you will have to ask them for explanations.
- Then, you will have to get down to the business of *managing* those expectations—that is, respond to your stakeholders by modifying your performance, negotiate with them on some of the unrealistic and unreasonable expectations, open up channels of communication to get frequent feedback from them, use any other sources to help you in this process—so that in course of time, your job performance totally resonates with your stakeholders' expectations.
- Then you go one step further. You start *delivering more* than your stakeholders expect. At this point, managing expectations is not just a defensive manoeuvre to play it safe, but a potent soft skill known as 'under-promising and over-delivering'.

You will find that this four-step process is an iterative cycle. As you meet or beat the expectations of some of the stakeholders, newer stakeholders may emerge or the expectations of the stakeholders will change repeatedly, thus needing to be managed and delivered upon, *ad infinitum.* Something interesting happens when your job performance and your stakeholders' expectations are in line. You notice a complete transparency in your work environment. You are perfectly clear about the expectations they have of you and they in turn, find your performance to be totally consistent. In fact, your performance will be so boringly predictable that they will even count on it. Predictably solid performance, that is.

Exceeding expectations and delivering some real, positive surprises is the closest one comes to achieving workplace *nirvana.* Just imagine, in the example of PQ Inc. in Snapshot 8.1, if you told your boss that the report would be ready in one week, but actually delivered it in five days. Or, had a section in your report on end user computing or something that is an extra even for him. Or got it 'proofed' by one of your senior colleagues, so that it read well. By 'exceeding expectations', you are delivering much more than consistent performance—you are delivering consistently *better and better* performance with every passing day.

Of course, if you beat expectations, it is highly likely that your boss will have even higher expectation of your job performance the next time. But then, that is okay. Once you have figured out how to exceed expectations, you can always do it again. And again.

Managing expectations is as much about competency as it is about managing hype, relationships and risks. It is certainly not about putting up a shoddy job performance and somehow hoodwinking your bosses into thinking you did a fantastic job. It is not about window-dressing and smooth-talking. Quite the opposite—it is about working hard and toward clear goals and conveying this sense unambiguously and accurately to whoever it matters.

8.2 Find Out Who Your Stakeholders Are

Like it or not, you have several stakeholders who watch over your job performance and act as judges and arbiters. Your manager, your customers (if you interface directly with end customers), individual project managers, suppliers, colleagues and even the administrative assistants—they all have a stake in what you do and how you do it. Even your organization may have some expectations of you—that you put on a tie and a suit when you travel on business, for example. But, it is usually a trivial exercise to figure out that among the many masters you serve, the *supremo* is your immediate supervisor and his judgement carries the most weight. Usually, his list of expectations about your job performance will be so broad and exhaustive that it will include the main points of other stakeholders. So, your task is now made simple. Just get his list and follow his directions and this may be sufficient to satisfy other stakeholders. This list we are talking about, may be a general-purpose list, covering your performance for the entire year, or could be a list specific to individual assignments like writing a feasibility report. However, for the purposes of our discussion, the list can be any list of expectations. Please remember that the list referred to is usually an ethereal one. You have to surmise and infer this list from what your supervisor says or implies. It is also in your interest to convert this ethereal list into a real list, document it and run it by your supervisor to ensure you have not missed anything. But don't hold your breath in assuming that your supervisor will read your list, much less comment on it.

Your boss may also appear to be a very subjective and partial person. While he may expect you to finish your report in ten days, he may expect a more senior person to complete an even bigger report in just five days. And he may be very forgiving of a new employee and give him twelve days to do it. Although everyone in your team may do similar assignments, organizations realize that there are differences in experience level, training and abilities among employees. Therefore, bosses throw a different list of expectations at different workers. Even if some items in your list may be common with your items in your co-worker's list, you may have an entirely different passing grade set for you. This is not surprising if you consider the equation we saw earlier in this chapter. As your boss's expectations of you are higher, it is obvious that your performance should also be correspondingly higher to give him the same level of satisfaction. Your boss's evaluation of your performance, vis-à-vis his expectations, will also be unique to you. So, make sure that what you get from your boss is *your* list of expectations.

Lastly, there is an even bigger stakeholder than your boss or anyone else—a stakeholder who should be even more demanding of you—namely *yourself!* Your expectations of your own performance should always be far more stringent and tougher than anything your boss can come up with. Your boss may expect the report in one week, but in your own mind, you will want to get it done within five days, by firing on all cylinders.

The winning recipe then is very clear. Once you get your boss's list of expectations, use that as a guideline and generate a parallel list of *your* own expectations of your performance. (Of course, you don't have to show this list to anyone, much less your boss.) Your list will be so stringent that in comparison, your boss's list may look watered-down. You then operate according to your list. And if you *meet* your own very high expectations, then you have automatically *exceeded* your boss's expectations. You win!

Given below is a sample table (Table 8.1) comparing your boss's list of expectations with your own. You may notice that on the whole, your internal standards are much higher. On some parameters (such as the due date of the report, in Table 8.1 below) your boss's expectations may seem more aggressive. But, we would like to give you the benefit of the doubt and presume that this is a simple case of his being unrealistic or being more aware of market demands.

Table 8.1 ***Boss's expectations and set your own bar higher***

Boss's Expectations	**Your Own Expectations**
Include a section on LAN and database management	Go beyond that. Include a section on the client's Intranet servers and mail servers.
Give comparative numbers from similar successful bids we had in the past	Not only give numbers from our past bids, but also include some competitive analysis for comparison.
Finish the report by Friday	Finish the report by Monday (negotiate with him on this)
Should have two years revenue projection	Has five-year-revenue projection using multiple projection techniques.

8.3 Explicit and Implicit Performance Expectations

Expectations come in several flavours. *Explicit expectations* (see Box 8.1) are those which spell out the details clearly and unmistakably. Company norms, standard practices and formal instructions are examples of this category. Within the explicit variety, some expectations are also *quantifiable,* where precise numerical targets can be assigned to them. Expectations regarding cost, budget, time, output, some resources, etc. are examples. When expectations are quantified, it is a little easier to judge the performance objectively. Examples of explicit as well as explicit and quantifiable expectations are given in Box 8.1.

Box 8.1

Explicit and Quantifiable Expectations

Examples of Explicit Expectations

- I want the report to cover LAN.
- Don't include pricing in the report.
- Keep your uniforms clean and neat.
- Include that module in the beta version.
- Install the latest version of the tools.

Examples of Explicit Quantifiable Expectations

- The report should not be more than twenty pages long.
- Get it done by this Saturday.
- Test for 200 hours.
- Keep the cost to below Rs 200 per person per hour.
- Keep the number of bugs below five.
- We are going live on 12 February.
- Ensure that the top three accounts are never lost and have a growth of 25 per cent each year.

The next category of expectations is *implicit* expectations, where a stakeholder is silent about some of his expectations, but springs them on you and eventually holds you accountable to them. For example, after you get back from a business trip, your boss's implicit expectation is that you will brief him about your trip the day after you are back to your office. It is your responsibility to use your judgment and infer these implicit expectations and document as much of these as possible and make them explicit expectations.

The last category of *vague* expectations is the one that is generic and fuzzy and you almost never get the hang of it. There can be any number of reasons why your boss keeps some expectations vague and some other expectation under wraps. Maybe, in his mind these expectations are quite clear-cut and obvious. Or maybe he is unable to articulate his views very well. But quite often, it is because both you and he never had a chance to sit down together and discuss them.

Unless you understand your boss's implicit and vague expectations of you, they can come back and haunt you. It is important to realize that implicit and vague expectations are subject to interpretations (See Figure 8.2). Hence, you must gather as many such expectations from him as you can and with his help, translate them into explicit expectations. For example, if your boss says something as vague as 'I expect you to improve your work-quality,' you must corner him several times and ask him what exactly he means—can he suggest some metrics of quality along which you can improve? Can he suggest some specific targets to achieve?

Some examples of vague expectations and how you can convert them to explicit (and sometimes even quantitative) expectations are given in Box 8.2.

Box 8.2

Implicit/vague Expectations and how to convert them to explicit expectations

- Your written communication skills must improve. ➔ There should be less than two clarifications sought by your customer on your report.
- You should be more focused on what you are doing. ➔ You should not miss any of your deadlines.
- In future, I expect you to be a self-starter. ➔ You will have to do this without being prompted by me.
- You should write better code. ➔ Your code should have less than 2 bugs per 1000 lines of code.
- In future, I expect you to be a fast learner. ➔ You must be able to get on to the next version of the product in half the time you took for this version.

Fig 8.2 *Implicit and vague expectations are subject to interpretation*

8.4 Managing Your Boss's Expectations of Your Performance

It is not always easy to control or manage the boss's expectations – they have their birthright to have expectations But some of the things that you could do proactively to temper his expectations are:

Negotiate expectations: As soon as you compile a list of your boss's expectations of your job performance, sit down with him to negotiate on specific items on the list. While discussing with him, err on the side of under-promising and over-delivering. Point out those expectations that may be too difficult to meet because of various reasons. Maybe you don't have the time to do everything the way he wants. Maybe there are crucial dependencies and the other person will not finish things in time for you to get going. Perhaps you don't have the technical expertise in some areas and maybe your boss's expectation of a hundred-page report in two days is just too unrealistic. Hold your ground and don't let him sweet-talk you or intimidate you into impossible situations. On the other hand, don't be unreasonable yourself. Don't give him the impression that your enthusiasm-level is low. Instead, appear hungry for work. For comparison, find out what expectation levels he has set for the others in your group. Find out the industry benchmarks.

You should have follow-up sessions as often as needed. You might have to review your list in light of any new developments. Maybe your initial performance targets were too optimistic. Perhaps, too pessimistic. Or maybe you just uncovered a new implicit expectation your boss had been harbouring all along and need to discuss it with him. If he has difficulty verbalizing his implicit expectations, help him with words. Usually, after two or three such sessions, your list should be pretty much 'frozen'.

Remember the parallel list of *your* expectations you had compiled, for your eyes only; based on your boss's list? Take care to update it every time you make changes to the official list.

Adjust your job performance: You have to modify your job performance based on your boss's list and get it in line with his expectations. You just cannot keep doing what you always did and hope that one day, your boss will finally accept your way of doing things. When you do modify your performance, make sure your boss notices it and approves it. This modification process may involve learning new things or going through some sort of training, but most importantly, it involves a change in your mindset and giving up old ways of doing things.

Communicate often with your stakeholders about your performance: The cardinal rule is to be in constant touch with your stakeholders and get regular feedback on your performance. Do this as often as necessary and through as many channels as possible. Instead of your boss intimidating you with his expectations about your job performance, you must be the one beating down on him for feedback and encouragement.

With his help, set short-term, intermediate-term and long-term goals for your performance. Take the initiative to schedule quarterly and perhaps even monthly meetings with him to review your most recent performance. Ask for his comments on your report soon after he reads it. Once-a-year annual review alone is not enough to get his complete feedback on your performance. Ask him to compare you with some of the more successful employees he has had. This can be a nice baseline to have. Ask him about how he himself improved his performance and came up to his level. We will discuss this more in Chapter 28 on Performance Appraisals.

Communicate through e-mail and document that you have met or exceeded some of his expectations that he had laid out for you. An informal lunch break conversation can suddenly shed light on what your boss expects your work quality to be for the next year. Talk to third parties about your performance and pick up some pointers.

Exceed expectations, but don't overstep your authority: Eventually, your job performance will reach equilibrium with your boss's expectations and you will reach a plateau called meeting the expectations. From there, you will proceed toward the final destination—meeting your own internal list of expectations—also known as exceeding your stakeholder's expectations. Quite often, your internal list of expectations will be simple extensions of your boss's list and reaching there would only involve incremental hard work and cleverness.

However, in your quest to overachieve, do not take matters in your own hands. Don't look for tricks and short cuts to get there. Don't undermine your organization or overstep your position in the organization. Exceeding expectations is important, but the means are as important as the end.

8.5 When Your Performance Always Exceeds Expectations

When you consistently exceed your stakeholders' expectations, you will be tagged as a special employee by the management. Most organizations reward their expectation exceeders handsomely. By the same token, failing to meet expectations is often the reason for demotion or lower bonuses. The corporate world is full of workers who are every bit hardworking as any but who did not follow the organization's script and ended up with directionless careers.

When you keep exceeding expectations, your stakeholders will identify you as that special someone whose job performance is always on the upswing. This will do wonders for your confidence and self-esteem. Like we mentioned earlier, your organization will no longer look like an Amazonian jungle, but instead its vision and practices will become very transparent and clear to you.

This brings us to the other thing that happens when you consistently exceed expectations—you are no longer just a consistent performer, but you are also an embodiment of the vision and philosophy of your organization. You now represent it. You become the trusted lieutenant of your organization—and your boss. Your boss feels so confident about you that you become his double and substitute him in crucial meetings. Perhaps, after you write that superb feasibility report, your boss includes you too in the contingent that goes to France—you win the bid and say hello to a nice quarterly bonus.

Just like personal accountability is done by people for its intrinsic reward of satisfaction, so also, exceeding expectations is done by people for its own sake, without any consideration for extrinsic rewards. A person consistently exceeding expectations invariably steps up to the plate, as discussed in Chapter 10.

8.6 In Summary

As we had said at the beginning of the chapter, performance-expectations management starts with setting the right expectations. Even before that, you should know whose expectation you should set right. Thus,

> First, find out who your stakeholders are.

Once you know who the stakeholders are, not all their expectations will be explicitly stated by them. So,

> Find out their implicit expectations as well.

Once you know the explicit expectations and have made a guess of the implicit expectations, you should document the expectations, then review and negotiate this list with the stakeholders. This becomes the living document for you. Make sure you

> Review the expectations and job performance often with the stakeholders.

As you review your performance and expectations often with the stakeholders, you will find that both their expectations and your performance will change with time.

> Be ready to make several mid-course corrections for both your performance and their expectations.

Finally, you can always come out a winner by working towards expectations that are much higher than what your stakeholders expect of you.

> Set your bar higher than what anyone else expects of you—always under-promise and over-deliver.

9

The Art of Time Management

"You will never find time for anything. You must make it."
–Charles Buxton

Snapshot 9.1

Sheetal, a junior HR manager with PYM Computer Systems Pvt. Ltd., has been feeling very hassled of late. She has no time for anything any more. She feels as if she is on a treadmill—she has to keep running, even to stay in one place. It is rush, rush, rush.

There are not enough hours in the day to get things done. Even before she can finish a pile of work, two more piles are waiting on her desk, begging for her attention. With her deadlines and appointments falling by the wayside, she doesn't think she will ever catch up with the backlog. She is always late—late to get up, late to get to work, late in her activities at work, late to get home, late for this and late for that. She feels that she is slowly losing control over her life and hopes she is not heading for a quick 'burn-out'. Her mind and body are crying 'enough is enough' and she wants to hit the 'reset' button.

It is not that Sheetal doesn't try hard. She spends nearly twelve hours each day at work. But somehow, she is slightly out of phase with everything. Just this morning, she missed the nine o'clock meeting and she is already late for her first interview of the new candidates. This delay will have a domino effect and she will be late for all her interviews and appointments today.

As she gets more and more entrenched in this vicious cycle, Sheetal's personal life and office life merge into a continuum. She makes lengthy phone calls to her friends while at work and often carries home a laptop full of office work. She hasn't had a free weekend away from work in two months. And with the campus recruitment season just around the corner, she doesn't think she can go on this much-deserved, sanity-restoring vacation that she was planning for a long time. She also has a whole bunch of e-mails awaiting her reply and a boatload of phone calls to return and if she doesn't get to them in a few days, the statute of limitation might run out on them. And she is deathly afraid of walking by Mr Godbole, the Mumbai area manager's office, for fear of being cornered by him and asked about that final summary report that was supposed to have been done a month ago. Sheetal has almost finished it, but every time she flips through it 'one final time', she discovers new errors and grammatical mistakes. She hopes to fix them and embellish the document some more, to make it look like a super-report.

It is not as if Sheetal is being singled out for this third degree treatment and made to suffer through long days with crowded schedules and high expectations. Her colleague and friend Shilpa, has a similar workload and routinely has ten to twelve hour workdays, but seems quite unfazed by it. She comes to work at the normal time (putting in a half hour of *yoga* before that), makes pleasant small talk with co-workers in the hallways and even has time to pursue romantic interests on the side. How does she do it? Does she have an invisible helper in her cubicle?

Sheetal's cell phone is beeping to remind her of her group meeting in a few minutes. Another e-mail pops up on her screen. Visions of a half-done report stream in her mind, along with flashes of other things she must get done before the end of the day.

'Giddyyap, girl. Your break is over. Hop on to the machine,' a little voice instructs her. And off she goes again on her timeless treadmill.

9.1 Time Management—What Is It?

Haven't we all felt Sheetal's anguish sometime or the other? What can we do when overwhelming demands are made of our time by so many people and so many things? Why is it that some people like Sheetal are caught up in a turbulence, whereas some others, like Shilpa, can handle a similar job effectively and even thrive in the same get-it-done-yesterday atmosphere? Are Sheetal's problems entirely her doing or can we blame it on her heavily-globalized, high-pressure corporation?

Let's look at the last question first. The modern workplace indeed heaps an unprecedented amount of work on its workers. The ever-shrinking product life cycles, short project durations, fierce global competition, and high level of customer service all push the workers a wee bit harder and spin them a wee bit out of control. The sheer volume and complexity of today's work assignments can rattle the faint-hearted and induce all kinds of time-related problems. We can either wilt and wither like Sheetal or figure out how we can handle it like Shilpa and reap the rewards of working for a modern corporation.

To be successful today, we should learn how to cope with the constant chase of deadlines, schedules and deliverables and how to ration our available time, prioritize our tasks and learn to be in-sync with other people (some half a world away). And on top of that, we should make time for our personal lives as well. In other words, we should have an active and disciplined time management system in place—not just when things go awry, but all the time.

Time management is not about being obsessive-compulsive about time and glancing at the clock every two minutes. Nor does it mean being a slave of the clock, going to bed precisely at 9.58 every night or eating lunch everyday exactly at 1.02 p.m. Rather, time management is about developing a nice internal rhythm within ourselves and then tuning our internal clock to that giant external clock. Time management is about planning and executing our activities as best as possible. It is about debugging our 'time-honoured' bad habits relating to time. Time management is really an easy soft skill to acquire. Like all other soft skills, it requires a little bit of discipline and some dedicated practice. The idea is to control time before it starts to control and pressure us. (see Box 9.1).

Box 9.1

***Tell-tale symptoms of time management problems*:**

- You have missed or forgotten an appointment recently.
- You have missed a deadline recently. You defaulted on your deliverable.
- You were late to more than one appointment/meeting in the last two weeks. You are habitually ten minutes late for some meetings, even if they are on-campus.
- You have e-cobwebs in your e-mail Inbox or Sent Items box or Outbox
- You feel that you have plenty of free time on hand and you sometimes don't know what to do with all that time or what task to take on next. You find yourself drifting randomly. (This symptom may be rare, but some people can have it.)
- You have to switch off your cell phones at least during a part of the workday so you can get on with some of your tasks uninterrupted.
- You don't have a 'list of things to do' or you have not updated it in the last many weeks.
- You have a huge backlog of things and activities that are not yet 'closed' properly.
- You live life on the edge—barely making it to trains, buses and flights. You do things at the last minute. You often feel rushed.

- You do many personal activities at work and work-related activities at home. There is a blur between your personal life and professional life.
- You have not been able to have uninterrupted personal time for yourself.
- You forgot important dates like birthdays and anniversaries of close friends/relatives. Even when you remembered a few dates, you were too busy to call.

9.2 Time Management—Attitude Is Everything

The first thing to realize is that time management is a matter of attitude, reinforced by strict discipline. You have to realize that there is not an unlimited supply of time, even though it may seem like there is always a tomorrow. We all have to realize that we should not let time pass us by, but rather, actively partition our workdays into time slots and allocate them appropriately to different tasks and carry out this plan perfectly.

This attitude can be further characterized along the following angles:

Time is Money: Time is precious and you should treat it exactly like you would treat money or anything that you only have a limited supply of. Do not treat it unwisely and squander it away. You can figure out approximately how much one hour of your time is worth and perhaps this conversion can help sensitize you to the value of time—then you won't waste thousands of rupees worth of time on silly activities like idle net-browsing or parking yourself in front of the TV. Looking at time as money gives a certain involvement and urgency to what we do. Besides, it also makes us appreciate other people's efforts and the time they put in to do things. No wonder modern corporations put a tremendous premium on time and constantly try to streamline their own dynamics.

Time is opportunity: Time also brings us unique opportunities. Today's moments are today's only and cannot be got tomorrow. So, we might as well savour the present and make best use of it. The special circumstances of today, spent on today's projects, today's activities, today's challenges, will present us with all kinds of possibilities and may not come again at any other time in the future. Likewise, the quality time we spend with our parents, children, friends today is something to be cherished—for tomorrow will be a different day.

Timeliness and punctuality mean trust: Timeliness means trust. Often we will have to synchronize our schedules with others' and do things cooperatively with them. We should honour this unwritten code of trust and come together in harmony and keep our part of the commitments. Modern businesses—and in fact, the modern world—runs on specific things happening at specific times, in consonance. If you are a 'no show' or if you default on doing your share of things, you are going to be viewed as unreliable. And if you have chronic punctuality problems, it is only a matter of time (pardon the pun) before a time-conscious person comes in, steps into your shoes and edges you out.

We would like to point out that some people can have a contrary view of time and its role in one's life. There are rebels among us who disdain the modern busy lifestyle and who prefer to do things leisurely and spontaneously. They would rather live for the moment than crowd up their day with busy activities. Some others would wait for the right moods and inspiration or auspicious times. Casual and passive activities are condoned by several others. We have no disputes with them and wish them a lot of luck in their non-professional careers outside the modern corporations.

Taking these three dimensions of attitude of time management—money, opportunity and trust—would cause a fundamental paradigm shift in your ability to manage time. This sets the scene for a systematic approach to managing time that we will discuss in the next section.

9.3 Steps in Time Management

The essential steps in effective time management are outlined below:

1. Look ahead and make a map of what needs to be done and when.
2. Prioritize the tasks under various dimensions.
3. Estimate the time needed for each task and fit it in the calendar.
4. Document the schedule.
5. Refer, track and revise the schedule as necessary, as changes unfold.

Let us now look at each of these aspects in more detail.

9.3.1 Planning Your Time

Planning is everything! For any activity, 'failing to plan is planning to fail', an old saying goes. This is especially true of a resource like time, which cannot be gotten back once lost. It is absolutely essential that we start off our time management by asking ourselves the following questions:

- What are my long-term priorities?
- What is the big picture that I need to see of myself and my organization?
- What are the intermediate milestones that I need to achieve in my journey?
- What are the burning issues that I need to address?
- What are the things I need to do in my other roles—personal, social, spiritual and so on?
- What skills do I need to acquire or hone to achieve all the objectives? Have I allotted time for acquiring these skills?

The questions given above are indicative but not exhaustive. Having answers to at least some of the questions above, constitutes the first step in planning. Planning is half the battle won. In Snapshot 9.1, the single biggest cause for Sheetal's chaotic workdays is the lack of planning. Sheetal may have some intuitive mental picture of how to slice and dice her workday into time slots and allocate them to different activities. But she would do well to put it on paper (or in her electronic scheduler) so that things get done and any potential confusion and conflicts can be avoided. At a minimum, high priority items and important appointments should be clearly scheduled and these should set the pace for one's workdays. Planning and scheduling and making appointments are not just for the big bosses. Everyone needs them—and you are no exception.

There is a mistaken notion that planning means planning only work-related activities. Far from it, an important aspect of planning is *factoring in breaks and personal time.* A big problem with Sheetal was that she got extended in every single activity and this left her with no time for breaks. To prevent this from happening, you must schedule adequate breaks. It may be tempting to keep going forever while doing some activities, but we must remember the law of diminishing marginal returns and the fatigue factor and force ourselves to take a break. It is a good idea to block a small slab of time as free time each day and not book it for anything.

Another sin that Sheetal committed was that she let her personal time coalesce into her work-time. Some of this overlap is inevitable in today's business world, but we strongly suggest that you make a clean exit out of the office every day and get to your personal chores or recreational activities in your personal time. Don't linger on in the office many hours after everyone has gone and alternate between office work and personal chores. Likewise, don't look at your home as a home-office and your nights as a second shift and schedule office work at home on a regular basis.

The underlying principle is that you should finish a required amount of work each day—even if it takes some extra time. But try to do it in the office as much as possible, and make sure that this 'extra time' does not become a regular feature and is not so huge that it severely eats into your personal time. If in spite of your best efforts in time management, you see yourself being overworked (and under-rewarded) it is time to have a long chat with your manager.

By taking the step of planning, you arrive at a list of what you have to do. This list will obviously be like a laundry list and will definitely contain more things than you can accomplish. Hence you need to *prioritize* the tasks.

9.3.2 Prioritizing the Tasks

Since we all have so little time and so many things that clamour for our attention, we prioritize our activities and then schedule them, based on their relative importance. High priority items have precedence over everything else and we must make sure we allot enough time and resources to getting them done in the required time. The core or routine activities—like Sheetal's interviews—must be done, no matter what. And then, there are some other things in life that are worth just five minutes of our time. We should learn not to waste too much time on them.

Prioritizing tasks involves ranking and ordering of those activities that you would do in a week or a month or any given period. While most of us may know what needs to be done, it is determining the priority amongst the tasks that distinguishes effective and ineffective management of time.

Some of the thumb rules you can follow in prioritizing are:

Identify those activities that you absolutely have to get done in the given time period: These include the deliveries expected of you—the programs, putting in place the quality-improvement steps, the interviews you have to conduct and so on. These also include the supporting activities you need to perform, like attending meetings, sending in status reports and so on. These are driven by deadlines that are usually tough to avoid. These are what Stephen Covey[1] calls 'urgent' activities.

Make sure your manager agrees with your order of priority and, if required, approves the amount of time you plan to spend on high, medium and low priority activities. Just because an activity is deemed 'low priority' you cannot forget about it and wish it away. You will have to make time even for such back-burner activities.

Squeeze in time for those things that you don't have to get done immediately, but need to get done anyway: There are always activities that you need to do but never get around to doing because there is no one breathing down your neck to get them done. These are what Stephen Covey calls 'important but not urgent' activities. These include the skill upgradations you always planned to do, the book on soft skills that you planned to read, the thirty minutes of exercise that you promised yourself you would do every day and things like that. You will generally do all these activities only when there is a crisis. You will try to learn that new tool when pushed into a corner with a project deadline looming large—and then you will do a shoddy job. What about your exercise? Welcome blood pressure pills to swallow every day! And what of that soft skills book? Oh, that can wait till next year! The challenge is that we will all have a temptation to put off these important but not urgent activities till they become important *and* urgent; by that time we are in fire-fighting mode and it becomes too late or too ineffective. Figure 9.1 depicts an adaptation of Stephen Covey's urgency-importance dimensions to time management.

Once you consider the time needed for all the activities in the 'important' category and add it to the time needed to finish the 'urgent' activities, you may find that you need to work fourteen hours per day! A person with habitually poor time management skills will be stretched for time even more and may have to toil for long hours just on these categories. So, what does one do?

One way to break from this shackle is to consciously allocate some time for the 'important but not urgent' activities. Initially this may entail that you work extra hours to make time for the 'important but not urgent' activities. But if you consciously set

---

1 Stephen Covey, *The 7 Habits of Highly Effective People* (New York: Simon & Schuster, 1989).

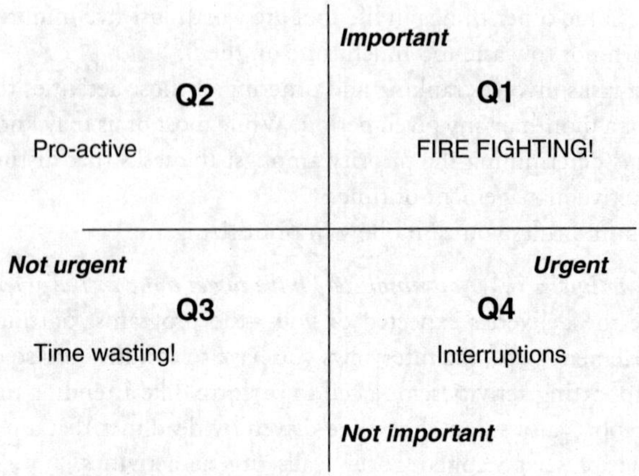

Fig. 9.1 *Urgency/importance dimensions of time management*

aside a certain time every week for such activities, you will be surprised at how much you can accomplish.

Identify tasks that you need <u>not</u> do during the time period: We can hear you asking 'How can I ever set time aside for anything except fire fighting, as after all, we live by deadlines and pressure all the time?' To answer this, ask yourself, 'Am I *always* doing only things that are important and urgent?' Alternatively ask yourself the question, 'Don't I *sometimes* do things that I need not do or should not do and thereby waste precious time?' You will find that most likely your answer to the first question is a 'no' and the second question is 'yes'. Let us be more specific. Reflect on these questions:

- When a phone rings, don't you feel tempted to take the call immediately, unless it is a call from some irate customer you want to avoid? (Thank God for caller IDs)
- Don't you have the urge to check your e-mail every few minutes?
- Don't you spend time on something that is low priority in your work, but that gives you the kicks to do it and thus you push it up the priority list?
- Don't you, every now and then, go Googling on a random walk to the no-man's-land of cyberspace?
- Don't you tweet to your friends about the delicious pasta in the new Italian joint down the road?

Most of you would answer 'yes' to the at least some of above questions. These activities can be viewed through a different set of classifications as given in Figure 9.2. A good lot of time management problems arise when one spends too much time on 'interesting' but low-priority activities, at the expense of important, pending matters.

Very few of us are lucky enough to find a perfect fit between what we would *like* to do and what we *need* to do. Given a choice, we choose those activities that we *like* to do. There is an inertia that forces us not to choose the activities that we don't like to do, even if they *need* to be done. This drains the time we have and leaves less time available for those activities that we actually need to do, thereby making our time management less effective. The approach then should obviously be to move from the quadrant of 'like to do and don't have to do' to 'don't like to do but need to do'. This obviously needs an understanding that life always comes as a package, you cannot simply choose and do only those 'cool' activities (see Box 9.2).

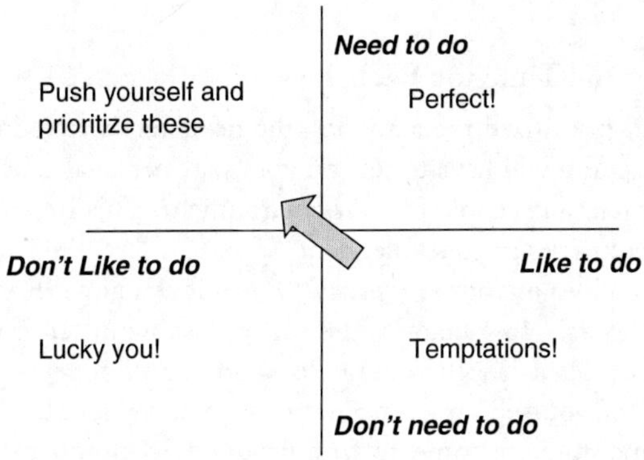

Fig. 9.2 *The 'Like to do' and 'need to do' dimensions of activities*

Box 9.2

Some tips for finding more time for important activities and not being always in fire-fighting mode

- Don't take phone calls during important activities.
- Earmark specific times of the day to check and respond to e-mail (preferably not more than four times during a work day).
- Set aside a certain time of the day for the important activities; unless pushed, don't use this time for any other activities.
- Rejuvenate yourself by taking periodic breaks. And don't use your break times as buffer times for your unfinished work.
- Take a few minutes off on a regular basis for deep breathing or similar relaxation exercises.

Within each category (top half of each of the two graphs in Figures 9.1 and 9.2), list out relative priorities of each of the activities: Even after all these classifications, there are likely to be many activities than you can handle. Hence, go to the next level and rank the activities in the upper half of the graphs by priority. Is the training more important or is rewriting the code more important? Is the new technology feature more important or is certifying against a new operating system more important? Obviously these are not easy questions to answer and you may have to seek advice from others as well as use your discretion in prioritizing the activities. Spending some upfront time doing this prioritization will definitely help you get the maximum bang for the buck for every minute you spend.

9.3.3 Estimating the Time for Each Task

Having classified and prioritized the activities, the next step is to estimate the time required for each task. You will have to rely on your past personal experience as well as on those of other relevant people in your environment. This step enables you to effectively slot these activities in your calendar.

You should have an idea of your *productivity rate.* How many HR interviews can you handle in four hours? How many slides can you show in ten minutes? What do you expect to accomplish—both qualitatively and quantitatively—in the schedule you have made for yourself? Big corporations, mainly manufacturing houses, do what is called 'time study' to come up with productivity numbers for individual employees and expect them to work at that rate.

If you are asked to work more aggressively and you don't think it is possible, talk to your manager and ask for extra resources to help you do your job.

Sometimes the time taken for an activity is also used as a parameter to prioritize the activities. When we have a list of twenty things to do in a day, sometimes we take pride in completing as many activities as possible. In this case, picking on the shortest activities and completing them can give us a sense of satisfaction. But, it is important to ensure that we don't just pluck these apparently low hanging fruits. Picking the shortest activities to do first may eventually lead to a backlog of the longer—and perhaps the more important—activities.

Picking shorter activities for execution can also be useful in another context. Suppose you have a half-hour break in-between meetings. You cannot possibly do half of something that will take an hour during this time. Instead, you can pick an activity that perhaps takes twenty minutes to complete. In this way, you earn a ten minute break as well.

You should also remember to use the time you have estimated for an activity only as a guideline. Expect that the task may take plus or minus a few minutes off your estimate and budget it. Don't stop the activity midway because the time you allocated for it was up; you may spend more time picking up the threads and doing context-switching when you restart the activity later. If you are close enough to completing the activity, by all means try your best to complete it, keeping the impact on the other activities to a minimum. But don't go beyond a certain threshold as that will have a domino effect on the time allotted for your other activities. Beyond a certain limit, put the activity on hold and go onto the next.

Don't forget to make allowance for transition time between appointments. If one meeting ends at 10.30 a.m. and another meeting starts at 10.30 a.m., then surely you are going to be late for the second meeting even if the meeting is in the same venue. You should allow a few extra minutes in your schedule to migrate from the first meeting to the second. If you have a say in the matter, do not schedule back to back meetings. If you are going out of town to attend a meeting, plan the travel time carefully by factoring in the potential airport delays, traffic jams and so on and allow extra time as a buffer. Good planners know that there are always lag times and lead times (the time between your ordering something and actually getting it) and are very good at figuring them out and incorporating them in their schedules. Be cognizant of holidays, factory shutdowns, general strikes and so forth before happily making aggressive schedules.

Often, the dates and times of activities will be imposed on you by external sources and you will have to build the rest of your schedule around it. If you have a prior commitment and a new meeting time clashes with it, sort it out right in the beginning and ask to re-schedule one of them, so that both your commitments are taken care of. (In case of a tie, the prior commitment should have greater priority.) As a rule, do not overbook or crowd up your days, if you can help it.

9.3.4 Documenting the Schedule

Having prioritized, estimated and allotted activities into time slots, it is important that you document this. You can use any of the following for documenting (and monitoring) your schedule:

- The old fashioned 'to-do list' on a piece of paper
- One of the 'organizers' with flashy leather covers and a tabbed section on 'to-do lists'
- Any cell phone of today that usually has a to-do list in its organizer (provided you are able to use the cell phone's small keyboard)
- Laptop, where you can integrate your mail with appointments and notes.

The specific tool itself is not as important as how effectively you use it. Even a back-of-the-boarding pass planning of your time that you use effectively can be far more effective than using a high flying Blackberry-based to-do list that you don't use at all.

Using the tool you have chosen, you can do your planning for different time horizons—years, weeks, days. Let us first look at short-term time horizons, days and weeks, and look at longer term horizons later. When you schedule activities in your planner, you need to enter when the activity starts (day/time) and when it ends (day/time) and mark the entire duration of time to be spent on it. (If your activity is a half-hour meeting beginning at 3.00 p.m., mark the entire half-hour slot between 3.00 and 3.30 p.m.) If the meeting you are interested in is long and you cannot attend the entire meeting, see if you can attend just a part of it. Find out exactly when your part occurs and negotiate on participating in that abbreviated session.

Some of the meetings we are invited to, might require that we 'RSVP'—or tell them clearly ahead of time whether we will attend or not—in which case, make sure you inform them of your decision. Conversely, if you are the meeting organizer and request your potential participants to RSVP, keep track of the participants who have confirmed. (In a country like India, where RSVPs are not taken very seriously, we should make allowance for 'confirmed participants' not showing up or the unexpected presence of people who never bothered to send their RSVPs—see Chapter 24 on 'Meeting Management' for more points.)

Another important aspect of documenting a schedule is keeping others informed. Spend adequate time in documenting vacation/leave plans and make sure you communicate your vacation dates to the concerned people in advance, especially your immediate manager, so that they can factor that in and arrange for substitutes in your absence.

9.3.5 Referring, Tracking and Revising the Schedule

Finally, remember that your schedule is a dynamic and live document and is subject to change. Don't forget to update it as things develop. Always keep the schedule current and make sure people who need to know your schedule are kept well aware of any changes. This is especially important in a geographically distributed team. Visits by people from a different country should generally be planned ahead and should be the last in the pecking order to get shuffled around and the people involved in it should be among the first to be informed, should there be a change.

9.4 Time Management—Best Practices

Be a role model for punctuality: Be painstakingly punctual for all appointments, especially in high-priority activities and more so in cases where a lot of other peoples' time is involved. If you are going to be severely delayed, but can still make it to the meeting, communicate that to your meeting organizer or the other party. If you are habitually late to your appointments—like Sheetal—you have a huge time management problem on your hands. You will not be taken seriously as a contributor to the proceedings and will not be entrusted with responsibilities.

You should be equally punctual about breaking away from meetings and appointments. If the meeting or appointment seems to spill over beyond the time limit, look for a logical break to terminate the session. If this cannot be done, telling them that you need to hurry to your next activity (or letting your phone alarm ring) is a good enough way to end the face-off. You can always make another follow-up appointment if needed or contact them offline.

Follow your natural rhythm: Different people have different styles of working. If a task requires four hours to complete, some people may start quickly, 'frontload' their efforts and try to finish the task as soon as possible and enjoy any leftover time later. Some others though would start slowly, but backload their efforts and pick up steam as time goes on. Yet others work at a uniform rate. Some people work in spurts and streaks. They work intensely on some days and on some activities they like. But they slack off on some other activities. People also have their own ways of taking breaks. Whatever may be your style, you should work at a pace dictated by your natural rhythm. Be conscious of time, but don't let a clock set the pace for you, i. e., don't keep on looking at the clock and feeling tense. Work is not like running a race against time. If you run a bit over or under the scheduled time, it is okay. But if you are way off, then you will have to resolve it with the other party or your manager. The hallmark of a true professional is being consistent in delivery through all kinds of tasks, even if his pace of work varies with time.

Make efficient use of free time and break time: Some time-efficient people tend to put even break time to good use and get refreshed efficiently. They may utilize a part of their break time to do filler activities like replying to e-mails or making phone calls and so on, but would not misuse it to do heavy-duty activities. It is an art to use break time or even to factor in break time into schedules. People who just run from meeting to meeting and take pride in the fact that they don't have even one minute of spare time because of their tightly-packed schedules can burn out easily and may not always be successful, as such schedules lead to inflexibility and that in turn leads to ineffectiveness.

Synchronize with others: Even if you work at your natural pace, your work will have to be integrated into other people's work. This will require you to synchronize with others at periodic intervals. Sometimes you may have to slow down your pace and sometimes you may have to accelerate. So, time management is not just about how well you manage *your* time, but also how you have integrated your time into a *common* time with your team-mates.

Don't lose sight of 'important but not urgent' activities or activities that you need to do even if they are not what you enjoy doing: People who manage time effectively perform Stephen Covey's 'Q2' activities (i.e., important but not urgent activities) before they become 'Q1' activities (i.e., important and urgent activities). Similarly they do not give into the temptations of doing only things that they like. They realize that there are things that they need to do to take things to completion and to see the benefits of the 'cool' things that they have done and have enjoyed doing.

9.5 Time Management—The Killers

In spite of good planning and execution, we may still lose our control over time due to various reasons, some of which are discussed below. We need to have alerts in place to warn us that we are straying from our plans. We should also have appropriate mechanisms to bring us back on to the charted course.

Tasks taking longer than scheduled time: By far, this is the biggest reason why most of our time management goes for a toss—that a scheduled activity takes much longer to complete than envisioned. This could be due to any number of reasons—inherent complexity of the task, unforeseen complications along the way, lack of proper resources, poor definition of what needed to be done and so on. If you sense that a delay is a possibility in your task, warn your upper management about it well in advance so that they can step in and try to remedy the situation. Otherwise, negotiate down to a new, extended deadline, reduced deliverables or more resources. If you do need to go with a revised schedule to accommodate the task in hand, that might push out your other commitments, you may have to re-jig your entire future calendar, generating a huge chain reaction. Also, make sure that you understand the root cause behind the delay and ensure that such delays do not recur in the future because of the same reasons.

Improper closures: In a sense, this is just a variation of the previous point. Here you achieve a significant number of goals of your activity, but you still have a few more that have not yet been completed. Yet you consider the activity as done or 'closed' officially, with the understanding that all the loose ends will be tied in a reasonable time *unofficially, offline*—which also means that even though the schedule for this task is officially over, like Sheetal and her summary report in Snapshot 9.1, you will be stuck with completing the task 'on the side', adding to your time burden. *Clean closures* are absolutely important and in case you are faced with such a not-so-clean closure, try to officially extend your schedule, instead of doing it in your spare time as extra work.

Meetings and appointments running over the limit: This is yet another variant of the earlier point. If such overruns happen regularly, make sure they don't affect your subsequent meetings or important commitments. If you are in an executive meeting or a client visit with no clear end in sight, take turns with your colleagues to attend parts of it.

Interruptions: When you are neck deep in work, it is not uncommon for someone or something to interrupt you and demand immediate attention. The phone, for all its utility, is probably the biggest interrupter of all. If you must answer it while toiling away, keep the conversation very, very brief or do not answer at all, if you think it is not a critical call. Switch it off when you want absolutely no interruptions. Set up a voice mail box and instruct your potential callers to drop messages in it or to send you SMS messages.

After the telephones, the next big interrupters are perhaps the bosses. They are not subtle about marching into our offices (just when we are in the middle of a critical activity) and asking for that Walmart report we did three months ago. Or they may ask us to come to their office for five minutes, which will drag on for half an hour. We will then have to spend an extra half-hour afterwards to get back to where we left off. Remember, it is his prerogative to approach us for all kinds of information when he needs it. So, build your schedule with enough flexibility to accommodate such managerial incursions.

Meeting/Appointment cancellations due to 'no show': In a one-on-one appointment, if you are the person that is being stood up, then it is appropriate to consider it cancelled after a ten-minute wait time. If you have a lot at stake, call and find out why the other party is a no-show. If there is no answer or contact from the other party, you have every reason to be upset. But you may still have to complete business transactions with that person in spite of this—so control your emotions and go through with it. Put a large tick mark against this person and be careful the next time. If you are the customer and this incident upsets you, then be sure to express your feelings.

Ineffective multi-tasking: Multi tasking is for computers, not all human beings are equally efficient at this. In general, we do not recommend multi tasking as it reduces the overall efficiency of any task you do. Certain kinds of multi-tasking like talking on the cell phone while driving is an absolute no-no for safety reasons. Certain other kinds like participating in a meeting while having lunch is okay, depending on the context. You have to be objective in ascertaining when you would multi-task and when you won't. When in doubt, serialize the tasks.

Procrastination: This is probably the single most significant factor why our time management goes haywire. Just postponing an activity that you can do today to tomorrow for no valid reasons (except you have to watch that TV programme today) is one major reason why the important activities never get done till they become urgent. In your time manager, have a column that indicates how many times you postponed a given activity. If you find a lot of activities that are constantly getting postponed, you are a chronic procrastinator. Give yourself a good overhaul with the principles and practices we have outlined in this chapter. If only certain specific activities are getting postponed again and again, then it clearly means a lack of prioritization among the activities. Maybe, the activity can be shelved off to a later date, in which case reset the schedules appropriately. If the activity should not be shelved, it should not be procrastinated either. Make sure you up the ante on this activity.

A poor attitude of 'they can wait': Sometimes people get caught up in respecting their own time so much that they trample upon other people's times. Making other people wait for scheduled appointments presumably gives them a sadistic pleasure and makes them feel that they are more important than others. Sometimes people habitually come late for meetings just to appear important and busy. This is simply not acceptable and will not endear such people to their environment.

Being ultra-perfectionists and embellishing reports and e-mails: Some people think they are perfectionists and keep on refining and making changes to their programs, documents and e-mails and thus consuming more time than what was planned. For any activity, there is a point of diminishing returns, beyond which 'perfecting' will not get any mileage. Effective time managers know where to draw this line.

Biting off more than what can be chewed: In an effort to 'fill up' their calendar, people sometimes end up committing to more things than what they can possibly deliver. Some people get sucked into doing chores, unscheduled activities and being 'volunteered' by others or make it appear they are considerate to others. Helping out others and being a volunteer is good, but this should be done only when the right bandwidth is available. If you hang around the office with that foolish grin and the 'look, I am free' kind of look, you can bet that someone will commission you to do something and drain your time.

9.6 In Summary

India is not a traditionally clock-oriented culture. Fortunately, rapid globalization is accelerating the spread of time consciousness and time management and bringing about a sea-change in the Indian way of life. Now, it is either effective time management or a perpetual ride on that dreaded treadmill.

While the Sheetals of the world are struggling to find their bearings, some others are moving into the paradigm of 'just in time'. This concept is predicated upon very precise adherence to time and deadlines, well-coordinated responses—and above all, a total trust in each other that deliverables will be handed as promised. It makes it possible to operate 'just in time' and eliminates any time buffers or time uncertainties built into our plans, thus freeing up a lot of time for other activities.

And maybe in future, someone will discover a way to add a few extra hours to a day... Until that time, here is a brief summary of ways to best utilize the time we have:

- Internalize the value of time. Time management is an attitude, not a superficial skill.
- Prioritize your activities; embark on an organized and planned schedule each day.
- Use all the productivity improvement tools you can get.
- Don't be an ultra-perfectionist and spend undue amount of time on one single activity just to be perfect in executing it.
- Track and revise your schedule often.
- Have a sense of your natural rhythm.
- Use your free time effectively.

- 'Close' activities completely, without things hanging loose or left in limbo.
- Learn to handle interruptions and time over-runs and how to recover from them.
- Avoid procrastination and ineffective multi-tasking, which are poor time management habits.
- Learn to appreciate others' valuable time.

"I know you want to do a good job of time management. But, don't you think this is a bit too much?"

Fig. 9.3

10

Stepping Up to the Plate

"If you have accomplished all that you have planned for yourself, you have not planned enough."

– Edward Everett Hale

'Stepping up to the plate' is one of those American sports metaphors that is widely used in the business world. It has its origin in baseball, where the word *plate* is synonymous with *base* (actually a little plate is kept at each *base* to mark its location) and 'stepping up to the plate' means taking your turn as a *batter* at the *home plate* to face the *pitcher.*

In management terminology, this phrase has several broad interpretations. In its simplest version, it means 'to face up to one's responsibilities or meet one's obligations'. However, the 'responsibilities' implied in this idiom are not run-of-the-mill type, but have an element of 'taking on a challenge'. For example, we can say that the XYZ Inc. stepped up to the plate and built a community hospital to show it is a responsible, corporate citizen. Similarly, if we say that Mr Verma, an XYZ Inc. employee, stepped up to the plate in his project, we may mean that he took on a *challenging assignment* in the project—perhaps something that nobody else wanted to touch even with a ten foot pole—and executed it perfectly.

Stepping up to the plate, in the context of soft skills, refers to an attitude of going the extra mile and taking on accountability for areas beyond the normal call of duty. In our opinion, it is the same thing as leadership behaviour. It is leadership by example, which goes over and above the demands of regular professionalism. It is an intense way of connecting to the environment and eventually becoming a star in that environment.

This chapter is about that special breed of people who relish challenges and leadership opportunities–and what happens when they 'step up'.

10.1 ANATOMY OF STEPPING UP TO THE PLATE

Snapshot 10.1

Mr Verma is a junior programmer in XYZ Inc. His Java development project is in full swing and if all goes well, it is slated to be completed in another three months. But Mr Menon, a senior Java programmer on the same project, is suddenly involved in a nasty road accident and is hospitalized with multiple fractures. The prognosis is that he will be bedridden for nearly a month and his neurologist has advised him not to do any intense, work-related activity for the next several weeks. Of course, Menon's well-being is foremost on everyone's mind. All his colleagues wish him well and offer support to the affected family.

But, back in office, if you are the project manager, you will be worried about your project's future progress. Menon is a lead programmer in the project and his magical Java skills are the reason why the project is proceeding at rocket speed. The last thing you want is a project delay or a drop in work quality. You can always get another Java programmer—perhaps even two—from some other project, to fill Menon's shoes. You may even be able to steal that Java whiz kid from the CBA Project. But they will still need time to come on board and ramp up to speed on the project. On the other hand, you can redistribute Menon's responsibilities among your guys—because they know the project—but you know that a lot of them are already overworked. You call a project meeting to thrash out the issue, hoping against hope that someone in your team will come forward and take up the slack for Menon. But there is a deathly silence and everyone is avoiding eye contact with you. You wonder if it is time for you to unilaterally impose your back-up plan on your team.

That's when a minor miracle happens. Verma, a junior member of the project team, approaches you unsolicited and volunteers to take on a lot of Menon's responsibilities—especially in wrapping up some of the crucial modules. Verma knows that his Java skills are nothing compared to Menon's, but he tells you that he will try to learn and improve along the way. Even though he is busy, he will re-prioritize his work to accommodate his new responsibilities. He may be a bit green behind his ears, but Verma promises you that he will get the job done. In effect, Verma is offering to go as the seventh down batsman, trying to steer his team to a victory, even as they still need eighty runs off, say, ten overs. Verma is stepping up to the plate.

Although you are a doubter initially, you still take your chances and let loose Verma in his new role (of course, you introduce several new checks and balances to manage this new 'risk'). Come three months, Verma has delivered on his promise, the project coasts to a smooth finish and a new star is born in XYZ Inc. End of story.

Fig. 10.1 *A new star is born*

Before we go any further, a couple of caveats are in order.

You don't have to have a colleague getting indisposed as a trigger point for someone else to step up. There can be a lot of other circumstances too, where an intrepid team member steps up to the plate and bails the project out. A serious lack of leadership and management control, rampant infighting among team members, conflicting signals and poor support from upper management, financial constraints, technical difficulties, poor customer interface, chaotic work environment—and you can add your favourite project-killer to this list—all create a perfect backdrop for a Verma to emerge. But the beauty of stepping up is that often, even when nothing goes wrong around you, you can still find a way to step up.

Also, stepping up to the plate is not just about glory and being in the spotlight. Quite often, the path to meeting a challenge will be paved with unglamorous and painstaking activities.

10.2 Some Components of 'Stepping Up'

An in-depth analysis of people like Verma will throw some light on the 'stepping up to the plate' process and what makes them so different from the vast majority of workers who are content with simply eking out a living. We present a short list.

Appetite for a challenge: People like Verma have this passion for challenges. They cannot pass up a crossword puzzle or a computer game or a jumbled-up Rubik's cube or whatever teases their right brain. They are easily lured into physical and athletic challenges—they get into friendly running races, 'push-up' contests and even take the street-corner cricket games seriously. In their student days, they are the ones who raised their hands to do extra assignments and projects that went beyond the standard classroom fare.

They don't view such challenges as boring or burdensome. Nor do they have this 'Why do it? Leave me alone' kind of attitude. They really have fun delving into the challenge in hand, unfazed by its 'difficulty'. It is their opportunity to display their talents and pick up some wisdom in the process.

The responsibility factor: Verma also feels tremendously responsible for his team and his employer. The success of the project is essential for him, because it serves the greater good of the larger community. He knows that his corporation and his team in particular, have invested so much in the project—and so much progress has already been made—that now is not the time to lose momentum. Besides, there are legal, contractual obligations with the clients. So, *he* must pitch in and do something.

Verma feels that he is the project. He is the team. And he is XYZ Inc.

Confidence about meeting the challenge: There is a *chutzpah* factor in what Verma is doing. And some people may even think he is crazy. But Verma's decision to fill in for Menon is a studied response and not a split-second, impulsive act just to endear himself to his managers.

As much as Verma likes a challenge, a gambler he is not. He knows that the challenge is do-able and he has reasonable confidence in his abilities. He is aware of the kind of help he can get from his environment. He also knows his territory and the range of his skill-set and interest. Java programming yes, but he would not step up to do computer animation. Not just regarding skills, he is also very aware of time horizons and deadlines and is reasonably certain that he will get things done in time. He is sure of not only himself and what he can and cannot achieve, but he is also perfectly cognizant of what the synergy is between the needs of the environment and his strengths.

Ingenuity and innovation: Verma knows that virtually nobody is going to hold his hands and guide him through Menon-land. Not only does he have to program like Menon, but he will also have to be effectively his own project manager for that leg of the project. He will have to figure what Menon has already done, plan/schedule his Menon-impersonation and be in lock-step with the rest of the project. The onus is on him to be ingenuous and innovative, given the time and resource constraints. Devising clever tactics for one's stint at the bat is an important component of stepping up.

Tapping into one's full potential: Since Verma will have to elevate his Java programming ability, he will dig into his inner reserves and push himself hard. In that process, he will discover skills and potential that he never knew he had. Like a sprinter who not only wins the race but also sets the world record, Verma too will come up with a neat trick or two that will completely astound the others in the project (and sometimes he may even surprise himself).

Stepping up can be a major self-discovery process. You will discover and unearth not only some amazing hard skills (like being able understand cloud computing), but you will also gain a slew of soft skills, like report-writing, testing, time management, inter-personal communication and much more that will stand you in good stead for a long time to come.

It is beyond simple volunteering: What Verma has done is much, much more than, say, offering to pick up a bag of potato chips on his way back from lunch. Not just in terms of effort, but also qualitatively—because he came forward, while others in the project team were either too disinclined or were still deciding about taking on Menon's load. By stepping up to the plate, Verma is making a statement about his character. He is setting himself up to be a new leader, even if he is still a few steps away from being a complete leader.

10.3 How Life Changes After Stepping Up

Verma's is a classic tale of 'a challenge is an opportunity'. Following his successful 'stepping up to the plate' episode, his life and career in XYZ will change forever. Let us see what we mean.

Stardom and superstardom: The main takeaway from Verma's story is that at the end of it all, he has managed to break out of the pack and differentiate himself from the rest of his co-workers. 'Stepping up to the plate' is probably the closest any organization comes to conducting a 'star search' and Verma managed to present himself perfectly. Not only will he be recognized and rewarded immediately, Verma will also become the poster child of XYZ Inc. He may be called upon to defuse another challenge somewhere else in the organization or be placed in a leadership or management position. His career will be put on a 'fast track'. And if Verma's stepping up directly resulted in a bunch of very happy customers, you can bet that his star status will be enhanced even more.

It is 'baptism-by-fire': As a professional experience, 'stepping up' is truly valuable for Verma. It enabled him to mature several notches. His initial act of volunteering, his impromptu project planning, improving his Java skills on the fly, discovering the depth and scope of his potential, and his final, successful delivery—most of it self-directed—are things he will cherish for a long time. This is stuff you don't pick up from any business school course.

You win, even if you don't completely deliver: There is good news and bad news if you are not 100 per cent successful in your effort with the bat. The good news is, that depending upon the degree of success, you will still reap rewards. The bad news is that you will get credit for only what you accomplished and not for your intentions.

The bottomline is that stepping up presents a golden opportunity, with very little downside.

A final point. What happens when Menon returns to work?

Perhaps nothing. Menon should return to work without any misgivings or fear of losing his place to Verma. Any growing organization will have room for both a Menon and a Verma and in fact, now XYZ Inc. is in a much stronger position.

However, we would like to caution you that a stepping up to the plate need not be a 'stepping on others' toes' experience. One has to be aware of the functional division of labour in one's organization and learn to respect it. Don't poach others' territory and don't do other people's job for them just to prove that you can do it better. (if indeed there is a better way to do a job, teach them and don't hoard that from them or steal their thunder) Step up only with the blessings of everyone around you.

10.4 In Summary

Project teams—and even organizations—lose out big when they don't have people stepping up to the plate. Let us summarize what the impediments to the stepping up process are and what positive steps we can take to replace them (see Box 10.1 and Box 10.2).

Box 10.1

Excuses, excuses, excuses for not stepping up!

- I want to keep my life simple.
- Why bother?
- I don't want to take on risky assignments.
- Let others, who are more enthusiastic, do it.
- It is not my job. Somebody will surely step in and step up.
- I don't care to be a hero.
- I cannot do that—I am not as qualified as Menon, even though I am also a Java programmer.
- If something goes wrong I will be blamed.
- I am not empowered.
- I don't have the bandwidth.

Box 10.2

Step up with zeal!

- I am going to be stretched, but let me give it a shot.
- Somebody has to do it. I guess I will be that somebody.
- It is not going to be easy pickings. Let me see what I can do.
- There is a risk of project delay, but I will try my best.
- I guess since no one wants to do it, I might as well take a crack at it.
- It is not up my alley, but let me see.
- Hey, I should do everything to help out with the project.
- I can never be as good as Menon in Java, but it is crunch time.
- I will try. But I am sure I will need help and I am also sure I will be able to get the help I need.
- I will have to clear that with my manager, but I am sure he will be okay with it.
- I may have to sit down with the clients to better understand some of the deliverables. Let me take care of it.

11

When Things Go Way Wrong at the Workplace

> *"Life is not a matter of holding good cards, but sometimes, playing a poor hand well."*
>
> – *Jack London*

It may seem odd that we are dedicating an entire chapter to a negative and almost taboo topic, 'When things go way wrong in our workplace'; especially, when most of us have visions of sailing through our careers and retiring with glory—and a gold watch. But today's globally competitive, dog-eat-dog world is more like the rough seas, exposing organizations to corporate equivalents of tsunamis and typhoons. And if an organizational disaster indeed strikes, many corporations these days simply implode and self-destruct under the impact, causing widespread damage and deeply painful consequences.

At the individual level, a corporate storm has the potential to ruin many, many careers and professional lives. If you are in its path, you will not be spared, no matter whether you are a bit player or a major player. Given this brutal reality, we should be open to the idea of a possible career disruption due to office events and must do at least a bare minimum of risk management and disaster-recovery planning, in advance. To see what we mean, take a look at the following Snapshots illustrating the deadly nature of today's workplace disasters. They will show you why disaster-planning is not just for the disaster-prone and paranoids, but in everyone's interest.

Snapshot 11.1

NNA Corp. has always been your top customer. It is an MNC with a presence in practically every street corner in the world and it is a matter of pride that you have them in your client list. Not only that, every year the account is getting larger and larger with you poaching projects from your rivals. In fact, your company dedicates a separate department (including 'hot line' phones) to molly-coddle NNA. Then one day you hear the news that your big rival has trumped you and stolen the NNA account from you—lock, stock and barrel. The 'unhappenable' has happened. Within a few days, you find yourself sitting squarely on the 'bench', waiting for the next assignment. You start thumbing through old COBOL manuals.

Snapshot 11.2

You work for Fizz Bottled Drinks Inc. Your company has ambitious plans of entering and capturing the juice-drink market. You and your colleagues in research and development labour for months and come up with formulae for several juice-drink flavours. The first such product—called Mang-Jooz, a mango drink, is test-marketed in several parts of the country and based on the positive marketing results, it is introduced nationwide, with celebrity brand ambassadors and promo videos and all that jazz. But within a month, the bubble bursts and Mang-Jooz turns out to be one of the biggest fiascos in the industry. After enormous losses, Fizz not only gives up on the mango drink, but also puts the entire line of juice-drinks follow-products in permanent cold storage. You were counting on the success of this line of products to vault you into higher orbit. But, now you are re-assigned to an insignificant job of doing minor chemistry experiments in a jungle of test tubes and round bottomed flasks. Your program manager was not so lucky. He got transferred to your Antarctica office. Or something like that.

Snapshot 11.3

You work in AB Mutual Funds Company. You earned huge bonuses and incentive pay just last year when the entire country was hungrily grabbing up shares of your mutual funds. But this year, with the global economic downturn, there are no takers for your mutual funds even if you gave it to them for free (well, almost). Stock trading activity has come to a crawl and your company makes a tough decision to close its Kolkata office and lay-off the entire staff—including you.

There are some things in common to all of the three Snapshots. Firstly—and fortunately—they are all hopefully low probability events that presumably happen only once in a rare while. Secondly, they are devastating and can completely destroy everything we worked so hard for—our family, our mental and physical health, our financial security, our careers, etc. Next, we can be impacted by such events even if we are several degrees removed from the trigger point. We may have the natural instincts to survive such calamities described in the Snapshots, but an ounce of prior-planning can give us a solid advantage while facing the ordeal and help us navigate out of the mess, to safe grounds.

As the Snapshots illustrate, we are talking about the sky falling on us—the kind of disaster that can rattle even the strongest among us—and not about everyday mishaps like a hard-disk drive crashing. Myriad things happen to us when we go through such a crisis. We would get anxiety attacks—not knowing how long or how deep the crisis would be. Internal and external pressures would mount. A potpourri of emotions would occur—right from fear, anger and helplessness to downright shame, defeat and guilt. We may even have to go through a job change and be transplanted to an unknown and alien environment. Even if we held on to our jobs, our roles in our organizations can get marginalized. Yet others may be so traumatized that they will be in a 'reactive' mode, swept away by the tide, powerless to do anything about it.

But, one doesn't have to be despondent. In this chapter, we will outline a five-pronged approach to disaster planning—the 5A approach focusing on the 'before, during and after' phases of a crisis. We will tell you how best to pre-plan for such potential disasters, how to ride out the storm and what will help us lick our wounds and move on to the next innings of our lives.

We also believe that some of the elements you will pick up in this chapter will go beyond crisis-management and help you even in your every day activities at work.

1. Disaster-planning can be a part of our overall career planning strategy. Some of the ingredients used in disaster-planning like risk management and planning for contingencies, are also used in our career master plan.
2. Some of the habits that go into effectively dealing with disasters—such as anticipation, accepting that not everything can be anticipated, ice-cold nerves, alertness, sharp observation powers and instincts and carrying forward the lessons from a disaster—are good traits to have even under normal circumstances.
3. We will see that we need a large dose of this soft skill called *resilience*—the 'never say die' attitude—to tide over any calamity and to thrive in the post-disaster world. Understanding resiliency will be an important part of this chapter.

In good times, everyone will look like a winner—as long as you don't mess things up. But it takes a crisis to differentiate the strong, the poised and the resourceful ones from the rest of the flock. The fittest not merely survive the ordeal and rise from the ashes like the mythological Phoenix, but also go on to become even more successful. Thus, resilience and how you handle crisis situations can really be a major differentiator as you progress further in your career.

The approach to handling crisis is given by the 5A formula:

- ▶ *A*nticipate what could go wrong.
- ▶ *A*ccept that you cannot anticipate everything!
- ▶ Be *A*lert, and have your antennae up during execution.
- ▶ *A*ct on alternatives when things do go wrong.
- ▶ *A*ssimilate your learning to encounter crisis better the next time.

11.1 Anticipate—Be Prepared!

We cannot lightning-proof our lives. But we can do a thing or two by way of preparation, just in case a crisis descends down on us. Let us see how.

Anticipate what could go wrong: Being prepared is winning half the battle. Your first step should be to anticipate what things could go wrong and what kind of disasters or risks can strike you or your project. You can enumerate the possible disasters in two levels—first the category of disaster and the next the specific instances of possible disasters within that category. Table 11.1 lists some of these.

Table 11.1 ***Anticipate disaster category and example***

Category of Risk/Disaster	Examples
Political	▶ Terrorist attacks ▶ Embargo or sanctions ▶ Travel/visa restrictions
Project	▶ Customer throwing in a sudden unrealistic deadline ▶ A seemingly insurmountable bug that has caused a lot of customer dissatisfaction
HR/People	▶ Key person has left the project ▶ Huge increase in attrition because of the arrival of a competitor in the city
Technology	▶ Sudden changes in technology making the current technology and project obsolete ▶ Difficulty in finding support for older legacy technology
Market changes	▶ Financial crisis like the ones in 2008–09

Develop early warning systems to understand symptoms of potential disasters: A lot of disasters brew and slow-cook for some time before they erupt. The mango-drink fiasco in Fizz in Snapshot 11.2 probably developed over many months and we could have picked up the warning signals ahead of time if we were perceptive, and kept our eyes and ears open to the environment. Advance warning is crucial to taking any kind of counter measure.

Look for troubling signs: Such signs would include an uncharacteristically frowning or introspective manager, too many closed door meetings, an unusually busy admin and of course, a yelling and screaming client who is threatening to pull out—just about any unusual activity. Keep checking on the health of your project in particular, through various sources. Read all e-mails carefully to see if there is anything between the lines. Check with other companies in your industry to see if there is a major systemic problem developing across the industry. Talk to outsiders and ask them for their insights. Are there unusually large numbers of people confined to the bench? Has the recruitment of new employees stopped? Are there any major contracts cancelled or scaled down? Have there been any shake-ups in the organization? Are there reports of any important strategic or tactical shifts in your company? Is there any hint of major belt-tightening?

Make sure that all the early warning signs add up. Quite often, we are not good at interpreting what we see in our radar screens and many times, early troubles may not be indicative of future bad trends. Sometimes a single piece of bad news can produce a knee-jerk reaction to jump into unnecessary alternative plans. That single piece could be an aberration that is unlikely to be indicative of any trend. The main point in developing these early warning signals is that the signals should show some *consistent* pattern.

Develop contingency and mitigation plans of how to react in a disaster, should the disaster materialize: Businesses manage their risks by coming up with alternative plans to complement their original plans, just in case the unexpected happens. So, whether you work in the administration or on the factory floor or in a BPO project, you will be required to operate out of a 'Plan B' in times of crisis. Discuss with your manager about your particular contingency plans, well in advance.

Determine the risks in your own job and see if you can devise back-up plans at the personal level. For example, if you are a software developer in an off-shoring project, what are the consequences if you cannot complete a critical module by a given deadline? Can you then re-negotiate the deadline? Can you deliver just a subset of the deliverables on the said deadline? Should you ask for more resources?

Contingency plans are very, very important. Sometimes they incorporate as much ingenuity as the original plan. The good ones are not only pragmatic, but also have the essentials of the initial plan and thus the impact of deviating from the main plan is minimized. Enough thought should also go into the disaster recovery part of any contingency plan, so that we are still on track to achieve most of our broad strategic goals we have set for ourselves.

Contingency plans apply not only to the project you are doing, but also to your own career and personal life. You have to ask yourself questions such as 'Will I have adequate cash flow to maintain my standard of living in case something drastic happens? For how long?' and so on. Of course, we caution you against dwelling on the negatives or spending too much time and effort on planning for contingencies.

One of the main ways of anticipating what could go wrong is to *stay connected.* Liaison with colleagues from your group as well as from other functions, your external business contacts and just about anyone who can add to your knowledge of the big picture. There is no better source of information than the human tongue. Of course, you should not spend half your work day chit-chatting or rabble-rousing. But don't exist in a clamshell either, completely isolating yourself from everything else.

Also, you should know when to ring the alarm bells and embark on back-up plans. A moment too late and you will find yourself in a bigger mess. On the other hand, you don't want to use contingency plans in non-emergency situations. Don't break that piggy-bank yet, just because you are running a rupee too short!

11.2 Accept That You Cannot Anticipate Everything

As much as you gaze through a crystal ball, you can never completely foresee and anticipate everything. The most well laid out prognosticating plans can go haywire and there can be new, totally unexpected, disasters that can hit you every now and then. Be aware of this and accept this reality.

But, that doesn't mean that you should abandon the process of 'anticipating' or figuring out your risks!! If you do not even attempt to anticipate anything, your situation will be far worse. Some people give the excuse, 'Whatever risk planning I do, some new risk always hits me! So why I should I waste my time anticipating any risks? Let me take a shotgun approach and face things as they develop, rather than waste any time in anticipating possible risks and disasters.' This negative approach will not take you anywhere nor will it make it easy for you to work with your colleagues.

Your plan should anticipate risks as well as have a proviso or contingency for unanticipated risks as well. You can call them 'buffer' or use any other name, but the process of identifying the possible risks and accepting there will be ones that you cannot anticipate, will definitely help you to tide over times when things go wrong.

We, as individuals, could not have prevented losing a valued client or losing one's job. But the steps mentioned here can mentally prepare us for such things in advance—right from working on alternate contingency plans ahead of time, to developing a professional veneer even in the face of impending disaster.

11.2 Be Alert and Have Your Antennae Up!

This section is about the beginning stages of the storm. What started off as latent and somewhat subtle warning signals earlier, have now developed into major alarms and it is time to face the impending disaster and execute on your plans. For success in execution, you need to be on a high degree of alert and have your antennae up even more—for, you need to follow the developing events closely and make the relevant tactical adjustments. Here are some points to consider as the storm just gets started.

Recognize and react to the alarm bells: For example, when a project is about to enter crisis mode, things can start to go very wrong. The concept of ownership and accountability will likely go for a toss. People may blame everything around them and may make lame excuses for missing deadlines or for their poor performance. Accusatory e-mails may fly all over the Intranet. There may even be a steep fall in morale and a total lack of motivation to keep going. All these signals start off as being subtle, but soon become blatant and you need to be an alert radio man with a powerful antenna. It will be good if you can register these signals ahead of others to give you more room to react (but do not fall a prey to being a source of these signals yourself!)

Don't compromise your professionalism: Your professionalism should be impeccable even in the face of a brewing disaster. Any way you act, you should not compromise your professionalism. Even if things are crumbling around you, you should play for professional pride until the last whistle is blown. Like professional athletes who give their much-clichéd '110 per cent' effort in *all* the games—not just in the games they are winning—you too, should be duty-bound and perform in your job at the highest level. So, keep those reports, documentations and testings coming till the bitter end.

Also, whether it is your job or not, if there is anything you can do to avert any organizational disaster (or at least mitigate it), you are required to do it. In other words, it is mandatory for you to be a Good Samaritan, if you are in a position to do so. We have discussed more on this in Chapter 10, on 'Stepping Up to the Plate'.

All this might sound like it is too much to ask of anyone. But your professionalism is far more important than any job or project. You just cannot bail out ahead of everyone else for selfish reasons.

Don't have the 'I told you so' attitude: the last thing people want to hear is a smart aleck co-worker loudly proclaiming his superiority just when a crisis is about to erupt in the background. 'I told you so' are such empty words—and definitely the most irrelevant piece of hindsight. Such an attitude simply reflects an unhealthy cynicism toward one's colleagues and the management.

If you are a chronic dissenter or a constant 'I told you so' person, odds are that you not only make your life miserable, but also spread the gloom around—crisis or no crisis. You will not relate well to your environment. Remember that while extraordinary insights and heroism are always welcome, a 'holier-than-thou' attitude—especially when dire things are happening to your organization—will only result in your getting isolated and picked on.

Refrain from any public display of emotions: Even when major work-related disasters occur around you, you are supposed to deal with them with quiet dignity and nerves of steel. It behooves you to control extreme emotions such as rage, frustration and panic, or breaking into tears. Staying cool and poised in the wake of bad news—with a dash of dark humour—is the preferred approach.

11.4 Act on Alternatives When Disaster Strikes

One day when you sit in your cubicle and it feels like the middle deck of a sinking Titanic, be aware that your office storm is just touching down. It can be a flurry of pink slips in case of AB Mutual Funds or a complete re-drawing of the organizational chart as in the case of Fizz Bottled Drinks. In any event, once the disaster starts to unleash, you have time only for tactical response and you will have to simply rely on your dynamism, reflexes and instincts.

Press the 'survival mode' button: Your first instinct should be survival. Be on high alert and grasp every single thing going on around you. Talk, listen, see and feel. Be aware of time progression of the crisis. Is it over yet? Mentally try to comprehend what is going on. Through all this, don't slack off or give up. Keep yourself well organized and keep information readily accessible. You never know which report, document or e-mail will be asked of you by your bosses. Above all, don't do anything silly to attract the wrong kind of attention and jeopardize your job.

This is also the time to work closely with your management team and be sympathetic to their plight. Volunteer to put in extra work, if you can. Show moral and real support to your colleagues on the team and extend your helping hand wherever possible. Remember that you are all in it together.

Till the last ball is bowled, stay connected with your customers—if you interface with them at all. It may be annoying sometimes when they constantly call you for updates and news. But be patient and courteous. During conversations with them, remember not to give out any privileged information. An 'I don't know, sir' or 'I cannot talk about that, madam' is an appropriate response—and better than not picking up the phone at all.

Assess the damage: Once you have figured that the storm has just passed, it is time to assess the damage. Start with yourself first. How will your job change? How much damage did your organization or your group suffer? Get out of denial mode and do some serious *ad hoc* analysis with the initial data. Don't overreact or go out of control—we know it is hard to be calm—but there is life even after the worst office crisis. Do not hesitate to take any help that is available and that you may need.

Choose the most appropriate of the alternative plans: In the earlier stages, you had drawn out some contingency plans. Now is the time to revisit these plans and make a hard choice of which one you want to implement. Ask yourself questions like:

- Has the situation changed from the time that I drew up this plan to now?
- What new risks do I face for each of the alternative plans?
- What new benefits do my alternative plans have now?
- Can I consider *status quo*, i.e., not do anything as an option?

The last question is often something that is ignored. It is okay to continue in *status quo* mode in the face of a crisis if you *consciously* choose to do so. Not doing anything should be a conscious choice – it should not be a choice by inertia nor should it be due to ignorance of alternatives available.

11.5 Assimilate the Lessons Learnt

Once the eye of the storm has passed you, it is time to start rebuilding your lives and move on to your next *avatar*—perhaps in another role, and perhaps, even in another organization. And when you do so, you should have the same energy, enthusiasm and professionalism within you. All traces of the crisis—besides the lessons-learnt part—should be confined to the annals of history.

Such things may seem easier said than done, because a crisis—even an office crisis—can cause deep psychological scars which may take a long time to heal. Here is where 'resilience' comes in to help you spring back to life, time after time, crisis after crisis.

The Merriam-Webster dictionary defines resilience to be the 'ability to recover from or adjust easily to misfortune or change'. But, you need to understand it better and take a close look at its many elements, so that you can develop it into a very powerful weapon in your war chest of soft skills.

Resilience means keeping your spirits high even in times of crisis: A significant calamity like a job loss or a major setback to your project—even if you eventually land another job or project—can leave you an emotional wreck, with a serious damage to your spirits. With your body and soul feeling so lousy, how can you quickly rebound to your old positive, cheerful self? How do you get back your zest for life, rather than wait for time to do its healing?

First off, realize that with every passing day, the crisis that traumatized you, is going farther and farther away and there is no point staying angry or depressed or in lapsing into long bouts of brooding. Instead, try to tell yourself that it is useless to cry over spilt milk and that careers can be rebuilt. Get a perspective and focus on your new job and the positives it brings to you. Draw inspiration from others' success stories and anecdotes about perseverance. Remember that *nobody can break your will unless you let them.* Set new and realistic goals for yourself, your project or your organization and be happy when you reach them. Finally, remember that you are not the only one to go through such a crisis. It has happened to others (may have even been a lot worse than what happened to you) and it may happen to you again.

Resilience means being enterprising even after a crisis: Suffering through a crisis can sometimes result in a 'once bitten twice shy' attitude, where you become completely risk-averse and ultra-conservative in your outlook. But this is exactly the wrong lesson to learn from your experience. Like a child taking stutter steps even after a fall, you too, should continue with your spirit of enterprise and take risks again. Maybe not the same amount of risks, may not even be the same kind of risks—but risks nonetheless.

With this renewed risk-taking, you regain your confidence. This confidence should restore your faith in your fundamentals. This in turn should result in fresh optimism. Resilience is about believing that no crisis can keep you down for too long.

A word of caution though—be careful about becoming too cocky and reckless in your desire to quickly make up for the previous time.

Resilience means being stronger and smarter the next time: Debacles like the ones described in the Snapshots, can change a persón, hopefully, for the better. Here is where resilient people have an advantage, because usually, they are also good learners. They pick up the right lessons from their bitter experience—they shed a lot of their bad habits and try to eliminate their mistakes, they will add more skills and knowledge to their repertoire and try different approaches and tactics in their new jobs. They don't just blindly repeat what they did the previous time counting on luck to bail them out this time. Instead, they try to strengthen their performance by doubling their efforts and by using better techniques and resources. Resilience is about the hunger for success in the next opportunity.

Resilience implies perseverance: Resiliency is not just about wanting to redeem an earlier failure with a resounding success—it is also about the burning desire to get that one more chance. It is the perseverance to go after more and more chances should disaster keeps striking again and again. Resilient people are good at looking around and spotting their next opening and they even create one if none exists.

In addition to being persistent and enthusiastic, they also view any opportunity as god-given and try to pounce on it and take advantage of it. They look at their new job—even if it is a come-down from their previous job—as a source of opportunities. They don't view it as a consolation prize or the 'no choice but' choice. The new job may be their third or fourth assignment in their career, but they will still treat it with the same fervour and believe that maybe this will be their calling. History is full of examples of how an actor got her first break in her sixth movie and so on. Instant tea was a failure when it was first introduced, but when it was re-introduced as an ingredient in a new product called 'iced tea' it was a big success. As someone said, '*There are no failures. Only feedbacks.*' Sure, the agony of defeat is difficult to erase, but moving on can be a very positive experience if you have the right attitude.

The net summary of the 'assimilate' phase is the need to do a thorough after-the-event analysis of any calamity or crisis that hit you. Resilient people perform a thorough analysis of what went wrong and what went right and draw the right lessons. The analysis produces a comprehensive list of 'lessons' you learnt. It is imperative that these lessons are the 'right' lessons and not emotional, knee-jerk reactions. Discuss with friends and advisers about your inferences and record your findings in your diary for later reference. This exercise should give you a practical set of rules to follow in the immediate future. As someone said, it is only when you are intimidated and get pushed against the wall, that you learn serious lessons in life. Maybe, this is the only silver lining in a crisis.

11.6 In Summary

It is always a good idea to trust Murphy's Law. Anticipating what all could go wrong would make you better prepared to meet adverse situations and surprises.

> Anticipating what all could go wrong and planning for it can reduce the impact of the wrong things, if and when they do happen.

Even if you can anticipate what could go wrong, but don't have a system to track them, it is not going to help you much.

> Have early warning systems that alert you to impending crises—keep your antennae open.

Even if you anticipate and plan a lot, be clear that you cannot anticipate everything. Hence,

> Have contingency plans to deal with emergency situations.

During a crisis, do not hesitate to take help or ask for help; likewise, during a crisis in other parts of your organization, volunteer help if you can. Most importantly, in whichever crisis situation you work (whether or not you are successful in tackling the crisis), learn from the crisis and what you did or did not do to make sure such crises do not recur in future.

> Prevention of a crisis is better than fire fighting.

When you are under pressure and working in a crisis situation,

Do not display your emotions in public.

And when you find your team in a crisis, don't take a holier-than-thou attitude and

Never say 'I told you so before that this won't work.'

A crisis is a challenge to you to learn something new. It is not meant to act as a deterrent for you to try out new things.

Just because you went through a crisis or had a setback, do not stop taking risks—nothing ventured, nothing gained!

"..and you need to go to the basement to see the rest of our sales performance...."

Fig. 11.1

12

Tying It All Together: Work Your Way to Success

"The people who get on in this world are the people who get up and look for the circumstances they want, and, if they can't find them, make them."

–George Bernard Shaw

We have seen several different soft skills pertaining to attitude, starting from 'seeing the big picture' to 'resilience'. Finally, it all comes down to execution and delivery. This means *work.* Ever since man 'invented' work—perhaps around the time he was hunting and gathering food—he also invented the notion of hard work. From time immemorial, hard work has been universally revered as an important work ethic, transcending cultural boundaries and cutting across different generations. But 'hard work' has assumed different dimensions in the context of the vastly complex, global work environment of today.

More than anything else, hard work today is a matter of *attitude* and is the key to achieving success. It has assumed more than just a physical dimension (as we will see in the next section). Hard work starts with an insatiable hunger to work well and be successful in our careers. This attitude results in willingness to put in long (and often extra) hours on the job and the perseverance to chase after lofty end-goals. This attitude makes us enjoy our work and not view it as a burdensome chore standing between us and better things in life. Remember that in this globalized world, if we are not interested in doing our job well, there is always someone elsewhere—perhaps in the Philippines or South Africa—who will gladly do it and send us home. Our work is not just something that needs to get done. Hence, however old fashioned hard work may sound, there is no denying the fact that it is absolutely an essential soft skill to have even in today's environment. It is only what constitutes hard work and how you leverage the hard work and get the best mileage from it that has changed.

In this final chapter in the attitude dimension, we will see more details about this soft skill called hard work. In Section 12.2, we will discuss the different dimensions of hard work. In Section 12.3, we will present how to get the best mileage out of your hard work. We conclude this chapter after discussing some of the common myths about hard work and some 'work killers' that tend to undermine the benefits of hard work.

12.1 Dimensions of Hard Work

Hard work today is no longer just slogging away and sweating it out till we are dead.

In today's professional world, simply sitting at one's desk and plodding along mechanically will not get us anywhere. But minus those long brutal hours of 'hard work', we will never become successful. In our fast moving, tension-filled age, hard work is actually comprised of three dimensions—*physical*, *mental* and *informational*. Only when these three dimensions are recognized and a judicious balance is achieved between them, can you really expect to get the best leverage out of your hard work (see Figure 12.1).

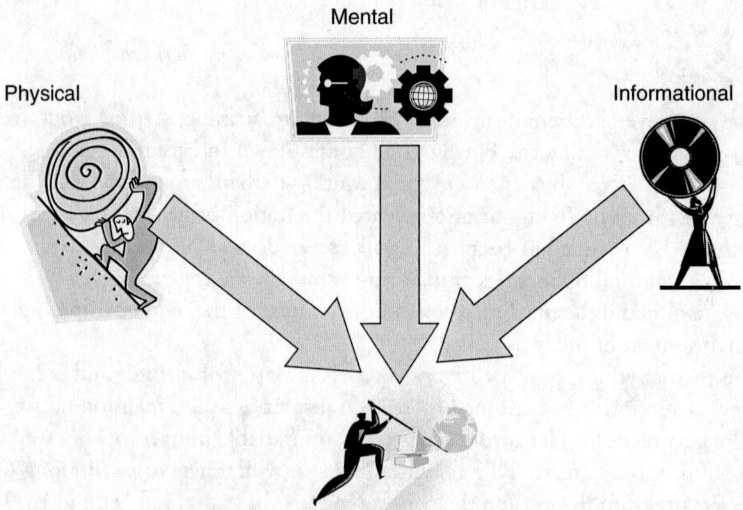

Fig. 12.1 *Components of leveraging work*

First, hard work obviously has a physical component to it. Nothing can replace it completely. Being physically fit is absolutely essential for you to have a positive attitude and being ready to take on hard work. Burning out physical stamina by neglect of basic hygiene factors like work–life balance, diet and exercise will undoubtedly decrease your ability to succeed in your environment, especially in the long run. Tiring yourself out early or peaking prematurely with your energies will definitely make your career reach a plateau that is difficult to scale further.

Even though hard work might seem only like physical work, a good part of hard work is actually mental and it calls for a certain mental tenacity to keep working hard for long hours. It is the same mental faculty that also identifies any recurring patterns in your work. You start applying intelligence to your work. When you do repetitive work routinely, it is likely that you will invent short cuts and other tools that will make your work simpler, error free and more efficient. The 'work hard' at this juncture starts incorporating the 'work smart' components.

Do not underestimate the chance that you will first hit mental fatigue before you become physically fatigued. What you may think is manifested as physical fatigue could actually, well be mental fatigue. If this happens, it can impair judgement and cause you to commit mental mistakes that translate into execution errors. Watch out for any little warning signs your mind gives, so that you can take a break and refresh yourself. If you have several different assignments on your job, and several kinds of activities, rotate them, so that you have more variety.

A third component of getting the best mileage out of your hard work is informational. This is perhaps the single most differentiating factor that sets apart a hard worker of today with his counterpart a few years ago. New concepts are emerging—we now tele-commute, e-learn and Pod-cast. We have become smart about working hard and 'employee productivity', as it is called in management parlance, always seems to increase year over year. If we are going to be intimidated by technology, gadgets and overabundance of information, we are not setting ourselves up for success.

You live in times when you almost need a degree in 'Wiki-eology' to be successful and you need to know the precise method to Google-search for a needle in the haystack. Googling has become an accepted verb! Effective use of the Internet and other technology resources involves figuring out the appropriate Web sites, blogs (and even Twitters) and joining the relevant forums and relentlessly pursuing what you want. It also means that you will stay on top of new developments and trends, new directives from the government and the industry.

For example, if your organization wants to choose between Nairobi and Lagos for its African sales office and asks you to find out rough-cut information about these two African cities, you should know exactly which sites and forums to go to and for what information. You should not only get narrowly focused direct information, but also some 'related information' that can come in handy to help you do a detailed analysis later. Thus your hard work can take you through more miles than it is ever possible to go without the informational dimension.

To be of the best breed of employees today, you need to have a judicious mix of nascent hard work, smartness and being information savvy. Your bag of tricks should include ways of getting maximum output for your physical hard work, the intelligence to identify and use resources, the temperament to acquire and use knowledge and the aptitude to pursue and solve complex problems along the way.

12.2 Hard Work—How to Get Most Out of It

The steps to maximizing the results of your hard work, considering the three dimensions discussed above, are:

1. Visualize
2. Organize and prioritize
3. Practise
4. Exercise judgement
5. Recharge yourself.

12.2.1 Visualize

It is important that you understand the big picture (Chapter 2) and in particular your role in your organization. This will give you a context and a perspective to your job and will work as a motivator to do hard work. If your organization is a huge puzzle, which little piece are you and what is the value you bring to the table?

Know the organizational structure and the work flow in your immediate vicinity. Do you know who supplies you with your assignment and gives you the inputs to do your job? Who takes your output and uses it in his or her job? Who are your stakeholders? What are the expectations from you in terms of schedule, productivity, deliverables and so on? Who do you complain to, if there are problems? What kind of paperwork and data entry do you have to do?

Figure out your physical environment. What are the limits to what you can do?

What is going on around you? What resources are available to you in your immediate vicinity? Are there any people who can help you or resolve things for you in a crunch? Such elaborate understanding of the big picture can give you a psychological comfort-zone to operate out of.

12.2.2 Organize and Prioritize

It is a good idea to organize yourself and your space before you go full throttle on your job. Like we already discussed in Chapter 9 on Time Management, scheduling and prioritizing your activities are important and you need to execute your commitments in a certain order. Even if you don't have very many activities crying for your attention, try to make at least a short list of things to do and operate according to it. Simply making a laundry list of your pending tasks will bring clarity and control to your workdays and give a direction to your hard work.

It is important that you keep your workspace clean and clutter-free. An organized workplace in itself can improve your productivity by cutting down on the time you take to search for things and so forth. There is a home for everything in your work area—the files, the letters and the work pieces—and make sure you dock them in their appropriate places. Likewise, un-clutter your computer too and have a neat directory structure of folders, files and e-mail boxes. File away information and paperwork in a timely fashion instead of laying them on the nearest flat surface. Of course, such things are easier said than done and in spite of your extreme meticulousness, mess will find a way to creep up on your space and you may have to do periodic housekeeping.

12.2.3 Practise

Even if it is clichéd, let us state this: *practice makes you perfect.* When you are engaged in hard work, you are so focused on the work in your hand that your only goal is to execute it as best as you can. There will be periods when you will be bored, but you will still need to keep going after taking timely breaks. As a professional, you have to be disciplined enough to put in hard work day after day after day—like how Tendulkar puts in several hours of practice every day, even if he is on top of his game. Discipline is the key to working hard consistently. You cannot work in spurts or only on 'good days'. While going through your work, keep an eye on the numerical targets you had set for yourself, the time factor and the quality of your work.

When a professional sportsman like Tendulkar hits hundreds of balls in practice, to an outsider it might look like a mindless, repetitive exercise. But upon closer inspection, you would see that Tendulkar was actually focusing on making subtle improvements to one of his strokes and in fact, was getting better and better as he kept practicing. Researchers like Geoff Colvin,[1] Anders Ericsson and colleagues argue that you too should view the hard work you put in your activity as a practice session toward improving some of your skills. A hundred hours you put in writing C code, in effect, is like a hundred hours spent by Tendulkar in practice—although this analogy is somewhat stretched. The point is, once you see your hundred hours as a means of improving, say, your C skills or interpersonal skills, you will derive more out of the activity and what's more, you will actually improve those skills on top of delivering the C code.

Ericsson et al call this *deliberate practice* (meaning deliberately practicing a particular technique to get better at it) and outline it in a three-step process, which is roughly:

1. Focus on technique as opposed to outcome
2. Set specific goals
3. Get good, prompt feedback, and use it.

At the gruelling practice session—whether it is you writing C programs or a Crickete hitting balls at the net—you should not worry much about the output, but concentrate only on improvement. Your level of natural talent doesn't matter here

[1] Geoff Colvin, *Talent Is Overrated: What Really Separates World-class Performers?* (New York: Penguin Books, 2008).

because excellence is accomplished through deliberate practice. This recipe is a mental exercise and you should tell yourself that this time you are going to improve such and such skill and focus on that while you go about working hard. This is yet another place where you bring smartness to your job.

Realize that everyone who is successful in your organization has paid the devil its due and has put in many, many hours of hard work before moving up. Remember that work equals hard work plus everything else. If someone like Tendulkar has to practise so much, we all also need practice to smooth out any rough edges in our work and get the best mileage out of the hard work we put in.

12.2.4 Exercise Judgement

One of the indications of working smart is the ability to comprehend things and make judgements. Whether you are reading an article or simply visually observing something, you should be able to see the main points—and the subtleties—and be able to connect the dots and draw inferences.

A lot of jobs would demand this skill. If you are a loan officer working in a modern bank, you might be processing, twenty loan applications a day. Although you may have some initial quantitative screens to shortlist applicants, eventually you will have to make a subjective decision on whether to issue the loan to an applicant or not. The ability to pick out the deserving applicants out of a pile, the ability to decide whether A is better than B, will give you a solid edge over the others. Poring over sample case studies, prior examples in your organization and so on, can help you hone your skills in this.

12.2.5 Recharge Yourself

Modern workplaces are high-voltage environments—definitely no place for pussyfoots—and you should have the stamina and the toughness to perform your job. Most jobs these days are not of the nine-to-five variety—especially if half the members of your team are sitting on the other side of the globe. You may be asked to attend a high-powered meeting at seven in the morning, followed by two hours of intense client visits, then two acrimonious conference calls and just when you are packing up for the day, you may be asked to finish a report that is urgently needed. Not only should you have sufficient energy throughout the day, but you should also know how to ration it. Otherwise you will end up looking harassed. Remember that you cannot sprint all the time and you don't want to burn out prematurely.

You should try to schedule in some sort of a physical activity every day to build up your stamina and endurance and also to afford you that personal time for yourself. It can be a brisk walk around your house, jogging on a treadmill or biking, *Yoga* or a workout in the office gym. There is nothing like a well-conditioned body to take on hard work.

12.3 Some Work Killers and Myths About Hard Work

Fig.12.2 *Myths about hard work*

There are a number of myths about the concept of hard work that we would like to address briefly and present the underlying reality (see Figure 12.2):

'Only some jobs require hard work': This stems from the misconception that hard work is essentially physical work. A white collar, typical nine-to-five job, it is argued, does not require hard work. There is no job on earth, however 'cool' it may be, that is exempt from hard work.

'Hard work is others' perception of how I work': Hard work, as we have defined it here as a soft skill, is intrinsic and stems from an attitude of '*I will give my best.*' It is not just staying back in the office till late night and doing nothing (or meaninglessly chit chatting away); it is about doing whatever it takes to do what you have set out to do—of course, within ethical limits. When you do *real* hard work, you will not care about others' perceptions; you will know from your own heart.

'Short cuts will eliminate the need for hard work': Short cuts and improvisations are always good. These improve your effectiveness and efficiency. But don't forget that you get to learn these short cuts only by hard work! Once you know these short cuts, you will not cease to do hard work, but you will rise to the next level of work and start the hard work at that new level all over again.

'You should work smart, not work hard': People who voice this opinion are fundamentally viewing working smart and working hard as mutually exclusive and tangential. As we discussed in the previous paragraph, you will learn the methods of working smart only by working hard. Working smart will leave you more time to work hard on loftier goals.

'I am a visionary and thinker...hard work is for lesser mortals': It is argued that there are two classes of people—those that think of the great ground-breaking ideas and those that are supposed to work hard to achieve those noble goals, being cogs in the wheel, following and executing instructions like a programmed computer. When you look at the annals of successful business people, you will quickly realize that this is not true at all. Steve Jobs, Bill Gates, Ratan Tata or Azim Premji did not become business icons by simply conceptualizing great ideas. All of them worked closely on the ground with the troops to realize the goals. And they worked very hard indeed!

Snapshot 12.1

Why can't Akash Malhotra work too well?

Akash Malhotra is your regular IT professional who puts in ten-to-twelve hour workdays, but still something seems amiss in his work habits as his productivity falls way below the average. It is not as if he is a chronic poor-worker who sulks and feels lazy or indulges in time-wasting activities. Sure, sometimes he feels tired and slow—but it's nothing that a cup of good coffee won't fix.

The first thing we noticed about him was that he was highly susceptible to *interruptions and diversions* and could not recover swiftly enough to get back to where he was. We advised him to put on a big, virtual 'do not disturb' sign on his back sometimes when he worked and tune out any phone calls or meddling colleagues. (Looking busy in itself dis-invited a lot of people to his desk.) At other times, when interruptions are inevitable, we suggested that he parks his work at a logical point so that it would be easier to get back. Yet at other times a simple 'to-do list' can track where he was before the interruption so that he wouldn't be so lost getting back to the original point of his work.

He would also get sucked into *skunk projects*—those unofficial, yet highly interesting projects (sometimes simply because 'someone has to do it'). This may be as simple as spending half a day with a summer intern on his college project or writing a cute java applet that absolutely adds no value to anything. There is a time and place for skunk projects. If Malhotra has neither, he shouldn't be doing them.

Sometimes, Malhotra is hit by the *expanding favour syndrome* where someone asks him to do a simple favour, but the favour expands and consumes hours. A simple request to e-mail someone a report that he filed away somewhere in his computer under some godforsaken name can become a challenging project. Now Malhotra has learnt to limit the time he spends on such requests and suggests possible alternative sources for such information or asks them to wait until he is free enough to look for it. He doesn't quickly 'buy into' such requests.

Malhotra also exhibited the '*too many balls in the air' syndrome* because he didn't know how to say no to various assignments piled on him. (We will deal with this in Chapter 37.) He ends up taking on too much work and responsibilities and is unable to cope with them all. He told us he didn't want others to think badly of him for not being able to handle the workload. He should look at his plate first, before loading it up with some more work.

Occasionally he suffered from the *out of sight, out of mind syndrome* too, where he would discuss about doing something, but would not get around to doing it or completing it—unless the person who requested it showed up again and pestered him about it. Malhotra was simply scheduling work very poorly. Some other times he would *say the right things in a meeting, but not follow it through*. This, we pointed out, was because Malhotra didn't realize these were real action items and not idle discussions.

And finally, Malhotra also on occasions suffered from *over-promising and under-delivering*, where there was a major disconnect between him and his stakeholders on what the deliverables were. Now, Malhotra gets everything documented clearly and knows exactly what is promised and how and when he should deliver them.

Malhotra is back at work with a vengeance.

12.4 In Summary

We spend a good part of our lives at work. We even derive our identities through our jobs. (We are what we do, right?) We get all sorts of rewards and recognition through work. And for many of us, this is probably the only path to success available in life. So, it behooves us to be exemplary workers and make a mark at our workplaces. We should not be afraid to use every tool in our arsenal to achieve this. We collectively referred to this arsenal as the soft skill, 'work to succeed'.

Hard work starts with vision. But, it does not end there. As an old saying goes,

> The vision must be followed by the venture. It is not enough to stare up the steps—we must step up the stairs.

Hard work is not just about the number of hours you put in, but also what you get accomplished at the end of the day.

> It's not so much about how busy you are, but why you are busy. The bee is praised.The mosquito is swatted.

When people are not successful, they blame it on luck, without introspecting whether they have given the devil its due and worked hard. It is useful to realize that

> The only way to overcome hard luck is by hard work.

We will conclude this chapter with a quotation from Thomas Alva Edison, which summarizes the role of hard work.

> I never did anything worth doing by accident, nor did any of my inventions come by accident; they came only by work.

If that is the case for a genius like Edison, should we say anything more about hard work for lesser mortals like us?

Part II: Communication

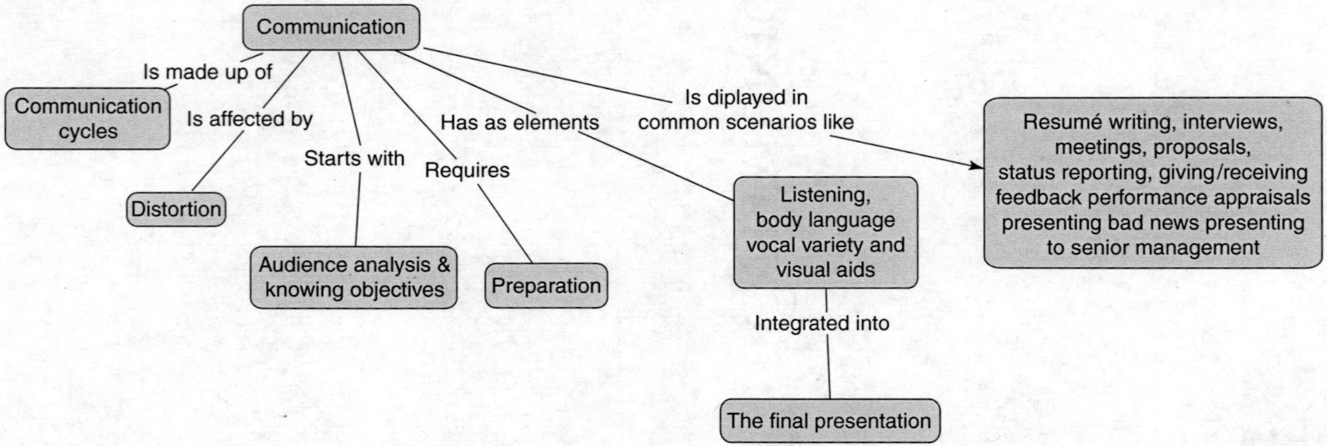
Communication
Is made up of
Communication cycles
Is affected by
Distortion
Starts with
Audience analysis & knowing objectives
Requires
Preparation
Has as elements
Listening, body language vocal variety and visual aids
Integrated into
The final presentation
Is diplayed in common scenarios like
Resumé writing, interviews, meetings, proposals, status reporting, giving/receiving feedback performance appraisals presenting bad news presenting to senior management

13

Understanding the Communication Cycle

"You can have brilliant ideas, but if you can't get them across, you won't get anywhere."

–Lee Iacocca

A dictionary definition of the word 'communication' has several meanings: to impart, to share, to succeed in conveying information, to pass on, to be connected, to transmit and to express one's feelings. Why do we human beings communicate? We communicate to make sure our needs are met; we communicate to co-exist and help each other; more than anything else, we communicate because it is our human urge. The human race will undoubtedly come to a standstill if communication ceased.

13.1 Communication and Communication Cycle

We defined soft skills as the skills required for an individual to succeed in his or her environment. Viewed in this context, we can look at communication as our physical link or the vehicle to connect to the external environment. Driven by passion and attitude, communication manifests itself as the force that binds us to the people around us. The following traits of communication also stand out:

Every communication has an objective: Communication is done to achieve a desired individual and/or organizational goal. You may attend an interview to get a job; you may make a sales pitch to a prospective customer to persuade him to buy your company's product; or you may simply be communicating with someone to build or nurture a friendship.

Communication establishes an ongoing relationship between two parties—the sender and the receiver: In most cases, communication is never a one-time deal. There may be a series of interviews you would have to go through to get a job; you would almost never close a deal in one shot with a customer. True communication is seldom a one-off transactional thing.

Every communication is made up of a series of communication cycles: Each of these cycles contributes to the objective, and builds upon the previous cycle. Each communication cycle is a brick carefully laid with other bricks to achieve the objective of communication. In this book, for brevity, we sometimes use the word 'communication' for 'communication cycle'. But, it is important to keep in mind that communication cycles are the atoms that build the molecule of overall communication that achieves a certain objective.

In this chapter, we will see the constituents or elements of a communication cycle. These are depicted in Figure 13.1.

Every communication starts with a *need* or *objective* and works towards achieving that. This need or objective of communication has to be very clear at the outset. Or else, you would be driving down the wrong alley.

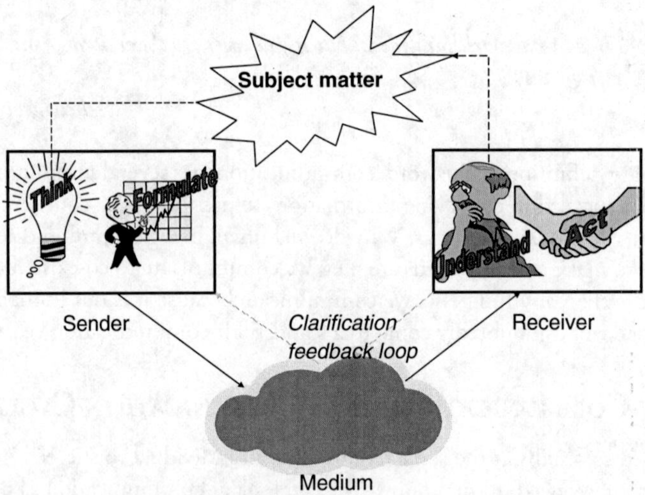

Fig. 13.1 *Elements of communication*

These objectives give rise to *subject matter* that needs to be communicated or transmitted in order to progress towards achieving the objectives. Communication is not a one-way street. It takes two to tango and it takes (at least) two for successful communication. There is a *sender*, who is the source of the matter to be communicated. The *receiver* receives the message that is transmitted through a *medium*. If you are the sender, hopefully you know your objectives. For the objective to be achieved, you should also choose the right receivers. This is *audience analysis*, and is closely tied with understanding the objectives of communication. These two inter-related topics are covered in Chapter 15.

A number of processes take place behind the scenes to effect this seemingly simple act of communication between the sender and the receiver(s). The sender has to first *think* and arrive at a thought process that he is comfortable with. Once the thoughts are clearly formed, the sender has to *formulate* his thought process and *encode* the message in a way that can be transmitted through an appropriate *medium,* in a form that can be understood by the receiver. This step of formulation entails being able to articulate the thoughts in a cogent way, codifying it using the right language and supplementing the message with other tools (like pictures or graphics) that aid in better understanding by the receiver. All these—thinking, formulation and encoding—together form *preparation*. The various aspects of preparing for communication are covered in Chapter 16.

A formulated, encoded and aptly supplemented message is then *transmitted* through the medium and reaches the *receiver*.

The receiver has to perform the reverse process now: he or she has to *interpret* and *understand* the message. While trying to understand the message, he also taps into his knowledge of the subject matter. This understanding may or may not be in synch with what the sender intended. Having understood the message (in his own way), he or she then goes to the next step of *acting* on the message. In an ideal situation, the way the receiver acts on a message is exactly the same as the way the sender intended the receiver to act.

But things are seldom ideal in the real world. There comes this unavoidable evil called *distortion* that spoils the sport. We will see the causes and effects of distortion in Chapter 14.

Sometimes, it is not obvious to the receiver what action he or she should take. An effective communicator will steer the receiver to act in a particular way that is intended to achieve the objective of communication. Also, since communication is a continuous process, there has to be ongoing *follow-through*.

There is a repertoire of *tools* available to perform effective communication. These include listening, verbalization, body language and visual aids. Each of these is covered in detail from Chapter 17 to 20. All these have to be put together to form a cogent whole and this is covered in Chapter 21.

Communication manifests itself in various communication scenarios like resumé writing, interviews, proposal writing, meetings, appraisals, presenting to senior management and so on, These are covered in detail from Chapter 22 to Chapter 30.

13.2 Modes of Communication

If you look at the different types of communication interactions we have, you can classify them into two categories: *synchronous* and *asynchronous* (see Figure 13.2).

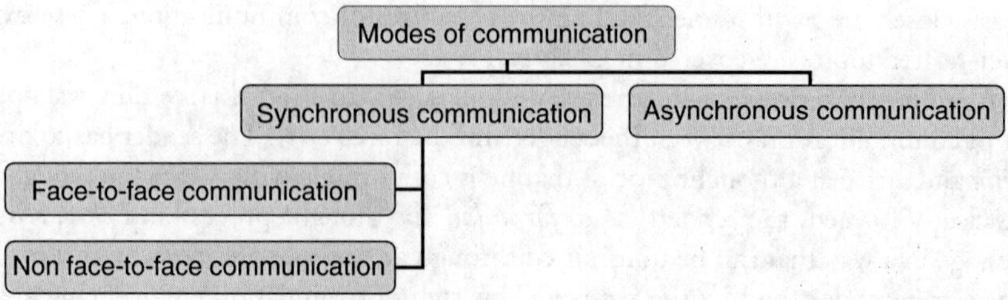

Fig. 13.2 *Modes of communication*

Synchronous communication takes place in real time—you have to act and react to scenarios as events unfold. You have little time to think, reflect and respond. Synchronous communication can again be classified into face-to-face communication and non-face-to-face communication. The meetings you attend, the interviews you conduct, the presentations you make and the classes you conduct in the classroom are all examples of face-to-face, synchronous communication. Some of the traits of such communication are:

- You should perhaps prepare more extensively and thoroughly for such a communication. Why? No one likes to look like a fool in front of others. When you are making a face-to-face communication, any mistake you make is likely to be pounced upon by the audience
- You should anticipate the objections and questions the audience may have well in advance and be prepared with the necessary answers. The audience will in all likelihood bring up questions and objections that, if you don't address to their satisfaction, will undermine your credibility and prevent your communication from achieving the desired results.
- You should keep your emotions under tight control. The objections and questions may turn personal or may be distracting. It is important not to easily give in to the temptation of 'getting one back on them'.
- You should watch out for any tangential deviation from the intended objectives of communication and be quick to steer the communication back to where you want. Having this control over the communication process is absolutely essential in this form of communication.
- You have access to studying and inferring from additional sources of information that the audience provides—inputs that you glean from their posture, their body language, their facial expressions and so on. You should fully exploit and utilize these other stimuli and inputs. Actions speak louder than words.

In the second category of synchronous communications comes non-face-to-face synchronous communication. These are the telephone calls and the chat sessions that you have. Here, you face all the challenges that you come across in the face-to-face case, with one more added challenge: you have lost those valuable cues of body language. You don't have any mechanism to fathom the implied meaning of any spoken word For example, you cannot look at the enthusiasm (or lack thereof) in the gestures and body language. You would not be able to look into the eyes of the recipient to make a judgement as to whether or not he is lying. You would not be able to ascertain his interest levels in the conversation—for all you know he may have put you on mute and switched on the television and gotten absorbed in the latest football score. What is more, you probably don't even know for sure who you are communicating with!

As against all these types of synchronous communication that take place in real time, we also often use asynchronous communication. In this case the sender and recipient are not necessarily available at the same time for communication. The e-mails and text[1] messages you send, the proposals and documents that you write, the faxes you send, the voice-mails you leave, are all examples of asynchronous communication.

Asynchronous communication eases out some of the challenges of synchronous communication while introducing some unique challenges of its own. In asynchronous communication, you don't need to get too concerned about being taken off-guard with an unexpected question that you would have to respond to in the spur of the moment. You can take your time and respond back appropriately in an objective, dispassionate and meaningful way. But at the same time, you must remember that your recipient also has these same advantages and that may turn out to be disadvantageous to you! For example, your recipient may receive the message when he is not in a good mood and hence (perhaps unreasonably) take out that anger and vent it on your message and send you a nasty and perhaps unreasonable reply. You don't hold your audience captive during asynchronous communication and that may be to your disadvantage. You may have to produce extra effort to ensure that your recipient reads your entire document or e-mail and gets its underlying message the way you want him to get it and takes actions that you want him to take. In addition, compared to face-to-face synchronous communication, you also lose the huge advantage of observing the non-verbal signals of body language, eye contact, voice modulation and so on. Finally, asynchronous communication will leave a trail of written proof and hence, you have to be doubly careful about what you say in asynchronous communication as it may have legal implications as well.

It is not as if one mode of communication is better than the other. Each of these modes of communication has its own advantages, disadvantages and applicability. Table 13.1 summarizes all the above discussions and provides a comparison of these modes of communication.

---

1 In India, text messages are referred to as SMS; 'text' is predominantly a term used in the USA and not in India.

Table 13.1 ***Comparison of the various modes of communication***

Attribute	**Synchronous, Face-to-face Communication**	**Synchronous, Non-face-to-face Communication**	**Asynchronous Communication**
Description	▶ The sender and recipient/audience are in the same place (virtually so, in the case of video conference) and at the same time. ▶ All interactions and responses happen in real time.	▶ The sender and the recipient exchange messages at the same time but are not face-to-face.	▶ The receiver is not receiving the message at the same time as the sender is sending it.
Examples	▶ Interviews ▶ Meetings ▶ Live presentations	▶ Telephone calls ▶ Instant messaging	▶ E-mails ▶ Reports and documents
Advantages	▶ Gives access to non-verbal stimuli like body language, eye contact and voice modulation ▶ Enables fine tuning of communication based on audience response ▶ Reduces the time needed for coming to a conclusion ▶ Provides best opportunities for rapport building	▶ Provides limited access to non-verbal cues; voice modulation can be used, but not other cues like body language and eye contact ▶ Enables fine tuning of communication, although to a lesser degree	▶ No need to respond back immediately to objections ▶ No danger of getting side-tracked ▶ Leaves a written record ▶ You can put a lot more thought and present a more cogent delivery.
Challenges	▶ May get unexpected questions from the recipients that need to be addressed on the spur of the moment ▶ Need to respond quickly to objections	▶ Not having access to body language and eye contact may reduce the effectiveness of communication ▶ Distortions in communication channels (e.g., telephone lines) will be detrimental to communication	▶ Don't have control over how and when the recipient processes your communication ▶ Likely to result in delays in communication outcome

Attribute	Synchronous, Face-to-face Communication	Synchronous, Non-face-to-face Communication	Asynchronous Communication
	▶ May get side-tracked	▶ May not be able to get undivided attention of the recipients/audience	▶ The written trail may be misused against you ▶ There is almost no possibility of 'small talk' that can help in rapport building
Disadvantages	▶ Have to think on your feet!	▶ Possibility of noise in channel (e.g., telephone lines) ▶ Lack of inputs from body language and other stimuli	▶ Takes long time ▶ Would not be under the direct control of the sender ▶ Leaving a written trail may have legal implications
Applicability	▶ Best suited for teams in the same location ▶ Very useful in the initial stages of a relationship-building between teams in different locations. A face-to-face meeting greatly aids in better understanding and rapport building.	▶ When the teams are geographically separated ▶ Useful for teams to keep in synch on a continual basis without having to go through expensive travel (especially makes sense with technologies like VoIP that reduce costs compared to normal telephone calls)	▶ Formal documentation is achieved ▶ When the teams are geographically separated ▶ Most economical way for teams to stay in touch

13.3 In Summary

In this chapter we have seen the different elements and modes of communication. We have also briefly outlined the advantages and disadvantages of each of the modes, thus leading to an understanding of the scenarios of applicability for each of the modes. There is an important new element that comes into play in the real world that affects the existing elements and also influences the mode—it is *distortion*, the topic for the next chapter.

14

Distortion in Communication

"I know that you believe you understand what you think I said, but I'm not sure you realize that what you heard is not what I meant."

–Robert McCloskey

Why is it that a prospective customer buys our competitor's product after (what we thought was) a hair raising, absorbing and convincing presentation? Why is it that at the end of a status-review meeting, the boss blows his top saying that the project is going nowhere when you thought all was kosher? It simply means that the receiver has not acted the way we intended him to act. How many times have you had misunderstandings while communicating with someone and said, 'That is not what I meant!' or 'I am being quoted out of context'? With all good intents and excellent content, there is no guarantee that the recipient will receive, interpret or act upon the message in the way that the sender actually wanted. The result? Broken relationships, unsuccessful deals and a whole lot of heartburn. What is the cause for all this? *Distortion.*

In this chapter, we start with identifying the different barriers to communication and trace how distortion sets in at each stage of communication because of these barriers.

We also suggest some measures to reduce distortion at each stage. After looking at how distortion occurs in some common scenarios of communication, we conclude the chapter with common-sense tips to minimize distortion.

Fig. 14.1 *The ideal world of communication*

14.1 Barriers to Communication

There are several barriers to communication. These barriers manifest themselves in different ways and affect different phases of communication. In Table 14.1,we have summarized the common types of barriers to communication and how they affect the different phases of communication. The net result of these barriers is that they give rise to distortions.

Table 14.1 *Different barriers to communication*

Type of Barrier	How the Barrier Affects the Various Phases of Communication
Organizational barriers	In a very hierarchical and bureaucratic organization, information may have to flow through several channels. Hence, distortion through the various layers is possible. Also not all the relevant information may be available to a speaker, because of hierarchy. This may affect the thinking and formulation phases.
Status barriers	Closely tied to organizational barriers, the status consciousness of a speaker or listener can lead to bias and hence distortions in the formulation, understanding and action phases.
Language barriers	In a multi-lingual team, language barriers can come in and these may affect the formulation and understanding phases.
Background barriers	The background of the speaker and listener can be very different. For example, a speaker may be highly technical and use highly technical terms. These may be incomprehensible to the listener. This can introduce distortion at the understanding and acting levels.

(Continued)

Table 14.1 *(Continued)*

Type of Barrier	How the Barrier Affects the Various Phases of Communication
Cultural barriers	Cultural barriers may place limitations on the way a person thinks; it may also restrict how a thought is expressed, including the use of certain body-language gestures.
Media barriers	As we have discussed earlier, media can be a cause for significant distortion.

14.2 Distortion Through the Stages of Communication

Snapshot 14.1

In the old days, trains were classified as 'passenger trains' and 'express' trains. Passenger trains were the slower trains that stopped at all the stations, while express trains were the ones that stopped only at a few stations. Also, each train had a three digit train number.

One day, a passenger train almost met with an accident. Here is a conversation thread that goes from the first person, who saw this first hand, to the subsequent people.

First person: 'Passenger train 423 had a minor accident and just avoided being derailed; no one was injured.'

Second person: 'Passenger train 423 had an accident and almost derailed; someone may be injured.'

Third Person: Passenger train 423 derailed; not sure of injuries.'

Fourth Person: 'Train derailed; 423 passengers injured.'

As you can see from Snapshot 14.1, each person just makes a 'minor' change to the input he got, but eventually, the compound effect of all the changes resulted in a complete change of meaning!

Distortion is anything that causes the recipient to understand, interpret or act upon the transmitted message in any way different from what the sender intended. Why does distortion happen? Distortions come from several sources. In Chapter 13 on communication cycle, we presented the elements or stages of communication. We reproduce that figure here (see Figure 14.2).

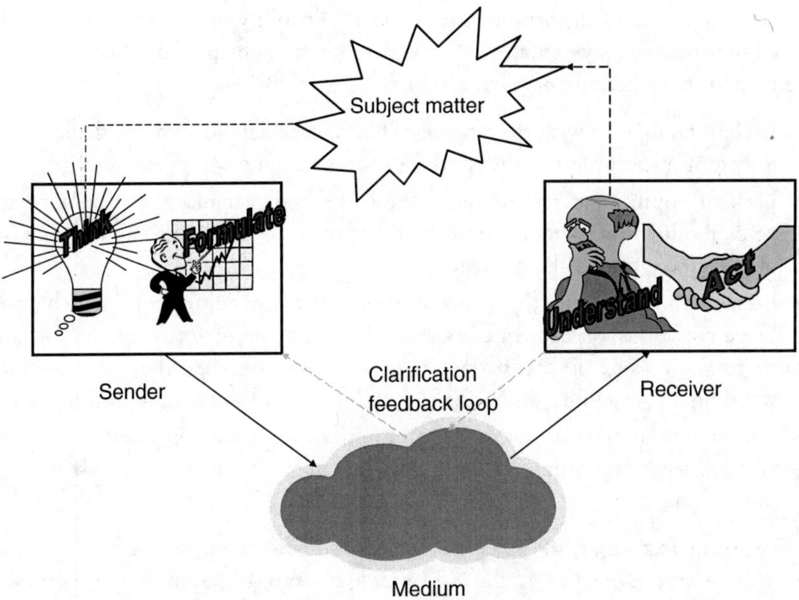

Fig. 14.2 *Elements of communication revisited*

Every stage can—and does—add distortion. Distortion feeds on itself. Each distortion that is added compounds the possibility of misunderstanding exponentially. Eventually the final message that the recipient gets is completely different from what the sender intended and hence, the action taken by the recipient is completely different from (and sometimes opposite of) what the sender actually intended. Let us now see how distortion gets introduced at every stage of the communication process.

First of all, a sender has to *think* through what he wants to communicate. There may be problems in this *thought process* itself. It is possible that the sender does not have adequate knowledge about what he wants to communicate. When the original understanding is poor or muddled, it is obvious that the expression will also be unclear. There is only so much you can sugar-coat plain ignorance. The person may have to do more research on the topic and may not have the time or resources to do it. He may have his personal biases and blind spots that prevent him from thinking along the right directions to enable effective communication. A possible antidote to help minimize distortion at this level could be for the speaker to only communicate about topics he is familiar with (or even passionate about). If he is not fully familiar with the topic, he should do sufficient research and dig around and arm himself with the required information.

The next source of distortion could be in the inability or ineffectiveness on the part of the speaker to *formulate* and articulate his thought process effectively. This could come about because of several factors:

- Lack of familiarity with the language: This is especially true when the language of communication is not the speaker's mother tongue or native language.
- Lack of appropriate reinforcing stimuli like body language, eye contact and voice modulation: These stimuli may not only not reinforce the message but may even contradict the message!
- Lack of familiarity with the media of communication: Some people may become 'stage conscious' or 'camera conscious'. They may be perfectly decent communicators on a one-on-one basis, but may get put off when they have to speak standing on a podium, under the glaring lights of a camera or a projector.
- Creeping in of nervousness while communicating: A fully prepared person may get cold feet while communicating and this may mar the effectiveness of communication.

The most effective way to overcome the distortion due to ineffective formulation is through continuous practice. In the case of spoken communication (especially presentations), it is essential to practice, rehearse and perfect the delivery as much as possible.

Distortion can be introduced by the *media of communication*. When you use a phone, the lines may be bad. When you use e-mail and have painstakingly formatted the message with various fonts and colors, it may get lost because of poor rendering of the e-mail at the recipient's end. When you use video conferencing, the ghostly, jaded movements you see because of communication latency may act as a distraction. Media is just a part of the overall environment. When you are using a projector with a remote control, perhaps your lack of familiarity of operating with the remote control can make your presentation look jaded. Even being in a new environment or room can add to distortion.

To account for such media/environment-related distortions, it is important to reinforce the message through multiple media. Such redundancy serves to balance out any possible disadvantages of a single medium. You can follow up a phone conversation by a 'MOM' or documented minutes of the meeting; you can augment a mail exchange with a personal visit where possible; you can SMS a person if the mobile signal is not very clear. All these methods of redundancy and reinforcement appeal to common sense. Of course, such reinforcements do come with the additional cost of time and effort but if they achieve to synch up the parties involved in communication and reduce any misunderstandings, they may all be well worth it.

Distortion can be caused by the *receiver's inability to understand the message* as it was intended. This can arise from bias or preconceived notions that the receiver may have about either the subject or you, the speaker. Just as your inadequate thinking process can result in distortion, the receiver's inadequate thinking process, or lack of knowledge, could also result in distortion. A possible mitigation strategy to reduce distortion due to this source is to do a thorough audience analysis (discussed in

Chapter 15). You might have to educate the recipients about the subject matter or get them to have favourable disposition towards your point of view so that they can understand the message as it was intended. Also, the use of redundant media discussed in the previous paragraph would also help improve the understanding of the recipient.

If a recipient does not understand a message as intended, there is recourse to a *feedback loop*. The feedback loop is supposed to minimize distortion. But in geographically distributed teams (using media like e-mails, phones and chats), this avenue of feedback loop is not always used effectively. In order to use the feedback loop effectively, the recipient should use some of the common-sense approaches like asking questions or for clarifications, paraphrasing what he heard and by the process of *active listening* (see Chapter 17). Distortion due to ineffective use of the feedback loop is exacerbated by the inherent shyness to ask questions that we see in Indian engineers.

Finally, as we saw earlier, the intent of communication is to make the recipient act. In an ideal situation, the way the receiver acts on a message is exactly the same way in which the sender intended the receiver to act. But distortion can prevent this from happening. In addition to all the distortion caused by earlier stages, inability to act in the intended way is in itself a distortion. One of the causes for this could again be inappropriate audience analysis. At the end of the day, if the audience does not act on the message the way the sender intended, then it defeats the purpose of communication. The mitigation strategies we have outlined against distortion in the various phases can help steer the recipient to act in consonance with the sender to achieve the original objectives of communication.

In Table 14.2, we have summarized the above discussion covering causes for distortion in each phase and how to minimize the adverse effects of distortion due to these causes.

Table 14.2 *Distortion in the various phases*

Phase/Element of Communication	Causes for Distortion	Ways to Minimize Adverse Effects of Distortion
Subject matter	▶ Subject matter itself is very nebulous (as it may happen with new technologies)	▶ Conduct up-front research about the subject ▶ Having a subject matter expert's advice
Thought process of the sender	▶ Thought process of the sender not clear ▶ Sender not intimately familiar with the subject matter ▶ Bias of the sender	▶ Communicate only on topics you are intimately familiar with (not always possible) ▶ Get familiar with the topic by taking advice of subject matter experts and doing up-front research ▶ Go with an objective and open mind for the communication, setting aside personal biases

(Continued)

Table 14.2 *(Continued)*

Phase/Element of Communication	Causes for Distortion	Ways to Minimize Adverse Effects of Distortion
Formulation of the message by the sender	▶ Lack of familiarity with the language of communication ▶ Lack of or inconsistent use of supplements like body language and voice ▶ Lack of familiarity with environment and media ▶ Excessive nervousness	▶ No easy solutions for the language familiarity issue—there is a need to keep working on it or to have an interpreter if it is a presentation ▶ Practise effective use of body language and other channels discussed later in this book ▶ Spend extra time and effort to become familiar with the environment and media ▶ Use nervousness to your advantage (see Chapter 21)
Medium of communication	▶ Noise introduced by the communication channel ▶ Technology limitations ▶ Lack of familiarity on the part of sender in utilizing the communication channel effectively	▶ Choose the right medium to minimize these effects ▶ Supplement the communication using multiple media so as to introduce redundancy and thus reach higher fidelity
Inadequate or ineffective feedback loop	▶ Insufficient avenues for feedback ▶ Ineffective or insufficient questions asked ▶ Cultural or language barriers for the feedback loop	▶ Through synchronous face-to-face communication, practising active listening (see Chapter 17) ▶ Through periodic questions and clarifications throughout the communication ▶ Get sensitized to cultural nuances ▶ Get more familiar with the language and/or use interpreters as necessary
Receiver not physically understanding the message correctly	▶ Language and cultural barriers that the receiver has ▶ Poor understanding because of the distortion introduced by the medium ▶ Receiver's biases	▶ Combination of methods used in the other factors

(Continued)

Table 14.2 *(Continued)*

Phase/Element of Communication	Causes for Distortion	Ways to Minimize Adverse Effects of Distortion
Receiver not acting on the message as intended	▶ Receiver's biases ▶ Inadequate follow-through by the sender	▶ Receiver to be more open minded ▶ Proper audience analysis so as to minimize audience biases ▶ Proactive addressing of the biases and dispelling of doubts ▶ Constant follow-through by the sender till the objective of communication is achieved

14.3 How Distortion Occurs in Various Business-Communication Scenarios

Later chapters of this book discuss the various communication scenarios that present themselves in typical business environments. In this section, we will see how distortion sets in these different scenarios and what can be done to minimize distortion in such cases.

14.3.1 Presentations

Distortions sneak into presentations quite easily because of several factors:

Nervousness: Presentations can give cold feet to an inexperienced person or sometimes even to the most seasoned pro. When a person is nervous, the most appropriate words don't always come out and sometimes even the most inappropriate words, that convey the opposite of what was intended, may be used. All this can lead to distortion.

Lack of preparedness: Presentations in which a presenter is confronted with a possibly heterogeneous audience calls for a lot of preparation. Preparations include audience analysis and understanding the objectives of communication as well as anticipating the questions that the audience will ask. If the questions are not anticipated properly, it can lead to answers that are not clear and can in fact lead to straying away from the message to be conveyed, thus leading to distortion. Also, when questions are not answered properly, it erodes the credibility of the speaker and sets in bias in the mind of the receiver.

Ineffective use of visual aids, body language and voice channel: Sometimes the different channels of communication give conflicting or confusing messages, different from what is spoken. For example, a slide in a presentation may indicate certain data is contradictory to the argument being put forth; the body language and/or the voice may betray a lack of enthusiasm and energy. These can muddle up the message being conveyed and hence, lead to distortion.

Ineffective time management: Time management is crucial to a presentation (as much as to any form of communication). As we will see in Chapter 21 a presentation has to have a proper closure wherein the presenter stresses the key points. Ineffective time management, when a presenter spends an undue amount of time in a part of the presentation, can lead to insufficient time for the closure part and hence the audience may walk away with different notions than what were intended.

14.3.2 Group Meetings

Distortion in group meetings often arises because of two major reasons:

First, not everyone is on the same page. People may be straight-jacketed about their own piece of work without really knowing the big picture. People may be oblivious to or not empathetic to the needs of others. This may result in people taking stands that create bias and hence, the message gets blocked.

Second, inefficient meeting management can result in people not taking turns and can thus cause cross talk and poor understanding. When a group meeting is over a conference call or video conference, distortion could be even worse because it is even more difficult to take turns. Lack of reinforcing and redundant face-to-face contact and body language further increase distortion.

As we will see in Chapter 24, effective meeting management entails setting a clear agenda, making sure that all the people know their roles and responsibilities ahead of time and following through with lucid minutes of meeting and action items. We have summarized these by the acronym ***PROOF***—***P***lanning, ***R***eaching out, ***O***rganizing, ***O***rchestrating and ***F***ollowing through.

14.3.3 Status Meetings

Distortion in status meetings generally arises because of the unwillingness of people to candidly share the status. Especially when there is bad news, people may sugar-coat the bad news to make it appear that things are kosher. As a result, people (especially managers) may walk out of status meetings with a feeling of complacence only to be given rude last-minute shocks later on. A clear mapping of 'planned vs. actual' for every week and also putting together a clear plan for the upcoming period would help in getting some objectivity in status meetings and thus minimize distortion.

In Snapshot 14.2, see how distortion sets in a status meeting. The text in italics below gives the comments about the specific interaction.

Snapshot 14.2

Manager: So folks, what is the status of the invoicing module? *(Very open ended.)*

Ravi: My program for pricing is almost done, have a few bells and whistles to complete. *(Very generic.)*

Manager: Good to hear! When would the program be complete? *(Has not gone into details.)*

Ravi: Later part of next week.

Deepa: Wait a sec, unless you complete the pricing program, I cannot test my bill printing program. I will get delayed.

Manager: Ravi, can you accelerate the pricing program and get it done by Tuesday? *(Has not explored all the options available.)*

Ravi: Boss, not unless there are 30 hours in a day! I am already here till ten every night.

You can see that there is distortion everywhere in the above meeting. The manager seems to meander without any clear goals. Ravi is not being specific about his work. He does not seem to be aware of the implication of his work for Deepa. Finally, the manager has not explored all possible options for resolving the issues. A better approach to the above scenario that would minimize distortion and increase clarity could be as follows (see Snapshot 14.3):

Snapshot 14.3

Manager: So folks, let us get on the same page on the status of the invoicing module. Let me start with Ravi. What is the status of the pricing program? *(Shows control and makes the intention of getting specific answers very clear.)*

Ravi: My program for pricing is almost done, have a few bells and whistles to complete. *(Very generic.)*

Manager: Good to hear! Can you be more specific? Have you completed the GUI? How about validations? You know Deepa needs the basic logic to work so that she can test the program. When would you be able to get this done? *(Has gone into more details.)*

Ravi: I have completed the validations and the basic GUI. I still have to fine tune the interface and also put some of the logic for discounting into the program.

Manager: What is your plan for achieving this? *(Giving Ravi an initial responsibility to chalk out a course of action.)*

Ravi: I plan to complete the GUI portion by Tuesday and the discounting logic by Friday.

Deepa: Wait a sec, unless you complete the pricing program, I cannot test my bill printing program. I will get delayed. *(Specific dependencies start coming out.)*

Manager: Deepa, if Ravi can give you the basic logic of the pricing program that should enable you to start your work, right? *(Generating new options.)*

Deepa: Yeah.

Manager: Ravi, can you reschedule your priorities and get the discounting logic part done by Tuesday so that Deepa can start her work and you can then go on in parallel with the GUI stuff… this way you also won't be stretched too much… *(He has anticipated the objections from Ravi and preempted them.)*

Ravi: Okay, sounds fine.

Manager: Deepa, okay with you?

Deepa: Yep.

14.3.4 Written Communication

Distortion in written communication is highly prevalent in geographically distributed teams. Even if India and the USA use 'English', the two 'English' es could be very different in style and substance. The metaphors, language, spelling are all very different. As this is a crucial aspect for communication across global teams, we have dedicated one full chapter (Chapter 39), to address the issues of writing styles and to give some common-sense suggestions to achieve clarity and consistency.

14.4 Distortion in Communication Within Globally Distributed Teams

The avenues for distortion increase significantly in globally distributed teams. We have already mentioned the effect of language in causing distortion. Culture is another major dimension that causes distortion. For example, while the US culture is to speak candidly, the Indian engineer may tend to be 'soft'. The metaphors—especially sports metaphors—tend to confuse people and convey the wrong message. Even some of the gestures are different across cultures and this may have a negative impact in making sure that the sender's message reaches the receiver in the desired way and causes the receiver to act in the intended way.

14.5 In Summary

If we were to summarize three key points in minimizing distortion in communication, they would be the following.

The devil is in the details.

More specific the details you go into, lesser the chances of distortion. This minimizes the chances of misunderstandings, assumptions and biases.

Have empathy.

If you put yourself in the shoes of the audience, you can get a better 'under-the-hood' perspective of how they look at things. This will help you to think and formulate the message in a way that will reach home for them.

Reinforce with redundant channels.

Where possible, reinforce your message through multiple channels—verbal, vocal, visual aids, body language, etc. Always follow up spoken communication with a written confirmation.

Despite all the precautions you take, remember that complete avoidance of distortion is simply not possible. Just accept it, watch out for it and make a conscious attempt to minimize it (see Box 14.1)! Someone said that in life, only two things are certain—death and taxes. You can modify it to add distortion in communication to that list.

Fig. 14.3 *The real world of communication with distortion*

Box 14.1

Distortion Minimization Checklist

- Are you clear as to why you are performing this communication?
- Are you sure you are the correct person to perform this communication?
- Do you know the subject matter that you are communicating intimately?
- Have you done the necessary research on the subject matter?
- Have you chosen the right audience for the communication?
- Have you chosen the right media for communication?
- Have you chosen the right mode (synchronous/asynchronous) of communication?
- Have you chosen the right language for communication?
- Have you reinforced the communication using multiple channels?
- Have you kept the options open and flexible to address audience questions?
- Have you rehearsed the communication sufficient number of times?
- Have you followed up on the communication to ensure it has the desired effect?

15

The 'Why' and 'To Whom' Parts of Communication: Knowing the Objective of Communication and Audience Analysis

"Wise men talk because they have something to say; fools, because they have to say something."

–Plato

Snapshot 15.1

A saint was meditating. A cat that was moving around was disturbing his concentration and hence he asked his disciples to trap the cat under a basket while he meditated. The trapping of the cat under a basket by the saint's disciples when he meditated, became a daily routine. Over the years, the same phenomenon continued with the saint's descendents and the cat's descendents. One day, there were no cats in the hermitage. The disciples got panicky and searched for a cat saying, 'We need a cat; only when we get one, can we put a basket over it and only after that can the saint start meditating!

There are times when communication in the business context is as muddled as the work of the disciples in Snapshot 15.1. People don't fully comprehend the *purpose* for which they are working and as a result they end up doing activities that don't add value. The purpose is closely tied to understanding the big picture. Once a person understands the big picture and his or her role in it, it becomes easier to grasp the purpose of each communication.

In this chapter, we propose a few basic tips for understanding the 'why' and the 'to whom' aspects of communication.

> Why you communicate is as important as what you communicate.

Of course, you may also be communicating with someone you know very well, without any purpose, simply to kill time! But, since we are discussing *business* communication, we will not consider this case any further. When we start communicating, sometimes we forget the very purpose why the communication was initiated in the first place. It is useful to step back and ask ourselves the objective(s) we want to achieve in a given communication. When people who enter into communication do not understand its purpose, communication goes off into tangents and not surprisingly, they don't get any worthwhile results.

15.1 Starting to Understand the Objectives of Communication

How do you get an appreciation of the objectives of a given communication? You could start off with the following questions:

Am I communicating to *educate?* If you are taking a class or a training session for a customer (or for your employees), you will be communicating to educate the audience. In this case, you should clearly know the experience or skill levels of the audience and prepare and use educational material that is appropriate to achieve the educational objectives. Typically, such a communication is always accompanied with visual aids like PowerPoint slides (covered in more detail in Chapter 20).

Am I communicating to *inform?* This may be the case when you are sending in a status report of a project or formulating the minutes of a meeting. This may be oral communication but, in general it is either accompanied by or replaced with written communication. The nuances of status reporting and formulating the minutes of meeting and such 'informational communication' are covered in Chapters 24 and 26.

There are many instances when you are communicating to inform, and at the same time, also subtly trying to educate the audience. When you are updating your manager about the status of the project, you would necessarily have to have a judicious mix of informing and educating.

Am I communicating to *entertain?* This may not happen too often in business scenarios. Hence, we would not consider this much in this book. But remember that your communication should be entertaining and enjoyable regardless of the motive of communication!

Am I communicating to *sell* something or *persuade* someone? This is something that happens ever so often in the business context. When you make a product presentation to a customer, when you are trying to present a case to your venture-capital partner, trying to justify your architecture or approach to a problem in front of your CTO or trying to get funding for your project, you are communicating to sell. It is said that almost all communication is about selling something and persuading your audience about your viewpoint. Hence, it is fair to say that almost every chapter in this book has some aspects of this type of communication. Specifically, resumés (Chapter 22), interviews (Chapter 23) and proposals (Chapter 25) fall under this category.

Am I communicating to *establish rapport?* This is something that happens very often, especially in a globally distributed team. When the team members are located in the same place, there is a lot of opportunity to build rapport by way of hallway talks, coffee table chats, and so on. But, when the teams are geographically distributed, you have to make up for the lack of these opportunities and yet build rapport by other means like e-mail, chat, etc. Cultural and linguistic barriers make such rapport building even more difficult. Such cultural barriers not only show up at the communication level but would also surface in the attitude and the etiquettes levels. One such rapport building communication is in the form of small talk covered in Chapter 35.

Is this communication intended to be *formal* or *informal?* Formal communication places a lot of restrictions on the delivery, style and language that is used in communication. Informal communication, on the other hand, is a lot less restrictive. Sometimes you may have to make a choice of whether to use formal or informal communication based on the need. More often, these two have to supplement each other effectively. Some examples of formal communication are appraisals (Chapter 28), presenting to senior management (Chapter 30) and reports (Chapter 26). Small talk is an example of informal communication.

Which aspects of my objectives are sacrosanct and cannot be violated and in which aspects do I have some leeway? As an old adage says, 'If everything is important, nothing is important!' Any communication would have multiple objectives to accomplish; it is important that you prioritize the objectives and identify which cannot be compromised and which are negotiable. Once you have identified what are the non-negotiable objectives to be achieved, you would be in a better position to fine tune your approach to the presentation. This may also call for choosing a different set of audience. Thus, audience analysis and understanding the objectives of communication are intricately related as illustrated in Figure 25.1.

Do these questions appear too 'obvious'? You bet they are. But, how many times are such 'obvious' things missed out? We have seen instances of an engineer trying to show off his knowledge of technology with all the buzz-phrases and three-letter acronyms to a CFO who was looking at the *business* impact of a product and who did not really care about all the technical nitty-gritties. There are people who assume that a communication is an informal one and take a casual approach, whereas the recipient was looking for a very formal communication. In our view, not stepping

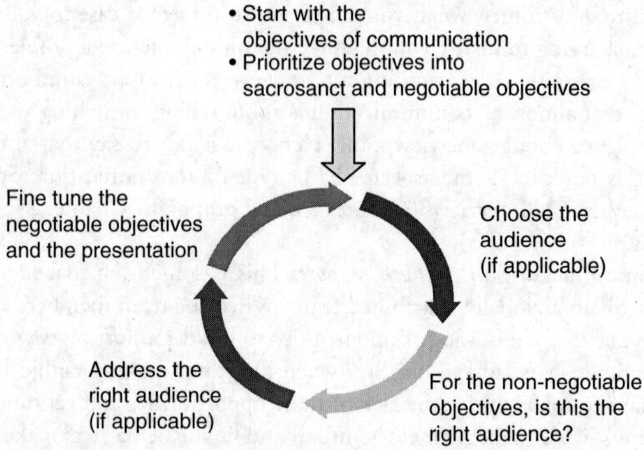

Fig. 15.1 *How understanding the objectives of communication and audience analysis are inter-related*

back a bit and understanding the objectives of communication, causes more failure in communication than anything else.

The various questions or objectives discussed above are not mutually exclusive in a communication. As we will see in section 15.2 on audience analysis, it is possible that you would have a *heterogeneous* mix of audience, each of whom may have a different set of expectations, tastes, skills and experience levels. You may have to address some of them to educate them, some of them to sell to and some of them to establish a rapport. For example, when you are presenting the status report of a project to an audience comprising your partners from other locations, bosses and teammates, your approach should be a combination of educating, informing and selling. The challenge is to structure your communication in such a way that it addresses all these seemingly disparate objectives. Table 15.1 gives the typical objectives and nature of communication for the various stakeholders in an organization.

Table15.1 *Typical nature and objectives of communication for various stakeholders*

Who?	Type of Communication	Comments
Sponsors	To sell an idea or to report to them about progress	Tend to be very formal; usually in the form or written reports, presentations and negotiations.
Line managers	Status reporting; Work allocation	Tend to be more tactical in nature; usually a mix of formal and informal communication and a mix of written communication and meetings.

(Continued)

Who?	Type of Communication	Comments
Partners	Regular, operational communication that involves exchanging information about the project being executed, future plans, etc.	These are typically teams working in other locations; for example, when a software development team is distributed between the USA and India, the two teams work as partners and need to communicate with each other.
Other groups within the organization	Spoken and written communication to set, execute and discuss 'service level agreements'	These are typically infrastructure teams like HR, administration, etc. as well as other project groups on whose work your work depends.
Government	Extremely formal communication; mostly written communication	These could be for issues like visa processing, exports, imports, taxation, etc.
News Media	Needs to be formal; also should not be done without prior authorization from the superiors	These could be for press releases, product announcements, new partnership announcements, etc.
Vendors	Involves spoken and written communication; a mix of formal and informal communication	These are typically for product sourcing, sub-contractor (vendor) evaluation and choice and execution.
Customers	Communication to inform, to persuade, to educate and to build rapport with; mostly formal communication	Sales presentation; support calls and problem resolution; regular status updates and review.

15.2 Audience Analysis

Once you have addressed the 'why' (objectives) of communication, the next issue to address is the aspect of 'to whom' or audience analysis. Though we are presenting these two—understanding objectives and audience analysis—as two sequential steps, they are actually inter-dependent, iterative (as illustrated in Figure 15.1). You start with some initial objectives for communication and make some initial assumptions about what audience you would get. Once you know the actual audience, you fine tune your objectives, or at least the finer details like the negotiable parts of the objectives. Sometimes you may not have a choice of the audience—you may be forced to communicate with an audience you didn't expect; sometimes you get lucky and have the luxury of making a choice of your audience. In either case, you would have to do a quick analysis of the audience and hone your strategy for communication.

For the chosen objective, am I addressing the right people? If you have the luxury of choosing the audience, then this becomes a very vital question. If you want to make the customer sign on the dotted line of your contract, you must obviously be communicating to the people with the right level of authority. If you are convincing someone of the technical capabilities of your product, you better be talking to the technical folks. If you are communicating to persuade a customer about your product's value proposition, your audience could be a mix of technical and management folks.

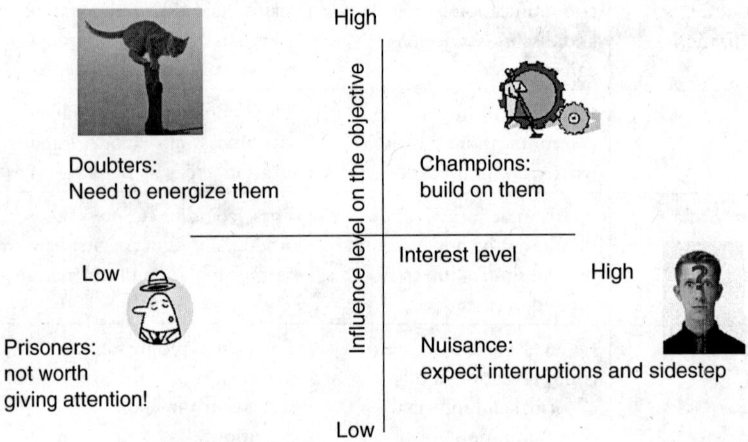

Fig. 15.2 *Quadrants of audience analysis*

Is the audience heterogeneous in terms of age group, educational background or experience levels? A heterogeneous group is likely to have different preferences, tastes or biases that you would have to be prepared for. This could also give rise to potential conflicts in the approaches that you may have to take to communicate to the individual audience members.

Are they there 'as prisoners' or by their own will? Sometimes, the people attending a presentation or a meeting or a training programme come on their own and sometimes, they come at the behest of someone else—willingly or unwillingly. When they come on their own, their motivation level to be interested in the subject matter is likely to be more. Else, you may have to work harder to educate and motivate them.

What are the audience's likes and dislikes? What if some members of the audience have a strong dislike for any issue, topic or concept? If so, it is important for you to decide how you are going to tackle this. An approach that can be very effective would be for you to anticipate their objections and preempt them by directly addressing such objections and allaying any fears proactively. Another approach could be to simply side step the objections, but that would require you to speak from a position of strength. In all probability, the second approach is likely to leave the audience less satisfied.

Are there people in the audience who need 'special attention'? The special attention could be needed either because they are influential or because they simply need ego boosts. It would be immensely useful for you to know about such people beforehand. Remember, in any communication involving a large audience, it would almost be impossible to divide your attention equally among everyone. A more capitalistic approach of picking your targets in the audience, who need extra attention, is likely to earn you better dividends. You should know the influencers, champions, nay sayers or decision makers. *Influencers* are those people who have a say in the subject matter that will affect the objective you are trying to achieve. They may have some 'hot button' that you feel you can touch upon and turn them into your spokespersons. *Champions* are those that have (at least) a partial concurrence with your objectives and hence, if molded properly, can be your spokespersons. *Nay sayers* are those who could spoil the show in terms of your not achieving the objectives. You may have to keep them at bay and proactively address their concerns. Finally the *decision makers* are those that have to be finally convinced.

Another way to look at the special attention spectrum is to look at the two dimensions of *interest in* (or *favourable disposition to*) your objectives and the *ability to influence* the decision in your favour. When you take the 2x2 cells, you see that there are these groups:

- Those with low interest in the subject matter who have low influence on the final outcome are prisoners in the communication, dragged into the net not out of their own free will. They will be happy to get out of the meeting 'asap' and get on to 'real work'. You can identify them as they will be in the back benches, constantly checking stuff on their laptops or using their cell phones (for text or games!).
- Those with high interest in the subject matter and low influence on the outcome. They generally ask a lot of nitty-gritty questions and are insistent upon stealing all the air time and perhaps showing off their knowledge. You need to silently side step these questions and move on with others.
- Those with high interest in the subject matter and high influence on the final outcome. They are your champions. You need to give them attention, use them as your lever to mobilize the last class of people discussed below. You would have to do your homework on these people.
- Those with low interest in the subject matter you are presenting (or those having little concurrence with your view point or being less favourably disposed to your idea/product) but with high influence in the decision. Along with the previous set, these are the decision makers. These are the nay-sayers or doubters. These people probably require maximum attention from you to get them to your side, as they are likely to be fence sitters to start with. You will need the leverage of the previous set of people to achieve this.

"And the 'Ah-Oh' shampoo not only cleanses your hair follicles, but also conditions your hair."

Fig. 15.3

What do I bring to the table? Why would the audience be interested in communicating with me on this subject matter? You should clearly articulate your personal credibility and make it compelling for the audience to listen to you and communicate with you. For this, it is not enough if you simply read out PowerPoint slides. You must show conviction that what you are presenting is indeed something you strongly believe in. And, what is more, you have to prove that given your personal credibility, your conviction is something that is significant. Any personal experiences or anecdotes that you can quote from your own experience can richly enhance audience interest.

15.3 PUTTING THE OBJECTIVES AND AUDIENCE ANALYSIS TOGETHER

After getting some idea of the objectives of communication and having done the audience analysis, it is worthwhile putting together a table like the one in Snapshot 15.2. It helps to have a clear understanding of the various constituents of the audience, their roles and importance and their expectations, needs, wants, hot buttons and bugbears. This would enable you to prepare your strategy for communication so as to achieve the set communication goals effectively. This would also enable you to preempt any questions and objections that each constituent would have.

Snapshot 15.2

Example of Audience Analysis

You are an R & D engineer and have hit upon a new product idea that would cut down users' operational costs by 30 per cent. Your objective is to productize the idea. You are making a product presentation for a new product idea to the people who would play a vital role in productizing it. The table below includes the typical audience, what each of the audience members expect, what could be their potential objections and what your planned response to those objections are likely to be. The purpose of this table is only to illustrate the process behind audience analysis and not to exhaustively stipulate the constituents for the given scenario.

Constituent	Their Role/Importance *Vis-À-Vis* Your Objective	Their Objection/Concerns	Your Planned Response to Their Objections
Your manager	You need your manager to be your voice to the senior management.	▶ Recognition for the group ▶ If there are any competing ideas from other groups within the company, the advantages of this idea over that proposed by other groups. He or she does not want to have a large risk of failure and hence may play devil's advocate (at least before the idea is allowed to be presented to the senior management).	Address the technical, financial and political objections that your manager raises upfront. Also, try to understand the internal compulsions and pressures that other groups may put on him.
Your colleagues	'Your' idea should actually be bought by key players within your group (including your manager).	▶ They don't want this to be perceived only as 'your idea'; they want a share of the glory.	Make sure you highlight their contributions to get their buy-in

(Continued)

Constituent	Their Role/Importance *Vis-À-Vis* Your Objective	Their Objection/Concerns	Your Planned Response to Their Objections
Head of the manufacturing group	If the manufacturing team does not sign up to your idea, it cannot be productized.	Manufacturability issues; scalability issues; economies of scale; break-even point;	You should talk to these people ahead of time and understand these issues. You should also work with the marketing team and understand the viability of the break-even point based on projections.
Head of sales and marketing	Both your CEO and CFO will lend their ears to the sales-/marketing head; eventually these are the people who will turn your idea into real money	▶ How is this product better than that of the competition? ▶ What feature benefits does this product offer over competition? ▶ Who are the target audience? ▶ Will this cannibalize any existing product?	Even if you are a 'pure techy', your presentation will not fly unless you think through these aspects. Here is where a close collaboration with your manager would help immensely. Make sure you have a business view of the product idea and not just a technology view
Head of HR group	This is the group who have to get people to realize your product.	▶ Can I easily scout for the talent required for this product? ▶ Can I use any internal resources?	Make sure your presentation addresses the human resource requirements to productize the idea. This should include the academic qualifications, experience, ease of getting the people, lead time required for training and so on.

(Continued)

Constituent	Their Role/Importance *Vis-À-Vis* Your Objective	Their Objection/Concerns	Your Planned Response to Their Objections
CxO	They want to ensure that if they spend money on your idea, it gets the best risk-return factor or best bang for the buck.	▶ What is the risk-return factor for this product vis-à-vis other ideas in the pipeline? ▶ What are the best case, worst case and normal scenarios for the product? ▶ Can the product be manufactured with the equipment (or people) we have or do we need fresh investments? ▶ How much capital would we need? ▶ What impact would this have on operating costs, margins, working capital and so on?	Obviously not all these are down the alley of a 'techy'. Here is where good teamwork becomes essential when the engineering group works closely with the finance and marketing groups proactively.

15.4 When You Don't Know Your Audience in Advance

We can hear you say, 'All that is fine; but what do I do when I don't have any details about the audience?' Valid question. When you go on your marketing spiel, you don't always get to know any details of audience preferences. When you are in a customer support job, you don't know the next customer who is going to call you and what his hot buttons or gripes are. If you don't know your audience *and* don't know your objectives of communication, the communication will meander into meaninglessness. If you know your objectives well, but come in with a rigid framework of what and how you will communicate, then again you will fail as you would not be able to adapt yourself to the situations. What you would need when you don't know your audience beforehand is

- A flexible approach to the communication
- A clear understanding of what aspects of the objectives are negotiable and what are not
- An ability to map the (unknown) audience's needs and preferences to something that you know already.

When you are addressing an unknown audience that is small in number (i.e., not a mass presentation), it would be a good idea to introduce yourself to them and in turn ask each person his or her name and their position. You would have to ask yourself the questions we asked earlier about audience analysis, but you would have to do so and come to conclusions 'on the fly', as you meet them and make a judgement.

When you are doing a mass presentation, it is important to make sure that you are addressing the right forum. Such presentations are usually fairly generic in nature and hence, it is unlikely that you will target some specific part of the audience or you will customize your message.

15.5 In Summary

The summary of the above discussion can be stated simply as

> Start with the end in mind.

This is one of the seven habits propounded by Stephen Covey (referred to in Chapter 9). Unless you know the objectives of communication, you will not get anywhere.

> Clearly identify what you want to achieve and what is negotiable.

Remember, when you communicate, you should be clear not only about what you want to achieve, but also what you are prepared to compromise on.

> Put yourself in the audience's shoes.

This is even more challenging when you have a heterogeneous audience. You will have to visualize the thinking process of the key people in the audience and make sure you understand their hot buttons and gripes.

> Don't try to distribute your attention equally to everyone:
>
> Be selective.

You need to identify the key targets on whom you should put more focus and attention. Trying to be socialistic in distributing attention will not be worthwhile.

Knowing the objectives and audience analysis lay the foundation for effective communication. They go on iteratively and may influence each other. While you don't always have control over who the audience is going to be, you absolutely must have your objectives—at least the non-negotiable ones—absolutely clear in your mind. If this is not the case, it would be akin to driving in a new city without a map or a guide. Knowing the objectives and understanding the audience now leads us to the next question—how to prepare for the communication? This is the topic for the next chapter.

16

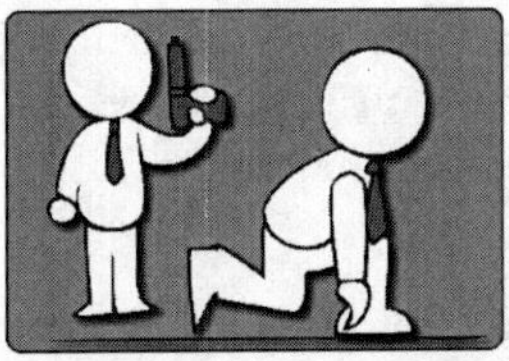

Preparing for the Communication

"Spectacular achievements are always preceded by unspectacular preparation."

–Roger Staubach

Having got a clear understanding of the objectives of communication and performed audience analysis, now is the time to get to the logistical preparations for the communication. This includes:

- Gathering and organizing all the necessary support data
- Finalizing the mode of communication
- Deciding the location of communication
- Ensuring that all the infrastructural elements are in order
- Notifying all the participants with agenda items and logistical details.

Obviously, the last three will be applicable only if the medium of communication is a meeting and if it is not a written communication.

16.1 Gathering and Organizing All the Necessary Support Data

The type of preparations you would do for a communication depends upon the type of communication you are going to have. We have covered the details for some common types of communication. Regardless of what communication you are going to have, the following steps—that you can remember by the acronym ***ICEAGE***—will always be required as preparation before you embark upon the actual communication (Also see Box 16.1).

Identify the stakeholders you need to engage: The stakeholders whom you need to engage to gather data may not be the same as the audience to whom you are presenting. For example, you may be making a product presentation to the prospects (who are the audience for the communication). You may have to talk to the product developers, architects, support people and sales people to get various perspectives and potential data.

Communicate with the various stakeholders to gather the required data: Once you know who the stakeholders are, you would have to communicate with them to get the required data. For example, if you are preparing for a status review meeting, you may have to talk to your team members to get the status of the project, to the infrastructure groups to identify any bottlenecks and so on.

Enumerate all the required data: The data that you gather from the stakeholders must be in a form that can be analysed and aggregated (in the next step). To this end, you may have to identify some common formats and templates that you could use, not only to gather data but also to record data.

Aggregate the data: The data supplied by the stakeholders whom you talk to may be at a fine-grain level. You may have to aggregate, summarize and reformat the data in a more concise form in order to make the data useful for the audience.

Generate the agenda and the communication plan: With all of the above, you should be able to generate a clear agenda (details of which are covered later in the chapter).

Box 16.1

As examples for some of the preparations, consider a project status review meeting Some of the questions you would have to address will include these.

- Have you gathered all the data from your team members or other stakeholders as appropriate?
- Have you identified any deviations from any planned activities?
- Have you identified the root causes for any deviations?
- Have you identified any corrective actions for the deviations?
- Have you identified any preventive actions for such deviations not to occur again?
- Have you consolidated, aggregated and organized the data in a way that makes sense to the recipients? For example, if the review meeting is with the senior management, you may need to highlight some of the very key accomplishments and challenges and sieve out unnecessary details.

Elicit concurrence and ensure participation of the stakeholders: You should vet your final agenda with the stakeholders. This will ensure that in whatever aggregation you have done, you have not misstated or misinterpreted what the stakeholders said.

16.2 Finalizing the Mode of Communication

In Chapter 13, we have already discussed the various modes of communication and where each is applicable. When you have decided to have a communication, a key thing to decide first is the medium you will use.

The first option is a face-to-face meeting. A face-to-face meeting is most effective in situations where you need interactions, discussions and brainstorming. Where you require flexibility, where you need to build rapport, where you have cultural or language barriers, a face-to-face meeting will definitely help in minimizing any distortion. In some cases, when it is required to build personal rapport or when the infrastructure is available only in one place (e.g., for a demo), this may be the *only* option. Where there is more structure, the flow of the meeting is quite linear and where there are travel constraints, face-to-face meetings are not necessary. In some cases—when the teams are geographically distributed—a face-to-face meeting may not be an option at all.

The next option is a telephonic conference call. This may be the next best option to face-to-face meetings. This can give access to the vocal channel of communication. It may also not be very expensive. Of course, you can include in this category, channels like voice chat that serve the same purpose as a phone call.

You may also choose video conferencing, which adds some rudimentary body language aids to communication. This may require more infrastructure and hence, is logistically more difficult than a telephonic conference call.

As an alternative to all these synchronous forms of communication, you may simply choose to have an asynchronous written communication to provide written records and to reduce scheduling and infrastructural logistics issues. You can give yourself more time to plan and ensure fewer execution surprises as well as give the recipient more time to respond. The specific mode of communication you choose will depend on factors governing synchronous and asynchronous communication given in earlier chapter 13.

16.3 Deciding the Location of Communication

If we need to have a face-to-face meeting or any other synchronous mode of communication, where should a particular meeting be held? In the case of routine meetings, they are usually held within the office premises, in a conference room or in the boss's room. While this is very convenient, it is easy to get distracted with frequent interruptions–due to visitors, 'due to the urge to look at that important bug to be addressed' or 'because of that one single e-mail that I will respond to and return'. Or you may be passionately making a pitch for your latest idea to your boss's superior and he may suddenly get called to attend some other meeting. Hence, sometimes a meeting is held offsite, in some remote location, removed from the office. Of course, with the Blackberries and iPhones that have proliferated in society, whether you are within the office or outside does not really matter. E-mails and phone calls haunt you wherever you go. If you really want to focus on the communication and not get distracted, it is only a question of personal discipline.

Sometimes you may have a communication in a client's location. Your degree of freedom in this case, will be a lot less. And, all the planning that is described here becomes all the more important in such a scenario.

If an outside location (or a customer site) is chosen, you need to check out the following:

How long is the normal travel time? This will enable you to allow the right amount of time to get to the meeting on time. If you are driving down, it may be a good idea to look at something like Google Maps to know the route and the approximate travel time required.

What extraordinary conditions do you expect? For example, during winter times, you should expect fog in Delhi and that all flights out of Delhi to be delayed. Hence, don't count on having a vitally important meeting at 9.30 a.m. in Bangalore and plan to take the 6 a.m. flight from Delhi. While such a schedule would normally make sense during summer months, it is quite risky to rely on this during the winter months. Also—especially in India—make sure you read the local newspaper about any possible processions and '*bandhs*' that may bring the city to a standstill. If you have a meeting at the other end of town and you found out that morning about such factors, alert the audience ahead of time either of possible delays or even consider rescheduling the meeting. The last thing you want in a meeting is for the people to arrive in a bad mood, keep looking at the watch or the news alerts for traffic jams and be worrying about getting back home quickly.

If the location is outside your town, have you finalized the travel plans and stay details? Taking care of travel and stay logistics would be essential if you need to show up at the place of meeting on time. During peak travel seasons, it may be very difficult to get bookings unless you start planning early.

Do you know how to get the various necessities there? You might like to check that the various infrastructural elements are in place. (More about this in Section 16.4.)

If the meeting is in an outside location, it would be great if you can visit the place ahead of time and understand all the above issues. Obviously, this is not always possible. You must, at least, gather as much of this information as possible ahead of time, so that you are not in for last minute surprises that distract you from the actual subject matter that you need to prepare.

16.4 Ensuring That All the Infrastructural Elements Are in Order

Whether you are conducting a meeting within your office or in an outside location, it will save you a lot of last minute heartburn if you can ensure that all the infrastructural elements are in order in your meeting location.

- Do you need to make a presentation? If so, are you carrying your laptop? If not, is your presentation already loaded into some server from which you can download it? Or are you carrying your presentation in a pen-drive or some such portable device. If so, are you allowed to use those devices? (It is a good idea to build a bit of redundancy and carry your presentation materials in more than one device—for example, in a pen-drive and in a CD.)
- Do you have the right projection equipment and screen? (Projecting is commonly done on a white board but it hurts the eyes because of the glare.) Is the projection equipment compatible with your laptop?
- Do you need network connection? If so, do you have all the details and access rights needed to connect?
- Do you need to write anything during the presentation? If so, do you have a white board and/or some flip charts? Also, are there markers to write on these—markers that don't keep going dry? (And, hopefully the markers that you use are not permanent markers.) Make sure there is an eraser too. Remember that your shirt sleeve makes for an expensive eraser.
- Is the arrangement of chairs and tables like what you want? Can they be reconfigured? For example, if you want to have group discussions, you may want round tables. If you have a smaller group, you may not want too big a room. If you are in a typical board room with a fixed large center table, then it may not be conducive to having multiple break-up groups.
- If you are using a phone conference, do you have good speaker phone equipment that is truly multi-directional? Have you seated the people to be not too far from the phone so that everyone is audible on the other end of the phone line?
- If you are using multiple parties in a conference call, have you arranged for the bridge number to which they can dial in? Alternatively, if people have to be dialled out, have you got the numbers to be dialled out?
- If you need video conferencing equipment, have you booked a room where such facilities are available? Usually, these are scarce commodities in an office.
- If you need hand-outs and any other material to be given to participants, have you planned the right arrangements to make these available?
- If you need to make photocopies or need extra stationery, do you know how and from where to get them?
- Have you taken care to know where the other 'necessities' are around the meeting place e.g., coffee machines, photocopying machines, restrooms, and so on?

Fig. 16.1 *Communication infrastructure*

16.5 Notifying All the Participants with Agenda Items and Logistical Details

Once you have done all the above groundwork, you should notify the participants with a clear set of agenda items. Making sure each person comes to the meeting fully aware of what is expected of him or her is a good first step to a successful meeting. A good agenda should have:

- Details of the venue and time of the meeting
- Any information on 'how to get there', if required
- Unambiguous description of the objectives to be achieved or the purpose of the meeting
- A complete list of relevant items to be discussed
- A clear owner for each item to be discussed
- An allotted timeframe for the discussion of each item.

A well-laid out agenda acts as a road map to steer a safe meeting. Like all well-laid out plans, a meeting even with a good agenda in place, may go in all possible directions if the meeting is not managed properly. We will revisit this later in Chapter 24.

16.6 Ensuring That the Execution Is Perfect

All preparations are great, but the key is in proper execution. You need to keep your antennae open during the entire time period leading up to, including and following the communication. Trust Murphy—If anything can go wrong, it will go wrong, notwithstanding all planning. If you have any past data, try to see what has gone wrong in the past and have Plan B up your sleeve. If you don't have any past data, start the habit of gathering, recording and referring to past data. Mutual funds advertisements may say 'past performance is not a guarantee of future results', but ignoring all past performance is surely not the wisest thing to do. As a saying goes, 'Wise men learn from other peoples' mistakes, fools from their own!'

16.7 In Summary

A number of ideas, techniques and principles discussed in this chapter are closely tied to those discussed in Chapter 24 on 'Meeting Management'. The preparations we have listed in this chapter apply not only to meetings, but also to other forms of communication like presentations (and even written communication). To paraphrase an old saying,

> Failing to prepare is preparing to fail.

Some of the infrastructural elements that need to be checked (that are listed in this chapter) may appear too trivial. But experience shows that these 'trivial' things are indeed the ones that badly derail a communication. Remember,

> You don't fall down banging against a tall
> mountain, but only by slipping on a small pebble.

All planning and preparations are fine, but as we mentioned earlier, execution is the key. In order to execute effectively, we need to utilize the repertoire of various tools that we are endowed with for communication. These include active listening, vocal variety, body language as well as external visual aids. These communication elements are discussed in the following chapters.

17

Listening Skills

"To listen well is as powerful a means of communication and influence as to talk well."

–John Marshall

God gave us two ears and one mouth. The ears are exclusively devoted for hearing whereas the mouth is supposed to do both speaking and eating. Perhaps, God intended that we should do four times as much listening as talking. More often than not, it is the reverse! Most people tend to do more talking than listening.

In our school days, we are taught reading, speaking, maths and a host of other subjects. But do we ever have a formal course on listening? Even our teachers, in their pressure to 'teach' the subjects, very seldom find time to listen to the feedback from the students, whether they (the students) have understood the message or not. The myriad self-improvement programmes that exist in the market make no more than a passing mention of listening skills, let alone offer concrete suggestions for improvement. The purpose of this chapter is to look a little deeper into listening and provide practical tips to improve listening, in our quest to improve communication.

Perhaps, the best way the importance of listening is highlighted is by one of the seven habits propounded by Stephen Covey (referred to in Chapter 9): 'Seek to understand before seeking to be understood.' Listening is the process by which you seek to understand someone else's communication and point of view and thereby, relate to the environment better.

Right from our school days, we have to spend almost seven hours a day listening in the classroom (although most of time we only 'hear'!). This continues into our work environment, where very seldom do we get closeted into one man armies. We need to work in teams and this involves a lot of listening to and empathizing with others' point of view.

Listening starts with the physical process of hearing. But it is more than just hearing. Listening is to hearing what observing is to seeing. All of us see or hear; but not all of us observe or listen. Listening is the process of comprehending what the speaker said and understanding the speaker's point of view. *More importantly, listening also involves making the speaker understand that the listener has understood what the speaker has said and meant*. This is what is generically referred to as *active listening*—the process by which a listener listens, understands the message the way it was intended and conveys to the sender that the message is understood as intended. Any other types of listening (if it can be called listening) are what we will term as *passive listening*. From now on, we will only discuss active listening and the steps towards sharpening it.

17.1 Steps in Active Listening

In order to achieve effective active listening, there are a number of steps that have to take place:

Understand the purpose for which you are listening.

Understanding why you are listening and what you are listening to: This is the essential first step in listening. Are you listening for *exhaustive comprehension* like in a training programme or in a class? If so, you would have to sustain your 'listening energy' over an extended period of time. Are you listening *selectively*, i.e., you are specifically interested in just a part of what is being said? If so, you need to up the ante during certain periods, while you could afford to slacken in listening at other times. For example, in a long product presentation by a vendor, your role may be to understand the technology part of it and hence you may have to selectively listen to this part with more attention. Are you *listening to critically evaluate* what is being said? For example, when you are evaluating a vendor's presentation or performing a project review, you should be prepared to think on your feet and pose challenging questions. Are you listening *empathically?* For example, one of your staff needs a one-on-one with you to discuss some of his grievances. In this case, you should constantly try to put yourself in his shoes when you listen. You should also given him confidence that you have understood his point of view (though you may not agree with it). The various purposes for which you listen are given in Table 17.1.

Knowing the purpose of listening enables you to put sufficient energy and focus at the right times during a communication transaction.

Tune out unnecessary signals.

Just like an antenna tuned in to receive a specific broadcast filters out all other signals, the listener has to tune out all unnecessary signals. This is both a physical and mental process. On the physical side, the listener should

- Turn off unnecessary distractions. For example, turn off mobile phones, laptops and any such communication equipment.

Table 17.1 *Various types of listening needed*

Type of Listening	Scenarios Where this will be Needed	Tips and Challenges
Exhaustive comprehension	Training programmes; classroom settings	▶ Sustaining listening energy and concentration over extended period of time ▶ Taking notes can help in this.
Selective listening	When you are assigned a specific responsibility to understand a specific part of what is being said	▶ 'On demand' upping the ante for listening ▶ Being aware of when to tune in and when to tune out
Evaluative listening	When you have to give your feedback and evaluation on part or all of a presentation	▶ Would need upfront preparation to understand the evaluation factors ▶ Would need to ask the right questions ▶ Should be able to go into detail, and at the same time, understand the big picture
Empathetic listening	Typically applies when you are in an appraisal meeting or listening to customer complaints.	▶ Need to put yourself in the shoes of the speaker and appreciate his perspective ▶ Empathy need not mean that you fully agree with what the speaker is saying; all you are doing is to acknowledge that you have understood the speaker's perspective; this is a delicate balance.

- Minimize exposure to diversions. For example, instead of sitting overlooking a glass window, try to sit facing the wall.
- Consciously cut off other distractions like looking out of the window or scribbling on a note book or bringing up irrelevant topics for discussion.
- Refrain from side conversations with others in the room.

On the mental side, tuning out unnecessary signals involves:

- Putting away any distracting thoughts ('how will the traffic be when I am returning home?')
- Stop thinking about those urgent pressures like deadlines.
- Put your biases and judgemental feelings about the speaker or the topic aside so that you can listen objectively.

Tune in to the speaker.

You should not only tune *out* unnecessary signals, but also tune *in* to the speaker. This is again like how an antenna works by amplifying the required frequency. Tuning in to the speaker involves:

Using a posture that favours understanding and conveys confidence to the speaker: This point and the next one apply to body language (which is covered in more detail in Chapter 18). Sitting back in your chair as if you are watching a boring cricket match is neither going to increase your listening ability nor is it going to inspire any confidence in the speaker whom you are listening to (see Figure 17.1). Ditto to if you are lying down with your head on the table (Figure 17.2). At the same time, if you sit very straight it may be construed as intimidating. The best posture for effective listening is to sit bending a little forward (Fig. 17.3). This shows a sense of anticipation, almost like the person in a relay race ready to take the baton. If there is a table in front of you, leaning forward with your elbow every now and then will be a good posture for listening. Make sure you don't get physically tired of whatever posture you choose. Else, your focus will only be on your physical discomfort and not on the subject matter you are listening to.

Fig. 17.1 *Bad posture for listening: too laid back*

Fig. 17.2 *Bad posture for listening: conveys lack of interest*

Fig. 17.3 *Good posture for listening*

Providing eye contact to the speaker: Just as a speaker should provide selective eye contact to the listeners, the listener should provide periodic and selective eye contact to the speaker. The same benefits of eye contact that apply to a speaker also apply to a listener.

Perform the physical process of hearing.

Again, it is important to remember that this is more than a physical process. Some of the steps given below transcend sheer physical functioning and bring in a mental and psychological angle.

Look for the main ideas: Any communication you hear would have the main ideas that are substantiated by details and supporting facts. It is important that as a listener you catch the main ideas and sieve them from the details. This is especially true if you are performing critical listening or evaluative listening. Some speakers highlight such main points by phrases like 'the point to note is…' or 'what I would like to stress is…'. Some use effective voice modulation (including pauses and suspenseful silence). But, some others just don't give such cues. Regardless of whether the speaker gives these cues or not, the listener should develop the habit of looking for main ideas and separating out the essence from the details (see Box 17.1).

Box 17.1

Key Phrases to Look for to Get the Main Ideas

'The important point is…'
'What I would like to stress is…'
'Note here, ladies and gentlemen… '(and a poignant pause before the next word)
Special effects on the visual aids….

Put your emotions aside while you listen: Emotions are valves that shut off hearing and listening when they feel like it! Emotions and strong biases will make you hear what you want to hear and not what the speaker wanted you to hear. You will end up with a jaundiced view of the inputs that is not going to help you get an objective understanding of the message.

Defer all judgment and conclusions till you finish listening: As an extension to the previous paragraph, remember, do not try to be judgemental when you listen. Do not let the communication go tangential because of counter-arguments stemming from your predetermined mindset. You will end up in an unnecessary adversarial position with the speaker that is not going to take the communication too far.

Reflect on what you heard.

Reflecting on what you heard is what distinguishes active listening from passive listening. Reflection means conveying to the speaker your understanding of what you heard. This can enable the speaker to ensure that you understood the message as he intended you to understand. Reflection can be done by:

Expressive body language feedback: For example, as a listener you can nod your head when you agree, shake your head when you disagree, twitch (or mildly frown) your eye brows when you don't understand something (see Figure 17.4 and 17.5). And you can smile, clap and even thump on the table if you strongly agree with the speaker. Some of these instant feedbacks could enable the speaker to do any mid-course corrections to facilitate the correct message to reach you.

Fig. 17.4 *Body language feedback for active listening: frowning / twitching of eye brows*

Fig. 17.5 *Body language feedback for active listening: nodding the head*

Voice feedback: Occasional 'ah ah's and such vocal feedback (that does not necessarily involve words) could supplement the body language feedback discussed above (especially if the conventions of body language are not fully consistent or understood). We can also include generic verbal feedback such as 'that's interesting' or 'you must be kidding me' kind of interjections.

Paraphrase: Occasionally—especially for the important points—paraphrasing or restating the message in your own words would provide reinforcement for your understanding and give clear feedback to the speaker as to the extent of your understanding. Some of the phrases you can use are 'if I understand you right…', 'let me restate what you said in my words … let me know if I have misunderstood anything', 'sounds like…', and so on. While paraphrasing, it is important to ensure that you don't repeat what the speaker said verbatim like a parrot. It is also important not to do the paraphrasing for each and every point made by the speaker as it would affect continuity (see Box 17.2).

Box 17.2

Key Phrases Use for Paraphrasing

'If I understand you right …'
'Are you trying to say …'
'Here is my understanding… correct me if I have got it wrong.'
'Let me state this in my own words…'

Ask questions: This is absolutely essential to make sure that the message is fully understood by the receiver. And, this is one area where there exists a cultural divide in a global team. For example, some people don't ask questions for the fear of appearing naive. In the classes we have taught and in the training programmes we have conducted, we find this to be a major hurdle. If, as a speaker, you don't find the audience asking questions, you should assume that they have not followed your message. You should then paraphrase your message in different words and/or ask leading questions to your audience.

17.2 In Summary

Listening requires a synthesis of not only words that we hear, but also other signals like vocal variety, body language, visual aids and so on. For example, the speaker may be saying that he is very enthusiastic about a proposed project, but his demeanour may suggest that he is not too excited about it. You have to 'listen' not only to his words, but also to his body language.

Listening is a holistic and whole-body process—you 'listen' to words, actions, slides and the whole works!!

Listening entails not only an input process (of hearing and grasping), but also providing feedback.

Listening is an input-output process, not just an input process.

Listening should complete the feedback loop between the sender and the receiver. It is like a switch in an electrical circuit. Only when it is on and closed, will current flow through the circuit.

Listening is seeking to understand what the speaker communicated, and assuring the speaker to understand that the listener has understood!

As we saw, body language is an essential part of effective active listening. Body language, in fact, is useful for much more than just active listening. We will see more details of this in the next chapter.

Fig. 17.6

18

Body Language

"Actions speak louder than words."

—*Unknown*

When we send a message as part of a communication, it can reach the receiver in more than one way: through the *words* (verbal channel) we use, through the *voice* (vocal channel) we use and through the body language (*action* channel or what is broadly considered as 'non-verbal' channel).

Imagine you are writing a letter to a person A, talking to a person B over phone and meeting a person C face-to-face and trying to convey the same message in all the three cases. Who do you think would receive the message most clearly? In all likelihood it is person C.

In 1971, research[1] published by Albert Mehrabian[2] showed that

- Words account for 7 per cent
- Tone of voice accounts for 38 per cent
- Body language accounts for 55 per cent of the message.

Just think about this: More than half the message that a receiver gets is from your body language! While it is not always possible to have access to this important

---

1 While this study only mentions the effectiveness of body language in the context of expressing strong likes and dislikes, we believe that it is reasonable to assume that body language forms a potent channel for any communication.

2 Albert Mehrabian, *Silent Messages* (Belmont: Wadsworth, 1971).

channel (especially in a geographically distributed team), it behooves us that we explore how to maximize its benefits when available. This will be the subject of discussion in this chapter.

While there could be many contributions to body language, we will consider only the following:

- Posture
- Use of hands
- Eye contact
- Gestures

Each of these is discussed in detail in the subsequent sections.

18.1 Postures

Posture refers to how you stand or sit. This is a sure give-away of your attitude and confidence level. When you are standing straight and not slouching, it usually indicates a higher degree of confidence. When shoulders droop or when you are bending

Fig. 18.1 *Bad posture: a person slouching forward*

Fig. 18.2 *Good posture: straight and easy stance with hands free*

forward too much, it conveys a lack of confidence (see Figure 18.1). This does not of course mean that you should be extremely stiff, making a herculean effort to stand absolutely erect and straight! Nor does it mean that if you have a physical difficulty that causes you to bend forward or slouch a bit, you should try to stretch yourself. Stand as naturally as you can, because posture will have a bearing on your movements and gestures—very important components of body language that we will see next.

Posture also applies when you sit. As we saw in the previous chapter, leaning forward while sitting down could indicate a more keen interest in the subject matter. When you extend the leaning forward to almost lying down on the table, it will obviously convey a reduced interest in the subject. (Besides, such a posture can easily induce you to sleep!) Whether you are sitting or standing, a good posture would:

- Be comfortable for you
- Demonstrate your active interest and confidence
- Not hinder other communication vehicles (like gestures, movements, etc.)

18.2 The Use of Hands

How you use your hands has two implications: First—as in the case of posture—it indicates your level of confidence. Second, it determines how easily you can position yourself for effective use of gestures.

Fig. 18.3 *Bad use of hands: stiff stance (appears cold)*

Fig. 18.4 *Bad use of hands: a person with hands folded (shows defensiveness)*

When a person stands with very stiff hands, he will find it a serious hindrance to communication. He will not be able to move around freely and use other gestures. Also, he will appear cold, nervous and inflexible to the audience (see Figure 18.3).

When a speaker folds his hands across his chest, it indicates putting up an artificial barrier between him and the audience. When the overall situation is amicable and friendly, it can be interpreted as the speaker thinking deeply about the topic. But, in a serious or confrontational situation, it can indicate defensiveness on the part of the speaker. This is especially so if the speaker is leaning away from the listener. Sometimes a speaker may put his hands across his chest because he is feeling cold. In such a case, it would be useful to indicate the actual cause by saying it and perhaps by rubbing the hands.

If the speaker puts his hands in his pockets, it indicates a lack of openness and it would also be very distracting. Furthermore, the speaker has eliminated the possibility of other gestures we will see in the next section.

When a person uses his hands for some repetitive gestures like, touching a button of the shirt or coat or fiddling around with a pen or some object, (Figure 18.6) it is distracting, indicates nervousness and above all minimizes the avenues for deploying message-enhancing body language.

Fig. 18.5 *Bad use of hands: a person with hands in pocket (indicates lack of openness)*

Fig. 18.6 *Bad use of hands: a person with hands engaged in some form of distracting gestures (indicates nervousness)*

The best use of hands is as depicted in Figure 18.2 that we saw earlier. The speaker has given himself freedom to effectively use gestures. He is also conveying openness, confidence and trust to the audience. It is likely that such use of hands will result in better overall communication.

18.3 Eye Contact

Eye contact is another important aspect by which a speaker can reach out to the audience and the listener can synch up with the speaker. Let us consider the two cases one by one.

First, from the point of view of a speaker (no pun intended), eye contact gives a great opportunity to reach out to the audience better. Looking into the eye of a listener gives the speaker a possible insight into the listener's state of mind and how the listener is disposed towards the message. When a speaker is addressing multiple members of the audience, eye contact gives an opportunity to prioritize the listeners and to make the right message reach the right person in the audience more effectively. For example, when a speaker is making a product presentation to an audience comprising management and technical people, more eye contact can be given to the management people when talking about financial aspects and the eye contact to the technical people can be increased when going into appropriate technical details. Thus eye contact can be distributed on a targetted basis to different sections of the audience, based on need.

The amount of eye contact a speaker needs to give each member of the audience can be an indication of the importance of that member vis-à-vis the other members. By balancing the *duration* of eye contact and the specific *instances* of eye contact to specific people, a speaker can increase the chances of getting the message across more effectively.

As a thumbrule, when a listener asks a question and the speaker is answering the question, it is a good idea to give more eye contact to the person who asked the question. But if it is a long answer, then giving exclusive eye contact to the person who asked the question would likely lose the interest of the rest of the audience.

If you are chairing a group meeting and have specific agenda items for specific people, you can establish eye contact with the person to whom you are addressing each specific agenda item. If an agenda item is addressed to you, as a member of the meeting, you should give eye contact to the chairperson of the meeting while responding.

As a listener too, eye contact offers a very useful mechanism to convince the speaker you are with him. By establishing periodic eye contact with the speaker, the listener sends out a message that he is interested in the communication being made by the speaker. Such listening, coupled with body language like, nodding and verbal feedback (like 'ah ah' and questions), lead to active listening (discussed in Chapter 17 on listening).

Too much of anything is bad. This is true of eye contact as well. Constant eye contact with one member of the audience can be construed as intimidating by the receiver and could also send a message to the others in the audience that they are not cared for. Hence, periodic re-distribution of eye contact to the various members of the audience becomes essential.

Eye contact should not be taken in isolation. It has to be combined with other elements like posture and gestures to be effective. For example, direct eye contact coupled with a poor posture could send a conflicting message.

18.4 Gestures

Gestures involve two aspects, facial expressions and movements.

Facial expression should indicate a friendly, approachable disposition. Keeping a stern facial expression indicates outright hostility and should be avoided. Keeping a blank, emotionless, poker-faced expression can be good or bad depending on the situation. It could be good when there is a need to hide the true feelings, like in a negotiation scenario. But when you are having a normal communication in a team, a blank expression generally creates mistrust among members. A facial expression that is enthusiastic, sincere and expressive, stirs up interest in the other members participating in communication.

In general, communication begets trust when the speaker has a pleasant smile on his or her face. A smile conveys a friendly disposition and creates a feeling of trust. In addition, physiologists have established that a smile relaxes more muscles in your body and hence, contributes to better physical comfort and therefore, to an increased sense of confidence.

Movements form the second component of gestures. This includes movement of the speaker within the room as well as movement of the body parts of the speaker. If you are addressing a large audience from a podium, then moving across the podium, when done moderately will stimulate energy in the speaker and also give some change to the audience. But while making the movements, care should be taken to:

- Not move too far away from the lectern and mike, should you be using a mike (not a collar mike)
- Not move too far away from your laptop if you are using it for your presentation (unless of course, you are using a remote control)
- Not come in the way of projection of visual aids.

When you move about, it is important to be aware of the concept of personal space. Personal space refers to the distance beyond which people don't want you to approach. People guard their personal spaces passionately and it is not appropriate for you to get closer than what personal space allows. The amount of personal space depends on various factors like context of the interaction, relationship between the speaker and the audience and the culture of the participants. For example, in social settings, the personal space can be closer than in business settings; the personal space is lesser in India than in the USA. Having said this, it is important not to stereotype anything and to use your discretion. In general, in business meetings, keeping a distance of at least a couple of metres would work.

We will re-visit this later in our chapter on Privacy, Chapter 36.

Movement of hands can be a very effective reinforcement in several situations:

Fig. 18.7 *Hand gestures useful for creating a visual image*

- When you are indicating a process of counting, using fingers can be very effective for reinforcing your point. You can also move from left to right to indicate different options. For example, to illustrate three possible options, you can be on the left side of the table first to state the first option, then move a little to the centre and state the second option and then move further right and state the third option.
- When you are indicating progress—upwards or downwards—using hands in the appropriate direction would reinforce the message. Just make sure that the direction of movement is consistent with the words.

Nodding and shaking can be useful as body language enhancers but sometimes these could lead to confusion.

A word of caution about body language, especially in case of use of gestures: Certain gestures are taboo in certain cultures. Also, certain gestures mean completely different things in different cultures. Be sure to understand the local cultures and conventions before you use any gesture.

18.5 What Do You Do in the Absence of Body-Language Avenues?

Unfortunately, globally distributed teams do not always have avenues for using the potent force of body language in communication. This means that you may lose more than half the effectiveness of communication if you are not careful. With travel budgets being slashed ruthlessly, there is more and more emphasis on exploiting technology for better communication. Here are some practical tips:

- Try to include a face-to-face communication with business activities wherever you can. For example, there may be travel required for delivering a software product to a customer or for finalizing the details of a project. Maximize every such opportunity to have face-to-face communication so as to harness the benefits of body language.
- Whenever such opportunities for face-to-face communication present themselves, combine them with any non-work related or informal outings or meetings. For example, having a team meeting in a location outside the workplace (combined with some recreational activity like bowling) would put everyone in a more relaxed state and thus, make the use of body language and other communication elements more natural.
- Where possible, try to have more video conferences than just phone calls or chats.
- Always augment any chats or phone calls with minutes of meeting or a summary e-mail. This provides some redundancy that body language so effectively offers (although to a much reduced extent).

As is the case with any of the other element of soft skills, there is no one right way of doing things. Body language, voice modulation, visual aids and all the communication elements must be used judiciously and in such a way that they reinforce each other. That is something that comes through practice, by applying common sense.

18.6 In Summary

Body Language is the most potent vehicle of communication. It is absolutely essential to hone the skills in harnessing this vehicle.

> Body language supersedes everything else—your words, slides and even voice.

Different elements of body language work in unison—a positive improvement in one constituent usually has ripple positive influence on others. To start with, we may not have all the constituents functioning at the same level of effectiveness, but realizing the positive synergy among these constituents,

> Build upon your greatest strengths to fine tune what may not be so well developed.

In the previous chapter, we said that listening is a whole body process. Likewise, body language itself is part of the listening process. People 'listen' to your body language more than they listen to anything else—words, tone, visual aids and so on.

Actions speak louder than words.

Finally, you will find that effective body language can also add to your confidence and increase your overall communication effectiveness, which also includes effective use of other channels like voice (covered in the next chapter). Given this, it is fair to conclude the chapter by saying,

Improving body language is a low-hanging fruit and a great place to start in your quest to improve communication.

19

Vocal Variety: Using the Voice Channel

"Words mean more than what is set down on paper. It takes the human voice to infuse them with shades of deeper meaning."

– Mary Angelou

Your voice dictates who you are. People associate a lot of significance with your voice. People judge you by your voice. They come to conclusions about your confidence level, your well-being, your energy levels and your sincerity by just judging your voice. In fact, whenever we are asked to act according to our conscience, we are told 'to listen to the inner voice'! In this chapter, we will explore the various facets of voice—or more specifically what is called vocal variety. We explore the various components of voice and see how they all blend together for engaging, persuasive, enthralling and captivating communication.

19.1 Components of Vocal Variety

Our voice is a powerful instrument in communication that can make the delivered message more convincing and more appealing for the audience and could display your *passion* in what you are communicating. A good voice (or a vocal channel) can mean the vital difference between engaging your audience in the communication and lulling them to sleep; between a compelling, persuasive presentation and a mere ritualistic one; between achieving the objectives of communication and failing in your objectives.

What do we mean by 'good vocal channel'? Is it that we should all possess a wonderful musical voice or be doomed forever in communication? Is it *just* the voice? If we are not born with such a voice, can't we ever cultivate it? All these are indeed very relevant questions.

The good news is that a musical voice is not really an essential criterion for a 'good vocal channel'. Even better news is that you can develop a good voice by cultivating certain practices and habits. In fact, voice is just one aspect of 'good vocal channel'. There are certain important constituents of a good voice channel. These are:

- Pronunciation and Articulation
- Emphasis
- Pace
- Pitch
- Volume
- Pause

Let us look into each of these in some more detail.

19.1.1 Pronunciation and Articulation

Pronunciation refers to your ability to utter the words in the same way as is considered standard. This is admittedly a vague and inaccurate definition. The reason is that the meaning of the phrase 'standard way' is itself non-standard! What is standard in one place is non-standard in another place. For example, consider the words like 'can't' and 'fast'. While the phonetics of these words is standard, the way these words are pronounced by Americans and Indians are quite different. (Americans will pronounce the 'a' in these words like the 'a' in the word 'fat', while Indians would pronounce the 'a' as the 'a' in 'art'). Pronunciation depends on accent, which may override the 'standard' way of pronouncing a word. Also, pronunciation applies at a word level.

Articulation refers to coherence of the words and phrases in a talk. When a person is articulate, the message would be easier to understand for the audience. Articulation stems from proper pronunciation but is more than mere pronunciation. You may pronounce each word correctly, but when you combine the words and phrases together, they may wiggle into one another, thereby causing the entire sentence to be incoherent. Lack of articulation could arise from several sources:

- Excessive speed while talking: When you speak too fast, it may indicate you are thinking even faster. Before you complete one word, your mind has gone on ten words ahead and your spoken words are trying to catch up. As a result, either some words get missed out or the ending of one word gets eaten up by the beginning of the next word.
- Not using your natural or mother tongue: This stems from a cause that is opposite to the first cause discussed above. Normally, we tend to think in our natural or mother tongue first and then translate to the language in which we speak. During this translation process, we may lose some words, use inappropriate words or say the words with the wrong emphasis or pronunciation. This results in loss of articulation.
- Inability to utter certain special letters or sounds: For example, in certain East Asian cultures, 'r' is pronounced as 'l'. In some regions in India we tend to

pronounce 'r' as 'd'. This is not a pronunciation issue per se, but a cultural issue that results in what could be perceived as poor articulation.

Being conscious of some of the barriers to pronunciation and articulation could help you work on them and improve upon them. Clearly articulating every word and phrase in every sentence makes your speech more coherent and understandable. You will gain more confidence and will also gain credibility with the audience. They will begin to understand what you are saying, and this can leave you in a better chance of persuading them to see your point of view.

19.1.2 Emphasis

When you are speaking, not everyone in the audience tunes in to your speech the way you think they should. Each one would latch on to some specific word or phrase that he catches and then get stuck with it and this may lead to an interpretation of your message that is totally different from what you intended. The various techniques and components we have been discussing so far try to reduce the gap between what you intended to convey and how the audience interpreted it. Emphasis of words is another important tool in this direction.

When you have a sentence, not every word in the sentence is equally important. By emphasizing certain words, you can get the correct meaning across. If you utter all the words with the same stress, it becomes monotonous and each audience member could potentially walk away with totally different interpretations of your message. By emphasizing different parts of a sentence, very different meanings can be conveyed (see Snapshot 19.1 below).

Snapshot 19.1

The following was given in the context of gathering software requirements[1] to illustrate the effect of emphasis and how emphasizing different words can result in presenting different messages. In the following, the same sentence is spoken with emphasis on different words indicated by italics. The meaning conveyed is given in parenthesis.

Mary had a little lamb. (Emphasizing that Mary and not someone else, like John, had the lamb.)

Mary *had* a little lamb. (Emphasizing that Mary had a lamb and does not have it now.)

Mary had *a* little lamb. (Emphasizing that she had only one lamb.)

Mary had a *little* lamb. (Emphasizing that she did not have a big lamb.)

Mary had a little *lamb.* (Emphasizing that she did not have a little pup or kitten.)

Consider the sentence, 'Can you think of any better product than ours?' that you may use at the end of a compelling presentation. Which words would you emphasize and what effect would that have on the audience?

[1] Dean Leffingwell and Don Widrig, *Managing Software Requirements: A Use Case Approach* (Boston, MA: Addison-Wesley, 2003).

For best effect, you should combine emphasis of words with volume and tonal variation and supplement it with appropriate body language like movement.

19.1.3 Pace

Pace refers to how fast you speak. In general, in many cases, higher the pace of speech, the more persuasive it is. Higher pace gives an aura of confidence for the speaker but also gives less opportunity for the audience to intervene (see Snapshot 19.2). The pace with which you speak is decided by several factors.

Your passion in the subject: In general, more your passion in the subject matter of communication, higher your pace is likely to be. When you are passionate about what you speak, your internal energy levels tend to be higher and these invariably show up in the pace of the presentation.

Speed at which you think: This is a corollary to the first point. You are generally passionate about subjects on which you have command. And, when you possess that command and depth, you tend to think fast. Your speed of speech tries to catch up with your speed of thought. But it is never going to be really possible, as in general we tend to think 2 to 3 times faster than we speak. Just like peripherals cannot fully catch up with the CPU speed of a computer, one can never fully match the speed of talking with the speed of thinking.

Physical energy you possess: Speaking fast requires more energy than speaking at a slower pace. Some people possess indefatigable energy and can speak really fast for hours. There may be parts of a talk that would require you to talk fast (and loudly) to indicate emphasis. Make sure you know your energy reserves and allocate sufficient energy for such parts without expending all of it.

Your empathy towards the audience: While you may be a whiz kid in your subject matter, you should realize your audience may not be so. Similarly, the audience may not share your levels of enthusiasm on the subject matter. In communication, it is always good to empathize with the audience and accordingly pace your communication.

Cultural background: Some cultures and languages naturally favour a higher (or lower) pace of talking. For example, people from South India have a tendency to speak English faster than native English speakers like the British and the Americans.

Snapshot 19.2

What is a 'good pace' to use?

Well, there is no magic answer for this. Most speakers average about 120 to 180 words per minute. But this is not a hard and fast rule. For example, Franklin Roosevelt spoke at about 110 words per minute, while John F. Kennedy would race at about 180 words per minute! In general, a faster pace gives less time for the audience's mind to wander. Studies have shown that a higher pace while speaking generally excites the audience more.

The real issue is not whether you speak slow or fast, but how you use pace to communicate a message effectively. Some tips in this regard:

- Vary the speed. When you want to energize the audience, go on a faster pace; when you want to create an air of anticipation or suspense, you can slow down.
- Synchronize the pace with other elements of vocal variety like pitch, volume, etc. as well as with other channels of communication like body language and visual aids.
- Keep your antenna open about how the audience is reacting to your pace and accordingly modify it

19.1.4 Pitch

Pitch refers to how shrill your voice is – the baseline frequency of your voice. The pitch of your voice is dictated by the thickness and length of your vocal chords. Each of our voices has some limits within which we can 'stretch' them. Too much of stretching will be physically painful for the speaker and may be jarring for the listener. On the other hand, if we don't stretch our voices at all, it would become monotonous.

When we are under stress, our voice generally becomes shriller. That does not mean we should try to fake confidence by using a low pitched voice. What is important is for each of us to recognize our natural boundaries and provide variation within these boundaries, sufficient enough to be interesting, but not excessive enough to cause strain.

Sometimes the use of an extremely unnatural pitch, combined with high volume can produce good emphasis. Suppose you are showing the effect of electric shock in a presentation. You may display this by extending your index finger like the ET and shouting 'yikes' in high pitch and volume.

19.1.5 Volume

Volume refers to the loudness with which you speak. Some people habitually speak so loud that you wish you had a remote control button for controlling their volume! At the other extreme are people who talk so softly that they can barely be heard even when you sit close to them. To be effective you need to strike a balance (see Box 19.1).

Volume goes in tandem with other parameters like speed, pitch, and articulation. When you speak with high speed, you will generally tend to speak in a louder volume. Talking in high pitch and high volume may drain your resources fast. When you don't articulate well (like words blending into one another), it lowers the volume.

Volume can be varied to emphasize key points and to show gradation. For example, when you want to compare three different items, you can say, 'The first one is small, the second is bigger and the third is the biggest.' (The bigger fonts indicating louder volume). You can further combine this with synchronized body language to gain better effect.

> **Box 19.1**
>
> **Tips for Controlling the Volume**
>
> - Be cognizant of the environment. For example, if you are in a small room, speaking too loudly would be very irritating.
> - When you use a microphone, make sure you don't yell into it. Also, don't keep the mike so close to your mouth that it looks like you are ready to chew it.
> - Vary volume for effectiveness. Both loud volume and poignant silence can be very effective when used judiciously.

19.1.6 Pauses and Fillers

A good presentation should not be a continuous outpouring of words without any gaps. Periodic pauses during a presentation are essential. These enable you to recover your breath and also enable the audience to reflect on what you have said. The old adage 'silence speaks louder than words' is indeed quite true!

A pause can bring in a certain element of suspense and anticipation. If you remember seeing the results of the final round of any reality TV show the announcer would say 'the second runner up is...', then there would be a pause, some suspenseful music would be played (of course, in the real world, you cannot always have accompanying music!) and then ta da... the name would be announced. And when the first runner up (and hence, the winner) are to be announced, the pause is even longer! A pause in this case increases anticipation.

A pause can also be used for emphasis and better comprehension. You can say, 'I will present to you some important reasons for success of a business—you need sufficient finances, a strong management team and a talented workforce. But above all this, there is a very important success factor and that is (pause)... *a great and high quality product*'. The pause emphasizes that what is following (viz. the product) is the most important part. You can further highlight the effect of the pause by uttering the phrase in a higher volume and on a higher pitch.

A pause can also be used to separate out distinct parts of a presentation and to indicate that you are changing directions. For example, after presenting the technical details of a product, you can pause (may be sip some water), and then continue by saying, 'okay, we have finished with the technical details of the product, let us now look at the pricing options available.'

A pause can also give an opportunity for the audience to reflect on what you said and ask questions. This will engage the audience more, instead of making them hear (not listen to) a monologue from you.

A pause can also be used by you, the speaker, to regain your self-composure and thoughts in the event you are rattled by some questions from the audience. You can use this opportunity to collect your thoughts, sip some water, restore your energy and get back into action. And finally, a pause is the right opportunity for you (and the audience) to catch your breath, physically relax a bit and change one's posture.

But too much of pause can also be dangerous. This may be construed as the lack of confidence or lack of knowledge on the part of the speaker and that you are faltering. Some people try to cover up such long pauses with what are called fillers—the 'ah's, or 'umm's. Some even use words like 'and', 'of course' 'you know' and so on as fillers. When there are too many fillers in a presentation, it not only wastes time, but also distracts the audience.

Snapshot 19.3

An Example When Silence Speaks Louder Than Any Words...
Look up Steve Jobs' launch of the Macintosh in 1984. In total darkness when floodlights are focused on him, he walks to a bag that contains the Macintosh and in total silence he opens the bag and takes the Mac out. The suspense that rents the air, and the subsequent cheering provide a great example of the effect of a silence that is planned and executed to perfection.

"It was a good speech alright, but lacked a bit of vocal variety"

Fig. 19.1

19.2 How Do I Improve the Effectiveness of the Vocal Channel

Can we really improve our voice? Isn't voice a God-given gift that you either have or don't have? While we cannot change our voice per se (just like we cannot change the way we look), it is certainly possible to make the best use of what we have got, and what is even more important, improve the effectiveness of how we use our voice to get the message across.

We believe that vocal variety, like unadulterated innocence, is something that we are all born with as children and somehow lose gradually as we grow older. Do you remember how you said 'Baa Baa Black Sheep, Have You Any Wool....'? Did you say this in a monotone or did you go up and down like a sinusoidal curve? One of the best ways to cultivate good vocal variety is to awaken the child in you; spend some time and try to read a nursery rhyme or a kid's story book introducing a lot of vocal variety to show emphasis, emotion and variation. And, if you do it with your children, you may enjoy it even more! This may get you out of any inhibitions you may have to harness your vocal variety.

Speaking—especially with varying volumes, pitch, and so on—requires a lot of physical energy and good coordination between your speaking and breathing organs—lungs , vocal chords, jaws, etc. Doing some breathing exercises ahead of a speech would be worthwhile. Also, staying fit by avoiding not-so-healthy food (at least the day before a presentation and on the day of a presentation) would be useful.

Your throat may dry up during a speech. It would be useful to take periodic sips of water during your speech. You can integrate such mini-breaks with intentional pauses after asking the audience some question so that you can also use this to create an air of suspense.

19.3 In Summary

All the above can be summarized by the following.

> Be physically fit before and during the presentation.

Effective use of vocal variety requires a lot of practice. One way is to record your speech and listen to it again and again. In the old days, we would use tape recorders. With the ubiquitous cell phones mostly coming with features like voice recorders and video recording, the recording is a lot more high fidelity. Since vocal variety has to integrate with body language and other facets of communication, you can go one step further and video-record your presentation and see it. (In the old days when we had to see how we looked making a presentation, we used to stand in front of a mirror and practice.) All this can be summarized as:

> Practises, record, review, repeat and improve.

The previous step was about self feedback. You can also get feedback from your friends. If they have the time and willingness and are prepared to listen to you and give you feedback on how they feel about your voice, it would help you immensely. It is one thing for you to believe your vocal variety is good, but it is even better if someone else can give you constructive feedback.

Take feedback and act on it

As in other aspects of communications, variety is the key to effectiveness. You have to deploy variety in volume, pitch, pauses, emphasis and articulation. The variety should be within a reasonable range that your physical system can withstand naturally and should not become too predictable for the audience.

Variety is the key

Finally, the different aspects of vocal variety we considered in this chapter should work in unison with and synchronize with the other elements of communication like body language (discussed in the previous chapter) and visual aids (to be discussed in the next chapter). All these should work together in a harmonious way much like the different players of an orchestra jive together in a symphony. Remember, you are not merely making a presentation or a formal communication—you are performing!

Synchronize, synthesize and orchestrate all the elements.

"Wonder how they manage to communicate so well. They don't even use a powerful communication tool like the continuous annoying barking."

Fig. 19.2

20

Visual Aids

"'If your pictures aren't good enough, you aren't close enough.'"
–Robert Capa

Visual aids are things extraneous to the speaker that are visual and are used to enhance the effectiveness of the message. Visual aids act in consonance with the speaker, his body language, vocal variety and all the other elements discussed in earlier chapters. Visual aids include, but are not restricted to, white (black) boards, flip charts, posters, web sites, presentation materials (such as PowerPoint slides), models, working prototypes and so on.

Visual aids serve the following purposes:

They act as a reminder to the presenter not to miss the key points: Visual aids lead the presenter through the presentation. They give cues for sequencing the presentation so that the presentation proceeds in a logical (and planned) sequence.

They leave an impression on the audience as they get visual input: As we have seen before, the visual channel is the most powerful way of getting through to the audience. When a speaker uses visual aids, they act as significant reinforcement to the vocal and the verbal channel. Visual aids enhance the recall of a message by the audience.

They can incorporate transitions, graphics and other multimedia elements for added emphasis: A PowerPoint presentation for example can include effective graphics and multimedia effects to drive home key points. For example, to show sales rising over the years, a graph with the value of each year coming up one by one can convey a lot more information than any words.

They can be left behind as handouts with the audience for further reference: Copies of a presentation can be left behind with the audience so that these copies can be referred to as needed in future, thereby providing more opportunities to reinforce the message.

What visual aids are NOT meant to be:

They are not supposed to replace the speaker: Visual aids are just that: aids to the speaker. They are not meant to steal the thunder from the speaker. Visual aids cannot and should not replace the speaker. That is why, the same PowerPoint presentation given by two different people look as different as day and night.

They are not meant to be 'read aloud verbatim': Since the visual aids do not replace the speaker, it follows that the visual aids should not contain each and every word that the speaker is going to utter. They should only contain pointers that trigger or prompt the full presentation.

In the above discussion, we have tacitly assumed that visual aids mean things like transparencies, foils, canned presentations and so on. As mentioned earlier, visual aids can also be working models or demonstration prototypes of devices shown to the audience. For our discussion, we would only consider the first type and not discuss working models or prototypes.

20.1 Types of Visual Aids

There are various types of visual aids. These fall into two categories: prompted, interactive visual aids and pre-canned presentations.

Using prompted, interactive visual aids is appropriate to give an impromptu feeling to your presentation when you want to develop the entire storyline as you go along. Black (white) boards, flip charts and overhead transparencies are the common types of visual aids in this category. In each of these, the presenter writes on the board or chart or the foil during the presentation. The advantages that these media bring to the table are:

- They have a real-time, 'developing' feel to them and therefore present an opportunity for being more flexible and spontaneous than canned presentations.
- Since the presenter has to write on the media, it can slow down the presenter and give the audience more time to understand the presentation.
- These may leave a permanent record of the presentation and the direction in which the presentation went.
- Some of the 'low-tech' options like white board and flip charts would not get derailed because of power cuts and such infrastructural glitches.

Some of the disadvantages of this type of media are:

- Since no canned presentation is used, it is easy to forget some of the key points.
- Since the presentation is interactive by design, it is easy to get sidetracked .
- In the case of white boards and flip charts, the presenter would have to turn his or her back to the audience to write and during this time, he or she loses valuable chances of establishing eye contact and opportunities to watch and respond to the audience's body language.
- In the case of writing on an overhead foil, the presenter's eyes are obstructed by the glare of the projector and the presenter also obstructs the projection onto the screen. Anyway, this media is not much in vogue today, being replaced by a computer connected to projection equipment.

Most people today use pre-canned presentations as visual aids. PowerPoint, Flash and web pages are the most common types of tools used. Of these, we will focus only on PowerPoint in this chapter since a large percentage of presentations made by people use PowerPoint.

The next section focuses on the various aspects of PowerPoint. We don't intend this be a user's guide on PowerPoint. Rather, we have tried to encapsulate a few basic tips that we have found effective while using the software and have also tried to present a few common pitfalls that we have seen people falling prey to. We have also consciously stayed clear of giving operational instructions (e.g., menu options and actual key strokes) as these can change from one version to another.

20.2 PowerPoint Components

20.2.1 Slides

PowerPoint organizes a presentation into a series of slides. Each slide presents a unit of information and can act as an anchor for other slides. We can include multimedia content as well as information from other applications. In order to emphasize various points, we can further use animation and transitions of objects within a slide.

There are different formats for a slide:

Pure Text

Such a slide will have only text, usually in large fonts. Typically these may be used for emphasis and such text is usually self explanatory (see Figure 20.1). It is also common to use Word Art to spruce up the appearance of the text.

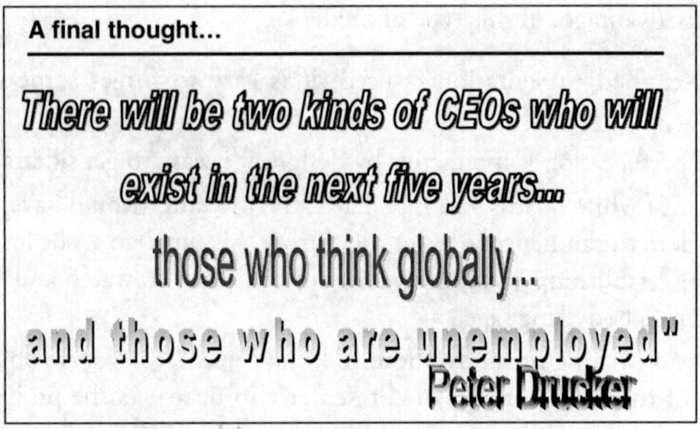

Fig. 20.1 *An example of a pure text slide*

Bulleted Text

A bulleted text would have a series of bullets; each bullet is a specific point or topic of the presentation that could be expanded in subsequent slides. You could have single level bullets or multi-level bullets. Typically, single level bulleted slides are used as agenda slides or to highlight the major points. The next level of bullets serves as explanations for the major bullet under which they come (see Box 20.1).

Box 20.1

Some General Tips About Using Bulleted Slides

- **Make sure there are no more than five bullets in a slide.** More numbers of bullets mean that there are too many points for the audience to remember. Psychologists have pointed out that the human brain can absorb 'seven plus or minus two' points at any time. We would be conservative and stick to the minus two option. When there are a large number of bullets in a slide, you cannot control what the audience chooses to absorb and chooses to ignore. (See Figure 20.4) Besides, as you increase the number of points or bullets, the font size decreases and this reduces readability.
- **Use fairly large font size and a readable font for bulleted items—e.g.,** Arial, 25. Since these are the major points the audience should take away, it makes sense to etch them clearly into the audience' visual memory.
- **Don't use more than two levels of bullets.** When you use more than two levels of bullets, the font size decreases and also, the focus gets diluted. When you have three levels of bullets, the chances are that the lower levels are details that probably warrant separate slides.

(Continued)

Box 20.1 *(Continued)*

- **Avoid putting full sentences as bullets.** The bullets are meant to be lead-ins for the speaker to make his points and not meant to be the very points to be made, presented in their entirety. If the bullets contain full sentences, the speaker may tend to read the entire sentence and the value addition that the speaker provides will be considerably reduced (see Figure 20.5).
- **Use bullets effectively with transitions.** We will discuss this point in more detail later in this chapter.

You will notice that the list in Box 20.1 is itself a bulleted list. It contains five bullets. What is appearing in bold is the bullet, while the rest are explanations that can be provided by the speaker, which would not appear as a part of bulleted text in a slide (see Figures 20.2 and 20.3).

Objectives of the session

- Identify the common "Great divides" between project groups and quality group
- Address how quality group can overcome these great divides
- Highlight how quality can be a powerful change agent in organizational excellence
- Leave you with litmus tests on whether "Quality"is moving in the right direction

Fig. 20.2 *An example of single level bulleted slide*

What are the types of maintenance?

- Corrective maintenance
  - Bug fixes
  - Enhancements...
- Adaptive maintenance
  - Porting
  - New versions of OS, database...
- Preventive maintenance
  - Database administration
  - OS tuning...

Fig. 20.3 *An example of multi-level bulleted slide*

System details

- The system has:
  - 25 Tables
  - 274 Columns
  - Average of 96 bytes per row
  - 12 Views
  - 14 Indices
  - 45 Synonyms
  - 3 Clusters
  - Distributed across three systems
  - Across two locations
  - Requiring no extra hardware
  - Runs as is
  - Can be maintained

Fig. 20.4 *An example of an ineffective slide with too many bullet points*

System design details

- The system design calls for having 25 tables, 12 views and 14 indices.
- With this, we would be able to meet all the current and future needs.
- You will also be able to run this in the current system
- Configuration that you have in your site. Hence there is no extra cost

Fig. 20.5 *An example of an ineffective slide with full text*

20.2.2 Graphics

Graphics can be a mix of graphs, trend charts, pictures, cartoons and multi-media. True to the old adage 'a picture is worth a thousand words', it makes a lot of sense to put in as many graphics as possible in a presentation (see Box 20.2). Some of the common uses of graphics are:

Graphs and Trend Charts: These can be used to pictorially present some of the results. These are effective in situations where details like sales figures, profitability analysis, competitive analysis, category distribution, root cause analysis and so on, have to be presented (see Figure 20.6).

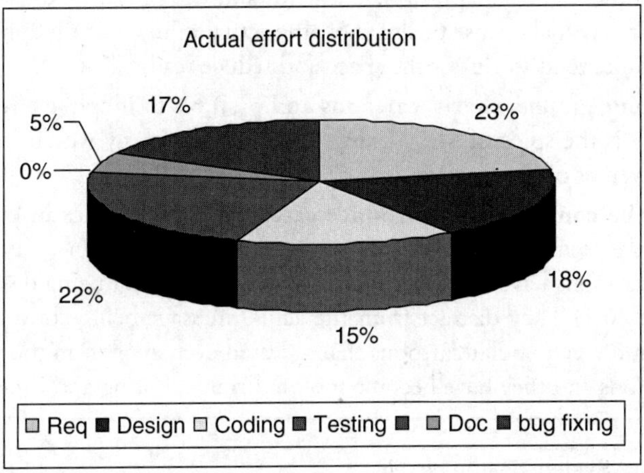

Fig. 20.6 *A graph showing percentage of errors in different phases*

Pictures and Cartoons: These are very effective in providing some lighter moments and variety. An appropriate cartoon can get the message across in a more effective way than pure text and it will also have a higher retention and recall value in the minds of the audience.

Box 20.2

Some General Tips About Using Graphics

- **Be conscious of colour contrast.** If, for example, you want to compare two areas of a graph, it makes sense to say 'compare the blue area and red area' rather than say 'compare the light blue area with the dark blue area'. Also, make sure that there is colour contrast not only within the graph, but also with the background. Sometimes the projection equipment distorts the true colours on the slides; hence it is a good idea to see how the colours look through the projection equipment.
- **Ensure that the graph is reasonably large.** This will increase the readability of the graph. When the graphs are too tiny, their purpose is lost. If you are using legends or titles, choose a reasonably sized font.

(Continued)

Box 20.1 *(Continued)*

- **Make sure there are appropriate legends and titles.** You want to emphasize the fact that the revenues and profits are going up while the expenses are going down. Putting appropriate legends and titles in the graph would help a lot. It may make sense to also show the actual values in the graph, but these sometimes tend to clutter the space and reduce readability.
- **Combine graphs, charts, cartoons and pictures to increase effectiveness.** Variety is the spice of life. Mixing these up judiciously would increase the effectiveness of the message.
- **Don't be compelled to introduce cartoons and graphics in every slide.** We have seen presentations where people use cartoons in every slide and these cartoons have absolutely no relevance to the point being discussed.(see Figure 20.7) They distract from the actual message being conveyed. There are some very popular cartoons that are used ever so often in too many presentations and they have become too predictable, boring and irrelevant.

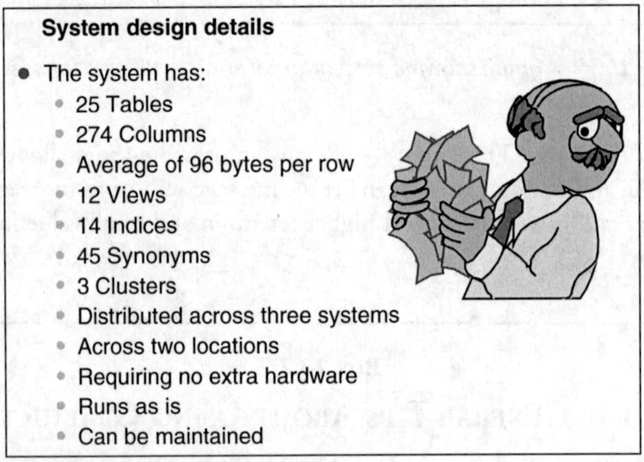

Fig. 20.7 *An example of an ineffective slide, with irrelevant clip art*

20.2.3 Use of Transitions and Animations

Transitions and animation will help you direct the audience to focus on one point or object at a time, without getting diverted (see Box 20.3).

When you have bulleted texts or objects (like cartoons, graphs, shapes, etc.) in a slide, you can make the bullets or objects appear one at a time. After you finish explaining the first point, you can press a key and the second bullet (point) would appear on the screen and so on. PowerPoint provides several ways to effectively use transitions.

- In case of multi-level bullets, you can control the *sub-levels* that appear together: make all the sub-levels of a bullet appear together or make the sub-bullets appear one by one. It depends on what you want to emphasize.
- You can control the *direction* from which the bullet or object appears. For example, you can make it come from top, bottom, left, right or from a diagonal direction.
- You can control the *pace* with which the bullet or object comes in. This is especially useful for emphasis. For example, if you want a tortoise and a hare to appear on the screen, you can make the hare come in really fast and the tortoise can come in slowly.
- You can add *special effects* for transition. For example, you can make the text or object come in with a diamond pattern, checkerboard, box, etc. You can further become very creative and use options like 'Box In', 'Box Out', etc.

As an example, consider Figure 20.8 that shows the evolution of global teams. You can use transitions and show one stage (the picture and the description) come up first, then the arrow would appear and then the next stage would come in. This will make the audience focus on what you say about each stage instead of getting distracted by the fourth stage when you are talking about the first one.

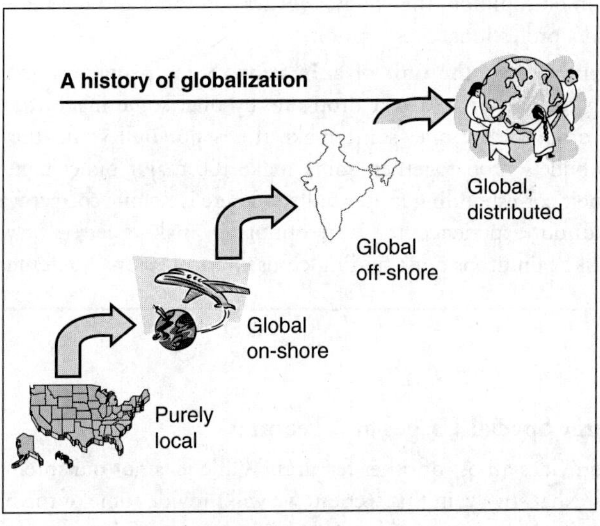

Fig. 20.8 *Transitions in slides*

Box 20.3

Some General Tips About Using Transitions and Animations

- **If you have included transitions and animations, make sure you utilize them.** We have seen presenters who make each bullet appear with a transition (key stroke). But they will put on that slide and then hit the enter key five times, make all the bullets appear on the screen and then explain *all of them* point by point! The speaker might as well have had no animation in the first place!
- **Don't have too many transitions.** Sometimes you may forget to hit the enter key. You may be thinking ahead of yourself and not notice what is on the screen. In this case, the animation may in fact have a negative or adverse impact.
- **Be aware of physical limitations.** If you are going to be on a podium with the laptop at one corner and you are moving around the podium, then having a transition that requires you to hit a key on the keyboard or click a mouse would require you to move back and forth. This may be very distracting. One option is to see if you can use a remote control.
- **Don't use too many special effects.** PowerPoint provides a large number of special effects like spinning, fading in, fading out and so on. While these are flashy, in our opinion, they do not always add value and tend to look out of place in a professional presentation.
- **Carefully choose the unit of animation.** Some people use the option of making each letter in a text drop one by one; some make the individual words drop one by one; some make the major bullet and the associated minor bullets drop together; some make the major bullet come first and then their corresponding minor bullets. There is no one correct way of using these. In our experience, the jazzy options of making letters or words drop down like rain drops don't find much use in professional presentations.

20.2.4 Some Special Usages and Features

PowerPoint provides a host of other features. While it is not our intent to cover all these features exhaustively, in this section, we will provide some of the novel ways in which certain elements can be used and also discuss some of the not-so-effective ways of using PowerPoint. Since most of these are best illustrated by looking at the actual slides, we will be including slides for these in the book's Web site.

Use of Icons and Pictures for Transitions

In the previous section, we discussed how to use single-level and multi-level bullets to introduce flow and structure into the presentation. These are slides that use pure text. As an example, suppose you are going to present on the various functions served by the offices in San Francisco, London and Bangalore, you could put together a bulleted list like the one given in Figure 20.2. An alternative approach could be to show a world map. When the mouse is clicked on San Francisco, the functions of that office can be shown as a pop-up. Similarly, when the mouse is clicked on Bangalore, the functions of that office can be shown as a pop-up. Since this approach combines graphics and transitions, it is likely to leave a better impact on the audience.

Use of Action Buttons

PowerPoint provides a set of action buttons that can be used to control the movement through the various slides. For example, each slide can have a next, previous, first and home buttons. The next and previous buttons when clicked, can take you to the next or previous slide. The home button can be the transition to the first slide of the presentation, while the first could make the transition to the first slide of a given set. Taking the previous example of the multi-location organization, supposing for each of the locations you need three slides of text to describe it, then in each of the three slides, you can put in the action buttons next, previous, first and home. Next will take the presentation to the next slide of the presentation (i.e., for that location), except for the third slide, where next is disabled. Similarly, the previous button from Slide 3 will take the presentation to Slide 2 and from Slide 2 to Slide 1 (all for that location). The previous button for the first slide is disabled. From any slide, home will take you to the very first slide of the presentation, while first would take you to the world map.

Use of Embedded Objects

Sometimes you may want to show an Excel spreadsheet or a Word document or some other object within a presentation. You can embed such an object within the presentation

Use of Tables

In general, we feel that tables are not very effective when used in PowerPoint, except when they are very small. The size of the cells and the space available reduce readability. It is visually far more appealing to link the slide to a table in Word or Excel and show those in full screen and then jump back to the original screen.

20.3 In Summary

First of all, choose the right type of visual aid to use for a given occasion. Flip charts and white boards may be the most appropriate for interactive communication while PowerPoint is more suitable for a structured presentation.

Choosing the right visual aid is more important than rightly using a visual aid.

While there are a lot of interesting features in PowerPoint, choosing what you need for the given situation is very vital. For example, while graphs may be the most obvious choice when you are projecting sales figures, photographs and animation may be most effective when you are trying to demonstrate the working of a product model.

Choose which features you need, don't just try to use all the features of PowerPoint!

As in other aspects of communication, variety is the key to the effectiveness of using visual aids. Your visual aids should have a mix of graphs, pictures, animation, transitions and bulleted lists.

Variety is the key!

Finally, visual aids like PowerPoint, present a lot of opportunities to synergize with the other communication elements like vocal variety, body language, etc. As we said in an earlier chapter,

Synchronize, synthesize and orchestrate all the elements.

Now that we have seen all the individual elements that aid communication, it is time to explore how all these work in unison—the topic for the next chapter.

21

Putting It All Together

"The whole is greater than the sum of its parts."

–Unknown

So far, we have looked at each of the components of communication in isolation. One common message that the reader would have observed is that we have constantly emphasized that these elements should be used together, in perfect synchronization and in an integrated manner. In this chapter, we will see how we can integrate these various elements together, to make an effective presentation.

If we were to use a sports metaphor, in the earlier chapters you saw the various parts of playing tennis–like forehand, backhand, serve, volley, etc. But in a real tennis match, you have to use all of these, integrating them and using them as demanded by the situation. As you grow from learning the building blocks to being a real player and then a champion, you will find that you will achieve this integration in a very seamless way and it will become second nature to you.

Let us look at this from another angle. In each of the elements of communication that we have discussed so far, we have seen various enabling components. For example, for body language we have eye contact, movement, posture, gestures, use of hands and so on. For vocal variety, we have pitch, modulation, volume, etc. If you consider a symphony orchestra, it has various instruments like the violin, flute and so on. Not just that, there will be several violinists and flautists. Not only will the individual violinists and flautists have to synch up among their own groups, they will all have to synch up together to make music. This then, is the topic for this chapter.

We have represented the process of integration and synchronization of the various components of communication by the acronym OPERA, extending our musical analogy from the previous paragraph.

O → Organizing
P → Putting it together
E → Embellishing
R → Rehearsing
A → Actualization

Let us look into each of these aspects in each of the subsequent sections.

"Sir, If only you can improve your body language, make eye contacts with the audience, modulate your voice a bit more, show more colorful slides and introduce a bit of humour, your speech will be fantastic".

Fig. 21.1

21.1 ORGANIZING

When you make a presentation, you may want the audience to go back with a few key points as take-aways from the presentation. But, each member of the audience may have different take-aways and these may be totally different from what you intended. As we have seen earlier, communication is a means to achieve a specific end. If the audience goes with a different take-away than what you aimed for, the goals of your communication may not have been achieved.

So, in essence, you must make the audience go back with what *you* want them to go back with, so that they will act in the way that *you* intended. This requires you to organize your presentation in such a way that the message you want to get across to the audience gets communicated effectively and with the right points highlighted.

Organizing a presentation is planning what you want to communicate and choosing methods of reinforcements that realize your plan. In order to make sure that the right points you want get highlighted, there is a simple but very powerful practice:

Tell them what you are going to tell them;
Tell them;
Tell them what you told them.

This organization broadly fits into the introduction—body—conclusion type of organization.

You first give an introduction of the major points you want to cover in the presentation. This is the 'tell them what you are going to tell them' part. This part sets the scene for the main body of the presentation, which is the 'tell them' part. The part in the end, the conclusion, summarizes the key take-away points from the presentation. This is the 'tell them what you told them' part. The part in the middle—the body or 'tell them' part—gives all the details and substantiating information or data for the conclusions. While you would dwell for the most part on the body of the presentation, the three parts must be designed to work in unison. Let us now see how you can make each part more effective.

21.1.1 Introduction or 'Tell Them What You are Going to Tell Them' Part

This is probably the most crucial part to draw in audience attention. It is said that in most interactions, the make or break happens within the first five minutes or less. Remember the old dictum 'first impression is the best impression'.

Your opening must serve two purposes:

- *Grab* the audience attention, so that they will continue to be in rapt attention
- Give them an outline of topics to be covered or the objectives to be achieved.

We consciously use the word *grab*. The audience should be compelled to listen to you; they should be filled with a sense of curiosity to get to the details; in short, they should be tuned in to your presentation, so that they are in a better state of mind to act according to your intentions.

How do we grab the attention of the audience? Here are some of the ways:

Take them by surprise by a most unexpected statement or expression: When Swami Vivekananda, at that time a little known preacher from India, started addressing the Parliament of Religions in the USA, he began his speech with, 'Brothers and Sisters of America'. This not only brought out his theme—universality of religion—but it also shook the audience to make them realize his power.

Show and (not necessarily) tell! Sometimes just displaying an object at the beginning in a most dramatic way in which one can immediately capture audience attention. The best example is Steve Jobs' launch of the Macintosh in 1984. He opens up the bag, puts the Macintosh out and it talks, 'Hello, this is Macintosh!' At a time when multimedia in computers was restricted to blinking cursors and a beep, this introduction captured audience attention in an instant and the rest, as they say, is history.

Use a quotation, a short story or a graphic illustration: If you are discussing a new product idea, you can use a quotation from a subject matter expert to present the technology trends and then use this to link up why the product idea makes sense. You can also corroborate this with a graph that shows the increase in user base for the technology area. A bit of topical humour can give you a nice opening, if done perfectly. Also, if you get greedy for attention, you can start off your presentation by showing a snazzy video.

There have been some totally ineffective openings that people sometimes use like the following:

- An inappropriate joke: Some people consider that in order for a presentation to be effective, there is a quota of jokes to be met!
- An apologetic statement that sounds defeatist and goes against the message of the topic being presented.
- A grandfatherly statement like, 'Did you apply yourself in this situation and stop to think . . .'
- A seemingly never-ending story going into gory details that are totally irrelevant to the topic in hand.

21.1.2 Body of the Presentation: 'Tell Them'

This contains the supporting details of the presentation. When putting this together, you should consider the following:

- **Have you got your facts researched correctly?** Before putting together a presentation, it is imperative that you have your facts well researched. You should expect that someone in the audience would refute your facts. Hence you should also have the source of your data at your fingertips (preferably in the slides themselves).
- **Are you considering the preferences and biases of the audience when you are presenting?** While you do not necessarily have to play up to the audience's whims and fancies, it definitely helps a great deal to know in advance about their reservations and biases—and technical and educational background. (See Chapter 15 on audience analysis and objectives of communication.) For example, if you are in a group which fervently supports alternative sources of energy, you should be cognizant (and respectful) of their viewpoints and sensibilities, instead of being seen as indifferent to the energy debate.

- **Have you considered the possible objections the audience may have for your point of view?** Anticipate questions and interjections from the audience and prepare appropriate responses. When appropriate, pre-empt such objections by including them (and your responses) in your presentation itself.
- **Have you sequenced the body in an appropriate manner?** The sequencing of the presentation of facts has a bearing on how the audience appreciates the facts. You should use the right level of abstraction for the audience and present the data in the right sequence. For example, if you are giving three alternative design solutions, one way to organize them would be to take each alternative and describe its characteristics and pros and cons. After presenting the three alternatives, you can summarize their relative merits and demerits.
- **Have you planned enough time for the entire presentation?** Timing is, of course, crucial. When sufficient time has not been planned for a presentation, it would indicate that not enough thought has gone into organizing the presentation. Oftentimes, this would end in a situation where not-so-important points are dwelt upon for extraordinary and unjustified length, while the important ones are either omitted or rushed through in the end.
- **Have you provided sufficient reinforcement for the key points that you want the audience to take away?** True to George Orwell's dictum, 'All are equal, but some are more equal than others', the most important points of a presentation need extra emphasis. These have to be reinforced, reemphasized and augmented by extra channels of communication. You might want to include some multimedia, graphs or demos to drive home such points.

If you are using PowerPoint slides as a visual aid, then by using an agenda slide and going from the agenda slide to each of the major points and then by returning back to the agenda slide by using action buttons (see Chapter 20), you can seamlessly link the introduction to the body.

21.1.3 Conclusion—'Tell Them What You Told Them'

This is the final part of the presentation. The audience has been sitting through the presentation and is ready to leave. You are approaching the final minutes of the presentation. Their thoughts are beginning to wander to their next meeting or task. You can be assured that they will not remember what your presentation said, much less what the third point of the thirty seventh slide of the presentation (where you have tucked away a very important point of the presentation) mentioned. You have to now make sure that they walk away from the room with the top points *you* want them to remember. Summarize the presentation highlighting not more than five, preferably exactly three, points that you want the audience to take away. These points:

- Should be the real vital summary of the presentation; they need not contain all the gory details
- Should take no more than about three to five minutes
- Should make the audience converge to your point of view
- Should preferably be visual and appealing (e.g., a picture or a model or a graph)
- Should call for action, guiding the audience to take the action you had intended them to take
- Should lead into the question/answer session naturally.

If you are using PowerPoint, it is a good idea to leave the summary slide on the screen during the question and answer session. This would enable stronger recall as this makes the points seep into visual memory for a long time. Some ineffective presenters have a trite final slide which says 'thank you' (or shows a pair of hands clapping!). Such concluding slides serve no purpose.

A common pitfall found in presenters is that they get so absorbed in the details of the body of the presentation that suddenly they find they are running out of time and hence run through the conclusion and summary in a great hurry. Just five minutes before the allotted time is over, they find they are on the 43rd slide out of 60. In a frenzy they keep going through the slides and either don't get to the conclusion slide at all or just skip that also. The result? It leaves the audience with the feeling that the presenter has come completely unprepared and is not clear of the message he or she wants to leave behind. This results in an orphaned communication, where the follow through is simply non-existent or not in a direction the speaker intended.

21.2 Putting It Together

Once you have your basic thoughts and the visual aids ready, it is then the time to put it all together.

- If the presentation links to other spreadsheets or documents or files, ensure they are all available in the proper directories.
- Make sure you go through the entire presentation at least once to ensure that there are no ugly 'file not found' message trying to access a non-existent web page.
- If there are any supporting documents or handouts that are needed for the presentation, this is the time to start assembling them. Make sure all the things you need for the presentation are available in one place.
- If copies have to be made, make sure you have sufficient copies made of whatever you need to hand over to audience. If you decide to give printouts of the

slides, it is better to defer this printing and copying till you have gone through all the rehearsal and modifications.

- If any brochure or promotional material needs to be given, make sure they are available.
- Compile a list of potential audience questions and objections. Highlight a few interesting ones in the presentation itself.

21.3 EMBELLISHING

Since you have the crux of all you want to present ready, now is the time to add the bells and whistles to the presentation to make it ready for prime time. Some common things to look for at this time are:

- Make sure you spell check every document and presentation. Typos in a presentation or document don't speak highly of your attention to detail and leave a poor impression in the minds of the audience. And, trust us, these stand out like sore thumbs and people—especially at the senior management level—spot these very quickly!
- Make sure you have the logos and any legal verbiage properly put in. These may include things like copyright notices, credits, acknowledgement of sources and so on.
- Try the presentation on the projection equipment and ensure that the colour combination, background, etc. are pleasing to the eyes and are readable. If the presentation is in a large auditorium, ensure that these are OK even at the far end of the auditorium. Check the microphone and the audio set up for any last minute glitches.
- If required, run the presentation and associated documents through the legal department to obtain any clearances.

21.4 REHEARSING

We have highlighted the importance of constant practice earlier in this book. Now that the entire presentation is ready, it is time to practice, practice and practice. For very important and crucial presentations, it is absolutely essential to rehearse under conditions as close to real-life as possible. This may not always be possible. Some of the practical techniques to rehearse are as follows:

- See yourself making the presentation in a full length mirror. This may give you first impressions and an outsider's view of your own presentation. While this is a good first step, this alone would not suffice as you may not be able to play it back and see it again and again nor would you be able to show this to your friends and get their feedback.

- Make a video recording of yourself making the presentation and watch it several times. See which movements you feel are natural, which ones are distracting. Listen to when your voice is showing proper emotion and emphasis. Judge whether the body language, voice and the visual aids are reinforcing each other.
- Make the presentation to a group of your colleagues and friends and ask them to give a critical and unbiased opinion. You should also ask them to play the devil's advocate by making them ask difficult questions.

The process of rehearsing is likely to shed some light on the organization, content and rendering of your presentation. Hence, based on the rehearsing, be prepared to iterate through the earlier steps—the organizing, the putting it together and the embellishing parts. One word of caution: do not try to be an over-perfectionist and keep on making changes. You should freeze a time to complete the presentation and make no further changes. Else, you will continue to make changes beyond the point of diminishing returns. And you will find that the final presentation has typos and errors that you forgot to check after some last minute changes.

21.5 Actualization: Get over Nervousness and Go for It!

After all the rehearsal and fine tuning, it is finally show time! Most of what we discussed in Chapter 16 on preparing for communication is directly applicable. Much as you have prepared and visualized the big moment, you are sure to have butterflies in your stomach. The bigger the occasion, larger is the likelihood of being nervous.

Is it okay to be nervous? *The Wall Street Journal* pointed out that public speaking was the number 1 fear in the USA—even the fear of death was ranked number 2! So, it is indeed perfectly standardize to be nervous! In fact, without any nervousness, our biological system would simply not rise to the big occasion. Nervousness keeps adrenalin flowing and gives you the psychological energy. Ironically, you need some of this 'nervous energy' not to be nervous during a presentation!

How can I reduce nervousness? While you cannot (and should not) completely eliminate nervousness, it would certainly make sense to reduce *unnecessary* nervousness. Most of the nervousness comes from fears such as, 'Will I look like a fool in front of the audience?', 'Will they ask questions I cannot answer?', 'How am I going to present to someone who may know more than I know?', etc. Some ways to reduce such fears and nervousness are:

- Constantly practice, do a thorough audience analysis and clearly understand your objectives of communication.
- Understand the big picture, know your role in it and take pride in it

- Don't try to be a perfectionist. Don't feel bad that you forgot the third point when you are talking about the seventh point—the audience would not know you had missed the third point unless you confessed to them
- Don't take public speaking (or any failure thereof) as a reflection of your actual self worth—there is more to life than this! Once you take this pressure off your chest, you will feel lighter and less nervous.

Am I nervous because I am a rookie? Believe it or not, even the most established pros do tend to become nervous. Regardless of whether it is a superstar playing in his fifth straight Wimbledon or a veteran politician making the speech of his lifetime or Wall Street's blue-eyed boy, or a CEO launching his company's latest gizmo, everyone has some nervousness during the big moment. The difference between these people and a rookie is not in how nervous they feel but how they channel their nervousness.

How can I use my nervousness for my benefit? Tap the nervous energy! If you feel your heart pumping, use the pace to add spice and energy to your presentation instead of biting your nails or fiddling around with your buttons. If you feel you are slumping down with nervousness, pep yourself up and start taking quick strides. If you are thrown an unexpected question from the audience, take a deep breath, rephrase the question and defuse the situation a bit. Just like you learnt in physics, convert nervous energy into some other form of energy that has a positive effect on your presentation.

The ultimate joy in a presentation is to actually perform it and see it going according to what you envisioned. All your hours of audience analysis, knowing your objectives, integrating body language, vocal variety and visual aids come to fruition with the presentation. Of course, you will still have to follow up on the presentation and take things to completion. This may require follow-up phone calls, emails and meetings. These will be discussed in the chapters that cover the etiquette of using these means of communication to arrive at the desired results.

21.6 Odds and Ends

In this section, we would address some of the miscellaneous topics you have to keep on mind when you are putting a presentation together.

21.6.1 How Much of This Applies to Written Communication?

Almost all of it! The principle of organizing in the form of 'tell them what you are going to tell them; tell them; tell them what you told them' very much applies to written communication. In any report you may prepare, there would be an 'abstract' section or an 'executive summary' which presents what is contained in the report, in brief. At the end of the report, there would be a 'summary/conclusions' section that summarizes the gist of the report. This is very much in line with what we have discussed for organizing a presentation.

The steps of preparation, embellishment and putting it together all apply *in toto* to written communication. In fact, in written communication, you need to prepare more as it leaves behind a record. And, as we will see later in the chapters on writing reports, proposals and other documents, getting the message across in a written communication can pose additional challenges because you don't have the benefit of other channels like vocal variety and body language. Hence the OPERA steps mentioned here has to be carried out with a lot more perfection for the written communication.

21.6.2 Should We Distribute Copies of Slides?

When you use PowerPoint slides for a presentation, should you distribute hard copies of the slides? Personally, we would not advocate giving copies of the slides ahead of time because:

- You may make changes to your slides at the last minute and this will make the printout go out of synch with the slides used.
- When you give out all the slides ahead of time, there is a tendency for the audience to look ahead to the following slides instead of focusing on the current slide.
- You may not want to leave hard copies of the slides for legal, confidentiality or other reasons.
- You may want to save some paper (and trees)

If you absolutely have to give handouts, then you can give them out after the presentation (and at least three slides per page to be kind to the environment). Alternatively, you can consider distributing the soft copies of the presentation (and ensuring they cannot modify them)

Should we stray from the prepared presentation? The answer is an emphatic 'no' unless you are a great orator or an expert in the subject matter or unless a speaker you stole your thunder by presenting your exact same content ten minutes earlier. We don't suggest that you memorize your speech verbatim, but you should try to stay on the prepared course as much as possible.

21.6.3 Potential Embarrassing Moments

We have seen it happen to others during presentations. Suddenly going blank in mid-presentation, or getting boggled by an audience question or getting into a lengthy verbal duel with someone in the audience or suddenly realizing in the middle of the presentation that it is a boring lecture that the audience is unhappy with (see Box 21.1).

Box 21.1
Some of the Most Embarrassing Moments During a Presentation

When power suddenly fails in mid-presentation or microphone dies or when audio has feedback: Pause momentarily. There will always be volunteers who would work on the problem. After a few moments, try to continue the presentation even without the electronics–unless the organizer of the presentation asks you to wait until the problem is fixed.

When you don't know the answer to an audience question: Remember that there will always be someone who will ask a clever question to which you don't know the answer. The best response is to lob praises at that person for asking an interesting question and that you will do your best to get an answer. Don't let your mind get boggled at the podium. Don't start solving the problem right there. Don't try to cover up by an answer you know is not appropriate.

Getting into a wordy duel with someone from the audience: When someone persistently argues with you, carry on the argument for some time and once it starts getting exacerbating, tell him or her you can discuss it off-line if he/she wants that.

When you go completely blank: This almost never happens in professional presentations. However, have a friend or colleague in the audience with who you rehearsed the presentation and he should give you the appropriate cues to get you back on track.

21.7 In Summary

The most important part of putting a presentation together is to remember the dictum,

> Tell them what you are going to tell them;
> Tell them;
> Tell them what you told them.

Since the steps described in this chapter are concerned with the grand finale of the presentation, hopefully leading to further fruitful action plans, the two principles we have been mentioning in the earlier chapter very much apply here, namely:

> Variety is the key—synchronize,
> synthesize and orchestrate all the elements.

The above principles would make sure that the machinery is well oiled and in synch. Your vocal variety, body language, visual aids and all the parts should work together as one unit. When you do that, you will find that

> The whole is greater than the sum of its parts.

Having looked at the basic principles of communication, we will now proceed to look at some common vehicles of communication in the next few chapters.

22

Resumé Writing

"If you call failures as experiments, you can out them in your resumé and claim them as achievements."

– Mason Cooley

Your resumé is the first gate to the heaven of getting your dream job. And there is as much stampede at this gate as on the first day of a newly released Bollywood movie with well known star cast. Studies have shown that typically, an organization gets several hundred resumés for every job opening. To handle this kind of crowd, the sentries at this gate have to display tremendous alacrity and sagacity.

Just consider the enormity of the task in hand for the recruiting organization. For every post they have to fill, they get, say, a hundred resumés. (By the way, it is pronounced *ri-zoo-may* with emphasis on the last syllable.) They would short list about ten for the first-level interviews and perhaps three for the next level of interviews, before selecting one. The biggest cut-off happens at the resumé scanning stage. And remember this as well—a person going to the interview stage gets about 20–30 minutes to demonstrate that he is fit for the job. But a resumé gets no more than 30–60 *seconds* of scanning before a decision is taken as to whether the candidate should be pushed through to the next stage or not. If you think it is very unfair on the part of the organization to evaluate your credentials on a mere one minute of cursory glance at your resumé, consider this: Even if they spend just one minute per resumé, they are expending close to 100 minutes (or a couple of hours) on scanning them! And this is only for one job. If you multiply this by the number of jobs that an organization has to fill up, you can well conclude that unless they are stringent about deciding the fate of a resumé in under a minute, they may well spend their time in scanning resumés rather than accomplishing the true objectives that the organization set forth to achieve.

So it is imperative that you, as the applicant, grab the attention of the person scanning your resumé so that he becomes interested enough to call you for the next stage. *And you should do this so that the right things catch the person's eye in under 30 seconds of glance at your resumé.*

Your resumé is not only your gate pass to go past this tough sentry, but it is also the tool that creates the first impression. You use this tool to demonstrate your professionalism, tout your achievements and most importantly make obvious the fit between your strengths and the organization's needs. Thus, a good resumé:

- Is a vehicle for crossing the first big chasm of screening
- Provides *quick* reasons for selection
- Demonstrates your professionalism
- Highlights a fit and synergy between (prospective) employer's needs and your strengths.

Fig. 22.1

22.1 Principles of Writing a Resumé

In order to achieve the above objectives, the basic tenets or principles to be kept on mind when writing a resumé can be summarized by the Five Fs:

- ***F**it*
- ***F**ocus*

- ▶ *F*uturistic
- ▶ *F*ormatted
- ▶ *F*actual

Given that the person scanning your resumé has no more than half a minute to devote to your resumé, he will only look for how relevant the resumé is to the position he is looking to fill. He should not consider you to be over (or under) qualified for the job nor of having a different set of skills than what is needed for the job. Thus, the *fit for the job* must be the top criterion you should concentrate on when you write your resumé. The resumé should be concise, to the point and should demonstrate *focus.* And of course, the focus should be on the fit for the job. To achieve this focus, you should be forward looking and provide a road map on why you feel the focus and fit are compelling. You have to list your past accomplishments as mere proofs of this *futuristic* outlook and not make it sound as if these accomplishments are laurels on which you will rest when you take up the new job. In order to achieve this futuristic focus and capture the conviction of the person scanning on the fit and the focus, the resumé needs to be *formatted* in a compelling and persuasive manner. Of course, as a matter of ethics, the resumé should be 100 per cent based on *facts* and should not make unsubstantiated or untrue claims.

As we go through each step of resumé preparation and writing phase, it is useful to keep the 5 Fs in mind.

22.2 The Process of Putting Together a Resumé

Fig. 22.2

Preparing a resumé has the following distinct steps:

Planning: In general, it is not a good idea to use a general-purpose resumé that you mass mail to all the companies. As we saw earlier the first criterion for an effective resumé is that it demonstrates the fit and synergy between your strengths and the organization's needs. In order to demonstrate this fit rightly, you don't simply start 'writing' a resumé the moment you see an opening. First, you research about the company, their business and their strengths. Ask yourself some of the following questions:

- Is the business of this company something that interests me?
- What have been the company's strengths?
- What are the technology focus areas of the company?
- What has been the recent press coverage about the company?
- Do I know anyone in the company? If so, can I talk to him to find out some more details?

The answers to these questions would enable you to identify the fit factor better. You can articulate your objectives and position your strengths and accomplishments to be directly appealing to the company's needs. This will also help you to speak confidently when you reach the interview stage.

Fortunately, the magical Internet and quick 'Googling' can help you find most of the above information. The few minutes you spend on this up front would well be worth it as it increases your chance of getting past the resumé stage and into the interview stage.

Laying out: The layout of the resumé is the next key factor. The layout should be compelling enough to highlight the right things at the very first glance. Laying out the resumé entails:

- Deciding the headings that are most relevant for the job: In the next section we would see various headings in a resumé—like objectives, accomplishments, etc. Not all would be relevant for each job. Having known the fit factor from the previous step, you can now decide which of the headings would be more appropriate.
- Sequencing the resumé giving the most important details first: For example, if you have multi-faceted experience that covers development in several technologies, you can use the knowledge about the company to decide which experiences and skills you will highlight first.
- Deciding the formatting so as to use meaningful highlights like fonts, bold, underline and so on: Deciding what to highlight and how to highlight at the outset, sharpens the focus, leads to better formatting and increases the fit.

You can choose to start with one of the readymade templates that is available in MS-Word and on the Internet and fine tune it rather than build the layout and formatting from scratch.

Filling in the content: Having got the structure and format decided, you can start filling in the content. We will go into more tips for the content to be filled up in Section 22.4, but just to highlight a few key points here:

- Do not state anything that is not true or make any tall claims that cannot be objectively verified. (Factual)
- Do not make the resumé sound like an autobiography. (Futuristic)
- Do think from the point of view of the person scanning the resumé rather than your own perspective. Whatever you write, ask the question 'Would this interest the person scanning the resumé and compel him to take me to the next stage?' (Fit and Focus)
- Do highlight the right things the resumé scanner will look for. (Formatted)

Reviewing and revising: Always review your resumé before you send it. We recommend printing out a hard copy and then reviewing as most of the alignment and formatting errors can be caught by looking at the hard copy. Pay extra attention to typos! Rest assured that these typos stick out like a sore thumb in the eyes of an experienced scanner in under thirty seconds! These typos are the most convenient excuses to reject a resumé.

22.3 The Structure and Contents of a Resumé

In general, a resumé contains the following sections:

- An objective section
- Highlights/summary
- Accomplishments or unique selling propositions
- Substantiating facts, made up of professional experience, academic achievements and other accomplishments.

An ***objectives*** section in which you highlight your career objective: This section should be full of punch and no more than a couple of lines (see Snapshot 22.1). And you can caption it 'objective', in block letters. It should create a stir in the person scanning the resumé and make him sit up with eyes wide open by sending a message to him, 'You want me as much as I want you!' The objectives should:

- Build upon the strengths you have demonstrated in your professional, academic and extra-curricular life. For example, if your objective reads 'to make a significant contribution to the important area of databases', then your accomplishments must demonstrate the basis on which you have nurtured this objective. In your interview too, you must be able to demonstrate your ability to realize this objective or vision with a lot of passion as well as positive proof.

- Have relevance in the company to which you are sending the resumé: The objective should make the prospective employer say things like 'wow!' and 'this resumé is *surely* worth pursuing'.
- Be more and more specific and cheeky/provocative as you go higher up in the career. For example, if you are applying for the post of a vice president of a software organization, your objective must not be something generic as 'to make a lasting contribution to databases', but should be something like 'to grow and head a large software product organization with independent profit center responsibilities'.

A ***highlights*** section typically follows the objective and gives a very quick overview of your career—at least those aspects that the potential employer cares about. (See Snapshot 22.2) Give it a suitable section heading like 'academic highlights or professional highlights or skills summary or computer skills' or anything else. This section should have

- A summary of your key strength areas, for example, strength in niche technology areas that the employer might be interested in.
- A demonstration of the breadth and depth of your experience (applies only if you have substantial experience).

Snapshot 22.1

Some Examples of the Objectives Section

If you are a software project manager, applying for a senior position:

To take on the responsibility of setting up and running a large product development organization, utilizing my eight years of experience demonstrated successfully in managing large projects.

If you have under two years of experience, applying for a new job:

To be a significant contributor to a high performance team in the area of open source software, building upon my strong academic career.

If you are a HR manager and looking for the post of head of HR in a large organization:

To take on lead responsibility in recruiting and nurturing people in a large organization, building upon my strengths of understanding the chemistry of people.

If you are applying for the post of process engineer in an electronics manufacturing company:

To develop new processes and applications using vacuum deposition techniques

- An affiliation with top institutions (especially applicable if you are from top brand name colleges and organizations).
- Your personal traits like teamwork, motivation and initiative that you are passionate about and proud of (which you can amply demonstrate through documented prior examples).
- A compelling unique selling point ('USP') that you have that is relevant to the potential employer.

A ***professional history or professional experience*** section that gives your employment your experience in reverse chronological order:

- Highlight only the most recent experience, especially if you have several years of experience; what you did ten years or even five years ago may not be relevant to the potential employer today.
- Among your most recent experiences, give priority to the type of experience that is relevant to the job you are applying for.
- If working in a certain organization or your affiliation to an institution that you have been part of is going to be considered valuable (for the given job), then do highlight your association with such an institution.
- Emphasize the job and role; don't put all the gory details of when you left a job, why you left a job and such.

An ***academic background*** Section in which you itemize your degrees and academic accomplishments: In this

Snapshot 22.2

Some Examples of the Highlights/Summary Section

Proven track record of growing an outsourcing organization ground up from zero to five hundred in two years, with a consistent record of increasing profitability and customer satisfaction.

Acknowledged expertise in the area of object technology, with fifteen international publications and three books.

Over ten years of experience as a financial analyst, managing assets over $20 million covering 15 high net worth customers.

Self motivated, energetic entrepreneur with a track record of setting up and running offshore centers. Known for strong knowledge of international operations and with excellent organizational and analytical skills.

Five years experience in sputtering and chemical vapour deposition technique. Extensive knowledge of photolithography and characterization techniques. Three years of experience in VLSI processing.

Graduate of IIT/Madras in Computer Science and recipient of Presidents Gold Medal.

- List the degrees in reverse chronological order.
- Highlight affiliation to brand name institutions.
- Don't make this section just look like a boring table of college—degree—grade! Rather, focus on accomplishments.
- If you have done any academic projects (especially those that are relevant to the potential employer or part of your academic requirement), highlight them.
- Put special emphasis on consistent, stand-out achievements like winning a national award. By the same token, be careful not to brag about the highest rank you secured in (just) one semester.

Other accomplishments section: Some people categorize this section as 'extra-curricular activities'. We prefer the phrase 'other accomplishments'. In this section, mention a few activities that are outside the professional realm, like participation in voluntary services like blood donation camps, social education and so on and any participation in activities that demonstrate patriotism and public work, like Scouts (and National Cadet Corps in India). If you have demonstrated abilities in sports (not just being part of your gully cricket team or being a great armchair critic), do mention it here. This section would be very relevant in bringing out positive attitudes, initiative, self-drive and social responsibility in you and your being a good team player that no amount of programming expertise can demonstrate.

The section layout and contents given above are only indicative in nature. They have to be adapted and customized based on your experience level, post applied for and company applied to. For example, while a generic objectives section would be okay for a relatively junior position, the same has to be very specific for a more senior position. The summary section has to be very compelling and specific as you move higher up in the ladder. The academic accomplishments section may be highly relevant for someone with less than a couple of years of experience (or when you apply for an academic position), but it may not carry any weight for more senior people. Also, if you don't have sufficient experience, perhaps you might like to put the academic achievements section ahead of the professional experiences section.

Regardless of which section of the resumé you are writing, your choice of words is as important as the content itself. The same content can be made very compelling or absolutely drab for the reader and may become a great reason for the rejection of your resumé. The way to make your resumé compelling to read is to use what are called ***power words***. These are nothing but buzz words that add marketability and value in the eyes of the reader. These are usually either action words (verbs) or qualifiers (adjectives). What we have provided in Snapshot 22.3 is just a set of examples of how you could deploy power words. The main points to keep in mind when you use power words are:

- Keep them full of punch
- Give specifics

- Keep the sentences really short
- Use a variety of key words and try not to repeat the same word or phrase
- Make sure there is a balance of action words and effective adjectives.

There are a significant number of web sites that give you the most popular power words to use.

22.4 Some Miscellaneous Topics

Should I write a cover letter? In general, if you are responding to an advertisement, a simple cover letter that specifies the job code and advertisement code (if any) would be appropriate. The letter should be personalized by addressing it to the appropriate person, with the address typed out. Don't use a generic template which does not carry in print the name and address of the company applying for, the job and advertisement codes, if any. The cover letter need not contain any flamboyant statement like, 'I would consider it a great privilege to work in your esteemed organization. Should you give me an opportunity, I will assure you that I will execute my duties faithfully and to the best of my abilities and your satisfaction.' It can be matter-of-fact and business like. It neither needs to be unduly long nor should it repeat the entire resumé.

Should I have a declaration and signature in my resumé? Some Indian resumés end with the 'solemn declaration' of 'I hereby declare that all the information furnished above is true to the best of my knowledge' and signed with date and place. This is completely unnecessary in the context of most MNC jobs.

Should I attach a photograph? It is a prevalent practice especially in Indian college campuses to have a resumé template with a space for photographs. Again, this is not necessary in the context of MNC jobs.

Snapshot 22.3

Examples of 'Power Words'

Achieved Distinction in BE
Streamlined the processes to achieve 50 per cent improvement in turnaround time
Doubled revenues within two years
Reduced expenses by 25 per cent by effective controls
Consistently accomplished on-time deliveries for six consecutive releases
Built a large offshore team from zero to 300 in a year

Should I give personal details? As we have stated earlier, unnecessary personal details should be avoided. Some commonly used templates in India have provision for date of birth, age, parents' names and so on. Except in extra-ordinary cases, these are unnecessary. (Even if you include date of birth, age is a completely useless column which only leads to inconsistencies.) Generic, unverifiable statements about your character should not be mentioned in your resumé. You can mention about your hobbies or extra-curricular activities only to the extent that they are factual and corroborate your credentials (e.g., being an organizer of blood donation camps displays initiative, team work and public responsibility)

Should I give references? In general, we recommend that you add a one line comment at the end of the resumé 'references available on request'. An exception to this is if you have exceptional references whose permission you have sought beforehand. Make sure you don't use the reference given in one context in another context/situation/purpose.

Should I provide a functional resumé or reverse chronological resumé? Essentially these are two ways of sequencing the information in your resumé. In a *functional* resumé, you highlight your skills in various functional areas. This works best for more experienced people who have worked in multiple functions. For example, a senior person may have played a HR role, an operations role, a project management role and a technology role. The resumé can be ordered in such a way that all related experiences (across different times) are clubbed together. In the *reverse chronological* resumé, you list your experience, from the most recent to the past. This usually works well for entry level and junior professionals as the nature of their work is likely to be more homogeneous and the resumé scanner would be interested in where and how the candidate gained any experience (or studied). Using the reverse chronological order ensures that the most recent experience stands out first.

22.5 In Summary: Some Dos and Don'ts While Writing a Resumé

We will conclude this chapter with a recap of the main points of things you should and should not do when you write your resumé:

Do:

- Use reasonably large-sized, standard fonts that are easily readable: Remember that the person scanning the resumé needs the slightest excuse to dump your resumé in under 30 seconds—poor readability is a good enough reason to do so!
- Use white space effectively: For the same reason as above, you don't want your resumé to look so crowded that the reader will have to scout around to find the important details.

- Use keywords listed in the ads or in the web site of the company. For example, if the organization is specifically looking for 'PMP certified project management professional' and you are certified, make sure you highlight that in your accomplishments.
- Write to sell, don't write to tell: Remember the old dictum in marketing—talk about benefits to customers and not just about the features in your product! This applies to resumés as well. You are writing a resumé to sell or market yourself so that you to go to the interview stage. You don't need to mention every little thing that you have done in your life.
- Strike a balance between consistency and variety in format: The resumé should not look like an essay full of long paragraphs nor should it look like a series of inanimate bullet points. There has to be a balance between various types of rendering of information—bullets, text and tables.
- Sequence in such a way that the most important points, from the point of view of the employer, stand out first. Present them in an eye-catching format.
- Have someone else review your resumé: A lot of times, we are not the best judges to find our own mistakes. Having someone else review your resumé will bring in new perspectives and enable you to improve it in ways that you might not even have thought of before.
- Since brevity is one of our goals, you should avoid using long sentences. Rather than writing 'I was the top ranker in the college and secured 89 per cent', you can rephrase this as 'Was the top ranker with 89 per cent average.'

Do NOT:

- Forget to put your name, contact phone numbers, address and e-mail id prominently.
- Start the resumé with a trite heading 'RESUMÉ' that too in large fonts: This wastes a lot of valuable space; you have lost five out of the thirty seconds the reader has for your resumé After all, he is expecting you to only send your resumé, not your horoscope
- Twist facts or state half-truths and untruths. (*Absolutely no compromises* on this!)
- Use too small a font size. Remember a small font size is a good enough excuse for a person to not read your resumé.
- Tell them everything. Try to make the resumé a sneak preview of the interview. The resumé should be like the trailer of a Bollywood movie—just show enough to entice the audience and to make them come to the movie!
- Use pronouns and complete sentences that span several lines: Pronouns like 'I' and 'We' have no place in a resumé. Whatever you state in the resumé is about

you and hence, 'I' is useless. If you use 'we', it leaves a doubt in the reader's mind as to what *you* specifically did.

- Use resumé as an autobiography. No one is interested in knowing the full details of all you did since your birth. Don't try to mention the award you won in your class for best behaviour when you were eight years old.
- Have any typos in your resumé. Typos stand out like a sore thumb for an experienced resumé scanner. Having typos is a give-away of your carelessness and lack of professionalism. If you don't care enough about your own self, how can you be trusted to take care of your job?
- Give irrelevant personal details. Besides family details, the other details that are generally irrelevant are things like height, weight and so on.
- Give all the details of the compensation you received in your previous jobs, the names and addresses of your supervisors and so on. These can be provided if asked later (and this gives you an opportunity to interact more in an interview).
- Let the resumé be longer than two pages (printed front and back on one sheet of paper). One page is preferable if you are an entry level professional.

A good resumé leads to a chance to appear in an interview—discussed in the next chapter.

23

Interviews

"Death will be a great relief—no more interviews."

–Katherine Hepburn

All of us have to go through selection processes for things we want in our lives. We seek selection in a school or college for a course of our choice; more than once, we may seek selection for a job; as a professional, we may seek to bid for a project or a contract. In all these cases, we work amid tough competition and going through this process could be a difficult, if not traumatic experience. In this chapter, we share some of the experiences and practices that could enable you to handle this stress better. While the selection process is a multi-step one, a major component of this process is the step of interviews. After a brief description of the process, we will dive deep into details of the interviews. As a professional, you would also be conducting interviews for aspirants. Hence, we would go into the perspective of the interviewee (i.e., the candidate) as well as the interviewer. Also, the style and philosophies of interviewing (and in fact the selection process) differ between India and the USA. We will devote one section to discuss these differences.

23.1 Some Basic Premises About Interviews

Going through an interview or selection process can be a nerve wracking experience for some. It is useful to keep certain points in mind so that the process can be taken in stride by the aspirant. It is not the end of the world if you don't get through an interview successfully; nor does it mean that a person who got through an interview is better than one that did not get through.

First, interviewing is a *sampling process*. The company shortlists people for interviews. It is just not possible for every applicant to be either short-listed or called for an interview. Any sampling process has its own vagaries and is subject to errors. All that can be said is that the process seems to work reasonably well—especially for experienced interviewers—and seems to get the type of candidates an organization wants most of the time, although it is far from 100 per cent foolproof.

An interview is a way of *ascertaining a fit* between the job and the candidate. If you are not selected, all that means—in the opinion of the interviewer—is that there is no fit for the job. That does not mean you are unfit for anything else!

Interviewers are also human! Even if you are the best available option for the job (at least in your opinion), the interviewer might have made a genuine mistake. Such is life—life just goes on.

So, don't take not getting selected for a job as an indictment of your competency or capability. Just move on.

23.2 Typical Selection Process

Different organizations follow different processes for recruitment. These involve a combination of the following (as illustrated in Figure 23.1). Like a funnel, at each stage filtering takes place and at every stage some candidate is eliminated from the process.

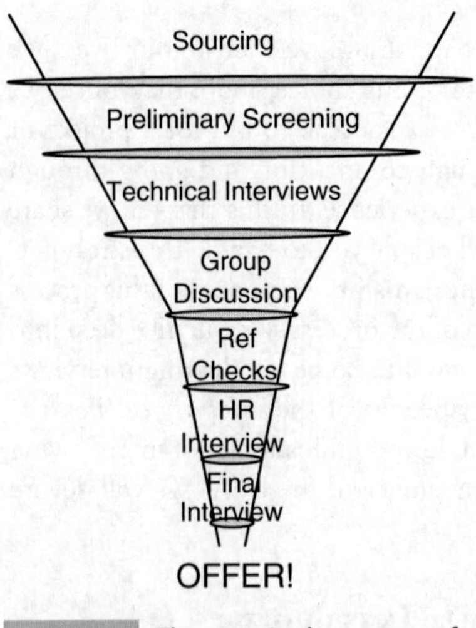

Fig. 23.1 *The steps in the process of selection of a candidate*

Sourcing: An organization sources candidates in different ways. They may advertise in newspapers or on the Internet; they may seek resumés from head hunters; most organizations post their openings in their Intranet and encourage their employees to take up new assignments or to give referrals. The resumés that come in are scanned and filtered and a shortlist of candidates is created. As discussed in Chapter 23, this hurdle (of going past the resumé stage) is usually one of the toughest to cross.

Preliminary screening: Candidates whose resumés get selected now go through a preliminary screening process. This may start off with a written test, which could be either the 'aptitude' or IQ type tests or a written test on your technical area (or a combination of both). The objective of this screening is to eliminate the people who don't clearly have the aptitude or the basic technical knowledge. This is followed by a preliminary interview. This is either a telephonic interview or a face-to-face one. Usually this interview is to ascertain basic technical and communication skills of the candidate. This is typically performed by someone who is not very senior in the organization. This stage of the selection process concentrates on the problem-solving skills of the candidate. An integral part of the problem-solving process is the ability to express the approach and the solution. This obviously requires good communication ability.

Technical interviews: The candidates who are successful in the preliminary screening go through several rounds of technical interviews, each one conducted by people more senior than the previous ones. (Usually, with each round of interview, your chances of being selected increases.) These technical interviews focus not only on the problem-solving abilities, but also on the veracity of the resumé. Typically, these interviews go deeper and deeper into what you have accomplished, both academically and in your previous jobs. As you go through to later rounds, there will be more of a 'HR flavour' to the interview when they test your soft skills and abilities like teamwork and communication.

Group discussions: Many jobs—especially at entry levels or those that focus on marketing, sales or customer-facing activities—would also have a group discussion component that requires the ability to get your point across in a group. This part of the selection process requires not only good communication skills, but also excellent general knowledge since most of the topics are of current interest. Sometimes the topics given are provocative or controversial in nature and you should be prepared to stick your neck (and tongue!) out. Silence is certainly not a virtue in this step.

HR interview: The HR interview, as the name suggests is conducted by the human resources group and usually addresses all the non-technical aspects of the job. This includes the soft skills as well as the financial aspects like salary and compensation.

Reference checks: Usually the organization would ask you to cite three professional references that they can check up for your credentials. It may be difficult to give someone who is in your current organization as a reference as you may not want the current organization to know that you are job hunting. You can give references from your previous jobs. While giving the references, make sure they are only professional references and not just personal acquaintances or thick friends or family members. Also, make sure that you have the referee's consent to be cited as a reference.

Final interview: This is usually with the head of the organization or the final decision maker. This is the last hurdle. This interview addresses the job fit, validates the findings of the previous rounds and unless you really mess it up completely, it is unlikely you will fall at this stage. In smaller organizations, the HR interview is combined with this level.

The above steps of screening may happen in any sequence—for example, the reference checks may happen only if you have cleared all the other steps. Also, how long the process would take also depends on the organization and the specific job. All the steps may get over in a day or can take several days or weeks. Be prepared to bide your time!

23.3 Before the Interview

The first step in preparing for an interview is to get your resumé ready. Make a clean, honest resumé. We have devoted one chapter, Chapter 22, for resumé preparation. The resumé usually goes through a first level screening and those shortlisted (as described in the previous section) may have to go through a written test (this is especially the case for campus recruitments and for people with relatively less experience). If you have cleared the written test, you may be called for a series of interviews.

23.4 Interview

In this section, we will give some general tips about interviews and walk you through the typical sequence of questions that would be asked in an interview and how you can tackle such questions, from an interviewee's perspective.

23.4.1 General Tips on Taking Interviews

Preparation

Before you go to an interview, some planning and research is required on the part of the interviewee.

- Learn a few things about the business of the company and some details of what they do. With the Internet, this is usually a breeze. You should find out from the Internet what products they make, what some of their buzzwords are, the technologies they use, the competition they face and their business size.
- Make sure that there is reasonable and significant overlap between the company's business and your strengths and interests. Some companies publish their job openings on the Internet. Looking at this would give some sense of direction for what the company is looking for and what the options available for you, the interviewee, are.
- Know the details of the logistics of the interview—venue, timing, etc. If the place is a new place, make sure you know how to get there and the time it takes to get there. The last thing you want to do is to arrive late for an interview! Most cities have hotels with similar sounding names (e.g., Taj Residency and Taj West End). Make sure you go to the right hotel, if the interview is in a hotel. Landing up in the wrong Taj at one end of the city may make you miss the interview.
- Assemble whatever you want to take–these may include copies of your certificates, testimonials and so on. (More on this later in this section.)

- If necessary, rehearse your short spiels about yourself that you are going to use in the interview.

Dressing Up for the Interview

The clothes you wear and your general appearance create the first impression in the minds of the interviewer. Hence, it is important to focus on these. Here are some common sense tips:

- There is really no 'dress code' per se to be followed when attending an interview. Use common sense and remember that the emphasis is on being subdued, neutral and conservative. Use clothes in which you will not feel uncomfortable. For example, if you have to travel a long distance by public transportation, it makes sense to wear a tie after you reach the place of interview (should you require a tie). Travelling in full suits in a crowded Mumbai train will make you arrive at the interview hot, tired and in crumpled clothes!
- Use clothes which are appropriate for the occasion. For example, if you are going for a sales or marketing job, make sure you go in a full suit or at least in smart casuals and a tie (for men). Generally, for technical positions in a product organization, smart casuals are fine. But, when going for an interview in a services organization, tie and formals are recommended for men. (If you are in doubt, instead of invoking any 'tie' breaker, just wear one–but make sure it is a staid, simple tie with no wild designs.) Decent 'dress' (leather) shoes are preferable. Don't wear sandals or sneakers even if they look reasonably formal and plain. The typical dress code for women can include traditional Indian attire like salwar-kameez, saris, etc. as well as western attire of a dress or trousers and shirts.
- Don't show up for an interview dressed in brand new clothes that you haven't yet had a chance to get comfortable in.
- We all probably know it, but we are still going to reiterate—don't make a fashion statement by dressing up in T shirts or jeans or cargo pants or shirts with wild and loud designs. It is recommended that men not wear ear rings and both sexes should refrain from wearing excessive jewellery.
- If your religion demands that you should dress up in a particular way or have particular symbols on your body (typically forehead), there is absolutely nothing wrong in donning these. US-based companies do respect religious practices.
- For men, it is advisable not to go with unkempt beards or with stubbles.

What to Take

It is advisable that you take with you any documents that could substantiate your claim for the job that you are trying for. But, don't go to the extent of carrying all your report cards from the first grade! Typically you should have copies (or originals if the company asks for them) of degree certificates, testimonials and experience certificates from all but your current job. Sometimes, the originals may be in the possession of your current employer. In such a case you can tell the interviewer that you currently have only the copies and the originals will be given at the time of joining (should you be selected).

In addition you can take your academic project report and any papers you might have submitted in the public domain if they are directly relevant to the job you are applying for. The key is to carry those documents that can augment your claim for the job and at the same time are not bulky to carry. What you don't want to do is to carry too many things on you and keep dropping them!

Fig. 23.2 *Carrying too many things to an interview*

Briefcases are fast going out of fashion. So, carry your documents in a nice-looking file, folder or portfolio. Carry a small notepad and a pen to take down notes during the interview when appropriate. Don't bring laptops, unless you have to show them demos of some of your work.

Entry

Before you enter the interview room, always knock. Do not barge in. Walk with confidence, neither too fast nor too slow. Do not sit until you are offered a seat. When the interviewer has asked you to sit down, sit on the designated chair and say 'thank you'. Sit straight, neither slouching forward (depicting anxiety) nor relaxing backwards as though you are on an easy chair watching a cricket match! Some people feel comfortable only when they cross their legs. Sitting without crossing the legs is preferable (especially if you are supporting a folder with your documents on your lap). If there is a table separating you and the interviewer, do not lean on the table.

Carrying Yourself

Carry yourself with quiet confidence throughout the interview. Continue the posture you had at the beginning, throughout. When you answer questions, establish eye contact primarily with the person who asked you the question and distribute eye contact among other interviewers as well. If a question or something they said is not clear, do not hesitate to politely ask them to repeat. ('Sorry, did not understand what you said, could you repeat it for me please?') Try and avoid any distracting gestures like fiddling with the buttons or tie, tapping the top of a ball point pen and so on.

Exit

While going out after the interview, do so only after the interviewer has said that there is nothing more to do now. At this point of time (after asking whatever questions you may have, as we discuss below), thank the interviewers and walk back to the door. Gently open the door and close the door gently after you. Not only should you create a good first opinion, you should also create a lasting final impression!

23.4.2 Common Questions and Flow

In this section we will see the typical flow of an interview, the typical questions that are asked and how to respond to them.

Warm-up Questions and Questions That Set the Stage

'Tell me something about yourself': This is usually the first question in an interview. This is an ideal warm-up question for both the interviewer and interviewee. For the interviewee, this is one question where he or she definitely knows more than the interviewer! Thus, it is a great opportunity for the interviewee to get rid of any nervousness and fear that he or she may be giving a 'wrong' answer! The interviewee can ease into the interview better and use this opportunity to start impressing the interviewer. Just like in a presentation, the first impression is the best impression. This first question is a great opportunity for the interviewee to create a lasting and positive impression.

Fig. 23.3

While answering this question, make sure you

- Keep the answer to about 3–4 minutes in length. Anything shorter would indicate a lack of self belief and pride; for anything longer, you are likely to be interrupted to stop and will be perceived to be boring. An exception to this is for people with long years of experience that spans 3–4 jobs. In this case, the answer to this question may take as much as 8 minutes. Of course, in this case, the interview time is also likely to be longer and the interviewer will probably be a senior person who has budgeted significant time for the interview.
- Highlight your accomplishments bringing in focus the synergy and intersection between your accomplishments and the company's (and the job's) needs. Focus on benefits the company will accrue from your accomplishments. The 5Fs that we talked about in preparing the resumé continue to apply during the interview as well.
- Highlight any affiliation you may have to any reputed names and institutions.
- Show your focus. Make statements like, 'I like taking up challenges in the area of databases'. Such focused, specific references will underline your confidence. This can also steer the interview into areas you are comfortable with.
- Demonstrate consistency. That is something that an interviewer always looks for. Make assertions like, 'I have *always* been in the top 5 per cent of the class' or '*None* of my projects have been delayed beyond the allotted deadline.' (Note the emphasis.)

- Cover attitudinal issues. Demonstrate all the facets of good attitude that we discussed in the first part of this book. Mention things like, 'One of the highlights of my career has been that I have *always* been a team player.'
- Demonstrate commitment and initiative. Prove that you have always gone the extra mile. 'I was a developer for the inventory module, but I also contributed towards our company's ISO-9001 initiative.' You can also highlight initiative in co-curricular activities, such as organizing a blood donation camp.

How can you do all these in 3–4 minutes? Devote a minute to your academic achievements, a couple of minutes for your work experience and a minute to summarize your consistency, initiative and focus. Some of the things to watch out for while answering this question are:

- Avoid sounding like a historical narration. You are not presenting a documentary on your life.
- Avoid detailed family references ('My father is a postmaster and mother is a school teacher; I have two sisters and a brother . . .').
- Avoid being excessively chronological to the point of being boring. ('From 13 September 1996 to 25 October 1998, I worked in ABC Corporation and then until November 2000 at XYZ Corporation . . .') While such facts are important, what the interviewer is looking for is a gist of what is relevant for the job.
- Avoid committing yourself to an area of interest that appears too narrow. ('I am really interested in doing Java development and nothing else.') Such a narrow specification of interest would indicate that you are not flexible or ready to meet the needs of the company.

As we discussed earlier, the answer to the first question sets the stage for your self confidence and also helps to steer the interview into areas that are your forte. A typical second question discussed in the next section provides an opportunity to build upon this further.

'What do you consider to be your major strengths?': This question gives you one more opportunity to steer the interview to areas that are your forte. Since interviewing is a sampling process, the interviewer has to decide how good you will be for the job, if chosen. One factor that will be used would be how good you were for the jobs you have done (provided of course, that what you have done is relevant to what you will do in the job, if selected). When responding to this question,

- Focus on *a few* related areas that are really your strengths. If you stretch this too wide, then you run the risk of being asked questions on areas that are not your forte; in addition, you will give an impression of not knowing your strengths. If your strengths are too niche, you run the risk of this being not interesting to the interviewer.

- Give *specific* examples to illustrate why you feel these are your strong areas. For example, 'Databases have always been my strengths as I got top grades in all the database courses, did a project on databases and have been working in this field for the last three years.'
- Highlight accomplishments in *teamwork* and *communication*. Don't let your strengths sound like you are a Superman or a Superwoman. It might intimidate the interviewer and give an impression that you are a difficult person to work with.
- Demonstrate your positive attitude by citing examples from your track record and show it in your body language as well.

A few words of caution:

- Avoid confusing strengths with skills. For example, 'problem solving' and 'object-oriented programming' are strengths, while 'java programming' itself can be viewed as a skill.
- Avoid bad mouthing areas that are not your strengths ('Development is my strength; who wants to do testing, which is not for qualified people like me.').

What happens when your area of strength is not in line with what the interviewer and the company is interested in? If the two are completely tangential, then you have not done your homework right (or the company has wrongly called you for an interview). If not, then try to project those areas of overlap and synergy between the two. By making sure your strength area is in line with what the company wants, you are increasing the chances of being successful in the interview.

Typically, with these questions, you are led into the details of your projects and accomplishments.

23.4.3 The Detailed Part of the Interview

The previous questions set the tone for the interview and will probably last for about 8-10 minutes (except in the case of very experienced candidates). The bulk of the remaining time would be dedicated to going into details of your projects, specific work experience, academic performance and so on. While presenting these details, make sure of the following:

- Answer what was asked of you and do not digress into irrelevant details.
- What you answer should be consistent with what is in your resumé (which of course should be honest).
- If there are any 'time gaps' in your resumé (either during your studies or in between jobs), ensure that you are ready with a valid substantiation of the gaps.
- Be confident and look into the eye of the interviewers when you speak. When there are multiple interviewers, distribute your eye contact among all of them, giving primary eye contact to the person who asked a question.

- If you are asked to use the white board or paper, write legibly. If using a white board and that is not empty, first ask the interviewer if it is okay to erase what is there on the whiteboard.
- Do not divulge any confidential information from your previous jobs. If a question is asked about such confidential details, do not hesitate to say that it is confidential and you are not in a position to divulge that information.
- Do not inappropriately use 'confidentiality' as an excuse to not answer questions in detail. This will surely undermine your credibility.
- While describing the projects you have worked on, put it in perspective. The interviewer should know the project at a macro level, the role you played in it and its relationship to the other players. Your description of the projects should bring out the challenges in the project, how you overcame the challenges and how you went the extra mile.

While describing your projects and accomplishments, you will find some common questions that the interviewers use to gauge your attitude and aptitude.

'Tell me what excites you most': When you describe the projects you have worked on or after you have described your accomplishments, one of the questions that are likely to come up is 'what excites you most'. Usually this question is a sure way by which experienced interviewers gauge the interviewee's interest and fit for the job. As an interviewee, you should have a clear idea of what is it that really excites you. This may be a *type* of work (e.g., software testing), a technology area (e.g., databases) or an aspect of *work environment* (e.g., liking customer-facing jobs and opportunities to interact with people). While specifying what excites you the most, remember:

- To be genuine, sincere and honest. Do not fake interest in an area that does not really excite you. Experienced interviewers can tear down that mask in no time.
- To see if the area of excitement is relevant to the organization. After all, if what excites you is mechanical engineering, what would a BPO company do with you?
- To make sure the area of excitement is not something that is either too narrow or just too trite or simply fashionable. For example, a number of interviewees say 'Java programming is what excites me most.' While this is not wrong per se, this answer came from so many people (during the heydays of Java) that interviewers tend to discount such a statement.
- To make sure that your accomplishments clearly demonstrate that you are indeed genuinely excited by what you are mentioning. (see Snapshot 23.1).

Snapshot 23.1

Let us recollect a vivid interview that the author did years ago, that still is fresh in his memory: One of the authors was conducting an interview for someone with three years of experience and they were discussing software development. While the interviewee was answering the questions, there was a lack of energy levels that was perceived in him. Then the author asked him what excites him most. He replied that it was software testing. When further questioned on software testing and quality arena, his face lit up and he was a completely transformed person. The energy levels displayed, the enthusiasm shown and the ebullience resulted were simply astounding. Now, this person is a very successful professional in the software testing and quality arena. If the author had not bothered to find out what excited him the most, the community would have lost a high calibre professional in software testing and quality.

'Tell me the biggest challenge you have faced so far': This is one of the questions that are asked to see your resilience. Your answer to this question should describe a specific technical or management challenge that you faced in one of your jobs (or in your academic career) your solution to which you recall even today with fond memories.

Try to make this as specific as possible. Making a generic statement like 'I debugged a ten thousand line program' or 'I had to be part of this crazy deadline driven project' will not hold water. If you did debug a ten thousand line program, then what specific debugging aspect was the challenge? If the crazy deadline project was the challenge, how did it specifically challenge you?

Not only should you focus on the specific challenge you faced, but you should also mention how you overcame that challenge. There is no use lamenting about a challenge for which you could not find a solution.

When you describe the solution, emphasize *your* contribution in overcoming the challenge. You may be asked a follow-up question as to what help you got from others for overcoming this challenge. Don't try to project yourself as a miraculous trouble-shooter saying that you handled it all by yourself with no help from anyone (worse, don't say that you overcame the challenge *despite* others!).

The challenge you describe should not be personally insulting to anyone.

By mentioning the challenge you may demonstrate that you were the 'go-to guy' in tough situations, but don't phrase it to be negative about others. Remember, teamwork is a paramount trait that interviewers look for.

Fig. 23.4

23.4.4 The 'Trick Negative' Questions

So far, most of the questions you have been asked have been about your positive aspects—what your strengths are, the projects you have worked on, what excites you most, the challenges you have cherished overcoming and so on. Just as you start feeling on top of the world, expect a couple of 'trick negative' questions. In reality these questions are neither trick nor negative, but when you are asked these questions, there is bound to be some trepidation on your part.

One such question you can expect is

'What are your weaknesses?': Most interviewees (especially those less experienced) get taken aback at these kinds of questions and are at a loss for answers. One immediate response is 'I don't have any weakness!' This is obviously incorrect as all of us have some weakness or the other and if we are not aware of our own weaknesses, it does not reflect well on our ability for unbiased judgement. Experienced interviewers can always rephrase this question in such a way that you will come up with your weakness! Some people who want to project an air of honesty and frankness come up with an answer such as, 'You know, my biggest weakness is that I am careless!' Would an employer even look at a candidate who is careless according to his own admission? Again, an answer like 'People get peeved off at me often!' is not something that will make your candidature appealing to the interviewer.

One way to tackle such a question is to be candid, but, at the same time, put a positive spin on it. 'I over exert myself till I get the results and sometimes that affects my health' or 'I am a perfectionist and sometimes expect the same from all my colleagues and that makes it difficult for them'. In each of these cases, the 'weakness' is brought out by the second part of the sentence, but such a 'weakness' is actually a result of something that is very positive and indeed very desirable (this appears in the first part of the sentence).

The same question may be asked later using different words to catch you unawares (especially if you have said that you have absolutely no weaknesses!). One such typical question is 'Suppose, I allocate 2 lakh rupees to you of training budget and you can spend it on anything you like (not of course, horse riding or watching a cricket match), what would you spend it on?' Be specific and at the same time not overly specific in answering this. 'I would like to improve my knowledge of the foundations of web security as this is in line with my interests and I need to acquire more skills in this arena.' Note how this answer shows focus and builds on the projected strengths. From the interviewer's perspective, he has come to know what you think are your weak or improvement areas.

Another such question perceived as trick negative is

'Tell me about the biggest mistake you have made': All of us make mistakes, but it is the ability to learn from the mistakes and apply the learning so as not to repeat the mistakes in future and improve ourselves that sets the more successful ones apart. The interviewer is looking for the attribute of *learnability* through this question. (We discussed learnability and lifelong learning in detail in Chapter 7) Some well-intentioned thing that you did might have bombed on you. Maybe you tried to add a new feature that was not in the plan for a customer and that messed up what was actually supposed to be delivered. Maybe you gave responsibility to a staff, with the hope of training him, but that person did not step up. What you need to highlight is that you were quick to spot the mistake and recover from it. And that you learnt a lesson from the mistake that you applied in the future. In the first example, your lesson might have been to first deliver to the specs and then take on new features; in the second example, your lesson may have been that you needed to put tighter controls. Never try to project an example where the mistake reflects a lack of sincerity or commitment—that is not a 'mistake', but cardinal sin!

Questions About Your Current (Previous) Job

When you are switching jobs or looking for a new job because you got laid off in the previous job, there are surely going to be questions about your current / previous job. If your resumé shows frequent job hopping, then there will definitely be questions about the reasons for the frequent changes.

One common question that comes up is

'Tell me why you left you last job(s)': Don't use this question as an opportunity to unleash your sob story of how stupid your boss was and how you could simply not get along with him. Don't just bad mouth your previous organization in order to get the new job. It won't cut much ice with the interviewer. He will go under the assumption that tomorrow you will do the same thing to him when you go for the next interview. Rather, your answer should be that you don't see a growth path for you where you are today and hence are looking to move out. Maybe you wanted to change your direction. Maybe the learning opportunities have dried up; maybe the financial viability of the company is uncertain and you feel it is risky to continue there; maybe the work they gave was not what they promised. Whatever be your answer, it should reflect that you are leaving the current job in good terms and that your reasons for leaving are for career growth and better learning.

Another question in this category is

'If I were to ask your boss to rate you alongside your peers (i.e., his reports at your level), what would be your rank?': The almost immediate answer one would like to give is 'Of course, numero uno!' If you are absolutely confident that this is the case and your track record justifies this and your general demeanor shows this, then by all means say so. If you are at rock bottom because of your dismal performance, then don't worry—the interviewer would have made it out by now and would not have wasted his time asking you this question. If you are in a highly competitive group, it is perfectly okay to say 'I am in a very competitive group and it is tough to put a number on this as this. I would say I am in the top maybe 2-3 (or middle 2-3).' A persistent interviewer may then ask you, 'What do you think you would have to do to be #1?'. You can use this opportunity to emphasize your learnability attitude and underscore what skills (soft or hard) you would like to pick up, given a chance.

23.4.5 Intention Testing Questions

While ascertaining your strengths and weaknesses, the interviewer would also find out your true motives for joining the job, if you are selected. One area of concern that interviewers have is how long the interviewee would stick to the job, if it was offered to him (or even whether he would really join if he were offered the job). After all, if you are the ideal candidate for the job by your skills and experience, but did not plan to take up the offer, what is the use?

There are different ways in which this question is asked:

'Tell me about your dream job': Some candidates, trying to placate or puff up the interviewer, immediately reply, 'Of course, working in this company! I have been dreaming about this ever since I entered college (or ever since I was in my cradle)!' This does not take you, the interviewee anywhere. Some immature interviewees answer, 'A job like yours which takes me to the USA!' This again is not going to be appreciated, as the interviewer would conclude that you will jump ship as soon as you land on the shores of the 'land of opportunities'.

An ideal answer to this question would be something like 'A job that utilizes my skills in the area of network security and gives me opportunities to develop these skills further' or 'A job that gives me more responsibilities and challenges'. Your 'dream' emphasizes long term thinking, a clear vision, knowing the big picture of how your skills fit into the environment, your pride in your accomplishments and your readiness to respect an environment that would be conducive for mutual growth. Not surprisingly, these are exactly the traits we have espoused in the attitude section of this book. In summary, you project your positive attitude in your dream job, convince the interviewer that you would view the job as one that supports this positive attitude and that you have the capability and potential to match the attitude.

'With all these qualifications, why are you not going for higher studies abroad?': One concern that interviewers have—especially in India when they are looking for people under 3 years of experience—is that the candidate may leave for higher studies. Hence, the hiring and training effort goes to waste. If the interviewee is actually planning to go for higher studies (abroad) immediately, he should not waste the company's resources to park for a couple of months. It is simply unethical. If on the other extreme, the interviewee, despite excellent credentials, is sure he is not going for higher studies, he can feel free to say that he is definitely looking for a job for personal or financial reasons.

23.4.6 Compensation and Financial Details

The final set of questions that will determine your getting the job is about the compensation and financial aspects. Two questions that are asked in this are:

'What is your current compensation?' and ***'What are your expectations?':*** For the first question, don't try to quote a higher number to extract a higher compensation from the job you are now seeking. It is easy enough to find out the truth. If the organization finds out you were inflating the numbers, your credibility goes out of the window and all the effort is lost, even if you were a technical whiz-kid. At the same time, do not just quote the fixed part of your compensation; include perks and the variable compensation you received in the last couple of years. Keep these two—fixed part and the variable compensation—separate so that the interviewer gets a clear idea of your net value as well as your being a high performer (especially if your variable compensation is high)

The answer to the second question depends on your seniority level. For relatively junior positions, it is best to leave it to the organization's standards. If the organization is a fairly large or mid-sized organization, then it is likely that there are norms that they will have for people at junior levels. For people at senior levels, however, it is always up to negotiations.

23.5 Differences Between the American and Indian Interviews

Having conducted interviews in the USA and in India for US companies and in India for Indian organizations, we have observed some basic differences, which we would like to share in this section.

Asking for family details: It is common to hear questions like 'What are your parents doing?' in some of the interviews conducted for Indian organizations. It is not legal to ask these questions when conducting an interview for a US organization.

Asking personal questions: Questions about marital status, sexual orientation and relationships should not be asked. Questions about physical disabilities should be limited to how it will affect the job function. For example, if you find an interviewee limping or using crutches, it is inappropriate to ask what happened to the leg (unless the job requires using the leg extensively like a salesperson who may have to cover a lot of ground by walking).

Commenting on personal appearance: Do not ask any questions about the interviewee's physical appearance. In addition to the questions discussed above, also avoid questions about the colour, height, weight, build or any other physical characteristic.

In the USA, it is not unusual for an interview to take all day or even two days. The candidate will meet several interviewers during the course of the interview, usually in one-on-one situations and talk in depth about not only technical things, but also about soft skills, with a view of finding out if there is the right chemistry between the job-seeker and the organization. In this format, the interview process loses its traditional question/answer form and develops into a probing conversation. The candidate is even taken to lunch and dinners (when the economy is good) to continue the interview process in an informal setting.

23.6 The Interviewer Perspective

As you grow in your career, you are likely to play an interviewer's role more often than an interviewee's role. Even though the latter's position may seem to be of higher pressure, there is an onus on the interviewer as well, to treat the interviewee properly. If the interviewee gets selected, it is obvious that he should have a good impression of the interview process. If not, even then, an interviewee could be an ambassador to carry a good impression of the organization. In this section, we will look at some of the things an interviewer can (should) do as a matter of courtesy.

Make the interviewee feel comfortable: It is essential to make the interviewee feel comfortable right from the beginning. At the very least, this would mean offering the interviewee to sit. If the interviewee appears nervous, it would also be common decency to offer a glass of water.

Make the interviewee understand the job role and functions: It is useful to start the interview by giving a brief description of the job function and the role to be played by the interviewee, in case he or she is selected. Should the job not offer any synergies to the candidate's interest, you can save some time. There are cases when an interview is not for any specific position. In such a case, it is worth giving an overall picture and letting the interviewee know that you are looking for a broad range of functions and roles.

Give the interviewee an opportunity to ask questions in the end: Just before the conclusion, you can ask the interviewee, 'Do you have any questions you would like to ask me?' This will serve two purposes: First, it will make the interviewee feel more at ease. Second, this will also act as a test for the interviewee's ability to ask *meaningful* questions. You don't need to answer all the questions. It is your prerogative. For example, one of the questions that the interviewee would ask may be, 'Am I selected?' You can then lead this to the next point given below.

Conclude with an indication of the next steps: Just like any communication should have a follow through, you should conclude an interview by mentioning the next steps that would be taken. You can say 'Well, I have nothing else to ask now. I will now forward this to . . . (next level/HR and so on) and you will hear from us.' The interviewee may ask you the timeframe when he or she would hear from your company. If you don't know, you can say something like 'That depends on the availability of our director.'

Do not allow any distractions: While conducting the interview, make sure you put your cell phone on silent. Do not take any call, unless it is absolutely urgent. If possible, don't conduct the interview in your office, so that there is no temptation to check e-mail during the interview.

Do not make any promises: Other than giving an indication of the next steps, do not make any promises of offer (or the compensation package), even if you are the CEO deciding the offer. You may just discover a more ideal candidate the very next day.

Do not ask any personal questions: As we discussed in the section on the differences between interviews conducted in India and the USA, it is taboo in the USA (and in US based MNCs in India) to ask personal questions. Any questions regarding age, religious/political preferences and family details are generally avoided in US companies.

Do not tolerate any nonsense: Some candidates may try to act smart by either asking very irritating questions ('Why does your product have so many bugs?') or some illegal questions ('How are the sales this quarter?'). Do not tolerate any nonsense. If the interviewee's questions are insinuating to the company or lack basic human courtesy and decency, politely and quickly conclude the interview so that you can minimize time wastage.

23.7 In Summary

We would like to conclude the chapter with a summary of what the interviewer looks for and what the interviewee should display and not display

What the interviewer looks for:

Attitude - Pride in past work and organizations.

Aptitude – Strength in what you do and willingness to learn.

Foundations – Trainable, not just trained.

Communication – Ability to articulate thought processes.

Ethics – Value systems, integrity and trustworthiness.

Focus – Self awareness and clarity of strengths, weaknesses and goals.

There is a thin line that separates what the interviewee should display and what he should not display.

Pride, not arrogance

Confidence, without condescension

Your accomplishments, not demeaning others

Your positives, not others' negatives

Knowledge, without showing off

Awareness of the company, without sycophancy.

24

Meetings

"Meetings are places where minutes are kept, but hours are lost."
–Unknown

Meetings consume a significant percentage of time for many individuals in an organization. Given the reality of globally distributed teams, not all meetings are in person; some of them are also video conferences. Whether the meeting is face-to-face or virtual (i.e., through conference calls), there are some unique challenges that meetings throw up. In this chapter, we will see some of these challenges and ways to overcome them effectively. We will start the chapter with some of the useful functions served by meetings and then take you through a step-by-step process for effective meeting management and to get the best out of any meeting. We will also look at some of the common complaints people have against meetings and how to address these complaints.

24.1 The Purpose of Meetings

Meetings provide an opportunity for the stakeholders to come to a common page: When all the stakeholders are brought to a common room, they can have a platform to share each others' views, understand each others' perspectives and hence, converge to a common understanding faster.

Meetings offer a forum for discussion: Meetings are necessarily synchronous communication vehicles and hence, as discussed in Chapter 13, they provide an opportunity to have healthy discussions and can throw up ideas and avenues that would not otherwise be considered.

Fig. 24.1

Meetings move things forward: Meetings will review the results of past action items and generate a fresh crop of action items to be done following the meeting. In this sense, it helps the progress of a project or activity.

Meetings can help create rapport: Since almost every meeting has some 'small talk' component or at least provides access to useful cues like body language, vocal variety and so on, they can aid in building better rapport.

24.2 Steps for Getting the Best out of Meetings

An effective way for meeting management can be summarized by the acronym PROOF:

Planning for a meeting
Reaching out to the stakeholders
Organizing a meeting
Orchestrating a meeting
Following through after a meeting.

The first three steps pertain to what needs to be done *before* a meeting; the fourth step is about what needs to be done *during* a meeting and the last step is about what needs to be done *after* a meeting. We will see each of these steps in detail in the following sections.

24.3 P: Preparing for a Meeting

Meetings are the cogs in the wheel to keep the communication process going. Just as any communication needs preparation, so does a meeting. Preparing for a meeting requires getting some clarity on the following questions:

24.3.1 What Is the Purpose of a Meeting?

As we stated in Chapter 13 on the communication cycle, the first step is to know the objectives of communication. In meetings too, it is important to get clarity on the purpose of the meeting. There are different types of meetings serving different, specific purposes. Some of the common ones are:

- **Status meeting:** This is probably one where teams spend time on a regular basis. This type of meeting helps to get all the stakeholders on a common page and helps everyone to take stock of situation and assess the progress of a project. It also helps in arriving at action items to take the mission forward. Such meetings are usually scheduled to be at the same time every week/day.
- **Brainstorming meeting:** This type of meeting is held usually on demand or to address specific needs (such as problem-resolution, new product features and so on) rather than being held on a regular basis. The purpose of such a meeting is to generate a wide variety of ideas on how to approach a given problem or situation.
- **Negotiation meeting:** This type of meeting typically takes place internally within an organization to meet a project's requirements as well as externally with customers to arrive at the project scope, cost and duration.

(Note that we are not going to talk about meetings where you are largely a spectator—such as an all-employee meeting.)

24.3.2 Who Should Be the Participants?

Two general thumb rules in deciding who the participants should be are:

- Call only those who can add value to the meeting and can contribute to it—and who participate in an activity discussed in that meeting.
- Try to keep the number of people to the bare minimum that you need. Carrying on a meeting with more than 15 people is likely to be less productive.

24.3.3 What Is Expected of Each of the Participants?

Most meetings become unproductive simply because the expectations are not properly formulated or communicated to the participants ahead of time. One way to guard against this is to formulate the agenda items for the meeting before approaching the participants and then getting it ratified by them (as discussed in the next section). Formulating the agenda items entails filling up a template like in Box 24.1.

Box 24.1

Template for specifying the agenda items for a meeting

Meeting Agenda:

Meeting Id / Description:

Date / Time /Venue:

Serial no.	Topic/Agenda Item	Who?	Time Allocated	Supporting Data Needed

While initially formulating the agenda items, keep in mind the following:

Achieve a balance between breadth and depth: Usually the time required for the number of agenda items far outweighs the time available. The dilemma is between covering all the items skimming the surface of each versus going into details of some of the items at the expense of other items. Neither approach is totally advisable. It is necessary to prioritize the items (hence, the serial number column) and make sure that the right items get discussed at the right level of depth.

Choose the most appropriate person to be assigned an agenda item: It is ideal to assign one individual for each agenda item. There may be agenda items that require several people to contribute. Even in this case, it is essential to reach out to the group of people, and yet, have them decide the one person who would be assigned initially to discuss this item.

Have a backup in case the chosen person is not available: If an agenda item is important and broad enough, it is essential to have a backup person who can handle this item in the event that the primary person is not available. Usually it is best to leave it to the primary person to nominate the proxy representative/substitute. It is important for this backup person to be sufficiently knowledgeable and empowered to articulate the views of, and take decisions on behalf of, the primary person. The idea is to have a discussion on the agenda item even if the owner of the item happens to be unavailable on a given day.

Provide reasonable time for discussions: The time allocated for the agenda item should not only give time for the owner of the item to present the facts and views, but also allow sufficient time for discussions and healthy debates. Again, there is a thin line between healthy debate and unnecessary digressions and the person conducting the meeting should use the time planned as a guideline to identify this thin line and make sure this is not crossed, when orchestrating the meeting.

From time to time, unscheduled but urgent agenda items may crop up and need attention right away. In such cases we should be flexible enough to change the meeting agenda on the fly. The point here is that while the agenda items act as guidelines for an orderly progress of the meeting to achieve its objectives, they should not always be cast in stone. There should be a balance between flexibility and discipline.

24.3.4 What Is the Estimated Time Duration for the Meeting?

Once we have the agenda items and the time required for each item, we can add these up to get an estimate of the total time needed for the meeting. If this time needed is substantially more than the time available for the meeting—constrained by availability of people, infrastructure or time difference between the locations—then we need to work backwards from the total time available and then scale down the time allocated for each item or even cut out some of the agenda items altogether. But one item that should never be compromised is the allocation of sufficient time for a proper closure of the meeting, which we will reiterate later in this chapter.

24.3.5 What are the Logistics Required for the Conduct of the Meeting?

After having worked out the details of the contents of the meeting, it is time to work out the logistics. A checklist for some of the logistical items for a meeting is given in Box 24.2. Please refer to also Section 16.4.

Box 24.2

Checklist for Arranging Logistics for a Meeting

- Have you located a suitable venue for the meeting?
- Is the venue easily accessible to a majority of the (key) people?
- Have you identified the supporting infrastructure needed in the venue (white board, flip charts, computer equipment, network connectivity, projection equipment to name a few)?
- Is the layout of the venue ideally suited for the type/objective of meeting? For example, a boardroom type of layout may not be suitable for break-out groups, while a classroom type of layout may not be suitable for formal discussions.
- If people have to be dialled in/dialled out from the venue, have arrangements been made for such dial-up?

(Continued)

- Have the parties to be dialled in been notified and their contact numbers got?
- Have you factored in time difference, especially during the time the clock changes (e.g., during spring and fall when the time is adjusted in most countries for daylight savings)?
- If video conferencing is required, have you communicated to the other parties to be present in the appropriate video conference room?

When all the initial planning has been done, it is time to go to the next stage of preparation—the reaching out stage.

24.4 R: Reaching Out

Having identified the objectives to be achieved in a meeting and ratified it with the stakeholders involved, the next step is to reach out to the stakeholders, ensure they are available for the meeting; that they understand their role and contribution to the meeting; and that they come prepared to maximize their contribution.

Make them know their roles: Discuss with the participants their role and value addition in the meeting candidly. Doing this before the meeting minimizes the risk of a participant not showing up for the meeting (or showing up unprepared).

Clearly state what data and other things they need to bring to the meeting: The participants may need to bring certain supporting data, models or prototypes to the meeting. They may also have to set up some demos. Ensure that they bring to the meeting whatever is needed.

Get their buy-in: Make sure you get their buy-in that they will come for the meeting prepared for the agenda items you would like them to take on.

Send them the agenda by e-mail to confirm their participation and role: This will ensure that they not only know their role, but also get to know the big picture.

24.5 O: Organizing for a Meeting

When the meeting has been planned and the participants have been identified, the next step is to carry out all the organizing needed to conduct the meeting. This entails:

Identifying the right place and time: Make sure the place is suited for the type of meeting. We discussed earlier that certain types of rooms are suitable for certain meetings. Take this into account before selecting the room (if possible). Also, make sure the room is easily accessible to the various participants. This consideration is especially important in organizations based out of cities like Bangalore. The various offices are spread several kilometres apart and moving from one office to another for a one-hour meeting could potentially waste the entire day in commute. Another factor to consider is the time of the meeting. When participants are distributed in different parts of the city, then the earlier part of the day would be ideal to beat the traffic. If the participants are in different time zones, then a mutually acceptable time should be chosen.

Get the right infrastructure ready: Make sure all the paraphernalia like flip charts, laptops, projection equipment, white board, markers and so on are all available. And, don't forget to check that the markers do *really* write! Make sure that the projection equipment works correctly. Minutes are wasted during the meeting by trying to make the projection equipment work correctly, and this eats into valuable discussion time. If you are the designated repository of data from various participants–to be distributed to the others during the meeting–ensure that you get them in time and in the format you were looking for.

If needed, remind the participants just-in-time: It is a good idea to send the final agenda to all the participants the day before the meeting by e-mail. This can act as a reminder to attend the meeting. More than any electronic gizmo, simply walking into the cubicles of the meeting participants a few minutes before the meeting and rounding them up, always works!

24.6 O: Orchestrating the Meeting

Orchestrating the meeting refers to an orderly way of going through the actual meeting. Here are some tips for this, especially if you are the person who is managing the meeting.

Arrive early! Make sure you arrive early and ensure all the infrastructure is in order. If other participants require any other infrastructure, encourage and persuade them to set it up before the meeting starts to minimize any distraction.

Prepare the seating arrangement: If you need to have specific seating arrangements, make arrangements for them. This may apply to brainstorming meetings when you want people from different backgrounds to sit together at a table to focus on different issues. Sometimes, when you are running group meetings, you may observe that some participants go at the back of the room, doodling and SMS-ing; you might like to draw these back benchers forward to make them participate.

Allow time for small talk: Whether you like it or not, some time at the beginning of the meeting would invariably be lost in small talk. If you are early and if some people have also trickled in early, the small talk time would not eat substantially into the meeting time.

Always start on time, respecting people who come on time: A major mistake is 'to wait for all others to come'. This is being unfair to the people who have been professional enough to come on time to the meeting.

Make sure the scribe is ready: Right at the beginning of the meeting, clearly identify a person who will take down detailed notes during the meeting. Some of the senior executives running a meeting would have their administrative assistant donning the scribe's role. But then, this is not a rule. In the excitement of jumping headlong into the meeting, you don't want to ignore taking down notes of the meeting to prepare the minutes. Hence, identifying or nominating someone to volunteer to be a scribe right at the beginning of a meeting is essential.

Review the agenda at the beginning: Start the meeting with a review of the agenda items. Some people have the habit of distributing the printout of the agenda and discussion items. While this may be necessary for formal meetings, you can consider replacing the hard copy with a soft copy projected on the screen and saving precious trees in the bargain.

State any protocol: Right after re-stating the agenda items and just before jumping into the items, it is a good idea to state any protocols you would like to follow during the meeting. These could include protocols for time management and how to signal and respect time-outs; how to take turns; when to interrupt a speaker; the roles to be played and so on.

Go sequentially as per the agenda: Assuming that you have put some thought into prioritizing the agenda items, going sequentially as per the circulated agenda will bring in order and predictability to the meeting. For each agenda item, try to stick to the allocated time; while doing this, provide a balance between flexibility and digression. Some amount of digression will necessarily happen and should be accommodated; trying to be a robot will not make a meeting conducive to effective decision making or information exchange.

Handle conflicts diplomatically yet firmly: As a facilitator of a meeting, when you allow discussions, conflicts are bound to spring up. It is your job to handle the conflicts effectively. While a very detailed treatment of conflict management is beyond the scope of this book, a few quick tips in managing conflicts in a meeting are:

- Allocate sufficient time for discussion so that it does not look like you are bulldozing or side stepping objections.
- Help the participants to articulate the nature of the conflict, making the conflict issue based rather than personality based.
- Acknowledge that you have understood what the different viewpoints are. Note that by this you are not accepting any one view point and are not taking sides.

- Impress that the goal is to arrive at a solution and not to finger point. To this end, paraphrase the problem and the various options available with the intent of arriving at a solution.
- When you (or the meeting) arrive at a solution, do not impose on people whose viewpoints are not agreed upon.
- If you find that it is not possible to arrive at a solution for an issue within the meeting, defer this agenda item (and any dependent agenda items) to a separate meeting focused on solving those unresolved issues. Ask the warring parties to bring extra supporting data to convince the skeptics.
- Eventually make sure that there is a shared ownership and interest in getting the problem(s) resolved. It should not simply be 'your problem'. It should be 'our problem'.

Allocate time for closing the meeting: Every meeting should have a formal close, wherein you recap what was discussed, what was agreed upon and what the action items are. When certain items take too long to discuss and when there is a lot of digression and tangential discussion or when the time is short, most often the time for closure gets the axe. Be conscious of this!

Cleaning up after the meeting: As a mark of courtesy for the people who will use the room next, make sure you leave the venue in a clean state. Wipe the white boards clean, remove any flip charts (these will also protect any confidentiality issues) and consign any remnants of food to the garbage can.

24.7 F: Following Through After the Meeting

Every meeting needs follow through for it to be effective. Some of the steps in following through are:

Sending MOM: The minutes of meeting (popularly known as MOM) is a written summary of what transpired, what was discussed and what was agreed upon during a meeting, highlighting any action items which may have been generated (more about this later). The MOM should be prepared with the help of the notes prepared by the scribe. The MOM should be distributed to all the participants of the meeting within a couple of days of the meeting when the memory of the meeting is still fresh in the participants' minds. This will enable identifying any misunderstanding or omissions at the earliest. Should any participant identify any such anomalies in the MOM, they should be corrected after due discussion and a corrected MOM should be sent to all the participants. It is a good idea to also blast off a copy of the MOM to other stakeholders and interested parties who, for one reason or the other, could not make it to the meeting

Distinguishing between decisions and actions: Every meeting is likely to have discussions of various options as well as decisions on the chosen option (with the responsibilities duly allocated). It is important that the MOM clearly demarcates discussions and decisions. The emphasis should be on the decisions as they represent how to move forward.

Structuring the action items: The meeting should generate a bunch of action items. These action items should unambiguously identify the three Ws—What, Who, and When: What is the action item? Who is responsible and accountable for the action item? By when will the action item be completed and reported?

Given below, in Box 24.3, is a sample MOM format:

Box 24.3

TEMPLATE FOR SPECIFYING MINUTES OF A MEETING

Project Id:

Minuted By::

Date and Time of Meeting:

Venue:

I. Attendee List

Attendee Name	Group	Present?	Represented By

II. Agenda Items

A. Pending Agenda Items from previous meeting(s)

i. A1 Review and Update of Action Items from Previous Meetings

B. New Agenda Items

i. B1 . . .

III. Decisions Taken

IV. Action Items

Who?	When?	Priority	Priority

The next couple of points pertain to other actions beyond the MOM.

Following through for action items: Once the MOM goes out, the coordinator of the meeting should follow through on the execution of the action items with their respective owners. In the case of periodic status review meetings, discussion of the action items from the previous meetings should form the first agenda item of a given meeting.

Communicating the meeting decisions to other people who are not participants: During a meeting, there could be several arguments and pros and cons could be discussed. Different people may have different viewpoints. But eventually, when a decision is made in a meeting, it is a group decision and everyone in the meeting should speak with one voice outside the meeting. Any difference of opinion expressed during the meeting should not go out to people outside the meeting.

24.8 The Participant Perspective

Most of the discussions above take the perspective of someone running the meeting. In several meetings, you may just be a participant. Here are a few ground rules for such situations (also, see Snapshot 24.1):

- Do come prepared
- Do come on time
- Do follow through on the action items assigned to you
- Do not be silent when your agenda item or action item comes up
- Do not feel tempted to hog all the air time.

Fig. 24.2 *Some meeting killers*

Snapshot 24.1

Rahul Sleeper: This is the person who dwells in the back seats of a meeting, daydreaming or lost in thought or simply, sleeping. He is also prone to fiddling with things or doodling in his notebook or having a conversation on the side with like-minded persons.

Anil Bore: This is the inverse of the above person. He simply puts other people into deep coma with his terrible communication skills, marked by a dull monotone or verbose diction. He is sincere alright, but people start to squirm one minute after his slides are loaded for display.

Sunita Unprepared: She is habitually late to the meetings and when she walks in, she creates a large enough disturbance that will probably be recorded in the meeting minutes. She often comes unprepared, looks hassled and not only brings wrong data to the meetings, but also makes lame excuses for doing so.

Sunil Nuisance: He is the time waster who will hijack a meeting and take it in tangential directions. He would go on and on and never come to the point. He loves attention and considers meetings to be the highlight of his workdays.

Jose Interrupter: He is pugnacious and argumentative. He always raises objections–from the most trivial, to the most logical, consensus decisions. He can derail meetings and be very divisive.

24.9 Common Perceptions/Pitfalls

Meetings are over, now let us get back to work: Meetings are often dreaded as a waste of time. This perception is primarily because unnecessary meetings are scheduled or unnecessary people are asked to participate in a meeting. One way to avoid such a complaint is to have a clear plan for the agenda and invite only those people who have direct stake and inputs in the agenda items. The key is to integrate meetings with work, by ensuring that important decisions are taken and communicated to stakeholders.

Having long meetings: In general longer meetings tend to drain out people and are unproductive. The mail withdrawal syndrome and the constant ringing in (even in silent mode!) of missed calls and text messages give people a sense of fear that they are missing out on something urgent. Ideally, meetings more than a couple of hours long should be discouraged and if you have to have longer meetings, split them into smaller meetings with focused agenda items. For example, if you have to hold a day long business planning meeting, split it into sessions for HR, deliveries, market expectations and so on. In such a case, also explore 'break out sessions' where each sub group meets for a shorter duration in a focused way.

Beating around the bush: Meeting duration typically increases because people don't come directly to the point of discussion. Beating around the bush, getting digressed with side issues, getting into personal mudslinging all cause unnecessary delays. The person running the meeting should take care that such things don't happen. Setting the right ground rules up front, allocating time slots and responsible people for each agenda items ensuring the rules and timeframes are adhered to are some of the ways in which the pitfalls can be avoided or minimized.

Postponing and procrastinating: Meetings become unproductive if people do not bring the right data to the meeting. In order to arrive at objective decisions, the correct substantiating data is required. If people don't come with the required data, it becomes a convenient excuse to have pointless discussions that can add to the perception that meetings are time draining activities. The plan of getting concurrence on what to bring for the meeting ahead of time can minimize or avoid this pitfall.

Not closing the meeting effectively: This is perhaps the most common pitfall in meeting management. The participants get too engrossed in the nitty-gritties of one or two agenda items when someone finally notices 'Ooops . . . it is 1 p.m. and time for my next meeting!' or someone knocks on the conference room door and says 'Excuse me, I have booked this room from 1 p.m.' and then everybody picks up their stuff and runs out of the room. An abruptly ended meeting will not feel like a serious meeting and therefore, suitable controls must be in place to formally complete the meeting in the set time. Every meeting should have allocated time for an effective closure—key decisions are restated, key action items are emphasized and the plans for the next meeting is laid out. As mentioned earlier, when planning time for every meeting, these 5–10 minutes should be factored in.

24.10 In Summary

We will conclude this chapter with a summary of key points to be followed if you are organizing a meeting and if you are a participant in the meeting. These are in the realm of etiquette, but it is worthwhile to summarize them here as they are intricately tied to what we have discussed in this chapter.

If you are organizing a meeting, please remember:

- Choose the people who should attend the meeting with discretion.
- Choose a convenient time and place. Generally the location which is convenient to most people is the preferred location (The one exception is that if the big boss is to take part in the meeting, generally his office building would be the venue).
- Depending on the travel time, it may be a good idea to have the meeting towards the end of the day or beginning of the day so that remaining worktime is not eaten away by travel.

- If people have to be dialled in, make sure you get the contact numbers right (and the time right when it is in a different time zone). If some of them have to dial in themselves, make sure you provide them the appropriate information (phone number with country and area code, meeting ID, pass code, etc.).
- Allocate sufficient time to discuss all the important issues, but do not make it so long that people feel they are wasting time.
- If possible, segment the meeting into smaller parts, where each person, relevant to an agenda item being discussed, can come in just for that part.
- Inform people of the agenda ahead of time and get their consent for participation. If they cannot participate, ensure that a reasonable substitute, who is empowered enough, can participate.
- For important meetings, try to remind the participants on the day before the meeting.
- Book the meeting venue well ahead of time.
- If the meeting venue is not in your home base, get familiar with the location ahead of time and get to know how to access infrastructure (e.g., printers, coffee machine, etc.)—and most importantly, get to know the administrative assistant who is in charge of this location and its infrastructure.
- Arrive early to the meeting venue. If you have access to the meeting room before the meeting, ensure that the necessary infrastructure is available.
- Identify a scribe at the beginning of the meeting.
- Stick to the agenda–don't let any one topic go tangential and steal the time from rest of the items.
- Handle conflicts delicately but firmly. Don't let anyone bully you or rest of the participants. Take charge firmly yet politely.
- Look for the people who want to interrupt. Honour such interruptions on a case by case basis.
- Always allocate a few minutes at the end for summarizing the meeting and stating the follow-through plan.
- Send out the minutes of meeting the same day or at most the next day.
- Diligently follow through on the action items and let these feed into the next meeting.

If you are an invited participant, then certain etiquette applies to you as well:

- If you are given an agenda item (and have signed up for it), prepare well before you come for a meeting. Don't have a shot gun approach to coming to the meeting and then thinking about the matter.
- Be punctual to the meeting. If your presence is required only for a portion of the meeting or if you can attend only part of the meeting, do inform the coordinator

ahead of time and ensure that the time allotted for discussing your agenda item is appropriately specified.

- If you cannot attend a meeting after you have promised to (because of some unforeseen emergency), do get in touch with the coordinator as soon as possible and convey the message. Try to see if you can send someone who could substitute for you and who is also empowered and capable to commit to action items or participate in discussions meaningfully.
- Do not walk in and out of a meeting repeatedly.
- Do not use your cell phone for talking or messaging during the meeting. Never leave your cell phone in the loud ringing mode. Switch it off or at least leave it in silent or vibrating mode.
- Do not work on your laptop while attending the meeting.
- Stick to your allotted time for discussion. Don't overshoot your allotted time as it will have a cascading effect on other agenda items.
- If there are other agenda items that you think you can add value, try to inform the coordinator ahead of time. If that is not possible, do not hesitate to contribute to the discussion on these items.
- Do not steal everyone else's thunder.
- If you have to interrupt, do it gently. Don't butt in abruptly or too often. Let whoever is talking come to some logical point (at least till end of the sentence).
- If certain action items are assigned to you, do what it takes to carry these to completion.
- Promptly report the status of assigned action items to the coordinator as soon as possible, at any rate not later than the next meeting.

25

Proposals

"Your customer is the best source to ask if you want to know how to write a winning proposal."

–Unknown

Proposals serve several purposes in a business context. Since a proposal is a written document, it has become more or less essential for contractual purposes. Customers use proposals for comparing different vendors. Vendors use proposals to demonstrate their superior position over other vendors

Proposal writing is one of the communication skills that would be called to play very often as a person advances in his or her career. While this applies especially in sales and marketing functions, the concepts presented here would apply just as much in an inward facing job like research and development.

From an external point of view, proposals are our ways of seeking opportunities for business from a prospect. Sometimes the customer need not be an external customer; he can be an internal customer also. For example, you may be running an offshore software center for a product development company in the USA and want to move some new work to the centre. This might require a proposal to be submitted that will be evaluated by the senior management of the organization. Almost no formal business gets closed without a proposal and a presentation.

In this chapter, we will first see some of the characteristics of effective proposals. We will then outline a process that can be followed for creating such effective proposals. One important aspect of the process of preparing effective proposals is the pre-writing research through which you find out what the customer's needs and wants are and how best to use this information to your advantage. We have dedicated one section to cover some aspects of this pre-writing research. Putting this all together, we have presented a structure for a proposal that can act as a starting point in many real-life cases. Proposal writing bears a lot of similarity with other scenarios of communication like resumé writing. We cover some of these similarities so that the reader can see the parallel and apply appropriate lessons from other chapters. We follow this up with a section on some of the pitfalls that we have seen in writing proposals and conclude with a summary.

25.1 Characteristics of Effective Proposals

There are some golden rules of writing effective proposals. Those proposals that follow these dictums are usually successful. While these are not exhaustive, these are certainly the most crucial.

Focus on benefits rather than features: A person writing a proposal should first realize that this is meant for a customer who has a problem that needs to be solved and that he/she is proposing a solution to the customer's problem. The entire proposal should be focused on the benefits the customer gets from the solution and not the outlandish features that the product you are proposing has. For example, if your software can run on multiple platforms, ask yourself 'Why is this relevant to the customer and for me to include in my proposal?' If the customer specifically asks for a 'Windows-only' solution, then, bragging about your product's super-performance on a mainframe does not add any value to the proposal. By including the entire product specs into the proposal, you may be diverting the focus of the reader to areas that don't contribute to your proposal being accepted over those of the competition (see Snapshot 25.1).

Snapshot 25.1

Consider selling a car that accelerates from 0 to 60 Kmph in under 3 seconds. This is a great feature. But, if you are selling this car essentially for city driving in India, then this feature is of absolutely no benefit to the customer. Rather than focus on this 'cool feature', you are better off on emphasizing things like ease of parking, fuel efficiency and so on.

Be customer-centric: To continue on from the previous point, the focus should be on the customer, not *excessively* on yourself or your product. This does not mean that you should not talk about your product, but talk about what aspects of your product will make it interesting for the customer. Your proposal should demonstrate that you have understood the customer's needs and wants; your solution should directly address such needs and wants. You should know the customer's hot buttons and address them (see Snapshot 25.2).

Snapshot 25.2

Imagine you are proposing a solution for a point of sale (POS) system to be used in checkout counters in departmental stores. The likely hot buttons that the customer would be interested in are reliability of scanning the bar codes (i.e., the code must be scanned correctly) and speed of scanning (i.e., there should be no need to swipe the item twice). Emphasizing that an item is guaranteed to be scanned correctly the first time 99.99 per cent of the times and guaranteeing the time of scan to be under a second would make the customer interested in the proposal. Focusing on the power of the laser beam or such technical details would not interest the customer.

Demonstrate credibility and track record: The customer is anxiously waiting for a solution to his problems. He has got several nagging questions like, 'If I go with the proposer, will my problems get solved?' 'Does he have the necessary skills and experience to solve my problems?' 'Will he be around long enough to support me if I have any ongoing problems?' 'Am I getting value for my money?' and many such questions. Your proposal should demonstrate credibility and a track record for solving similar problems (see Snapshot 25.3).

Snapshot 25.3

To demonstrate credibility and track record, include in the proposal,

- Solutions that have worked well in the same domain
- Solutions that are working in environments similar to the customer's environment
- Testimonials from people with credibility.

Highlight your USP: Not only should you demonstrate credibility and track record for solving customers' problems, you should also highlight the unique selling proposition for your solution. There will be several vendors who will tell the prospect that they can solve his problem. How does the customer choose your proposal over others' proposals? Are you delivering a better return on investment? Are you reducing total cost of ownership? Are you providing a better quality guarantee? Have you enjoyed the highest market share in the domain or similar areas? Do you own some exclusive intellectual property that is going to make your solution stand out? Do you have access to a large pool of manpower to expedite executing a contract? Do you have a demonstrated track record of low attrition (compared to your competition) that is comforting to the prospect? Whatever you consider your unique selling proposition, that sets you apart from the competition with respect to solving the prospect's problem, should be highlighted prominently.

Show need, affordability and worth from customer perspective: Perhaps the three best words that summarize what the prospect is looking for and needs to be convinced of a proposal, are need, affordability and worth. A proposal must meet the *needs* of the prospect. In fact, effective proposals go beyond the *stated needs* of the customer. They address the *implied needs* and sometimes the *un-thought-of requirements* of the prospect. Secondly, the solution must be perceived to be *affordable* by the prospect. 'Affordable' could be on any yardstick the prospect decides. It could be set-up time required for an off-shore team; it could be the per-transaction cost in BPO-like situations; it could be total cost of ownership for a piece of software (that includes license cost, cost of quality, maintenance costs and so on). It is important that the proposal addresses affordability in exactly the same terms and provide compelling evidence for it. Finally, we come to worth. The prospect must be convinced that the proposal is not only meeting his needs and he can afford it, but also he must see the *worth* or value in the solution.

End with a recommendation: When you are making a proposal to the customer, you are not only trying to sell something to the customer, but also demonstrating your professional pride and organizational strength. Your customer is trying to look for your value proposition and your judgement call on what solution you are proposing to his problems. If you are not proposing such a solution through a compelling recommendation, then the proposal is likely to be viewed as not useful or not compelling. Putting together a laundry list of 'here are the options available from my company and you can choose what you want' is not the right way of going about making proposals. After all, even when we go to a decent restaurant, we ask the waiter what his recommendation is!

Address important customer needs upfront with a great opening: Just like a presentation and a good resumé, the make or break for a reader of a proposal happens within the first few minutes. Hence, it is imperative that the proposal has a great beginning, says the right things upfront and gets the prospect interested in reading the proposal further. Demonstrating that you have understood the prospect's requirements, your recommendation of a solution that addresses the prospect's problem, the uniqueness of your solution, the quantifiable gains you can offer from your solution should all come out in a nutshell right at the beginning. Such a compelling beginning will augur well for the proposal to be considered favourably by the prospect.

Be brief and don't include irrelevant boilerplate material: Sometimes proposals look like huge binders or a Harry Potter book. This is not at all necessary nor is it advisable to have an extra-fat proposal. Effective proposals are brief and to the point, addressing customer requirements. All unnecessary boilerplate 'standard' stuff like full press coverage, detailed product specifications of all the products that the company produces and such are not needed in an effective proposal. Make it brief and punchy.

Make it free of typos: Just like a resumé, it is imperative that a proposal too, has no typographical errors. A typo is a clear give-away of the lack of commitment of the organization that is proposing. One more type of error, that is not really a typo but falls under this category, is using some other proposal and forgetting to change prospect's name. If such is the care given to a prospect, what would be the care given when the prospect becomes a customer! Rest assured that just like in the case of a resumé, these mistakes stand out like a sore thumb and seasoned campaigners will spot these in a moment's glance.

Balance the use of colour, graphics and the variety of visual aids: An effective proposal will have variety. Graphs, charts, colours, tables and pictures will be combined in appropriate proportion with the text. The presentation is as compelling as the content. At the same time, make sure that it does not contain an overdose of these elements to make it look flashy. Arriving at the right balance of these supplemental factors would add a substantial amount of weight to make the proposal serve its useful purpose in transforming the prospect to a customer.

25.2 The Process of Preparing an Effective Proposal

The process of preparing effective proposals can be summarized by Figure 25.1.

1. Prewriting tasks:
   (a) Put together a proposal team, if required
   (b) Qualify the prospects
   (c) Do background and foreground research.
2. Writing:
   (a) Prepare a draft proposal
   (b) Identify the things that are not clear about the prospect's needs
   (c) Talk to prospect if possible to clarify any unclear issues.
3. Quality assurance and final touches:
   (a) Get the proposal peer reviewed and make any changes as needed
   (b) Do a final check and put finishing touches.

Let us look at each of these in some more detail:

25.2.1 Prewriting Tasks

A proposal is used to convert a prospect into a customer, to materialize a sale or to make an idea into a product. Proposal writing—at least effective proposal writing—takes time and effort. For large proposals, it may neither be possible nor effective for just one person to put them together. You may need to assemble a team of people and divide the work among team members in a way that each team member does what he is good at, understanding and contributing to the over-arching goal of winning

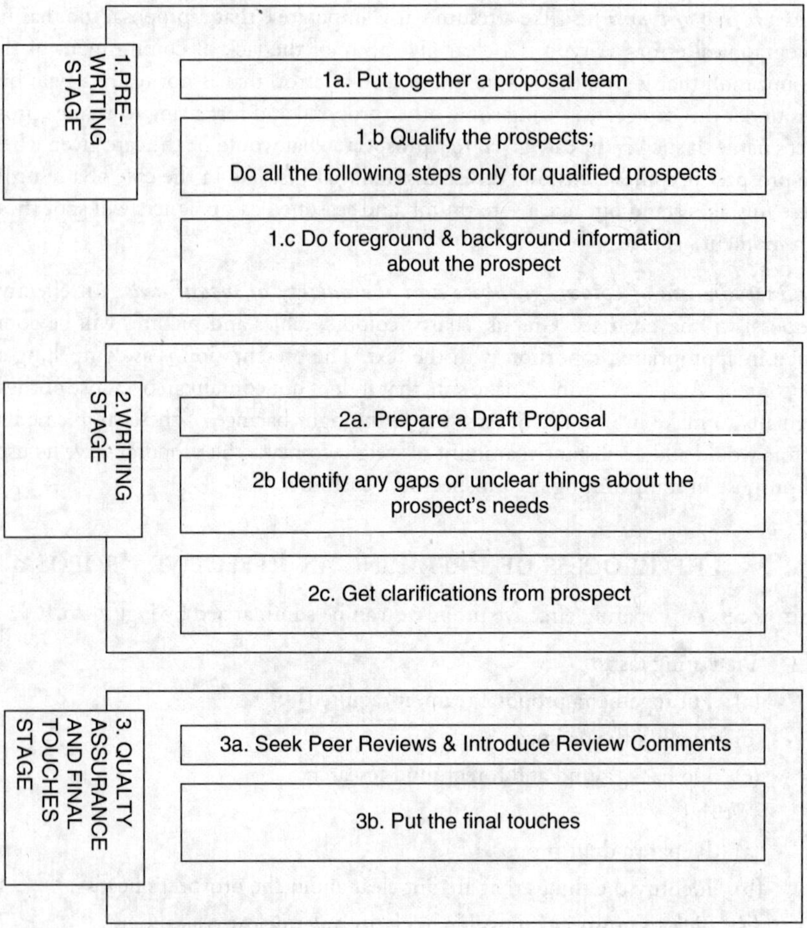

Fig. 25.1 *The Process of preparing a proposal*

over the prospect. You should not expend this energy for every suspect that comes along, but do it only for qualified prospects. Is the prospect serious about buying your product? Is he simply asking for a proposal to get into a better bargaining position with other vendors? Does he have a track record of wasting time by asking for proposals he never takes forward? Even if he really buys the product, is he a customer worth having? Can he become reference-able? If you are sure of answers to these questions, it would make sense to submit a proposal. You might also like to ask questions that are an introspection of your competencies and objectives. Do we have the competency for executing the work? Does this work align with my overall strategy? Would this work help in acquiring new skills?

The net summary of this point is that make a proposal only when you want to go ahead with the prospect.

Another prewriting task is to make sure that you gather as much information about the prospect's organization and needs as is possible. Go on the Internet, visit the prospect's Web site and understand his business model, value propositions and competitive advantage. Talk to the various sources and find out his pain points—what are the main problems he is facing and what he expects the solution to accomplish. What are the gains he is expecting? What metrics or yardsticks would he use to measure the value derived from a solution? What are his hot buttons? What are his likes and dislikes? These questions would look very similar to the ones we saw in audience analysis. After all, what we are doing here is indeed audience analysis. So, everything that we discussed in audience analysis does in fact, apply here.

A third prewriting task is to look at the projects or proposals you have done in your organization earlier and see which of them look similar to what this prospect wants. You can apply the learning from these earlier, similar proposals to make your current proposal effective.

More the efforts put out in the prewriting stage, more benefits are likely to accrue when you write the proposal to make it effective. However, you will surely be driven by timelines and there will be a point of diminishing returns beyond which preparations would not help. Like everything else, you have to bite the bullet at some point of time and get on to writing the proposal, which is what we cover in the next section. It is a good idea to put these all together in the form of an executive summary and get it reviewed by the appropriate people before jumping into the full proposal.

25.2.2 The Structure of Effective Proposals

There is no one single structure for an effective proposal. But there are some common threads that apply across the board (see Box 25.1):

Start with a courteous, customized cover letter: This cover letter should be on the letterhead of the proposing organization. The letter should be especially free of typos. It should be customized. The addressee should be named specifically, along with the title; the full address of the recipient must be mentioned. The salutation should be specific, if possible.

Include a catchy title page for the proposal, after the cover letter: Just like a resumé should not have a trite heading like 'resumé', so also, don't have a title called just 'proposal'. Make the title as customer centric as possible. For example, instead of having a title 'Proposal from XZY Corporation', you should use something like,

An opportunity for 50 per cent reduction in maintenance costs
for ABC Corp:
From: VSrinivasan
XYZ Corporation, . . .

Such a title can immediately stir up the reader.

Have a brief executive summary: The executive summary should ideally be one to two pages in length. As mentioned earlier, this should demonstrate that you have understood the prospect's requirements and that your recommendation of a solution addresses the prospect's problem. It should also highlight the uniqueness of your solution and the quantifiable gains you can offer from your solution using the customer's hot buttons.

Go through the same sequence in the body of the proposal: First, start with the prospect's problem you are trying to solve. Then, highlight the options you are proposing and your recommended solution, providing cost-benefit justifications. Highlight why your solution delivers more value than your competitors. In the body, make sure you have the right quality and quantity of graphics, illustrations, etc. as discussed earlier.

Have a few appendices to the proposal: Push things like company history and product specifications to appendices. Also include an appendix of testimonials, press coverage and any relevant white papers.

Provide a glossary of the abbreviations, acronyms and terms: Don't assume the prospect knows your acronyms and abbreviations. When in doubt, use simple English instead of acronyms and jargon.

Box 25.1

Possible Structure of an Effective Proposal

- Customized, courteous and concise cover letter (on the company letterhead)
- A catchy title page
- Executive summary that highlights the customer issues you are addressing and how your solution gives the best bang for the buck (be brief and to the point)
- Detailed body of the proposal covering
  - Prospect's issues and problems the proposal addresses
  - The options of solutions available
  - The recommended solution, along with cost benefit analysis
  - The unique selling proposition of your offer
  - Demonstrations of track record of accomplishment.
- Appendix containing
  - Product specifications for those products you are recommending
  - A brief company history
  - Testimonials, press coverage and so on.

While writing the proposal, you may need additional information. If there are no barriers, feel free to communicate directly with the prospect to clear any doubts that you may have about their problems and concerns.

25.2.3 Putting the Finishing Touches

Make sure that the proposals (at least the important ones) go through a stringent internal peer review. At least one of the reviewers should play the role of the devil's advocate and look at the customer perspective. Software developers use a technique called Fagan Inspection for important work products. This process has been found to be extremely effective for proposals also.

Finally, you should start doing the 'production copy'. Some of the things you should make sure of include:

- Printing on high quality paper
- Inserting the company logo in the pages where appropriate
- Giving each page its page number
- Taking care that each page is printed without blurred inks
- Confirming that the colours have come out well
- Ascertaining that the proposal is bound properly.

25.3 Similarity of Proposals to Other Vehicles of Communication

Throughout the chapter, we have highlighted some of the similarities of proposal writing with other communication vehicles. In this section, we summarize these similarities:

Being audience-centric: One of the first chapters we presented in the communications section was about audience analysis. Just like a presentation—in fact even to a higher degree—a proposal should *always* be focused on solving the prospect's problem. The language used in the proposal should be something that the customer can relate to.

Putting forth effort for preparations: Any form of communication requires preparation and rehearsal. Proposals are no exception. Subjecting proposals to peer reviews is crucial.

Having a great opening: First impressions are best impressions. This applies very much to proposals. Just like a resumé can be rejected in a matter of seconds because of poor, upfront presentation of key points, a proposal with a poor opening can be dumped by the prospect.

Fit and focus: We saw the 5Fs in writing effective resumés. Two of these—fit and focus—become more crucial for a proposal. The reader of the proposal is looking for the fit between his needs and the solution provided by the vendor. The writer of the proposal should put focus on demonstrating this fit.

Not having any typos: This is a given in any written communication scenario and applies 200 per cent in a proposal. This relates to the formatting Part of 5Fs

Ending with a punchy recommendation or call for action: Remember the dictum 'Tell them what you are going to tell them, tell them and tell them what you told them'. The recommendations that you give at the end of a proposal is an example of your making sure that the audience goes away with what *you* want them to take away rather than what *they* want to take away.

25.4 Pitfalls and Misconceptions in Writing Proposals

Here are some of the potential pitfalls and misconceptions to look out for while writing proposals.

A proposal should have detailed company history, upfront: Remember that a proposal is intended to highlight the match between what the prospect wants and the solution proposed. Company history (of the proposing organization) is not of much relevance. At least, it should not be the first thing to hit the eye.

A proposal should have the full product specification for all the products that your company makes: While it may be necessary to include the product specifications of the recommended product, it is certainly not necessary to include a laundry list of the specifications of all the products that your company makes.

Not ending with a recommendation: A proposal without recommendation is like a movie without a climax. Such a proposal betrays your lack of professional pride and most likely jeopardizes your chances in winning the bid.

Not explicit about the USP: Don't be too modest about demonstrating your USP. Include as much substantiation as possible to demonstrate the USP. If you assume that the reader will know your USP, tough luck. He won't. Also, make sure that the USP should relate directly to the solution you are offering to the prospect. Your company being a twenty billion dollar company is not a USP—unless it is going to solve the prospect's problem.

25.5 In Summary

Proposal writing is yet another soft skill that is going to occupy much of your time as you grow in your career, whether you are in the technical or marketing line of work. It is a communication vehicle and all the aspects of effective communication we have seen so far will also apply to proposals. Just to summarize the most important aspects of a proposal, it should be:

> Customer-centric, customized, clear, concise and compelling.

Since each proposal has the potential to add to your company's business or shape your career

> Pay attention to detail.

Attention to detail covers both the content and the delivery components—making sure the proposal addresses the prospect's needs, sets forth your USPs and is of course, free of typos as well as being colourful, printed on high quality paper and so on.

Just like in a resumé, make sure the right content appears right at the beginning, so that the reader does not have to rummage through your document to find what he wants. Remember,

> First impressions are the best impressions.

Finally, remember to have a few things that 'wow' the prospect's expectations.

> Winning proposals are those that go beyond just meeting the expectations—they should go far beyond.

26

Status Reports

"Reports that say that something hasn't happened are always interesting to me, because as we know, there are known knowns; there are things we know we know. We also know there are known unknowns; that is to say we know there are some things we do no know. But there are also unknown unknowns—the ones we don't know we don't know."

–Donald Rumsfeld

Status reporting is a typical upward communication done by an employee through an organization's hierarchy. Even allowing for individual situations, it occurs fairly frequently—typically on a weekly basis. In this chapter, we will examine the intended purpose of a status report, present a structure under which to organize a status report, give you tips on whom to send a status report to and on how to decide the most appropriate frequency of status reports. We will conclude the chapter with some of the common pitfalls that we have seen in the area of status reporting.

Of course, status reporting need not be limited to just one's managers and people higher up in the organizational chart. Project status reports can be also sent laterally to your fellow employees and even to outside stakeholders with whom you don't have a hierarchical relationship. But in this chapter, we will look at it as a vehicle of communication with your management.

26.1 The Intended Purpose of Status Reports

To inform: Status reports are a means of keeping the relevant stakeholders informed about how a project is going on. This provides a communication channel between an employee and the management (typically his or her immediate manager). The people who need to know, need to be informed and status reports provide this opportunity.

To track progress against plan: Status reporting is done for a given period (typically a week). They provide a window to understand the progress not only in absolute terms, but also against what was planned for the period. This obviously implies that there was a plan in place for the period.

To provide a signal for any corrective action: When what is executed is not in line with what is planned, it calls for corrective action. Either the plan has to be changed or the execution has to be tightened. In any case, status reports provide the primary inputs for deciding such corrective action.

To act as an escalation channel and seek required action: When a status report is submitted, there could be some action that is sought from the recipients of the report. For example, an employee may have a persistent problem with a piece of hardware and the vendor has not responded back. This may need to be escalated via the management channel. Status reports provide a channel to seek such an escalation.

To highlight red alerts: During the course of a project, there may be some 'red alerts'—those things that portend danger for the project and need corrective action from the upper levels of management. A status report should highlight such issues and give a heads up proactively, so that these can be addressed before extensive damage is done.

To outline the plan for the subsequent period: Just as the current period's status report stacks up the progress vis-a-vis the plan set forth at the beginning of that period, the current status report should outline the plans for the coming period. This will provide continuity of communication and the project objectives.

26.2 Organizing the Contents of a Status Report

In order for a status report to serve its intended purposes, it can be organized in the following simple heads:

- **What was planned for this period and achieved?** This would indicate things that are going as per plan.
- **What was planned and not achieved?** When this happens, it is important to perform a root-cause analysis of the deviation from the plan. When something that is planned is not achieved, it could either indicate a slippage or it could indicate that the original plan was unrealistic. In either case, some corrective action, that would include changing the plan, is needed.
- **What was not planned and was accomplished or consumed time?** If something that was not in the plan got done, it could either mean that there was some unexpected progress or that these unplanned activities that got done were simply unavoidable interruptions or unnecessary distractions. Again, in either case, it is necessary to understand why such interruptions happen and try to minimize these interruptions to make the plan as realistic as possible.
- **What are the really critical issues ('red alerts') that need to be addressed?** There may be some showstopper issues that the person writing the status report may

become aware of. He should bring it to the attention of the manager by highlighting such issues. Examples of such issues could be delays in getting hardware, unresolved problems in other modules, etc.

In addition to all this information about what happened over the previous tracking period, a status report should also give the plans for the next period. This part will act as the basis for the next report. Based on these, a sample template for status reports is given in Box 26.1.

Box 26.1

Template for Status Reports

Project Id:
Staff Name/User Id:
Period of Reporting: Start Date:
End Date:

Activities planned and completed

- ____________________
- ____________________
- ____________________

Activities planned and not completed (with reasons for any discrepancy)

- ____________________
- ____________________
- ____________________

Activities not planned and that consumed time (reasons as appropriate)

- ____________________
- ____________________
- ____________________

Plans for the coming period

- ____________________
- ____________________
- ____________________

Red alerts

- ____________________
- ____________________
- ____________________

26.3 Deciding the Recipients of a Status Report

The recipients of a status report must satisfy at least one criterion: They would need to know or be people who should act. The category of people who need to know would definitely include the direct manager of the author of the status report. It may also include others, depending upon the state nature of a project. For example, a project may be a high-visibility one for the senior management and top secret. For such a project, the highest levels of management, including the CEO, may be interested in the project's progress. In such a case, it would make sense to copy the required levels on the original status report itself. Or else, it will have to wade through multiple levels of the management and the subject lines will be full of 'Fwd: Fwd. . . .' to the extent that the CEO may not even be able to read the subject line on his screen (unless he opens the mail, which he won't unless he feels the mail is important). A word of caution on this: It is worthwhile to get a clear understanding of who the recipients of a status report should be from your manager (or someone higher up) ahead of time. Don't assume that your project is the super-project of the millennium for your company and copy all the CXOs.

For most common projects, the typical people who need to see the status report would include the direct manager and also the heads of the other groups who are either dependent on the status of the project or whose services the project needs (e.g., human resources or infrastructure).

The second category of people who need to receive a copy of the status reports would be people who should act based on the report. This again would include the immediate manager (as he would need to participate in most of the action!). In addition, this could include heads of other affected groups or dependent groups.

The recipients can change based on the stage in which the project is. For example, as a product approaches the release date, more people in several departments and at several levels (including the CXO) would need to be informed in a timely manner. It is a common practice to draw up a communication plan for a project right at the beginning, like the one given in Box 26.2.

Box 26.2

Example of a Communication Plan

Stakeholder	Project Phase	Medium of Communication (e-mail, meeting, etc.)	Frequency of Communication	What Needs to Be Tracked and Communicated
Testing Team				
Senior Management				
Infrastructure Team				
Development Team				
Customer				

26.4 What Should Be the Ideal Frequency of Status Reports?

The frequency of sending status reports depends on three factors:

(a) Duration/pace of project

(b) Current State of project

(c) Nature of project

The duration of a project is the primary driver to determine the frequency of status reports. The frequency of status reports should not be so rare that it does not add value to corrective actions. At the same time, it should not be so frequent that it is bureaucratic and not many changes happen between successive reports. For example, consider a six week project. At minimum, it may be required to have a status report twice in a week. This is necessary because, a considerable part of the project duration elapses (as much as 15 per cent) between reports if you have reports say once a week. This may be too long to implement any corrective action. If you have status reports as frequently as every day, it may be an overkill, because there would not be sufficient changes within a day and reporting every day would be construed as not adding much value. At the other extreme, consider a six month project. Then, once a week reporting should be more than sufficient.

Whatever be the duration of a project, each project typically goes through a crunch phase (normally towards the end of the project) wherein it is almost like a ultra-short duration project. For example, a six month release cycle for a product finally goes through a state close to 'actual release date'. All hell breaks loose at this time and almost everyone in the organization is interested in what is happening in the project in an hour-by-hour basis - it is almost like the last five overs of a 50-overs cricket match. Status reports are expected very often at such a time. Such reports can be very informal, but they should provide the gist of the information as very senior people in the organization may be interested in such reports (see Snapshot 26.1).

Projects can be broadly classified into two types: First are the routine projects that an organization executes on a day to day basis. These could be the periodic releases of software products that a software organization produces; projects to improve production yields or production quality in a manufacturing organization and so on. The frequency of status reports in such projects is decided purely on the basis of the first two factors—nature and current state. But, there is the other category of projects—the pet projects of the 'forces that be' in the organization, the top secret projects that the bosses are personally overseeing, the high visibility launch that will rewrite the company's history and because of which the bosses are breathing down your neck. For such projects that have high visibility or high stakes, all bets are off as to what should be the ideal frequency of reporting status. It could be very frequent—twice a week, daily or even hourly when the deadline is fast approaching. For such *ad hoc*

Snapshot 26.1

Imagine you are watching a limited-overs cricket match in which the team batting second is chasing a target to win. At the beginning of the run chase, the ticker at the bottom may say something like '320 to win in 50 overs at 6.4 runs per over'. This information is updated every over for the first 20 or so overs. But, as we approach the last five overs, the same information is presented in a different form. Instead of saying '37 to win from 5 overs at 7.4 runs per over', the ticker shows '37 runs to win from 30 balls'. This is updated after every ball and not at the end of every over. The reason for the change in format of this 'status report' is that the runs-ball difference is a better abstraction of the status for the batting team to see how many dot balls they can allow or how many boundaries they have to hit. Similarly, it lets the bowling team set a field either to block boundaries or block singles. Also, the reason why the status report is updated after every ball and not after every over, is that there are only five overs (or 30 balls) remaining and every ball is crucial to take an appropriate and timely corrective action. It is easy to extrapolate this example to a real-life project in any industry. Crunch-time reporting calls for different formats and almost always a more frequent status reporting.

status reports, be prepared to be flexible in format, content and media. These would be more of status updates than status reports. Be prepared to be creative in sending such updates by phone calls or even text messages/SMS.

26.5 What Should the Recipients Do with a Status Report?

Understand and acknowledge the progress: The worst thing that can happen to a sender of a status report is that he feels like the reports are going into a blackhole with almost no responses from anyone receiving the report. While it is not fair to expect the recipient to respond to every status report, it would definitely undermine his credibility if he does not acknowledge the progress at least occasionally.

Know what actions need to be taken—and take them! Sometimes the writer of the status report may not explicitly express the action required of the recipient. The recipient (especially if he is the direct manager) should take some extra effort to understand the actions required of him. As the eventual goal of a communication cycle is acting on the message, taking the appropriate action is absolutely essential.

Get the antennae up for red alerts: When a certain item is marked as 'red alert', the manager should keep his antennae up for any further developments regarding that issue. A red alert has the potential to blow up and hence, requires extra communication over and beyond the periodic status reports. This extra communication can be in the form of unsolicited synchronous communication like face-to-face meetings and phone calls, through informal across-the-hallway conversations or even by tapping into the grapevine.

Be prepared to read between the lines and see through any sugarcoating: When an employee does not want to tell a piece of bad news explicitly, there may be some sugarcoating or beating around the bush. The recipient should be able to read between the lines, infer any 'implied' bad news and talk to the sender to explicitly clarify any such issues. Such issues, when unattended could potentially blow up.

26.6 Some Common Mistakes in Status Reporting

Making it look like a superman adventure: Sometimes a status report contains all the gory details of a problem and the heroic steps taken to solve it. This is a common mistake made by technical people when sending a status report to a boss who has grown up through the technical ranks, under the assumption that the boss would get impressed by such details. While it is possible that the boss is indeed interested in these details, these are needed only to the extent of making him take the required action. Status reports are neither the forum where one shows off technical adventurism nor one in which the boss proves he is still technically minded even after moving to management.

Not having the right level of abstraction: To take the previous point one step further, the status report is read by an audience who neither has nor needs the full level of detail that the writer of the report has. The audience needs a level of abstraction that is presumably at a higher level than what the writer has experienced. For example, a manager who receives a status report is primarily interested in two things: First, is the project going on track; second, if not, who should do what. In particular, what should he do to get the project back on track. If this level of abstraction is not provided by the writer of the status report, there is the risk of the manager taking an action that is completely tangential to what the writer intended.

Not having continuity between status reports of various periods: As discussed earlier, the status report for a given period tracks the progress against the plan for the previous period and also sets the agenda or plan for the coming period. Thus, there should be continuity across project reports. In the first chapter of this part of the book (Chapter 13), we saw that communication is an ongoing process and is made up of smaller communication cycles. Viewed this way, status reports form the communication cycles in the overall project communication. Not having continuity across the status reports and making each period's status report focus on just that period's burning fires or flash-in-the-pan achievements undermines the usefulness of status reports.

Sugarcoating: The writer of a status report should not shy away from giving any bad news that is there. Postponing giving the bad news is only going to make matters worse. Some people have an uncanny knack of telling bad news in such a way that no one understands that it is bad news, but at the same time the writer can later claim that he already mentioned it. Such sugarcoating or camouflaging will reduce the credibility of the writer. Bad news, if present, is better conveyed sooner than later. Delaying the revelation of bad news or sugarcoating it only postpones and magnifies an impending disaster. We deal with more of this in Chapter 29.

Copying multiple layers of hierarchy: Sometimes, the writer of a status report does not understand who all he should mark a copy of the status report to. 'Just to play safe', a copy of a status report may be marked to the manager, manager's manager and even the CEO. This is perhaps the most *unsafe* option for several reasons. First, it unnecessarily clutters up the mail box of people at the senior management level. Second, the sender may be remembered by the senior management for the wrong reasons. In future, anytime the sender sends a mail to the senior management for a genuine reason, it may be ignored as yet another 'play safe' mail!

Having a red alert alive through several reporting periods: When a red alert continues to be alive over several reporting periods and if the project is progressing well, it would not be construed as a red alert at all! On the other hand, if the project is slipping and the red alerts continue to be flagged, then it means that appropriate corrective action has not been taken; either the manager or the person writing the report (or both) need to be held accountable for such a slip.

Not reading a status report and not following through on action items: The recipient of a status report (assuming that the report is sent to the right recipient) should carefully peruse the report, understand the action items expected of him and execute them within the timeframe agreed upon. A recipient (especially the manager) not following through with the action items will send a wrong message to the sender of the status reports that the reporting process is a bogus eyewash.

26.7 In Summary

Status reports tend to become a dreaded but necessary evil. While they are necessary, they need be neither dreaded nor evil. In order for a status report to be useful for the organization (or the recipients) and not intimidating for the writer of the report,

> Use status reports as a vehicle to highlight accomplishments.

From the manager's point of view, he would expect to know not just the good news, but also the bad news. If there is bad news, he'd better do what it takes to resolve the underlying issues. Resolution of an issue becomes more complex if the issue is allowed to stagnate for longer periods.

> If there is bad news, better tell it early in a status report.

Sometimes what is bad news to you may not be recognized as bad news by your manager. And he may take an action entirely different from what you wanted him to take. Hence,

> Don't sugarcoat a problem; be explicit; propose possible solutions

Every problem is not a red alert. If everything is important, then nothing is important (at least for the manager). So,

> Choose your targets correctly as far as red alerts are concerned.

As a recipient, a status report is not a mere tool to track progress against plan. A series of status reports can make interesting revelations about a project, a customer or an employee. So, as a manager receiving status reports,

> Make sure you do some aggregate analysis of several status reports to spot trends.

"So, your report says that other than the cost overruns, delays and shortage of resources, the project is going just fine."

Fig. 26.1

27

Giving and Receiving Feedback

"There is no failure, only feedback."

–Thomas Alva Edison

Feedback is a concept borrowed from engineering. It is a process where we extract information about the performance of a machine and use this information to tweak the machine settings, so that we achieve an improved performance. When applied to human beings, feedback is a moment of reckoning—when we let others observe us and suggest appropriate corrective actions so that our behaviour and performance become even better.

Of course, with us humans, things are not as simple as pressing buttons or designing appropriate electrical circuitry. We will have to deal with a whole slew of complex psychological factors while going through the feedback process.

Although most of us think that feedback is a good idea, most of us don't want to get negative feedback and criticism for fear of damaging the positive self-image we have of ourselves. When we do get criticized, we often tend to get very defensive and pooh-pooh the feedback. Most of us believe that we are reasonably good performers already and cannot possibly be coaxed into anything better. Even if we have an open mind about receiving feedback and changing ourselves, we are often too busy or too lazy to go through the process effectively. Of course, feedback can also be positive. We can get compliments on our performance and high marks for our strengths (just like we can identify the high-performance state of a machine). But, most of us don't know how to handle praise either—other than to look coy and sufficiently humble—and will end up squandering away an opportunity to get even better.

The workplace is a hotspot of feedback activity. A vast amount of feedback is given and received all the time—feedback about our jobs and how to improve our job performance, feedback about where we are with respect to our goals, feedback from our managers on how we rank compared to the rest of the group, feedback from our customers and business partners to nudge us toward better service and relationships. There are so many formal and informal channels of feedback available in our offices that a person interested in improving his or her performance can readily do so.

27.1 Features of Feedback Process

Let us first look at some features of a typical feedback process.

It is about a specific activity or skill: An ideal feedback is limited in scope. It concerns itself with a particular activity or competency you are associated with. For example, in case of performance appraisal[1], it focuses only on the job performance. It is not intended to be a master check-up of your entire life.

There is a feedback-giver and a feedback-receiver: The assessment of the situation is done by the feedback-giver—such as the managers who do the performance appraisals—and the persons who are being apprised are the feedback-receivers.

Ideally, it should lead to corrective action and performance improvement: The result of the feedback process should be a list of meaningful 'action items', which should be adopted and implemented by the feedback-receiver and should lead him eventually to better performance.

It comes in various forms: The performance appraisal questionnaire is but one form of feedback. There are several other ways to obtain feedback—right from non-verbal feedbacks to hallway conversations, as we will see below.

It has a relationship with the environment: As always, the big picture is important and you will have to relate the feedback process to the goings on in the surroundings and put it in context.

Ideally, it is an on-going process: It should not be a one-time deal or a once-in-a-year process, abandoned for long periods of time in between. Learning is a lifelong process and since feedback is integral to it, we should invoke the feedback mechanism as often as is necessary, till we reach a new peak of performance.

Feedback is not a passive activity. Nor is it a casual indulgence. It favours the prepared mind. It counts on good feedback-givers and feedback-receivers. No matter how hard an HR department tries, the annual review process can become ineffective, if not farcical, unless people are smart enough to take advantage of the process. A skilled feedback-giver for example, can not only spot your strengths and weaknesses—big and small—but will also help you with the corrective actions. He or she will also have the ability to teach new tricks to the old dog. The feedback they give will be timely and systematic. They can

[1] Performance appraisal is a specific and very important type of feedback. This is discussed in detail in the Chapter 28.

criticize you and still convince you that they are on your side. They will have your complete confidence—and your ears. A skilled feedback receiver, on the other hand, will be open to lifelong learning and self improvement. He or she will be good at identifying the right feedback-giver, parsing their suggestions into action items and asking them for even more feedback. He or she will get the full impact of the feedback, because they will be completely in tune with their environment. Handling the feedback process is a full-blown communication skill and in this chapter we will guide you through its finer details, so that you can become better givers and receivers of feedback.

27.2 Why Feedback?

Feedback serves many purposes. Let us list the top ones.

It is an important part of the learning process:

Snapshot 27.1

> ***Situation:*** *You are learning to drive a car. Your driving instructor is sitting next to you. He tells you that you are hitting the brakes too hard and shows you the right way of doing it. You try again, but you still don't get the hang of it. So, you go through several more iterations and with his help, you eventually learn the correct way of applying the brakes. He also teaches you a whole bag of tricks about driving a car.*

The teacher's feedback, such as in Snapshot 27.1, is absolutely crucial to any learning, be it car driving or learning to play the guitar or Java programming. A good teacher will give ample feedback to pinpoint your deficiencies, misconceptions, poor techniques and bad habits that hinder the learning process. He will point out subtle things to improve your performance.

Psychologists will tell us that the learning process essentially follows a logarithmic pattern called the 'learning curve', where the initial part of the learning is easy and fast and quite a bit can be picked up through self-learning. But, as we keep chugging along and reach intermediate and then advanced stages of learning, incremental proficiency gets more and more difficult. It is at these stages that we need good (preferably one-on-one) instructors to guide us to the highest level of skill. Even if we are excellent learners, sometimes we may not be able to see our own mistakes and poor practices. Earlier in the book (Chapter 7), we discussed learnability as an important attitudinal trait. Feedback is an essential ingredient of learnability.

Our jobs too, follow the standard learning curve and we do need coaches and mentors at work to help us reach newer plateaus of excellence. Our jobs evolve too and there is always a need to learn new technologies, software and new concepts—it is almost as if our job-training never stops. And inasmuch as this is the case, we need the feedback mechanism to help us get better and better at the job.

It can be used to get back on track:

Snapshot 27.2

Situation: *You are now a reasonably good driver. You are driving and your friend is sitting next to you. You need to go to M. G. Road, but you miss the turn and end up on some other road. Your friend tells you that you are off target and navigates you toward the right destination.*

Feedback is an important course-correction mechanism. From time to time, we tend to drift off-track in our jobs and sometimes we may not even be aware of it. A good external feedback will not only alert us about our straying, but it will also do so in a timely manner. For any organization to stay focused on its goals and missions, it is important that they have such feedback-based control of employee activities (see Snapshot 27.2).

It is needed in developing good interpersonal relationships:

Snapshot 27.3

Situation: *You and your friend are going on a long distance journey. As you start to drive, you adjust the air-conditioning and the seat, tune the radio to your favorite FM station, etc. Your friend tells you that the air conditioning is heavenly, but asks if you wouldn't mind changing to another, less annoying FM station.*

Interpersonal relationship is completely dependent on feedback. In the above case, your friend gave his reaction to your behaviour and based on his feedback (which spelt out his likes and dislikes) you adjusted or modified your behaviour—for the good of the relationship (see Snapshot 27.3). At work too, it is no different. Appropriate interpersonal behaviour, conflict resolution, team building efforts, etc. are all dependent on the feedback process.

It is used in ranking/rating people:

Snapshot 27.4

Situation: *You are driving with your boss. Suddenly the topic turns to driving habits. He tells you that Prakash is the best driver he has seen, Kailash the worst and that Thomas is okay, except that he tends to go too slow, even on highways.*

The feedback process can be used to rank and even rate various people under various criteria. Performance appraisal (discussed in the next chapter) is a classic example of this kind of a feedback. It is like a big exam that everyone writes and gets graded on (Snapshot 27.4). Such feedbacks are used typically to justify differential rewards and recognition. In such feedbacks, usually one giver assesses many receivers and so, he knows the relative performance of everyone in the group.

It is used to maintain service levels:

Snapshot 27.5

> ***Situation:*** *You are driving alone. You are thinking about what several of your friends told you about your car—that you should replace the seat covers and ought to keep recent movie-song CDs. You think they are right and head toward the nearest car upholstery shop.*

This is almost like customer feedback that is very commonplace. Such feedback is typically actively solicited from stakeholders and is used not merely to evaluate you personally, but also to find out how well the 'system' is serving. Is the level of service as it ought to be? Is the quality of service up to snuff? It is a 'many givers to one receiver' kind of feedback. If it is adverse or highly negative, it should ring alarm bells right away and call for immediate action (Snapshot 27.5).

It can be used to get an emergency response:

Snapshot 27.6

> ***Situation:*** *You are driving with your friend and as you turn a corner, he screams, 'Pull over to the side. My suitcase just fell out of the trunk.'*

When you get a forceful feedback such as the above, you have no choice but to obey immediately and unquestioningly, in view of the criticality of the situation (see Snapshot 27.6). Such a feedback can be negative ('stop the car right now') or positive ('Keep it up. You have just one more lap to go in the race') and it can come from any affected party, person of authority or from one of your well-wishers. But one presumes that the feedback-giver knows the situation and has figured out what should be the best response from you.

In addition to all these uses of feedback, there is one more that we will not talk about. And this goes under various names—ranting, venting, whining—where the feedback-givers loudly complain about the way things are and let out their angst. It perhaps serves the psychological need to get things off one's chest, but does not typically lead to any corrective action, and much less any performance improvement.

Box 27.1

Examples of Various Feedback-Givers

Who are the potential feedback-givers? How do we determine their effectiveness? This is determined by the technical expertise of the giver and also by the relationship that exists between the giver and the receiver.

- Givers such as *mentors* and *personal instructors* (and people such as *counsellors, doctors, physiotherapists and personal trainers* in a gym) are the most effective. This is mostly because they tend to be experts in their fields and so, we have complete confidence in their judgement. We are much more open about discussing our situation with them, because we know they will maintain confidentiality. Unlike our immediate bosses, they don't have a stake in our performance and this usually leads to a strong one-on-one relationship with them. They seem to be available when *you* want them and although they grade your performance, you know they will always put you on an improvement track, no matter what grade you got.
- Feedback coming from your *senior management*—the CEO and others—will have to be implemented without much argument, whether you like it or not.
- Next come people like your *immediate bosses* or *project leaders, teachers, instructors* in your courses at work or experts/consultants and senior colleagues. These are people who know enough about your performance to give feedbacks, but don't necessarily have a personal relationship with you.
- Then there is the army of people like your *friends, relatives or colleagues* who are your well-wishers. Even though they are not privy to everything that is going on in your professional life, they can still be tapped for their feedback because they know you and have your welfare in their minds.
- Finally, there are people like your *customers* and other *stakeholders* with whom you have little personal relationship—but whose feedbacks and suggestions need to be considered carefully.

Table 27.1 *Types of feedback*

Form	Example
Verbal feedback	Typical conversations
Visual feedback	Hand gestures, nodding
Off-line feedback	E-mail, letter of recommendation, personal
Official feedback	Performance appraisal

27.3 Receiving Feedback

Let us look at some pointers to becoming a good feedback-receiver.

Choose a convenient place and a time: Be serious and somewhat formal about receiving feedback, whether you or the other person initiated it. Make an appointment with the giver—this way, the giver too takes it seriously and organizes his thoughts, instead of giving you an on-the-fly response. Choose an appropriate place that is less susceptible to interruption—a secluded corner in the canteen, for example—so that your colleagues pretty much know that you people want to be left alone. Buy a large cup of coffee or tea and some snacks. Keep a notebook ready to record his key suggestions. And turn that cell phone off.

Confine yourselves to the specific issue/topic: Once you sit down, have a few minutes of warm-up conversation on an unrelated neutral topic, to establish a relaxed atmosphere. But once the feedback process starts, your discussion should be about a specific issue or topic. It should not be widely global, nor should it have digressions. Tell him at the outset, why and on what you are asking for his feedback. Describe your situation in detail and highlight the key points.

Rein in your emotions: When you give an account of what is happening, be as neutral as possible under the circumstances. Whether you are getting feedback about how to beat the challenges in your project or about how to handle a difficult colleague, try to present the situation almost as if you are an observer yourself. Don't convert this feedback session into a venting session. If a particular Java programming activity frustrates you and you have reached the end of the road, convey the givens of the problem, but don't sound so distraught that your learning process gets jeopardized. Remember that the feedback-giver is only going to guide you, but he will not personally get into the field and tackle the problem for you.

Also, be aware of the emotional state of the feedback-giver. For example, if the 'difficult colleague' is the one sitting across you giving feedback on how to defuse the crisis, there may be some residual animosity that you will have to work out. But be extremely polite and patient.

Listen actively: When the feedback-giver starts talking, listen to him actively—which means make the appropriate responses to let him know that you comprehend what he is saying. (See Chapter 17) Don't interrupt him so that he misses his train of thought, but ask him questions, almost any question on your mind. When he points to your mistakes, don't get too defensive or be in denial ('I wouldn't do a stupid thing like that'). Give him the freedom to presume that you are the guilty party, who fouls up everything from your job to interpersonal relationships in the office. Get his feedback on 'what if I did this' kind of hypothetical scenarios.

Learn to handle criticism and compliments: The feedback giver may dish out several highly negative or critical comments about you, in which case learn to swallow hard and take it on. Criticism is a tough thing to face up to and can poke holes in your self-esteem. Remember that your perception of yourself can be vastly different from others' perception of you. You know your intentions for why you did what you did. But, others can only guess and often, they would judge you merely on what you have accomplished, without giving much thought to the context. So, take off your body armour and accept inputs. What might sting you more is that some of the critical comments might come in areas in which you thought you were sound. For every critical feedback the feedback-giver gives, ask him to suggest a remedial course of action.

At the other end of the spectrum are the compliments. Gloat, if you wish, but once he is done with praising, ask for specific feedback so that you can get even better. Is there anything you can do differently, are there any mistakes you can eliminate and how can you enhance your strengths even more? High praise or hard-hitting criticism—learn to deal with both of them with a bit of stoicism.

Spring into action after the feedback: At the end of the feedback session, you should have a bunch of action items—a list of specific changes you want to implement in your behaviour. They could be new techniques you want to try in Java programming, shunning some old ways of interacting with customers or anything else. Whatever they are, they should be clear and practical and hopefully, they should lead to subsequent improvement.

Contact the feedback-giver a few days (or a few weeks) later to give him 'feedback' on the feedback session and tell him if you indeed saw any immediate improvement. Keep him in the loop on a continuous basis, but only if it is not an imposition on him.

Even if you felt the feedback was well off the mark and unhelpful, look for things to hang on to. Don't rationalize it or ignore it. Quite simply, don't do 'nothing' with your feedback (see Box 27.2)!

Box 27.2

Factors affecting feedback

The feedback process is colored by the dynamics between the giver and the receiver and also, by its relationship to the big picture. Some factors to consider when we receive feedback are:

- Context: Are there any conflicts with the giver?
- Emotional state of the giver: Are they in a position to give feedback?
- Relationship with the giver (boss/project-mate/assistant): Is that going to play into the feedback?
- Expertise: Does the person have expertise/competence in the matter?
- Vested interest: Are tangible rewards or punishment at stake?
- Usefulness: Where are you in the learning curve? How will the feedback help you?
- Relevance: Where does it fit in with your overall self-improvement plan?

27.4 GIVING FEEDBACK

As difficult as it is to receive feedback, giving feedback calls for even more sensitivity and maturity. Let us discuss some key points about giving feedback.

Detach yourself from the process: The most common mistake feedback-givers make is that they convert the meeting into an autobiographical session about themselves and frustrate the other person. Remember that although you are important to the process, the process itself is much more important. So, try to remove your personality from the proceedings. Also, make sure you are not pre-occupied with your own worries or in a lousy mood. Ensure that you don't have self-serving reasons for offering to give feedback. And no, don't subject him to your standard speech that you always seem to give at the drop of a hat.

If you initiated the feedback session—and especially if you are his immediate boss or the affected party—remember that the other person may only be a reluctant participant in the feedback activity. Try to reassure him that it is not to reprimand him or to give a piece of your mind that you want to have this discussion.

Appreciate that it is a delicate process: Even though the feedback-receiver might think of you as a mentor or a technical expert, present yourself as a simple down-to-earth guy just like him, with a lot to learn even now. This should establish a rapport with the other person. Quote examples of your own mistakes and poor judgement when you were like him. Use humour, voice modulation, appropriate body language and personal anecdotes to drive home the points. Be focused on a particular topic and use simple, direct language. The receiver will resist, argue and may not own up to his mistakes—in which case, you will have to win him over by delicately camouflaging your feedback with palatable suggestions.

Don't give feedback because someone is not behaving like you would like him to or because he is not meeting your expectations—unless you are the immediate supervisor. Remember that he is not giving you a whip to beat him. And no gratuitous, un-related, broad advice, please! We live in an era where we can Google-search our way even to self-enlightenment and the receiver is not as helpless as you think.

Be positive—turn it into a fun process: Start your feedback by praising the other person and highlighting their positive qualities. Be quick to compliment any good observations they make during the conversation. Be as specific as possible in the compliment for specific accomplishments ('You handled the problem situation of Amlong Corporation very well') rather than some generic praise ('wow, you are a superman'). Similarly be specific in your criticisms rather than make sweeping generalizations. As much as possible agree with them and sympathize with them, but be firm on the point that they will have to change some of their habits. Don't keep slamming them and their efforts. Even as a giver, you too should listen actively and try to turn the session into a conversation about how to do things right.

Don't be evaluative: Be candid, but make sure the receiver's ego is not deflated. Don't douse him with vague statements and general observations like 'you always goof up like that' and 'you never do anything right'. Also, avoid value judgement. Although you may give examples of other people, don't compare him with others and put him down. Remember that feedback is a very specific form of communication and not an inquisition. You should focus on the 'this is where you are today and this is where you want to be and this, I think, is how you can get there' formula.

Let the parting shot be positive, if possible: When you are just about done, summarize the key points. Or better still, let him summarize the key take-aways. Give him some more praise, a lot of encouragement and reassure him that you are on his side. Make arrangements to meet again and follow-up on the progress. If there are immediate rewards or avoidance of penalties at stake, find out how that went. End the session on a positive note

Minimize or avoid unsolicited feedback: Some people are quick to butt in and give unsolicited feedback, often, gratuitously. Giving unsolicited feedback is okay if you are a person of authority (like the manager), but otherwise you don't impose your suggestions or even help, if the other person is not interested. Ask them 'can I make a suggestion' or 'can I help you on this one' and proceed only if they answer in the affirmative. Some people are also perceived to be blunt and somewhat harsh when handing down negative feedback, not bothering too much about mixing praise with criticism.

Americans use a lot of what is called 'conditionals'—statements that are couched in uncertainty and doubt—when they give feedback. They would rather say 'I think it is a good idea to talk to Mr Bhagat', instead of a terse 'Meet Mr Bhagat'. They would use sentences like 'you might want to try this' or 'I would try this' (instead of plain 'try this'). This way, instead of dishing out direct commands to the person in front of you, you are simply expressing your opinions and offering tentative suggestions. It is just a polished way of achieving the same end results.

"You might want to clean up your desk"

"Clean up your desk NOW"

"Get the mess off your lousy desk, for Heaven's sake!!"

Fig. 27.1 *The good, the bad and the ugly feedback*

27.5 In Summary

Only a few among us realize the value of giving and receiving feedback. And even fewer people understand the subtleties of this process to use it effectively in their self-improvement efforts. Consequently, the feedback process has remained a largely under-utilized communication skill in our workplaces. A lot of us would rather isolate ourselves in our little cubicles and try to work it alone.

But we can reverse all that. If we look around us, there is an army of potential mentors and well wishers at work, who are perfectly willing to help us with their feedback. In fact, some organizations even have formal mentoring programmes to foster better feedback. We just have to take the initiative to reach out to those people and plug into their wisdom. Likewise, whenever possible, for the better of the organization and for the better of the individual who is going to benefit from it, we should give our feedback and spread our knowledge. A healthy and active feedback process not only helps you, the employee, but also makes your organization that much more vibrant and powerful.

In order to drive home the key points, we have provided below a summary.

If you are the one giving feedback,

- Be sensitive to the person receiving feedback.
- Listen to the other person actively.
- Give pointed and practical tips that will be useful to the listener, and not general, subjective and vague remarks.
- Don't be evaluative and judgemental.
- Give a lot of personal examples, but don't convert the session into an autobiographical session.
- End the session on a positive note.
- Afterwards, check with the listener periodically to see how he is doing after your feedback.

If you are receiving feedback,

- Be attentive and hungry for feedback.
- Be open-minded and not defensive.
- Talk clearly about your situation to the other person, by expressing your point of view in a non-threatening way.
- Learn to handle your emotions and to take on criticism.
- Take down notes, if you need to.
- Make use of the feedback and try actively to change the way you do things.
- Periodically meet with the feedback-giver and update him about your progress.

Performance appraisal, one important means of feedback, is the subject of discussion for the next chapter, Chapter 28.

28

Performance Appraisals

"The difference between God and CEO is that God sometimes forgives."
–Unknown

Snapshot 28.1

It is that time of the year again—when the migratory birds fly southwards and the managers scramble madly to complete the ritual called employee performance appraisals. Mr Arora, a production manager at QYW Pharmaceuticals, has already been at it for nearly a week now, but has hardly made a dent. This year, the human resources department seems to have gone overboard and added a hundred more questions to its already exhaustive questionnaire on each employee. The new questions seem more loaded and convoluted.

'Rate the employee's body language abilities in a customer meeting and whether it is suggestive of his being a self starter.' Of course, we are kidding about this question—but you get the drift—QYW employees are being evaluated on all kinds of things this year.

In a frenzied fifteen minute period, Arora quickly finished filling up two appraisal questionnaires, believing the spontaneous, gut level response to be more accurate and fair than a laboured one. But when he took the file of Mr Misra, his process engineer, he had to slow down. Misra was not particularly happy with the appraisal last year. Maybe, this year Arora can pre-empt a nasty situation by offering to send him on a junket to a 'workshop' in an interesting city to 'improve his skills'. Suddenly Arora felt the heat and agony of the whole exercise of employee review. He would rather be walking up and down the factory floor instead.

On the other side of the divide sits Mr Misra, your average hard working biotechnologist, wondering what the review process will bring him this time. He is still angry from last year's review, when he was given a three out of five on his written communication skills. When he asked Arora about how he could improve it to a score of four, Arora didn't have a clear answer for him. In fact, instead of getting a shot in the arm, Misra was de-motivated for a full week after getting his appraisal.

Misra knows that soon his file will be put in a pigeon-hole that holds his fate for the coming year. He thinks the whole thing is a charade and feels highly cynical about the entire process—no matter how hard he works, 'they' will find something wrong with him, just to neutralize his efforts and deny him the big pay raises and bonuses. 'It is a war I cannot win,' Misra thinks.

Next week will be rough for both Arora and Misra. What is supposed to be the next best thing to King Solomon's justice, will be reduced to a haggling session with both sides missing the point and feeling let down. Many managers are uncomfortable with it and many workers hate it—and some HR departments and businesses are even moving away from it. Yet, performance appraisal has been around for nearly as long as capitalism has been around and shows no sign of going away.

The already complicated process just got tougher with new concepts like 360 degree appraisals, self-appraisals and reverse appraisals . . .

Appraisals form the necessary evil that every individual in an organization has developed a love–hate relationship with! These are the sessions where an employee gets what is supposed to be objective feedback on his performance and tips on how he can improve. More often than not, these sessions are perceived as a way to 'justify' a lower bonus or hike, as we saw in Snapshot 28.1.

Most organizations have performance appraisals once or twice a year (and some even once a quarter), depending on the type of job and the nature of the organization. In this chapter, we will go into the details of what goes on (or rather is supposed to go on) in performance appraisals, how one can prepare—both as an appraiser and as one getting appraised—and how one can make these sessions painless and fulfilling (or at least less frustrating). We will also consider different variations in appraisals and conclude this chapter with a set of do's and don'ts.

As mentioned in the previous chapter on getting and giving feedback, appraisals are one form of feedback. Since this is probably one with the most material impact, it deserves a separate chapter. But the ideas we presented in that chapter apply equally here. What is more, you will find repetitions between the two chapters. Bear with us! We would rather err on the side of safety and repeat the stress on this important topic.

28.1 Objectives of Performance Appraisals

A performance appraisal session is meant to serve the following objectives:

- Measure the employee's performance during the period as objectively as possible.
- Evaluate how well the employee has accomplished the goals set for him at the beginning of the period.
- Recognize the contributions the employee has made, including those over and beyond his normal call of duty.
- Rate the employee's performance *vis-à-vis* others in the organization.
- Give the employee constructive feedback on the areas where he needs to improve.
- Provide a forum for the employee to give feedback or any inputs on grievances he may have.
- Use all the information above as the basis for determining the rewards the employee is to get in terms of salary hike, bonus and so on.
- Agree upon objective targets and goals for the coming period so that the same process can be repeated in the next period, hopefully better than the current time.
- Enable the employee to achieve continuous, measurable improvement.

While most of these are also the objectives of any other form of feedback, these become more significant for performance appraisals as they have a bearing on the employee's compensation and career growth.

28.2 Planning for a Smooth Appraisal

An appraisal can be an overwhelming experience for both parties involved. By following some of these common-sense tips presented in the rest of this chapter, both the parties can benefit.

Drill down from the overall organizational objective: It is essential that every employee gets the big picture of the organization (see Chapter 2) and understands his or her role in the system. Once each person understands this connection, the goals of the organization can be broken down into smaller parts. Each of these parts is assigned to a given employee and these 'sub-goals' of the organization become the yardsticks by which an employee measures himself, and gets measured by, in the appraisals. Once an employee understands why he is doing certain things and why he is being measured in a certain way, the motivation to perform would increase and the process of appraisal can become more objective and less painful.

Differentiate between 'baseline goals' and 'stretch goals': There are certain goals that an employee must achieve, no matter what. If these are not achieved, the employee's contribution to the organization is simply not acceptable. These goals are not negotiable. For a software development job, this could be sticking to the deadlines; for a maintenance job function, it could be achieving a certain amount of uptime; for a human resources position, it could be satisfying the staffing needs on time. These are part of the job and have to be achieved. These are what we call 'baseline' or 'non-negotiable' goals. Against this there are certain accomplishments that may be asked for or made that are over and beyond the call of duty that demonstrate the employee's potential. These could be things like participation in a ISO-9001 certification drive, contributing to profitability enhancement, participation in a cross-functional team or providing training and mentoring to the newcomers in the organization and so on. It is important to stress that these are over and above what is normally expected of their role and this is what really sets them apart. These goals, which we call 'stretch goals', should be achieved, but not at the expense of the baseline goals.

Snapshot 28.2

SMAART Goals

In order for goals to be meaningful both for goal-setting purposes and for tracking purposes, they should follow the ***SMAART*** principle. ***SMAART*** stands for

Specific
Measurable
Aggressive yet ***A***chievable
Results-oriented
Time-bound

Specific means that there should be no ambiguity in the definition of the goal; Measurable means that there should be an objective yardstick to measure the degree of success for achieving the goal; Results-oriented means the goal should have a direct contribution to the bigger goal of the project or organization. Time bound means that there is a finite timeline by which the goal should be achieved. We have consciously come to the aggressive yet achievable component in the end as it is perhaps the most difficult component to put one's hands around. The test here is to set goals that challenge the employee to a certain extent and make him go the extra mile to sharpen his intellect, to realize what he is actually capable of, removing any limiting thoughts he might have. At the same time, we want to make sure that the employee does not get completely demotivated by failure and hence, the 'achievable' has to be delicately balanced with the 'aggressive'. Some examples of possible SMAART goals are given below:

- To achieve a 50 per cent reduction in number of bugs in the next quarter, without increasing headcount.
- To grow the offshore centre to 400 people within the first year, with no more than 8 per cent attrition.
- To reduce bench size to less than 10 per cent, at the same time not losing any orders, by speeding up hiring for each post to under three weeks.
- To reduce order processing errors to less than ten per a lakh (100,000) orders.
- To improve quality to better than two defects per million tested.

Get a buy in from the employee: It is important that there is clear understanding between the employee and the (to-be) appraiser on the goals up front. Equally important is that there should be a clear understanding of what constitutes baseline goals and what constitutes stretch goals.

Identify the quality characteristics by which the employee would be rated: These include issues like communication ability, taking initiative, teamwork, ability to handle ambiguity, taking ownership and so on. These could be construed as subjective and hence, it is important to have clear data to justify why an employee is rated at a particular level. This is to make sure that he or she understands the rationale and also has a clear action plan for improvement.

"Anil, your computer skills are in the top 10 percentile.
But you need to improve your listening skills...."

Fig. 28.1

Document: The goals of a period (both baseline and stretch goals) along with the quality characteristic are documented into a ***Key Result Areas document***. (The Key Result Areas or **KRAs** as they are called). This document forms the basis for the appraisal. As we will see a couple of paragraphs down, using this document as an anchor for discussion even during the intermediate appraisals would make the whole process more transparent. At the end of the chapter, we have given a typical KRA form template.

Put in place a tracking mechanism: Both the appraiser and the person being appraised must come to an agreement on a reasonable tracking mechanism. The tracking mechanism could be in the form of intermediate feedback sessions (see the next point) or milestones to be achieved en route to the final target (e.g., completion dates of various phases of a projects that form the basis for the appraisal) or target numbers to be achieved during a given month (e.g., sales quotas).

Don't do a big bang appraisal—plan on several intermediate appraisals: Most conflict and disagreement in appraisals come about because of the setting of expectation in the minds of the person being appraised that he is on the right track and then finally getting a rude shock at the appraisal time that he has not done enough. This leads to a bitter feeling that the appraisal process is an eye-wash and is cooked up to substantiate the already decided compensation numbers. It is essential that the goals are reviewed very frequently throughout the appraisal period and constant feedback is provided so that there are no surprises in the end. If the official appraisal period is, say a quarter, once-a-month reviews and feedback will not only make the final appraisal a smoother process, but will also provide timely feedback to get back on track.

28.3 Planning for a Smooth Appraisal—Special Considerations for the Appraised

If you are the person being appraised, the performance review is also the time when you turn around and ask to be rewarded for your performance, loyalties and improvement in your attitude, skills (particularly soft skills). Come prepared to the performance review and don't be bashful about asking frank questions and even for a raise or a promotion (of course, not unreasonably!). If you squander this opportunity, you may not get another opportunity to discuss such things in a long while.

- Make a list of your solid achievements during the current review period. They should be in the format of 'category–specific achievement'. For example, 'I have done a good job in written communication' and quote the example of your report submitted for the XYZ project.
- Give examples of your solid achievements, for example, your hard work in the XYZ offshoring, your due diligence on QRS Corp., etc. Drum up evidence of your association and particular contribution to successful and profitable projects.
- Give examples of your soft skills—your loyalty factor, your leadership qualities, your communication abilities, etc.

- Offer examples of how you paid attention to your previous deficiencies and improved them. Give specific examples.
- Talk about your plans for the next review period, your expectations and your concerns.
- Discuss rewards/raise/promotions openly and to the extent you want to.
- Avoid making comparison with others—except to claim that you are heads and shoulders ahead of the others (with objective and indisputable proof).
- If the manager tries to lay blame on you for any shortcomings, hold your ground and give rebuttals wherever you can.
- Come prepared with a career-growth plan for the next period and get the appraiser's buy-in.
- If you disagree with the appraiser or are not happy with some things, talk clearly about what is on your mind, but don't resort to anger or go out of control.

28.4 During the Appraisal Meeting

Plan ahead and block the time: The appraisal time is sanctioned. Both the appraiser and the person being appraised should block the time on their calendars and stick to the time, unless there is a pressing emergency.

Make sure that there is enough time to prepare: Both the appraiser and the one being appraised need to come prepared for the meeting with *objective* data. This may require going back on the goals set at the beginning of the period as well as the actual performance. You do not want to announce an appraisal meeting at 3p.m. and have the meeting at 3.15p.m!

"Quick! Come to my office. Let us get done with your performance review and appraisal."

Fig. 28.2

Preferably, go to a place where you have privacy: There are two components to privacy: first, you do not want to be interrupted; second, you don't want to be seen or heard by anyone else. If you are in an office with large glass-paneled doors, we recommend you don't do an appraisal meeting there. If you really have to use a glass-door room, try to practise having a poker face! Similarly, don't do an appraisal meeting in an open cubicle.

Do not take calls, e-mails or allow any interruptions: It is important that the appraisal meeting is given the due importance it deserves. It must also be seen by the employee as an important activity that is not taken lightly. During the appraisal meetings, phone calls, text messages/SMS and e-mail as well as interruptions by anyone—including your boss—should not be allowed.

Preferably, sit at a round or a small table: It is not preferable to sit across a rectangular table (especially in the appraiser's office). This can look intimidating and can reduce the openness in an appraisal meeting. A round table or sitting side by side on a rectangular table is more conducive to an appraisal meeting.

Focus only on the goals and quality characteristics agreed upon: The focus of the appraisal meeting should be on the goals and quality characteristics agreed upon at the beginning of the period. Everything related to the goals finds a place in the appraisal meeting—these include the success achieved, issues faced and any instances of over-achievement and under-achievement. Any other activity or accomplishment should be discussed only to the extent to which it influenced the goals set forth or the overall organizational objectives, with justifications for how well the quality characteristics were achieved.

Have all the objective data available for discussion: In order to make the discussion meaningful, both the appraiser and the person being appraised should come prepared with data to objectively evaluate the progress towards the goals. This does not mean that the appraisal meeting degenerates into a legal battle of one-upmanship nor does this mean that it should be an impersonal, icy-cold affair bereft of humanity. This does not also mean that either party has to turn around to the computer, during the meeting, to unearth the objective data; nor does it imply that someone should print all the data, mail transcripts and so on to prove their points. If the preparations for an appraisal meeting are done well, such objective data will be natural and concise.

Fill up and print the KRA form: The KRA form that was filled up with the goals should be filled up to reflect the performance during the period. In addition, the quality characteristics should be rated. Sufficient explanations should be provided to justify the ratings.

Give attention to the entire period, not just the most recent accomplishments or mess-ups: The organizational memory is short, more so the memory of the appraiser during the period leading up to the appraisal meeting! If the person being appraised performed some heroics or caused a customer system to hang very recently, then it is likely that such recent activities may dominate anything else that might have been done five months ago. It is important not to put too much focus only on one incidence.

Look for and highlight consistency and patterns: The appraisal is for the entire period. While individual events are important, what is more likely to be indicative of performance in the future is consistency and predictability of patterns and behaviour. Is the person *consistently* delivering on time or is it a flash in the pan? Is the goof-up the person made for a customer-reported problem a one-off thing or have customers been *consistently* complaining about this person's service? High performers who have demonstrated consistency over several appraisal periods are the ones that need to be nurtured and developed. Identifying them will be no rocket science for the experienced appraiser as they will stand out.

Recognize any improvement initiatives an employee has taken: An appraisal session is meant to motivate an employee to enhance performance over the coming months and years. Highlighting any improvements shown by the person being appraised or even recognizing the positive and genuine attempts made by a person to improve would provide valuable positive reinforcement. The appraisal can then emphasize how the gains of such initiatives can be consolidated and built upon.

Have an open mind: During an appraisal meeting, both the appraiser and the person being appraised will get new perspectives and surprises. For example, a person who considers himself to be very friendly and approachable may get feedback that he is very intimidating; a person who thinks he has followed all the instructions of the boss may get a feedback that he is not taking any initiative. The boss (who is the appraiser) may think that he has set clear targets, but the person being appraised may contradict him. Criticism is not easy to gulp down and a natural defensiveness can easily take over. It is important for both the appraiser and the person being appraised to have an open mind and not have a pre-conceived notion that what the other party says cannot be right.

Listen! In the previous point, we said have an open mind. You cannot have an open mind unless you listen carefully. In the chapter on listening (Chapter 17), we stressed the importance of active listening in which you not only understand what the other party says, but also make the other party understand that you understood what they said. Nowhere can active listening be more useful than in an appraisal meeting–both for the one doing the appraisal and the one being appraised.

Show empathy: A very useful by-product of active listening is a show of empathy. Each party understands the point of view of the other party. Even if they don't agree with each other, at least they know where each is coming from. This can reduce the defensiveness in both and can make them more receptive to each others' ideas, thereby setting the scene for a smoother appraisal process.

Maintain calm throughout: Appraisal meetings can sometimes degenerate into hot debates that become personal and egoistic. In order to avoid such a catastrophe, it is important that both parties stay calm through the meeting and discuss only the issues, not taking anything personally. Of course, this is easier said than done. There is a higher chance of personal mudslinging boomeranging if the appraisal meeting happens to be a 'big bang', once-in-a-year meeting which brings in shocks. If there are more frequent and timely exchanges during the entire period, there is likely to be fewer surprises and hence, less scope for using the appraisal meeting as a platform to throw a fit of rage.

Don't sound confrontational or submissive: The appraisal meeting is not meant to be a bullying session where the manager can say what he wants and the person being appraised has to take everything lying down. Nor is it supposed to be an opportunity for the person being appraised to bash his manager. In order for an appraisal meeting to have its desired objectives, neither party should be confrontational or submissive.

Follow through: Always follow through an appraisal meeting with a written feedback that is received by the employee as well as the layers of management that need to see it, including the human resources department, for the appraisal to go into the employee's records. If an organization follows reverse appraisal, self-appraisal and 360 degree appraisal, then such feedback must also be in the records.

28.5 Challenges in Appraisals

When there is disagreement on clarity of goals: Most of the disagreements in appraisals come from the fact that the targets are not clear. Clearly demarcating the baseline and stretch goals using the SMAART criteria would greatly help in alleviating this challenge.

When there is disagreement on levels of accomplishments: This arises from having unclear goals, inadequate support data and also not getting sufficient feedback throughout the appraisal period. Having periodic intermediate reviews to look at the goals and correcting any misunderstandings can reduce the ill-effects of this challenge.

Appraisals not carried out in person: Sometimes in geographically distributed teams, the appraiser and the person being appraised may be in different locations. Face-to-face communication may not be possible; even video conference may not be possible in some cases. Appraisals being a sensitive issue, doing it over a telephone may be a little difficult as there is no access to important non-verbal communication channels. There is no easy solution to this.

Using a generic appraisal template with a lot of 'NA (not applicable)': Sometimes, the same appraisal template is used for different job functions and this may result in either a lot of 'force-fitting' the template to the job or a lot of columns with 'NA'. This will not be useful, either for the appraiser or for the person being appraised. It would be useful to have an appraisal form that contains two parts—one that is generic and addresses qualitative factors and the other with questions and factors specific to a job function. For example, an appraisal form used for a sales person would have appraisal criteria like ability to close a deal, negotiation skills and so on. But these will not apply directly to say, a programmer.

The ubiquitous bell-curve: One of the dangers that a manager faces can be that his group is a high performing group and everybody has contributed to the group's success. Yet, the various members have to be graded and placed along a 'bell curve'. A person who has apparently met all the expectations may be placed in the lower part of the curve simply because everyone else has performed 'as well' or even over-achieved. So, it leaves some employees to ask, 'I have done everything possible; did all you asked me to do and yet you say I have not done enough—why? What else do you expect me to do?' Unfortunately there is no easy answer to this question unless you have a methodical way of setting effective goals. In an earlier section, we talked of ***SMAART*** goals. The key is in the ***AA*** that stands for ***A***ggressive yet ***A***chievable. Those who achieve the aggressive (stretch) goals without compromising the achievable (baseline) goals would obviously move up the bell curve.

28.6 Variations in Appraisal Methods

Self appraisal: Sometimes, an employee is asked to fill up the appraisal form by himself and rate his performance before coming to the appraisal meeting. This is compared with the manager's appraisal. When there is significant difference between the two on a given factor or a goal, this can become a topic for discussion during the meeting. This can point to the need for a better and clearer goal-setting process. If an employee constantly rates himself 5 out of 5 in all the criteria of self appraisal, then it probably means that he has not been objective in his self-evaluation.

Reverse appraisal: Sometimes an employee is asked to rate his manager on various factors. This reverse appraisal is either shared with the manager during the appraisal or given directly to the manger's manager. When a majority of reverse appraisals about a manager indicate problems, it is time for senior management to have a closer look at them and take corrective action.

360 degree appraisal: In this system of appraisal, feedback about an employee is sought from his manager, his peers as well as his subordinates. The traditional 'downward' appraisal can give the manager's perspective. The peer appraisal can give clear indication of attributes like teamwork. It must however be mentioned that these processes are not universally followed.

28.7 In Summary

Performance appraisals are the dreaded periods of the year, whether you are the appraiser or the one being appraised. And, like taxes and death, these are certainties in one's professional life. We have summarized below the key points from an appraiser's perspective as well as the perspective of one being appraised.

If you are the appraiser,

- Conduct the appraisal in a place where there is plenty of privacy and minimum interruption.
- Sit down in proximity with your employee and go through the exercise carefully and diligently.
- Be objective and fair.
- Look at his performance for the entire period, not just at the most recent performance.
- Recognize the positives.
- Empathize with the employee and be sincere and open.
- Have all the data available to support your appraisal.
- Discuss only those goals and targets you had set out. This is not a general session to discuss everything under the sun.
- Promptly complete and print out the KRA document and give a copy to the employee.

If you are the one being appraised,

- Be punctual to the performance review appointment.
- Be prepared. Get a lot of documents to show your accomplishments and to corroborate your good performance.
- List all your questions and points on a sheet of paper and go through the list with your boss.
- Ask him for suggestions on how exactly to improve. Let him suggest specific targets—if possible quantitative targets—to help you improve.
- Even if you disagree with him, don't make matters worse by being combative.
- Be open, and don't be defensive.
- And finally, follow through with him on your work performance periodically to see if he is happy with your progress.

A Sample KRA document

Employee Name: Ganesh Venkatraman
Group: Head, Mobile Products Group
Manager Name: Ajay Kumar
Appraisal Period: Jan-June, 2009

Goals Plan vs. Performance

Area / factor	**Planned Baseline Targets (filled at the beginning of the period)**	**Planned Stretch Goals**	**Actual Achievements (filled at the end of the period)**	**Comments**
Deliveries	To complete five deliveries of various patches and releases, all within a schedule variance of 5%	Provide an initial version of a toolkit to make it easy for mobile service providers to integrate our product	➔ Three releases completed with zero schedule variance; one with 3% schedule variance; one with 7% schedule variance ➔ Toolkit well received by beta customers	Have met deliveries on time; the one with 7% variance was because of delays in approvals. Achieved the stretch goals in addition to meeting expectations of the baseline goals
Quality	➔ Number of re-opened bugs to be less than 10; ➔ Number of customer reported bugs to be < 10% of the bugs found out internally	Close all the pending bugs filed for the previous version	➔ Number of reopened bugs was 15 ➔ Number of customer-reported bugs = 50; internal bugs = 200;	Testing is not adequate; needs better focus on quality; could not do anything with the previous version bugs; Less than Expectations
New Features Implementation	Should plan to incorporate message translation into at least seven European and six Indian languages		Completed all the required European languages as well as ten Indian languages	Exceeds Expectations
Growth	Contribute to the addition of at least six identified new		Added five new accounts, including one that is bigger than the	Met Expectations

	major accounts for the product		targeted one	
Company Initiatives	➔ Participate in at least two campus interviews ➔ Be the group representative in ISO-9001 initiative and get less than 5 Non Conformances		➔ Went to IIT - Chennai, IIT - Kanpur and BITS, Pilani for campus interviews; ➔ The group had just two Minor Non-Conformances in the ISO 9001 audit; also was part of the Metrics Council	Exceeded Expectations
Self Improvement	➔ Be PMP Certified ➔ Enrol for an Exec MBA programme in a good college		➔ Completed the PMP certification ➔ Have got admission for Exec MBA program	Met Expectations

Quality Factors and comments

Initiative: Designed and conducted a training program for the fresh recruits on the architecture of the mobile interface

Team work: Worked collaboratively with the data storage group to resolve the Priority 1 bug reported by AXY Corporation

Communication: Maintained timely communication with the senior management, alerting issues well ahead of time in most cases. Customer kept in loop.

Tolerance to ambiguity: Took very broad specifications given for the user interface and came up with a real cool UI that became a hit with the customers

Add other attributes (persuasiveness, negotiation skills, presentation skills, conflict resolution, etc) as appropriate and relevant for the given job

Overall Rating

4/5

Fig. 28.3

29

How to Present Bad News

"Never awaken me when you have good news to announce, because with good news nothing presses. But when you have bad news, arouse me immediately, for, then there is not an instant to be lost."
–Napoleon Bonaparte

Let's face it. Bad things do happen from time to time and sometimes, the unpleasant task of delivering the bad news will fall upon us. Along with it comes certain responsibilities and expectations. For a start, we will be required to be thoughtful and considerate of the mental state of the person about to receive the bad news. Then, we will have to have the tact and the guts to break the bad news itself. Next, we are expected to deal with the recipient's reaction with poignancy and understanding. And finally, we are also supposed to act as psychological counsellors and assuage his grief and help him in the healing process—and we are supposed to do all this while trying to come to terms with the bad news ourselves. It is a difficult mission even for angels.

Our workplace probably generates the most number of bad news per capita. It is not surprising, considering that it is a beehive of activities and some of those activities are high-risk, with considerable exposure to internal and external factors that we have no control over. In fact, in difficult times, a ton of bad news will spew out of our organization—and a lot of it will understandably be about its own poor financial health and business performance.

29.1 Bad News at Work

Bad news at work comes in many, many flavours. (See Box 29.1 for some examples.) But in terms of dissemination, some bad news travel from the bosses to the junior staff top down and some others are delivered from bottom up, from the lower rank to the boss. Occasionally it is also transmitted laterally, colleague to colleague or business to business. Some bad news is localized and affects only a few workers in the office, whereas some others can have wide ramifications across the entire enterprise. Sometimes bad news will be delivered to a large group all at once and at some other times it is disseminated to a single person. Big groups have the advantage of eliciting a diversity of reactions and therefore, help bring out the full magnitude of the news. On the other hand, the intimacy and clarity of one-on-one communication can help analyse the situation in depth. Of course, in spite of these 'advantages', it is still tricky and difficult to convey bad news, irrespective of the group size.

If you think about it, conveying bad news is a skill too, although, perhaps, we won't highlight it in our resumé or want to be known around the office as the most skillful bad-news messenger. This skill is like that thick winter jacket that you have put away in the corner of your wardrobe, to be used only occasionally—but, whenever you need it, it should still serve you admirably. This chapter will take you through some essential points about delivering bad news, so that you can be more careful and effective the next time—or at a minimum, not bungle an already delicate operation. We will, of course, limit our discussion to just the communication of bad news and not go into what kind of follow-up actions should be taken in response. (This is covered in Chapter 11 on 'When Things Go Wrong At Workplace'.)

Box 29.1

Bad news galore!

What constitutes bad news is a matter of perspective. To some people a half-full glass can be terrible news. But instead of quibbling about the definition, we will list some 'major' bad news items that make their rounds in our workplace.

From managers to group members

- Poor financial performance
- Plant shutdown, layoff, closing of a division/merger
- Death/departure of a popular worker
- Natural disaster
- Bad economy, cut in bonus/pay
- Losing a customer/account
- Government probe/scandal
- Cancellation of a project/product
- Major policy changes affecting workers adversely

(Continued)

From workers to managers

- Missing a deadline
- Forgetting to do something
- Destroying a machine/part/product
- Disruption in production
- Any 'Murphy's Law' kind of violation
- Cost overrun.

Lateral

- Cancellation of joint project/contracts
- Not doing your part of a joint effort.

29.2 Some Commonsense Points About Delivering Bad News

Whether you are transmitting the bad news top down, bottom up or laterally, there are some common sense observations or practices about disseminating bad news.

Choose an appropriate time and a forum: Although emergency news will have to be told right away, you may want to choose the right place and the right time to reveal the bad news. The place you select should afford you enough privacy and the time you schedule should have enough leeway for their reaction and for possible follow-up. A project meeting or a specially called meeting ('can we all get together in my office at 3.00 PM'?) can serve as the right forum. Don't give bad news in a 'by the way' kind of fashion. And never, never convey it through cell phone, SMS messages, by shouting across the hallway or as you pull away in your car in the parking lot.

Being brutally honest vs wrapping it in sheets: Should we be brutally frank and dish it out straight or should we slow down and temper it with sensitive stuff so that it goes down better? It depends entirely on who is at the receiving end. Large groups lend themselves to the open, no-nonsense approach. With single individuals, a hemming and hawing approach works better. The best way, of course, is a hybrid approach, where you alternate between being super-candid and super-sensitive.

Don't give it in bits and pieces: Don't tease your recipients with the bad news, especially when they are too impatient to hear it. Don't drag it out or build unnecessary suspense. Don't give it in installments or omit key details. When you are done with delivering the bad news, clearly indicate to them that that was all the information you had. Forgetting a piece here and a piece there is understandable, but never deliberately hold back aspects of the bad news—either because they were too terrible or because it might aggravate the receivers some more. Likewise, don't have several versions for several people. Be consistent and true to the facts.

Give the bad news before they find out: The most fundamental tenet about giving bad news is give it early and don't procrastinate till the last minute! It is a human tendency to postpone telling the bad news and sometimes people even try to hide it. ('I was anyway going to tell you,' is a pretty lame statement.) If you are the point man to deliver the news and you didn't divulge it in time, your credibility and people's trust in you will be seriously damaged, once they find out about it. Remember that however much you try to hide the news, most workplaces have mechanisms to uncover such cover-ups and the unpleasant truth will emerge sooner or later.

Don't analyse, speculate or sell the news while still delivering it: Don't mix the delivery of bad news with bad news analysis. When you are in the delivery mode, stick only to that and come out with all the facts and details. Don't speculate or guess why or who might have caused it or who stands to benefit from it and so on. Maintain an element of impartiality and a TV newsreader kind of detachment. Don't think aloud or show your biases prematurely. Time for analysis will come later, after the details of the news are spelt out.

Don't have a neutralizing mentality: There is no way to gift-wrap bad news. So don't rush to find a silver lining in the whole thing, just because you feel sorry for the recipients. We are so used to rationalizing and seeing the good in everything that sometimes we become unrealistic. In fact, even if there is some incidental good news, that is relatively unimportant compared to the magnitude of the bad news. Also, don't wait for some offsetting good news to occur before delivering the bad news in hand.

Estimate the relative badness of the news: If you have worked in your organization for a while, it is likely that you have seen every kind of bad news that there is and you can pretty much categorize most bad news along a Richter Scale of 'badness'. This should help you come up with suitable ways of presenting various kinds of bad news. You probably even have precedence and established protocol on some of them already.

Look also for what other companies do under similar circumstances. However, remember that no matter how many times a bad event occurred previously, it still does not lessen the gravity of the situation. Nor should it desensitize you to the plight of the affected.

Handle emotions carefully: Remember that you too will be affected by the bad news So, first and foremost, try to control your emotions and calm down. Don't present the news if you are distraught yourself.

You will have to be even more careful about your recipients' emotional state as you break the news. Work toward reducing panic reaction among them. Don't whip up their fears or play on their passions. On the other extreme, don't overreact to the way *they* react or lecture them about controlling themselves or about time healing everything. Sympathize with them and tell them that you too, are with them. Don't be a 'bad-news monger', spreading it to anyone and everyone, planting prophecies of gloom and doom everywhere.

It happens all the time: Since we know that bad news can occur every once in a while, it makes sense to prepare ourselves and others in anticipation of such possibilities. Lower others' expectations ahead of time, especially if you see cracks appearing in your project. When you sign up for difficult activities with unrealistic expectations, temper others' enthusiasm right then and feed them the mantra of 'cautious optimism'. This is in line with what we have seen in Chapter 8 on Expectation Management and the equation 'satisfaction=performance–expectations'. If you are the boss, alert your workers to poor economy or difficult competitive environment well in advance, so that they see the trend. But, when the bad news does occur, don't trivialize it or gloss over it, 'because such things happen'. Encourage them wherever possible to get a perspective on the whole thing, although under no circumstances should you try to dictate how they should react to the news.

29.3 Top Down Communication of Bad News

Snapshot 29.1

Situation: *You are the big boss. You are at the podium, giving that 'we are a strong company today' speech. You point to the doubling of the Latin American business and 20 per cent increase in the Eurozone and almost like a non-sequitur you tell the crowd that to move forward they need a 'work-force rationalization' of two hundred workers. A stunned silence falls over the audience.*

Being the big boss, you get to drop such deadly bombshells (as exemplified in Snapshot 29.1) once in a while and given the nature of the boss–employee relationship, they will have no choice but to swallow hard and take it on the chin. Still, you can turn such a difficult event into a great communication exercise to rally your employees—or what is left of them. Let us see how.

Give the speech of your life: Even if you cannot do Nehru's 'Freedom at Midnight' kind of speech, rouse them with a well-prepared and well-delivered speech that touches their heartstrings. Let all your employees know that you are working hard for them and that you are looking out for them in such difficult times. Explain to them why so many workers are being laid off and what the other alternatives were that you considered. Detail the circumstances leading up to this tough decision. Bring all your managerial and public speaking acumen to the forefront. Admit that you yourself don't know the answers to some of the questions and that the decision is definitely an unfortunate one. Realize that the atmosphere will be super-charged and so, be ready to face the audience's ire (although most of them would have probably internalized their anger). Focus on the challenges of tomorrow and inspire your troops to join you on the march forward.

While delivering the speech, don't ramble on, don't sermonize and above all, be sensitive. Don't skirt the main issue or give a huge build-up. Don't confuse them with unrelated details. Sound apologetic, even if it is not your fault. Don't convolute your bad news with jargon—job loss by any name is job loss, even if you choose to call it the 're-equilibrization' process. Don't put blame on a particular person or organization. And don't be quick to put a spin on it.

Keep extra time for questions: End the 'bad news' speech quickly enough, but follow it with an elaborate question and answer session to give out more details. This will give the audience a sense of participation rather than making them feel like just passive spectators. Encourage them to ask questions and touch upon related topics when you answer their questions. Have all the other managers around and in case you need it, ask the relevant manager to come up to the front and fill the gaps in knowledge.

Give them time to react: Like a doctor breaking bad news to the patient, pause and solicit their response at every step of your disclosure. Give out a lot of facts and data. Make sure there are no loose ends in terms of topics to cover. Some of the workers may be too shy or too shell-shocked to ask any questions and so, get ready to answer their questions off-line. Have other managers respond to questions as well. Be there longer than you are needed. Try to offer all help and be genuine.

Have follow-up meetings: As people try to come to terms with bad news, they will have different sets of questions at different points of time. Hence it is essential to have follow-up meetings, provide an opportunity for them to aok these questions and get them clarified. Be patient, as they may take their own time to digest the news.

Let us look at another example.

Snapshot 29.2

Situation: *You are Javed's immediate boss. He has been eagerly waiting to hear about his promotion the past several weeks. You call him into your office, look him squarely in his eyes and tell him, 'Sorry, your promotion did not come through this year. But you are next in line and should get it whenever they open it up.' Javed freezes up in disbelief.*

What you told Javed in Snapshot 29.2 was bad news alright. He is going to react negatively and might even lose some of his enthusiasm for work. But you could have handled it better—by lowering his high expectation level (especially if the business climate is bad) or by explaining clearly how the promotion process works. You can point out that although he did not get the promotion per se, he did reap heavy rewards for his hard work, especially relative to the others in the group. In this way, you could motivate him back to his usual high enthusiasm.

29.4 Telling the Boss the Bad News

Snapshot 29.3

You tell your boss that the important report that you have been working on for days and nights—that is critical for the hot project in hand—will miss the deadline again. Although this is the two hundred and fourteenth time that someone in his group has missed the deadline this year, for the two hundred and fourteenth time, he flips the handle and starts transforming into a bulldog with a toothache. But you know that in the grand scheme of bad news, this one rates only a 'two yells and three screams' offence and after five minutes of hot air exchange, you both go back to your desks, pondering over the realistic date of completion of the report.

If you are an entry-level professional, you may be dealing with such situations, as shown in Snapshot 29.3, routinely. The bad news you bring to the boss will typically be a transgression or what is known in management lingo as an 'operations level problem'. The good news about your bad news is that your foul up is going to be limited in scope and will affect only a few associated activities. Still, bosses will come unglued when they hear about your lapse. You must remember that they take a lot of risks and count on things running smoothly. Let us look at some aspects of telling boss the bad news.

The most common bad news for the boss: By far, the biggest category of bad news an employee reports to his immediate boss, is his defaulting on some assignment, such as missing a deadline or not doing what he was supposed to do or not being successful in what he attempted. The best approach is to give it to him straight, take the heat and get right back to working on minimizing the fallout. Don't have that 'why are you making such a fuss about a minor thing?' or that 'look, I was being so honest. Why are you still giving me hell?' kind of attitude.

Granted, this might have happened in spite of your trying hard and putting in sincere efforts. But that still cannot absolve you. Prior to your 'miss', you should have taken sufficient precautions about warning him of delays or difficulties in the project.

When Murphy strikes: The next category of bad news that upsets the boss is the one where those unusual events and freak accidents that were never supposed to happen, happen. A server crash right in the middle of an important data transfer that set you back by three days. Such events are considered examples of Murphy's Law, which goes (paraphrased) 'If anything can go wrong, it will'. But your boss will not be so light-hearted or cool when you break the news and Murphy will be the last thing on his mind. He will have a thousand questions about the freak incident and will try to pin the blame on someone or something. He will try to even shoot you, the messenger. But, empathize with him and work with the recovery team in whatever capacity you can. A few days later, give him your inputs on ways to prevent a recurrence of the situation in the future.

Set the stage: One of the tactics often suggested is that you should not just convey the bad news, but also tell the boss ways of mitigating it or working around it. Be a part of the solution. You should have initiated some effective problem-solving activities even before you walked into his office, (Of course, if you haven't thought about it yet, don't start cooking up *ad hoc* plans between his yells.) List them in the order of the most practical to the most impossible. Accept ownership of these recovery efforts. The boss may have some suggestions, but he is not going to solve the problem for you right then and there. Also, let him not get the impression that you were always expecting the bad news and were working on Plan B right from day one. ('I knew the client would not be available today. That's why I never even prepared my slide show for him.')

Remember that managers will not be very quick to shift focus from the bad news to the 'what next' spin. Let him take his own time. Don't make light of the bad news or be in a hurry to put it behind you just because it is unpleasant to dwell on it. At the appropriate time in the session, try to pinpoint the root cause and be accurate about it. Note, however, that he will see through any lame attempts to shift the blame on a third party.

Recruit help and find strength in numbers: Maybe your bad news is a result of a systemic problem or event that also affected several other people around you. Perhaps everyone in your group is waiting for the same code from the development group. In such a case, it makes sense for several of you to go as a group and break the bad news to the boss. (Just make sure that this does not appear to be a mob attack!)This way, no one person will be blamed for breaking the bad news. Also, different people in the delegation can highlight different aspects of the bad news. Such powerful imploring might prompt the boss to escalate the matter to the higher-ups and request them to take care of the problem. But remember that if you have a weak case, approaching the boss in a group will not get you out of the situation.

Remember there can be long-term consequences: You might not think much about missing a deadline here or defaulting on a deliverable there. But, it is not just a short-term problem per se. Every time such a thing happens, your boss is making a note of it and if you are a repeat offender, there may be a price to pay at the end of the year, when it is time for the annual performance appraisal. Don't for a minute assume that he will quickly accept your explanation and move on as if nothing happened. His memory for your lapses is stronger than yours.

29.5 In Summary

In ancient Greece, in the days leading up to the War of Marathon, a warrior-runner named Phidippides had to run from Athens to Sparta and back (about 200 km each way, through a tortuous mountain terrain) to convey bad news about an imminent Persian invasion. Today, twenty five centuries later, it hasn't become any easier to dispense bad news. Presenting bad news is a frustratingly difficult task. For, right at the exact moment you are breaking the bad news, it may feel like the lights are going out in somebody's life (and that somebody can even be you). It is likely that with the passage of time, the bad news will play itself out and the affected people will move on. But if you are the one who doled out the news, you want to be remembered—if at all—as a person who handled the whole thing well, with your rock-solid emotional maturity, complete understanding of the bad news and above all, as the one possessing the intelligence to anticipate the recipients' reaction to the unfortunate situation.

Here is a quick summary of key points to remember, should you ever be put in the unfortunate situation of having to break bad news.

- Don't delay in conveying the bad news.
- Remember, there is a time and a place for conveying the bad news. Choose them appropriately.
- Give it completely, all at once. Don't give it in fragments.
- Use simple words and a straightforward approach to convey the bad news, don't sugarcoat, dilly-dally, beat around the bush or make it look unimportant. At the same time don't blow it out of proportion to evoke unnecessary panic.
- Give the recipients some time to digest the bad news before proceeding to analyse or discuss it.
- Be sensitive to the persons who are affected by the bad news.
- If you are the manager dishing out bad news to your employees, have follow-up meetings to discuss the consequences and to address their concerns.
- If you are an employee presenting bad news to your boss, set the stage and prepare him for the news as much as possible and then present him with the news—don't just sneak it in or worse still, don't try to cover it up.

"He is trying out a new communication technique to convey the bad news."

Fig. 29.1

30

Presenting to the Senior Management

"In large organizations the dilution of information as it passes up and down the hierarchy, and horizontally across departments, can undermine the effort to focus on common goals."

–Mihaly Csikszentmihalyi

Snapshot 30.1

The CEO vs You

Mr Swamy, the CEO of QRS Technologies, an automobile spare parts manufacturer, is naturally a very busy man. You are a junior process engineer and you have been developing a new forging process using a new instrument. Your immediate boss thinks it is a good idea for you to present your work to the CEO, make a case for the purchase of this Rs 12 crore new instrument, and get his blessings to incorporate your process in the mass production lines.

After much dancing around, they schedule you in an executive technology meeting and you spend weeks preparing gleaming slides and polishing your pitch. On the appointed day, you put on your best tie and step into the heavy, static atmosphere of the executive conference room, ready to bamboozle the company bigwigs crowding the room. Suddenly you feel uncomfortable and nervous. Perhaps you are at the wrong place.

Your turn comes and you start to talk like you are in a trance. The CEO is so near you that you can reach and touch him. You make eye contact with him because you had read somewhere about making eye contact. But you didn't expect that he too could look you in your eyes and unnerve you. Your pep and confidence are slowly beginning to vaporize. Not once does he smile or do anything to make you feel comfortable.

You are barely warming up, when his cell phone rings relentlessly and he rudely whips it up and answers it, leaving the whole conference room paralysed for the next five minutes. Barely a slide later, his administrative assistant barges in and kidnaps him for an interminable period and you are left to speak to a bunch of people who have very little stake or interest in the matter. Just when you are getting half-way comfortable, he walks in and asks that you continue from where you left. And right when you went back to that point, he gets his next phone call. Talk of non-linear narration.

Somehow you muddle through your talk. There is even a three-minute period where you find your flow. But he interrupts you constantly and derails your talk from your prepared sequence and no matter how hard you try to explain, he feigns ignorance and knuckle-headedness. At one point, you find yourself explaining the second law of thermodynamics that has almost nothing to do with anything you wanted to say. He thinks your explanations are poor. He asks for data on this, data on that, graphs and pie charts that you never knew would be needed. You become alternatively defensive and apologetic and your breathing becomes heavy. In one of your slides you have the name of the CTO of the company wrong (you were cutting and pasting from an older material and this inadvertently crept in) and he takes you to task for it.

'How many years have you been working here?' he dresses you down 'You have to pay attention to what you do.'

You think you could get help from your 'allies' sitting in the audience, such as your immediate boss. But they too join him and laugh at you. You look confused and foolish. Then the CEO leaves abruptly with a 'your case is not even close. Do your homework and get back to me later' kind of look. All your six months of solid effort—and the chance to gain visibility in the organization—are frittered away in a few minutes of poor communication with the man that matters the most.

Betrayed and humbled, you silently curse the CEO and return to the mundane.

Call it an opportunity of a lifetime or an ordeal that tests every nerve in your body, the rare occasion you get to present in front of your senior management is perhaps the ultimate test of your communication powers. Snapshot 30.1, although highly exaggerated, illustrates how a 'thoroughly vertical communication' with a CEO is fraught with landmines and crossfire. To win this war, we need to adopt a slightly different communication strategy, the essence of which is outlined in the following thumb rules and observations.

Much of what we are going to say about presentation also applies to the other big ticket activity that happens for the benefit of the senior management—namely the live 'demo' of products and prototypes that you may be asked to give every once in a while—and we will not discuss it separately.

30.1 Before the Presentation

Make sure you are aware of the following ground realities as you prepare your presentation.

Senior managers are a very busy bunch of people: Swamy and company are very busy people, who can't seem to have enough of phone calls and meetings. Often they multitask and pop in and out of several parallel meetings. They go out of town all of a sudden and will have no qualms about cancelling your appointment. You almost never get their undivided attention, even if you tie them down to their chairs. So, the best you can hope for is to try and get their divided attention between their phone calls and disappearing acts and make the best use of their limited airtime.

Preparation is everything: Spend a lot of time in preparation and organizing your materials and getting the right sequence for your talk—and on how best to handle interruptions. If it is possible, have a rehearsal before a crucial presentation. Make sure you run your slides through spell-check, verify that you have used the standard, official templates and also make sure your dates, names, numbers are all accurate and current, unlike the time when you had the CTO's name wrong in your slide show.

Pay attention to all the technical details. Make sure your flood of data is organized and that you don't get drowned in it yourself. Present your case in such a light that he realizes that your role is critical to the company and that you add tremendous value.

Gather a lot of related data that you may not even get a chance to present. The idea is that often a senior-management presentation could turn into a scenario-building activity and all kinds of risk-reward, 'what-if' and cost-benefit analysis will be performed *ad hoc*. A CEO, like Mr Swamy, will look for several ways to convince himself because he doesn't want to make a Rs 12 crore mistake. Go through such analysis and arguments in your mock session before the actual presentation.

If you are the messenger bringing in bad news, also give him a detailed analysis of what happened and your suggestions on how to mitigate it or recover from it. (For further details on reporting bad news, refer to Chapter 29.) Merely reporting the bad news and presuming that he will take care of the problem himself is poor judgement. He may be a very smart man, but he doesn't have the bandwidth to get into the nitty-gritties of the problem. You will have to shortlist the choices and guide him through the nuances, so that he can take effective executive decisions.

Basically, the senior manager wants you to get into his mind and speak his language. And he will be very frustrated and annoyed if there is a major disconnect with you. Your preparation should focus on his concerns.

Your talk should have an 'executive' structure: Give your talk a pyramidal structure, like newspaper stories. The first slide should pretty much contain everything you are going to say in the rest of your presentation. So even if you don't get through the entire presentation, the main points are not lost. Also, prioritize your points and let first things be first. You should have enough supplementary information that you can potentially have a follow-up discussion, should time and interest permit. If all this looks familiar to you, it is no surprise. These are exactly the tenets of a good presentation discussed in earlier chapters. 'tell them what you are going to tell them; tell them; tell them what you told them' is something that you have heard before. You have to muster all these skills to the highest level when you are presenting to the CEO or the senior management. If you are a regular presenter to the top management, you will eventually settle into a pattern and your slides will have a standard template and feel. But if this is going to be your first time, talk to your more experienced colleagues on the format and design of the slides and the presentation style. Basically, your presentation must make a nice package.

Your presentation should be modular: The CEO is not likely to stay through your entire presentation and watch you go slide by slide. You should try to grab his attention whenever you can get it. Instead of a long, linear narration, make your presentation modular to suit the CEO's short and highly fragmented attention-span. Your nuggets of wisdom should hit him like darts, right on target. Cluster-bomb him with several sound bites and takeaways, so that he leaves the meeting content and if needed, he will be able to later piece together the bigger story by himself. Repeat your main points over and over. If you paused your talk because he got interrupted, refresh him on where you left off. You usually don't have time for long-winded explanations, philosophical discussions or to campaign for your off-beat ideas. But if you are smart, in whatever minutes are available to you, you can still impress him with everything he expects, and more.

Your presentation should use a lot of graphs, visuals, analogies, etc.: Like a little kid, the CEO too loves colours, pictures, pie-charts and anything that breaks down complex data into intuitive inter-relationships. Remember that he is not an expert in your field and so you may have to interpret your pictures and graphs and explain to him what is 'good' and what is 'bad'. It is often useful to show him some benchmarks so that he knows what to compare your data to. He loves sigmas and statistics too.

The big bosses love standard pictorial tools like the Gantt charts, project network diagrams, flow-charts, decision-tree diagrams, etc. and therefore, become familiar with these and cast your information in these forms.

30.2 The Presentation Proper

During the actual presentation, be aware of the following points.

Get his attention, create a rapport: Given how limited his concentration is, try to lock him in a virtual strangle-hold when you have him in front of you. Make eye-contact with him and don't let go, even if you periodically move your gaze through the rest of the audience. Your body language should indicate that you are talking just to him. Address him by name every once in a while or drop in phrases like 'you have always said…', 'in the last all-employee meeting you emphasized . . .', etc. Agree with him on his points and try to connect to his understanding of the situation.

Does he fully understand the new forging machine? Does he understand *any* machines? Remember that you are the window into this technical topic for him and a good rapport is absolutely necessary to gently guide him through the maze. Slow down or speed up to conform to his speed. Be dramatic (as necessary), modulate your voice effectively and gesticulate so that his attention stays fixed on you.

Give it to him straight: Present your case in simple, plain English. Don't beat around the bush. No stories, preamble or embellishment with jokes or side-bar discussions are required. (But be open to such discussions, should the situation warrant it.) When briefing him and giving him project updates, remember there should be no misinformation or selective or partial information.

If you have bad news to report, give it without mincing words. Don't quietly slip it in or sugarcoat it. He is smart enough to see through. Tell him everything in the level he wants. Remember, he is your super-boss and he has the right to know. Be very focused and even if the discussion wanders off in a different direction, try to steer it back to where you left off.

Numbers can greatly enhance your communication. If you say that your Rs 12 crore machine can result in an eventual savings of Rs 3 crores per year, it might make a greater impact on a CEO like Mr Swamy. Similarly, if you can quantify the bad news and give it to him in terms of numbers ('delay of 3 days', 'cost over-run of Rs 10 lakhs', etc.) he would grasp the magnitude of things better.

Be prepared to explain the very basics: The CEO bunch is thorough and methodical in wanting to digest what you are presenting.

They may not be rocket scientists, but they would want to understand rockets. They are sticklers for details and sometimes don't mind if the entire discussion gets hijacked along a totally different path. They will often want the core concepts and basics to be explained to them. So be prepared to hold an impromptu 101 class.

When you do get down to explaining the basics, remember that they are smart people—otherwise they would not have risen to the top—and you need to explain only till a little light bulb gets turned on in their heads. They have their own ways of comprehending and systematizing knowledge and so, don't force anything on them. They know the big picture perfectly—and now they want to know more about the small piece of the puzzle you are holding and its relationship to everything else. In the bargain, people like Mr Swamy might also get to understand the second law of thermodynamics.

Get a lot of help: Plant your trusted colleagues in the audience. Enlist your immediate manager. Have support from your ranks—people who can be your back-up, argue your point or show alternate support data. If possible, keep some 'trump cards' ready, that lend complete finesse to your argument.

Make the time to meet with other managers in other functional teams who might benefit from your new forging process and get them to rally for you. But be forewarned that they will distance themselves from you if you make major goofs. As much as you want to make an impression on the upper management, they too want to look good.

Don't get flustered or confused and don't collapse: The CEO-bunch is also a very impatient lot. Make sure you are not on a slippery slope and ruin everything. If the big executive chews you up, hang in there, accept guilt and wear your best put-on smile. Only the less resolute will wilt under pressure and give up.

When he says, 'go back to the previous slide' it is usually a warning sign that he has spotted some glitch in your presentation. When that happens, take a deep breath and wait for the assault. Remember that you don't win by being cocky and combative, but by enamouring and gratifying him.

The super boss-underling relationship is highly unequal. So, don't take their insults and merciless dressing down personally. They do it to many other people in the organization as well and it is almost a part of their job description. Don't talk back to them or interrupt them when they are talking. Take their feedback as positive criticism and offer to bring the required information the next time. Take copious notes on what they want and arrange for your colleagues in the crowd to also take down notes. If you can think on your feet and *ad lib* your way out of the situation, then well and good. But don't get confused and confuse everyone else—or the big boss will start to lose confidence in you.

30.3 In Summary

Being at the big dance with a big boss creates interesting dynamics. It pitches your preparedness against his due diligence, your depth of knowledge against his breadth, your technical expertise against his managerial concerns and above all, it is a battle between your communication skills and his communication style. The keys to an effective presentation are total familiarity with the technical details and the ability to read his mind.

Who knows? In the next go-around, you may charm Mr Swamy so much that he not only buys you that forging machine, but also asks you to be on the committee to look into the modernization of the entire plant.

We summarize this chapter with a checklist of some of the key points to remember about presenting to the senior management.

- Do you have a complete set of presentation material—and in order?
- Is it reasonably simple, vivid and does it have a lot of pictures, graphs and other easy-to-understand objects?
- Have you carefully read through your material and eliminated silly typographical or factual errors in your slides?
- Do you have a clear idea of how long you have? Have you planned to use that time fully, and not ask for more time?
- Are you mentally prepared not to have the time you had planned for? In other words, should you have less time than what you had planned, have you prioritized what you would like to highlight?
- Have you translated all the benefits into an approximate rupee amount, instead of subjective, iffy, qualitative terms?
- Have you made sure you are not presenting an unrealistically rosy picture that is not rooted in reality?
- Have you got a concise and pointed summary of your presentation in which you have clearly articulated what is the action plan and what support you need from the senior management?
- Have you made a short summary report of your material for him to take home?

Fig. 30.1

- Do you also have a bunch of support data and extra, related materials handy, in case he wants to look at them?
- Did you go through a 'mock presentation' with your colleagues and immediate manager?
- Did you bring a few of your friends and immediate colleagues to the real presentation to support you, in case you need help during your presentation?
- Are you perfectly relaxed and loose on the day of presentation?
- And finally, do you know why you are making this presentation and where this fits in with the big picture?

Part III: Etiquette

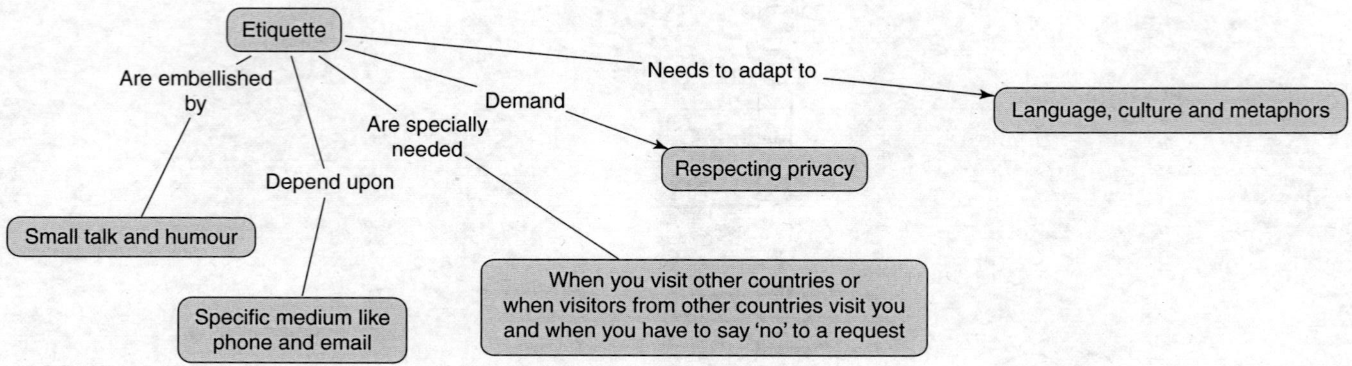
Etiquette
Are embellished by
Small talk and humour
Depend upon
Specific medium like phone and email
Are specially needed
When you visit other countries or when visitors from other countries visit you and when you have to say 'no' to a request
Demand
Respecting privacy
Needs to adapt to
Language, culture and metaphors

31

Phone Etiquette

> *"This 'telephone' has too many shortcomings to be seriously considered as a means of communication. The device is inherently of no value to us."*
>
> *–Western Union internal memo, 1876.*

The telephone has always been a beast of burden for business communication. Even some of the iconic images of last century's business world revolve around the phone—a serious businessman busily talking on the phone, a secretary taking down a phone message for the boss and the army of telephone operators (who were a subculture unto themselves) connecting phone lines and people. But, what used to be a simple instrument (with an annoying ringtone) tethered to your desks, has now evolved into a sophisticated gadget with all sorts of multimedia communication capabilities, elaborate storage possibilities with a number of organizer and productivity features besides being mobile so that you can carry it and use it almost anywhere in the world. The Blackberries, iPhones, 3G and what have you, have all ushered in an exciting era of communications, giving you many more choices (and many more annoying ringtones) and many novel ways to conduct business communication.

Once only in the hands of the elite—at least in India—phones have now percolated down to all strata of society the world over and are integrating entire humanity in a complex network of communication channels, making it possible for almost anyone to reach anyone else, anywhere in the world, at any time—a perfect pill for today's globalized business. Alexander Graham Bell may have invented the telephone. But, we are still discovering it and trying to come up with even newer applications for telephony.

India by and large missed the telecom and telephony revolution of the mid 20th Century. The good side of it is that India is not left with much of legacy baggage to carry on; a large number of Indians did not have to handle those brick-sized mobile phones, did not use answering machines and pagers, but simply leapfrogged into the mobile revolution. Indians have been quick to adapt to text messaging ('SMS-ing') and what is popularly called 'MCC' (missed call citizen), something a lot of older generation Americans loathe doing even now.

The bad side is that the legal aspects and etiquette of using telephones (at least as expected in a globalized business environment) have not been inculcated enough into the average Indian professional. Since we are in the 'catch-up' mode, most of us don't make the time to educate ourselves on these things. Instead, we prefer to go about our phone-business in an instinctive manner or pick up bits and pieces of information (some of it patently wrong) from a variety of sources, including hearsay. In this chapter, we will look at some of the standard business practices and telephone protocols that almost the entire world follows. At a microscopic level, this chapter will also talk about personal phone etiquette and how you can groom yourself into having a great 'telephone personality'. This can be a powerful asset in your soft skills portfolio and can make you a valuable member and a spokesperson of any international team.

31.1 What Is a Good 'Phone Personality'?

Phone communication is a form of synchronous communication. We have all the advantages and disadvantages of synchronous communications that we discussed in Chapter 13. Just to summarize these here,

- Since it occurs in teal time, you will get immediate responses
- You would be able to get insights about the recipient and be able to alter your flow.
- The 'out of sight'-edness of the other party can actually embolden you and help you get over your inhibitions. You may actually ask the boss about that bonus on the phone, whereas you may get tongue-tied and scared when he is actually, physically present in front of you.
- You can be freer as it is not always as formal as written communication.

But the major disadvantage is that it is not a face-to-face communication. Hence, we are left without the benefit of the important medium of body language. This can be a major handicap especially if you (or the other party) don't know the language very well and rely on body language. A good 'phone personality' can compensate for this shortcoming and can make our communication effective.

And what is a good phone personality? (Box 31.1) It is characterized by *courtesy* and *professionalism* during the call and *dependable follow through* after the call.

The basic expectation in any business phone call is that you be totally and unconditionally courteous and create a nice setting for a pleasant conversation and a possible business transaction. This means no sulking, no expressions of irritation and no caustic or sarcastic remarks and definitely no arguing or quarrelling with the party at the other end. It doesn't matter whether you are talking to your client or your vendor, your manager or a colleague way too junior to you; and it doesn't matter whether you are having a rough day at work; it doesn't matter who is right and who is wrong—you will have to display utmost courtesy on the phone. It is okay to disagree, but not okay to be disagreeable, especially on the phone! A good phone personality is *always* courteous, no matter what.

Professionalism in a call demands that you provide the information expected of you, address the things you are supposed to address and make commitments that you are authorized to make. But you do not take on-the-fly executive decisions or change project parameters during a private one-on-one phone call. Business phone calls have their limits and are no substitutes for a full blown project meeting. A good phone personality always maintains professionalism and knows where the line is between what he can and cannot commit to do.

A phone call is a part of the communication cycle, as described in Chapter 13. It is not a silo or an end into itself. A call can result in action items that need to be diligently followed through. A good phone personality always takes these action items to completion.

Box 31.1

Some Indicators of Good Phone Personality

While you cannot drastically change your voice and make it very musical, you have to hone your voice and make sure your voice modulation is pleasant to be a good phone personality. The problem with most of us is that we have never taken the trouble to listen to a recording of our own voices and see what we can do to improve it. So it helps to make a short recording of your voice and nudge it toward the right pitch. Some of the questions you should ask yourself about your voice, diction and conversation style are:

- How is your accent sounding?
- Can you make it more neutral and lively?
- Are you too loud or too soft?
- Are you stressing the right part of the sentence and are you putting in emotion, energy and exuberance into your diction?
- Since you are going to be invisible to the other person, what are the audible cues you will be giving (in the absence of body language cues)—the smirks, the laughs and the 'hmmm's, the interjections—how do they sound?

- Do you practise active listening and does the other person know that?
- Do you let the other person in on the conversation?
- Do you pepper your speech with enough humour and personal comments that relieve the monotony and keep the conversation interesting?
- Do you address the other person by his or her name often in the conversation?
- Is your conversation going in the right direction or is it meandering and waffling?
- Do you steer clear of controversies and proprietary matters?

Also, here are some things that you shouldn't do as a good phone personality:

- Don't multitask during a call (like checking e-mail while talking).
- Don't give the other party the impression that you are in the middle of something or not enthusiastic about the phone call.
- If more than one person is at the phone at your end, don't get into private conversations while on the call

31.2 Anatomy of a Business Phone Call

A business phone call roughly goes through the following steps:

1. Initial greetings
2. Establishing a (virtual) handshake with the other person
3. Getting down to business
4. Summarizing
5. Following through with the minutes of the call
6. Taking the action items to completion.

Let us look at each of these in detail below:

31.2.1 Initial Greetings

If you are answering a phone, basic courtesy demands that you don't let the phone ring till (what appears to be) eternity for the caller. Make it a habit to pick up the phone in no more than 3–5 rings.

When the phone rings and you answer it, do so with a courteous greeting:

- The universally understood greeting 'Hello' or variations thereof, like 'Hello, this is Ajay of RYZ Corp' or 'Good Morning, this is Ajay' or even 'Hi, this is Ajay Jaiswal' would be appropriate.
- If you are in a customer service position, an even better way of answering the call would be 'Good morning, this is Ajay of RYZ Corp. How may I assist you?'

- Don't use a rough-sounding 'Yes?' or 'Yeah?' or 'Jaiswal'. Or worse still, don't keep silent after attending the call, waiting for the other person to start the conversation.

When you initiate a call,

- Wait for the person at the other end to say 'hello'. It is extremely impolite to start talking even before the other person has had a chance to say hello.
- After the hello, identify yourself clearly to the person you called—don't presume your voice to be so familiar that people would recognize you right away.
- If you are making an unscheduled call, preemptively apologize for interrupting and ask them if it is going to be okay to talk for a few minutes. Most people should be okay with a short phone call even if they are busy. As a matter of courtesy, keep your call short and to the point. If they explicitly tell you at the outset that they are too busy, excuse yourself. But, find out when it is convenient for you to call them again and follow through promptly. Likewise, if you need to talk to them at length, find out when best to do so and call them back at a convenient time.

31.2.2 Establishing a Handshake

Establishing the identities of the parties involved in the call is the first part of the virtual handshake of a telephone call. The rest of the handshake is about establishing a rapport and setting the tone (no pun intended) for rest of the conversation.

The first part of the handshake is addressing. If the person at the other end is your customer and you don't know him or her well, address him as Sir or her as Ma'am. If you want to be very formal, you can use the 'Mr Gupta' kind of appellations. A lot of people these days don't mind being addressed by their first names or nicknames—in which case, do so. That might add a personal touch. (Some people may object to being addressed by their first name or nickname—so, be careful about being too informal)

The next part of the handshake is a very brief warm up. A reasonably short 'How are you? How are things out there?' kind of greetings would quickly and effectively provide a natural transition to the main point of the phone call.

31.2.3 Getting Down to Business

After the handshake, comes the main body of the phone call. Here are some general tips:

- Try to sound cheerful and energetic. Since you have to make do without the help of any body language, your voice should display the cheerfulness and energy.
- Remember to use a lot of polite words like 'please', 'sorry' and 'thank you'—sometimes even gratuitously.
- Be especially courteous when interrupting the other person. Make polite interruptive sounds or come up with a 'may I say something?' Don't aggressively butt in.

- While talking, you and the other party should go back and forth alternately, using short sentences and simple language. No one person should hog the conversation or try to overwhelm the other person.
- Allow gaps so that the other person can get into the conversation. If what you say is unclear to the other person, repeat it again. If it is still unclear, paraphrase your sentence.
- Use the methods of active listening described in Chapter 17 to ensure that you and the recipient are in tune.
- Keep a writing pad next to your phone and take down notes as you speak. String them together as an e-mail and send the other person a copy, just so that there won't be any confusion or misunderstanding later.

Snapshot 31.1

The meat of the conversation is in the middle. Let us say your name is Ajay Jaiswal and you are the quality test engineer at the computer peripherals manufacturer, RYZ Corp. When you interface with your counterpart Mr Rupak Shah, incoming quality test engineer of ECA Computers, you can have all sorts of phone conversations with each other—exchanging technical information, updating informally on the progress made, giving 'heads up' on what is coming, getting related information, etc. Mainly, you can have a serious and lengthy conversation on all the gory technical details ('I got only 4.95 milli-amps of current, when I set it to 5.0 milli-amps. It took me two hours to figure out the problem.')—something you cannot do in a full-blown project meeting, given the time constraints and that you don't want to put everyone else to sleep. You can give Shah partial results of your half-completed testing and he can in turn give you feedback on last week's quality tests and update you on what ECA might do next week in terms of volume and test requirement. This way, you and Shah not only develop a rapport, but also put your minds together to come up with some joint and concerted activities that you can bring to the table in the next project meeting.

31.2.4 Summarizing

The last part of a call is used for summarizing it. Such a summary should cover at a minimum:

- What is agreed to be done by each party, along with agreed dates
- Any actions that have to be carried out by other people and how those other people are going to be notified
- If you are going to formally document the minutes of the call (and we strongly recommend you should), when would that be sent
- When and how you are going to sync up again to review the follow up actions.

Try to end the conversation on a bright, positive note. A dash of small talk toward the end of the call is good practice. When you finish talking, make sure you actually utter the word 'bye' before ending the call. Just hanging up without a formal 'bye' is considered extremely rude.

31.2.5 Following Through with Minutes

Business phone calls arise out of action items. And they end up generating more action items and requests for information. So, it is important to keep track of these things or they will come back to haunt you. The first action item is that you quickly summarize these phone generated action items into a documented text and send them over by e-mail to the other party—and also a bunch of other team members, just to let them know what transpired. This way it will now become a part of the formal project paperwork. If anything is ambiguous, call Shah right away and resolve the issue. The tips we gave in the chapters on meeting management (Chapter 24) and will discuss in e-mail etiquette (Chapter 32) about writing minutes of meetings are applicable here as well.

A business phone call can also be used to compare your checklist of activities against the other parties checklist and formally close those items which have no loose ends. Again, circulate an e-mail announcing this 'off-line' transaction.

If you are the organizer of a regular conference-call, make sure you send out the minutes of the call as well as the agenda for the next call. And don't forget to reserve the conference room for the next call, should you require it. Again, these are in line with what we discussed in our earlier chapters.

31.2.6 Taking Action Items to Completion

The action items that were committed to during a phone call should be taken to their logical conclusion. If other people or functions are to be involved in executing such action items, make sure that you contact them soon enough and close the loop.

When the action items are taken to completion, acknowledge the people who made it possible. Also, if you have a follow up call, recognize this and document the completion in the minutes of that meeting/call.

Make sure you complete these telephonic action items according to the commitments that were made. If, for some unavoidable reason, you are unable to complete your committed action items in time, do inform the coordinator well ahead, so as not to cause unpleasant surprises.

31.3 Conference Call Etiquette

You can also connect several people from across the world to the same call and have an effective multi-pronged conference. International tele-conference or conference calls are so common place that some people participate in several of them each day. Your effective and active participation in your conference calls is absolutely essential for the success of your project.

Conference calls should be treated exactly like face-to-face meetings. You discuss project status, take decisions, assign activities to team members and so on over the phone, much like you would in a sit-down meeting. Here too, it is important that the meeting agenda are set ahead of time and after the call, minutes are noted down and published—especially the action items, the owners and deadlines.

Though conference calls are similar in intent and direction to a group meeting, they present several unique challenges that you don't see in face-to-face meetings.

- When a number of people participate in a conference call from different locations around the world, it may be sometimes confusing to figure out who it is that is talking.
- Accents could be very different, making understanding more difficult.
- The sound quality can be very poor and add to the confusion.
- Making interruptions and responding right away can become tricky in a conference call and you may have to try a couple of times before you can get yourself airtime.
- Time difference could reduce the focus of the participants who are participating in the call at what are unearthly hours for them.

Some of the methods to overcome the above challenges are:

- Make sure you have good multi directional speaker phones to make it possible for people sitting in far corners of the room to be audible.
- If you have to dial in any of the participants to the call, make sure you get their numbers correct.
- If the participants have to dial in themselves to a conferencing centre, make sure you e-mail them the number to be dialled in and any identification mechanism like meeting ID and password.
- Make sure all the international attendees know the local time in your location by giving your time as an offset from GMT. Make sure you account for any daylight savings.
- Accents and diction can help identify people sometimes. See if you can tag people based on their accents.
- When you dial in to the conference number, make sure you introduce yourself and where you are calling from. ('Hi, this is Ajay from Bangalore'). If there are multiple groups within Bangalore, make sure you identify your group as well.
- Speak even more deliberately and slowly than when you speak in person and only when it is your turn.
- Whenever you speak, it is a good idea to keep re-introducing yourself several times in the call, just to make sure ('Hi, this is Ajay from Bangalore, again').

- When you want to interrupt, make sure you choose an appropriate pause and say, 'Hi Ajay here again, I would just add to this point by . . . '.
- If you find the person speaking currently is not giving any chance to others by continuous, non-stop talking, you can interrupt gently by saying 'John . . . John . . . this is Ajay here, can I interrupt you for a minute?'
- Don't be shy about asking a speaker to repeat or re-affirm things if you didn't hear or understand what he said. It is wiser and more effective to ask him to repeat and get a common understanding than making wrong assumptions.
- Be very patient with people who are not particularly articulate or phone-savvy and try to help them by paraphrasing sentences. (But be careful about putting wrong words into their mouths.)

31.4 Some Phone Etiquette for the Modern Day

Nowadays, phones have features like text messaging, caller ID and voice mails that require some special etiquette. Here are some of them:

SMS/Text Messaging

SMS has got good traction, especially in India. The impersonal nature of SMS is a boon as well as a curse. It is easy to be more polite in an SMS than in speaking over phone, as you have time to formulate your message and there are fewer chances of getting sidetracked by synchronous conversations. It also helps you to respond back when you want.

- SMS is a good way of conveying short messages like 'I cannot attend the meeting' or some quick updates like 'the test was successful'. But obviously it is not a formal channel and you don't use it to order ten thousand units of a circuit board.
- Do not forward SMS messages recklessly.
- Be forgiving of poor spelling in SMS messages. 'That's hw u r supposed 2 deal wth it.'

Caller ID and Voice Mail

Caller IDs are godsends for us to ignore calls we don't want to take. Do use them, especially when you get a call while you are in the middle of a meeting. If you see a call coming from an unknown number or from someone you know but the call can wait, you should simply let the call pass. However, if it is a call from someone you know, do have the courtesy to return the call.

At work, set up a voice mailbox. Most Americans prefer to leave and retrieve voice mails than SMS texting. When leaving a voice message for someone, clearly identify yourself, your organization, your phone number and keep the message short. Make it a habit to check your voice mailbox frequently and retrieve messages in a timely fashion. Sometimes, when you happen to be away from your desk for long hours, this may involve remotely calling your central voice mailbox number and logging into the system. Do return the relevant calls promptly. The key word here is relevant. As in the case of caller IDs, you need not always return a call from an unknown number.

Contacts and Organizers

During the course of your work-related activities, you may get new contacts and phone numbers. Store them away at the appropriate place–and perhaps redundantly in more than one place.

Periodically, perhaps at the beginning of each work day, review your telephone activities for that day. Are there any phone calls you need to make/return soon? Are there any action items you need to follow through further? (Especially, are there any meetings you need to schedule, because of a recent phone call?) If you are the organizer of a weekly conference call, do you need to make calls to take care of it? Have you checked your calendar for any important, pending phone calls?, Remember that sometimes you may never get around to making that important phone call and this can come back to bite you.

And finally, take a few moments every once in a while to organize your contacts. How many times has it happened to you that the phone number you are looking for is the only one you don't have? The only way to safeguard against this annoying situation is to build some redundancy in your system and save a copy of it in your computer and perhaps even take a printout or e-mail it to yourself (so that you can access numbers when you travel). Don't be too quick to erase phone numbers from your contacts list. Likewise, organize the business cards you got from your contacts into a neat bundle and stash it away in a place you will remember.

31.5 Miscellaneous Tips About Phones and Phone Calls

- Never, never, never ask an international business partner for his or her personal cell phone or home phone numbers. Some people keep them a secret and even pay money to unlist their numbers from the directory. Instead, ask them how to contact him or her in case of emergency during the off hours and let them figure out a way.
- Do not communicate by 'missed call' with your international partner.
- When you are on the phone, don't multi-task.
- A corollary of the above—don't participate in conference calls while driving—even if you are using a 'hands-free' headphone. Driving in most modern cities requires total concentration on the traffic and conference calls also require a complete focus on the call. It is our opinion that you cannot do both of them well, simultaneously. Yes, the business call is important, but your safety and the safety of others around you is much more important. If you *really* must,

participate in the call, join the call in the passive 'listen only' mode and not actively take part in it.

- When abroad, obey that country's conventions and protocols on cell phone usage. Usually, it is okay to use cell phones in an already noisy environment such as airports, fast food restaurants and malls, whereas you are expected to desist from using them in quiet places like places of worship, group meetings or elegant restaurants.
- In some other places like hospitals and planes they may interfere with the radio equipments and you are not supposed to use them anyway. Please don't show off your importance to everyone around you by switching on the cell phone while the plane is still taxiing to the gate on the runway.
- Remember that it is generally not a good idea to carry on loud business calls in public (like in an airport) and letting others around listen to it. It is not only imprudent, but also very rude to the people around you.
- Use speakerphone only if you must. In such a case, inform the other persons that they are on speakerphone.

Fig. 31.1

- When giving out a phone number, say 2221 5515, don't confuse the international business partner by going 'triple two one double five one five' and so on. Most of the world does not use double, triple convention. Instead, combine two numbers at a time. (If the communication is very clear you can club three or even four numbers together) Say, for example, 'two-two, two-one, five-five, one-five'.
- Americans typically follow a 3-3-4 convention. Typically, they say 'Area code 415; 789 5672', with a pause after 415 and a pause between 789 and 5672. Or they say '415 (pause) 789 (pause) 5672'. It is a good idea to stick to this convention when you are in the USA.
- Indian numbers are somewhat non-standard, with a different number of digits for mobile numbers and landline numbers and different 'codes' for calling landlines from within India and outside India. For example, a landline number in Bangalore could be 080-25674292 while dialling from within India, whereas it would be +91-80-2567-4292 when dialling from abroad. And mobile numbers in India follow entirely different numbering conventions. Make sure you clearly say the correct number to be dialled from abroad – including the preceding international, country and area codes.
- It is illegal in many countries to record telephone conversations without the permission of the other party—but a lot of people are not aware of such legal restrictions. It is important to realize that the rest of the world expects us to follow such phone etiquette when doing business with them.
- And finally, the next time the phone rings and you are in the middle of something important, remember that you don't have to answer the darned thing!

32

E-mail Etiquette

"All the inhabitants of the earth would be brought into one intellectual neighborhood."

–Alonzo Jackman, advocating an Atlantic telegraph in 1846

We seem to receive a ton of it every day, both at home and at work. And in turn, we generate and send a few ourselves every day. Some people regard it as a necessary evil, whereas some others look at it as a fine art. And there are still others who would develop withdrawal symptoms if they don't check email every few hours. Bane or a boon, e-mail has been with us for over a generation now and has transformed business communication in ways we couldn't have imagined. Today, e-mails are the most common means of formal written communication, both for communication within an organization and for communication with external stakeholders.

Despite the obvious proliferation of this medium, it is often used inappropriately or ineffectively and does not achieve the intended purpose. The purpose of this chapter is to present some e-mail etiquette—common practices that you should follow as a matter of courtesy to your stakeholders as well as to increase the effectiveness of your communication.

We first summarize some of the obvious advantages and challenges of e-mail as a medium. We then identify the common types of e-mails that you would need to use in your workplace. We then take each of these in a separate section and present some tips on writing them and increasing their effectiveness.

32.1 Advantages and Challenges of E-mails

E-mails, being written communication, provide the following obvious advantages:

Provides a permanent record: As e-mails are forms of written communication, they leave behind a permanent record. E-mails are nowadays generally legally acceptable pieces of documents. This is a double-edged sword. While this increases the contractual validity of the document, you also need to be careful about the language you use in e-mails. Loose statements, bad language and false commitments in an e-mail are absolute no-no as you and your organization can be held liable for them.

Don't have to play 'phone tag': E-mails being asynchronous means of communication, you don't have to worry about whether the other person is present at the other end and if he would respond to you right away. You can send the mail when it is convenient for you and the recipient can read it and act on it when it is convenient to him. Obviously, this brings along with it all the accompanying advantages and disadvantages of asynchronous communication that we discussed in Chapter 13.

Cheap: E-mail today is among the most economical means of communication. It hardly costs you anything extra over and above a network connection (that is cheap) and given that delivery is almost instantaneous, the costs are far less than 'overnight delivery' (which, of course, is not even possible across continents). E-mail is also more convenient than physical mail in that you don't have to make that trip to the post office or lick stamps or worry about it getting lost. So, except in case of sending original documents or documents requiring signatures, e-mail can do everything that 'snail mail' can do–and that too, at the click of a mouse.

Ubiquitous: E-mails can be accessible anytime, anywhere. You can access e-mails through your mobile phones, laptops and so on. You can access e-mails in airports, at home, while in transit; you can receive alerts for incoming e-mails whenever and wherever you want. No other form of formal communication provides this flexibility.

Can handle most types of data: Whether you want to send text documents, drawings, photographs, presentations, spreadsheets, videos or voice recordings, e-mails can almost always handle all these as attachments. The online collaboration tools also allow you to share, modify and get to a common page (literally!) on these documents instantaneously. This makes e-mails suitable for technical communication (drawings, diagrams, etc.), business communication (contracts, spreadsheets, etc.), marketing communication (brochures, photographs, presentations, etc.) and just about anything else. Again, no other mode of formal communication can provide this much variety and such convenience at so little cost.

The challenges faced in e-mails arise by virtue of the fact that it is an asynchronous mode of communication and therefore, there is a time lag between when we send our communication and when the other party responds. Also, e-mail does not have a face-to-face component, thereby depriving the use of the body-language channel and the voice channel. In addition, you have no way to judge the recipients' moods or his immediate reaction. Words will have to speak for themselves, and this places that much more of a burden on you, the writer of the e-mail, to achieve the objectives of communication by just the written words, without any other help and without any immediate feedback.

In addition, because e-mails can be forwarded and copied way beyond your (the author's) control, your e-mail may land up with completely uninterested or even unintended and unauthorized people. Hence you have to be extremely careful about what you say in e-mails, to prevent misuse in unauthorized hands.

32.2 Common Types of Mails in Professional Environments

In business environments, there are a number of types of e-mails that are generated. Among all these, the most common types are:

Enquiry e-mails: You would need to find out information needed for your work from your colleagues, partners or customers. Enquiry e-mails serve this purpose.

Problem reporting e-mails: You may have to report problems in someone's product, complain about inadequate customer support or anything that does not meet the expectations. Problem reporting e-mails serve this purpose.

Problem response e-mails: This is at the other end of the spectrum for the previous category. When someone complains about your product or service, you would have to respond back with a problem response e-mail.

Status reports: We have already seen about status reporting in detail in Chapter 26. Most status reports are sent by e-mail.

Meeting minutes: Just like status reports, we have also discussed in detail how to document minutes of a meeting. Again, most of the meeting minutes are sent via e-mail as the participants are usually geographically distributed and the meetings are usually virtual meetings or conference calls.

Each of these types of mails requires different etiquette which we will discuss in the individual sections. We will first discuss some common etiquette to be followed, regardless of the type of mail.

32.3 Common Points About All Types of E-mails

No matter what type of e-mail you send, some points will have to be borne in mind. We will cover these in this section and then take up specific points about each type of mail separately.

Conversational style: Your e-mail should have a conversational style and should engage the recipient. Since you don't have access to valuable channels like body language, vocal variety and so on, the words of your written text should do the trick. The choice of words and the punctuation should clearly reflect the substance of the e-mail.

'Subject' line of your e-mail: It should concisely and unambiguously indicate to the recipient what is in store in the e-mail. It should be a compelling invitation to the receiver to open the mail. We all receive loads of mail everyday. Any subject that looks like spam (or a mail with no subject line) is an easy victim of not being opened and of being deleted ruthlessly (see Box 32.1).

Box 32.1

Some Common Mistakes in Etiquette in the Subject Line

The biggest cardinal sin is to leave the subject line blank. This is an invitation for the recipient not to open your mail. After all, if you as the sender do not think it fit to specify what the subject is, why should the recipient care to open your mail? A senior management person typically receives hundreds of mails per day. Out of these, crisis mails catch their attention with a compelling subject line and become the first targets to be opened. Then there may be the routine status and project mails which come from known people, which will catch his attention. If you are sending an enquiry email to someone and if your mail ID is not familiar to him, then you need to go the extra mile to make him open the mail. A blank subject line is not likely to entice someone to open the e-mail.

Another common mistake people make is to have the subject line as 'Hi' or 'Hello'. No one wants to take the time to open such mails from a stranger. Also, this subject line is too casual to be fit for a professional business environment.

Today, most of us receive a lot of spam messages with titles like 'Your Order', 'Invoice Enclosed', and so on. Such subject lines are likely to not even pass through the 'spam filters' in most organizations.

Thus, choosing an effective subject line is an extremely important rating factor in determining the effectiveness of e-mail. Just like most resumés get filtered in the resumé screening stage itself, an ineffective subject line like the ones above is a surefire way of ensuring the recipient does not even open your e-mail.

Addressing the person: You must address the person appropriately. If the recipient is your colleague—no matter what level of seniority he is in–an informal 'Dear Bill' should be fine. First make sure you know what his first name is and how he would like to be called and use that appropriately. If the recipient is a customer or somebody with whom you have to maintain a formal distance, than a 'Dear Mr Gates' is appropriate. But, if you have been corresponding with that person for some time, a simple 'Bill' by itself is okay. Note that 'Dear Mr Bill' or 'Dear Bill Gates' or 'Dear Gates' is inappropriate. If you know the recipient's nickname or any name that he prefers, use that. Some of our Indianisms like 'Respected Sir' or 'Dear Bill Sir' or 'Dear technical director' are absolutely not appropriate.

Sometimes you may not be able to guess the sex of the person from the name, in which case, a neutral sounding 'Dear Dipti' (or even 'Dear Dipti Patnaik') is fine. And don't misspell the name.

Closure: Similarly, keep your e-mail closure simple. Just say 'Regards' and in the next line 'Vijay'. (If you are sending it to a total stranger, 'Sincerely' would work as well.) If you have been writing to that person several times, you can drop the 'Regards' and simply sign off as Vijay. If you want to be formal and courteous in your closure, you can use 'Cordially' or 'Sincerely' Do not use expressions like 'Yours obediently' or 'Yours faithfully' or even worse, 'I remain, yours faithfully'.

Signature: When you are writing a business mail, we strongly recommend that you don't just sign off as 'Vijay'. Do have a standard signature that shows your full name, title and organization details (see the boxes below).

Length of an e-mail: There is no specific guideline on how long an e-mail should be. But in general, e-mails longer than a couple of screen scrolls are difficult to read and may force people to print the e-mail and read it later. Keep e-mails as short as possible. Should you really have lots of things to cover, consider giving a quick summary in the e-mail and put the rest in an attachment.

Giving the most important information upfront: Following through on the previous point, make sure you prioritize the contents of your e-mail and highlight the most important ones within the first few lines and definitely within a couple of screen scrolls.

Use of To, CC and BCC: There is a subtle difference between 'To' and 'CC'. People included in the 'To' field are primary recipients of the e-mail, whereas people who are copied are receiving the e-mail 'for their information' only, because the 'loop' includes them. If you need someone to take some action, their names *must* be on the 'To' list. If you want someone to be just informed and you require no specific actions from them, put them on a CC list. Use the BCC list sparingly, only when you don't want anyone else to know the recipient being BCC-ed.

Now let us look at some specifics of these different categories of e-mail.

32.4 Writing Enquiry E-mails

In a corporate environment, you may have to get information from other people (see Box 32.2).

Box 32.2

Common scenarios where enquiry mails are needed in business environments

Componentized development: Today, most software products are not developed in a monolithic way. Different components are developed by different teams in an inter-dependent way and these parts have to be assembled together to form an integrated whole, which is greater than the sum of its parts. Teams may need to interact with each other and get details about the functionality of the other parts and the interfaces they offer.

Geographic work distribution: Globalization has distributed work across geographies and time zones. It is common in software to find the global delivery model, where on-shore, near-shore and off-shore teams have to work together to produce complex pieces of software; in ITeS work originates in one place and gets executed in another location miles away. In manufacturing, design comes from different locations and the actual manufacturing occurs elsewhere. If all the teams are in one location, you can walk across to your colleague's office down the hall and ask him for any clarifications. But, with geographic separation and time zone differences, this option is foreclosed. E-mail is your only saviour.

Large organizations: When organizations grow in size, they become rather impersonal. When combined with geographical distribution of people and tasks, the only formal means of communication available, that is fast, economical and easy to use is e-mail. For example, you may need to find out about the problems encountered by customers by communicating with the customer-support personnel. The customer may be in New York, you may be in Bangalore and the customer support may be in Sydney. In such cases, e-mails are the best formal means of communication that leave behind a trail and resolve issues quickly.

Let us look at some practical problems in making such enquiries.

- First of all, you may not know where or to whom to send your enquiry e-mail. Large organizations tend to operate in silos in a somewhat impersonal way. For you to find out the right person to contact is sometimes not very easy.
- Even if you find out the right recipient, the person you send the e-mail to may not enjoy getting the e-mail or may simply choose to ignore your e-mail.
- If you are under time-pressure to get answers to your enquiries, that might compound the problem a bit more.

So how do you resolve this fundamental issue of whom to send the mail to?

- If it is an internal enquiry, you can determine who to send the e-mail to by looking up the intranet directory; usually most corporate intranets provide an easily searchable directory.

- Look up any work products like program source code or documents that you can lay your hands on. The person who last changed this program code or document would be a good place to start with.
- Use your network. You might have talked to someone in that group in a conference or a training programme. Dig out his contact information, pick up the phone and revive the contact. If that someone helped you with the e-mail ID of a valid contact, it is good manners to 'CC' the e-mail to that person as well, provided the matter you discuss in the e-mail is not confidential.
- Sometimes even a generic e-mail to the associate @customer_service kind of address might do the trick.
- Sometimes you may have to send your e-mail to multiple people in order to increase the probability of your enquiry getting answered. This should be your last resort, since whenever you send a mail to multiple people, each of the recipients may assume that someone else will respond back to the enquiry.

Once you find out whom to contact, there are a few more factors that you need to consider to make your enquiry effective (i.e. for you to get the information you want). These are:

- Use of subject line
- Simple introduction
- Building in some defense
- Proper wording of the enquiry
- Closure.

We have already seen the general guidelines to use for choosing an appropriate subject line. In addition to those discussed earlier, the following guidelines would be useful when you are sending an enquiry mail, especially to an unknown person.

- A subject line that specifies the topic of the enquiry that is likely to arouse interest in the recipient: e.g., *'Storage options: Request for information'*. Note that the topic (storage options) comes before the phrase 'Request for Information'. This is because the topic itself is likely to arouse more interest than the 'request for information'.
- A subject line that gives the name of the person who referred you to the person to whom you are sending the mail: e.g., *'Referral by John Collins: Storage options info request'*. If John Collins carries clout and is known to the recipient, this is likely to cause the recipient to open the mail.
- A subject line that carries a credible institution name: e.g., *'From IIT-Chennai: Request info on storage options'*. This again builds credibility by the name of the institution and adds to the interest of the subject matter (storage options).

A simple introduction of yourself is needed right at the outset, because the recipient probably does not know who you are or what exactly your functional role is in your organization. A possible introduction has been illustrated in Box 32.3.

Box 32.3

Effective Introductions: Example

I would like to introduce myself as Vijay Raghavan from Desi Computers Inc. in India. As you may be aware, Desi Computers Inc. manages MIRACLE's security environment. I am in charge of maintaining the directory and security database.

Note that the introduction clearly brings out your first and last name, your organization and your role in the organization–which set the tone for the authenticity and relevance of the body of the message (see Box 32.4 for same ineffective introduction).

Box 32.4

Ineffective Introductions: Examples

- 'I am Vijay. I am in charge of your security.' *(very abrupt, does not have sufficient context)*
- 'In my role as the directory administrator, I am . . .' *(again, not providing sufficient context and does not give the name)*
- 'I am Vijay, a distinguished graduate of IIT. I am currently at Desi Computers Inc., which was founded. . . .' *(very wordy and rambling)*

The next aspect of an enquiry e-mail is that you should build in some defence. You are sending this mail to get the information you want. You do not necessarily know whether the recipient is the correct one for the subject or whether he will help you. At the least, the recipient should not feel irritated by getting your e-mail. If he is not the right person to service your request, he should be happy to refer you to the right person or forward your e-mail to that person. A typical example of such a defence has been given in Box 32.5.

Box 32.5

I am looking for some information on LDAP security. Your name was suggested by your colleague Ms Mary Angelene. *(Note that we are establishing rapport and credibility, assuming Mary's name is well known to the recipient.)*

I would appreciate it if you could help me in this. If this issue is not in your group, I offer my sincere apologies. *(Again, note that you are preempting any feeling of anger by this apology.)* I would appreciate it if you could pass this on to anyone whom you think could help. *(You have stated what you want in a polite way.)*

(State your request)

Thanks in advance. *(Again a very courteous end to the mail that will make it difficult for the person to yell at you.)*

Regarding the enquiry proper, let the recipient see the importance, urgency and the need for your request, the sincerity of your request and the appreciation for a response. Try to remember the following points:

- Be specific; don't beat around the bush.
- Bring the crux of the matter within the first page (screen), possibly within just a few lines.
- Restrict the e-mail to a few questions; don't make it look like a laundry list
- Number the questions, so that they can respond question-by-question.
- Don't threaten a response.
- Don't give unreasonable deadlines!

But, make sure the urgency and the given deadlines are real and not fake and cooked up. And, don't use this criticality every time—that will reduce your credibility and the chances of the recipient responding to you (let alone responding to you in time).

What would you do if there is a real dependency and you must get the other person's response immediately? In this case, put some thought as to what you think is the right information to approach and state your viewpoint. If you have some idea of what the right action is and you are looking to the other person's inputs just for confirmation, you can include a default action ('deemed approval') in the mail and unless the recipient has serious disputes and expresses his reservations in a reply e-mail, the default action will be taken. For example, see Box 32.6.

Box 32.6

Looking at the issue, my understanding is that the appropriate solution is . . . Since the product release on 28 February is critically dependent on this information, can you please get back to me with any corrections by 10 February, if you feel my above understanding is not right?

Please note that this is not a foolproof method nor should this be used to cover yourself with a 'I told you so' later. Exercise caution and demonstrate professionalism in expressing the option you think is best.

Finally, have an effective, positive and courteous closure. Reaffirm your positive attitude (see Box 32.7).

Box 32.7

Since the product release on 28 February is critically dependent on this information, I look forward to your valuable inputs by 18 February and thank you in advance.

Regards
Vijay

32.5 Reporting Problems over E-mail

A problem-reporting e-mail arises because a problem has not been adequately resolved through regular channels. As the author of such an e-mail, your motivation should be in problem-resolution and not in lambasting the other person or otherwise venting your feelings. Also, you should be quite tactful in writing such an e-mail and make sure that it coaxes the other party to buy your viewpoint and nudges him into action. You should invoke the right tone, balance and list of suggestions. Remember that people generally do not like to get negative, complaining e-mails and so, your e-mail should project that you are a reasonable person with a genuine problem that you need to solve. Remember too, that such e-mails leave a trail behind and in the rare event the situation gets complicated, your e-mail messages will serve you as a record of the sequence of events.

Direct it to the appropriate person—look at the project plan or the intranet directory or simply ask around and figure out who to hit. At first, fire your e-mails just to that person. If this doesn't work out and you need to escalate the matter, 'CC' your e-mail to the person one level above the recipient. You may want to keep your own boss in the loop and 'CC' him as well. Here too, you have to address some key elements.

Such e-mails have the following basic structure:

- ▶ Addressing/Opening salutation
- ▶ Introduction of the sender
- ▶ Facts about the subject (problem report)
- ▶ Eliciting action
- ▶ Closure/Signature

The subject line should clearly and unmistakably introduce the problem to the recipient. As mentioned earlier, the subject line should motivate the recipient to open the e-mail. Vague subject lines like 'serious problem' or 'SOS' or 'HELP!!!!!' are inappropriate. The subject line should bring out two things: the urgency of the situation and a brief abstract of the problem being reported (see Boxes 32.8 and 32.10).

Box 32.8

Some examples of effective subject lines for problem-reporting e-mails

URGENT: A high priority security violation in the shopping cart application *(Note the word URGENT in caps and the specific description of the problem and the area.)*

Bug # 278902 from Timbuktu Airways, not resolved for 23 days *(Note the specific bug #, the customer name and how long it has been left unresolved.)*

Show Stopper: Year-end tax statements program crash at Country Bank of India *(Note the word show stopper upfront, specific information of what fails and the customer name.)*

The introduction part of the problem-reporting e-mail is similar to that of an enquiry e-mail. For example, see Box 32.9 for an effective introduction and Box 32.10 for examples of same ineffective introductions.

Box 32.9

Effective Introductions

I would like to introduce myself as Vijay Raghavan from Desi Computers Inc. As you may be aware, Desi Computers Inc. manages MIRACLE's security environment. I am in charge of maintaining the directory and security database. I am writing this note because of an unresolved, critical problem in the security environment that we have not been able to resolve through the normal channels. *(Note that the writer has introduced himself, his role and the specific problem he is encountering and that the problem is not resolved through normal channels—all in a matter of four lines.)*

Box 32.10

Not-so-effective introductions:

- 'I am Vijay. I am in charge of your security and there is a nagging problem.' *(Not a specific description; also a very negative word 'nagging' and on the surface, unsubstantiated.)*
- 'There is the problem . . . which I have tried umpteen times to resolve but feels like I am knocking my head against the wall. Can't you guys resolve these simple issues?' *(Very condescending—this mail can invoke fear but not perhaps co-operation from the recipient. He may resolve this problem, but you might have burnt the bridge for resolving future problems.)*

In order to get the best result adhere to the following:

- Report the problem clearly. Don't mince words trying to be nice or trying to report a problem that is not really important or urgent.
- State the original expectation and what the problem was. As we said in Chapter 8, satisfaction coming out of performance depends on the expectation setting.
- If possible, quote instances where the normal expectations have so far been met.
- Present facts to prove the existence of the problem, but do not over-inundate with data. Use only objective data and do not make claims that cannot be substantiated.

- Number the specific concerns you have so that they can respond to you concern by concern. Restrict to just a few so that you don't look like a perpetual moaner and end up getting solutions for none of the things.
- As with enquiry e-mails, don't sound threatening or give the recipient unreasonable deadlines.
- And finally, don't make any personal, caste- or gender-based remarks.

It is generally a good idea to have a separate, new paragraph for 'eliciting action'. Here you insist on a time-bound, reasonable and objective resolution of your problem. Be firm, but courteous. For example, see Box 32.11.

Box 32.11

Given the serious impact the availability of hardware has on our business, I would like to see the hardware (MBI Terminal Controller 3701, with 8MB cache, which is what was originally agreed upon) commissioned at my site in the next two weeks (i.e., before 15 February 2009). Please confirm the specific date of delivery by this weekend so that I can make sure my system administrator is available.

Regards
Vijay,
Vijay Raghavan,
MIRACLE Security Administrator,
Desi Computers Inc.,
234 Infantry Road
Bangalore 560001
Vijay.raghavan@desi.com
Ph: +91-80-2890-9809

For a problem reporting e-mail, the closure should have a full signature with the role of the sender so that the credibility and authenticity of the sender is established. Since there is already a call for action, no specific reaffirmation is required.

32.6 Responding to Problems over E-mail

The purpose of this type of e-mail is to respond to a problem assigned to you–either directly or by your manager. Responding to problems over e-mail requires certain mindset changes that you have to make in yourself.

- You have to be just as tactful, courteous and professional about writing these e-mails as in problem-reporting e-mails. Just as your aim in sending a problem report was to get your problem resolved, here also, your aim should be to resolve the sender's problem.

- Show understanding of the other person and his observation. Empathize with him. This does not mean you are agreeing that you are in the wrong. All you are telling the other party is that 'Okay, I understand you have a problem; let us work together and resolve this. I am equally interested in solving this problem.'
- Even if your instincts say otherwise, rein in your emotions. (It gets even more ugly and unpleasant if the sender copies several other people in the organization and escalates the matter.)
- Work towards resolving the real problem underneath the complaint. Don't be on the path to assign blame to any particular person.

No one likes to be told that there is a problem in what they do. Even though we asked that you should rein in emotions, it is easier said than done. What you don't want to do is type a nasty e-mail to the person who reported the problem and send it to the recipient before you have edited it, by mistake. Hence, we strongly recommend that you type the response offline in a notepad or word processing document, print and check it, make changes as appropriate and finally copy that into your mail and send it across.

Be very clear about who all should receive your reply. Some considerations in this regard are:

- Should your manager be cc-ed if he was not copied in the original complaint e-mail? Use your discretion. If the problem is not a very serious one, don't bug your manager. Save a copy for yourself and if needed you can show it to your manager or include it in your weekly status report.
- Should you copy the sender's manager? We would strongly recommend not to do this as it would sound confrontational and is likely to make the recipient more defensive and refuse to accept your solution.
- Should *you* escalate the matter to a higher level? Should you forward the original e-mail and your reply to any other persons? Again, unless it is a serious issue, we recommend that you do not escalate the mail or cc it to unnecessary people when replying.

The subject line is usually not an issue for these mails, because normally you would just need to hit the 'reply' button for the original mail. But, if there are too many replies and forwards, it is a good idea to refresh the subject line to avoid the multiple 'Re's and 'Fwd's that take up all the initial characters of the subject line.

In the body of the e-mail, there is no need to have an elaborate introduction since the sender probably knows who you are (or your role in the organization). Always start with a courteous and short preamble and apologize right away for the inconvenience caused, irrespective of what or who caused the problem (see Box 32.12).

Box 32.12

Thanks for the mail expressing your concerns. Let me take this opportunity to reassure you that things are under control and also address the specific points you have brought up.

If the problem message has a numbered list of problems, take them one by one. Even if the problem is not broken into components by the sender, see if you can paraphrase the problems by something like:

If I may re-state the issues you have brought up, they are:

1..

2..

Respond to the concerns with clear objective data, not just your perspective. Clearly document resolutions or actions for each item with 'what-who-when'.

Don't be overly defensive. But do not assume that you are always right or flawless. Be objective and focus only on the specific problem and present a solution that is mutually satisfactory. Do resist the temptation of 'getting one back'. Conclude with restating major action items and your (that is, your organization's) intent on customer satisfaction. For example, see Box 32.13.

Box 32.13

I hope that I have addressed all the points that you have brought up in the mail. I once again reiterate our commitment to achieving the common goals and would follow up on taking these action items to completion. I will get in touch with you again a week from now, by when the database backup issue should be resolved.

Regards
Vijay,
Vijay Raghavan,
MIRACLE Security Administrator,
Desi Computers Inc.,
234 Infantry Road
Bangalore 560001
Vijay.raghavan@desi.com
Ph: +91-80-2890-9809

Do keep your promises. Make a follow-through phone call after reaching a reasonable milestone. It is important to register small victories so as to restore or increase customer confidence. Follow the call after such a successful milestone with an e-mail, such as the one in Box 32.14.

Box 32.14

Thanks for taking the time for the call we had this morning. I am glad that everything is going as per schedule and we have achieved our first milestone towards resolving the database backup issue. I will follow up next week. In the meanwhile, if there are any specific issues you want to bring up, do not hesitate to e-mail / call me directly.

Regards
Vijay,
Vijay Raghavan,
MIRACLE Security Administrator,
Desi Computers Inc.,
234 Infantry Road
Bangalore 560001
Vijay.raghavan@desi.com
Ph: +91-80-2890-9809

Remember people do not care how much you know until they know how much you care!

32.7 Sending Minutes of Meeting over E-mail

The next genre is meeting minutes e-mail (which also encompasses minutes of conference calls and so on). These missives are aimed at all the attendees, including those people who should have attended the meeting, but missed it for some reason. Typically, a comprehensive mailing list is made at the beginning of the project and updated periodically. The mail should be 'CC'-ed to all the relevant managers, people who have been assigned action items and administrative persons, as necessary. The subject line should be crisp e.g., 'Meeting minutes—Lotto Lotteries Project—13 September 2009'.

The body of the e-mail should include the following information:

- Meeting at: (location)
- Attendees:

  Lotto Lotteries (customer):

  Desi Computers Inc.:

  (Names of those present and also of those absent)
- Agenda items:
- Discussions and decisions:
- Highlights:
- Red alerts:

- What action? Impact? Worst case (when required)?
- Action Items
- Who-when-what.

Prepare this offline and it is best to have a designated 'scribe' assigned to this task. Have a table of contents, with hyperlinks to other items in the message. Make sure highlights and appropriate red alerts come within the first two pages and make sure you don't 'hide' action items within details! Wherever required, seek feedback within a clear deadline.

32.8 Status Reports and Other Types of Reports

Status reports (and other reports like trip reports) are typically sent over e-mail. Part of the purpose of such e-mails is to archive a particular set of findings/observations and keep it as reference. The main report itself should be a Word document attached to the e-mail, with only the 'hook' of the report featured in the body of the e-mail. We have already covered writing status reports in Chapter 26.

32.9 Miscellaneous Topics

Here we will cover some miscellaneous etiquette considerations while sending e-mails:

Use of Attachments

- Avoid attachments if you can. Keep any short narrative inline; use attachments only when it is large or cannot be contained in under a couple of screens.
- Zip or compress anything other than a 'simple document', especially those that contain graphics and animations. But be forewarned that some organizations ban the use of such files as attachments.
- Avoid sending executables as attachment because of potential virus threats.
- Send only something small (our recommendation: < 5 MB); else post on a site and give the URL.
- Send only to those who absolutely need to see it.

E-mail IDs, Use of Signature and Footer

Most organizations have definite standards in assigning e-mail IDs to users. (Typically, <first name>.<last name>@<companyname>.com)

Even if no standards are enforced, choose a clear and meaningful e-mail ID, which reflects your name. Weird handles, nick-names and anonymous-sounding IDs are not proper in a business setting (e.g., avoid things like smartestone@myhome.com or jamesbond@myco.com).

It is also okay to have a descriptive signature file that you can use at the end of your e-mail (see Box 32.15).

Box 32.15

Vijay,
Vijay Raghavan,
MIRACLE Security Administrator,
Desi Computers Inc.,
234 Infantry Road
Bangalore 560001
Vijay.raghavan@desi.com
Ph: +91-80-2890-9809

Small talk, e-mail style

It is not out of character to indulge in a bit of small talk in e-mails to people who are somewhat familiar to you. This is especially appropriate if you are e-mailing to your group members in a different geographical location. For example, see Box 32.16.

Box 32.16

'The monsoons are here. Let me know when you are coming over, so that I can give you some monsoon survival tips. . . .'

You can introduce other personal touches as well. But remember that these things should be interesting enough that they instantly endear you to the recipient.

Some more miscellaneous points

- Be prompt in replying to e-mails, especially those that solicit information or request the resolution of a problem. Don't treat it as a very low-priority activity.
- Avoid chain mails and cascade forwarding.
- Don't use sexist or chauvinistic phrases or mails with offensive jokes.
- Do not copy your official mail to your personal mail ID on public accounts (Yahoo, Gmail, etc.).
- There is no place for profanity or swearing or in indecent language.
- Try to spell right, although cryptic spellings (and acronyms like IMHO and LOL) are increasingly being used and accepted.
- Avoid using all capital (upper case) letters.
- Do not send highly personal or intimate e-mails—remember your business e-mail should be so staid that they can be read by your boss or CEO.
- Remember your liability to yourself and your company!
- Use neutral date formats (like 13 September 2009, instead of 02/05/09).
- E-mails are not SMS messages. They should not be one-liners.

32.10 Chat, Blogs and Twitters

Although chats, blogs and tweets on Twitter are not yet the mainstream modes of business communication, they have their place in the modern business universe and who knows, they might become important channels of communication in future.

Chats or 'same time' or Instant Messaging (IM) or whatever they are called in your organization offer a real-time opportunity to get into a 'chat-room' full of people who log into the service. The advantage here is that unlike e-mails, you will know whether your party is in the chat-room and available. If so, you may be able to 'talk' to him back and forth and extract his immediate response on things. But unlike in e-mails, you will have to keep your communication terse and ask only simple questions. The other advantage is that since a lot of people in your group may be logged into the same chat-room, you already have a ready forum for an impromptu, albeit simple, discussion. If you are into social networking (Orkut, Facebook, etc.), make absolutely sure that your social activities are kept separate from your business communication.

The blog and its cousin, Twitter have now become well-established. Both can be ideal media for 'broadcasting' technical and product development information or for educating your customers about your company's products, philosophy, policies and so on. Forums associated with blogs can be good places to communicate with end customers and spread your organization's message. But blogs and Twitters are highly time-sensitive and critically dependent on being updated regularly. And finally, you will have to clear your blogging or tweeting activity—even your personal and non work-related blogs—with your organization before embarking on it, to make sure that there is no conflict of interest.

"You've got mail. But anyway you are not going to read it and so, I am going to put it in Trash....."

Fig. 32.1

32.11 In Summary

Email has indeed evolved from just simple text to much richer presentation styles; from just the pride of the elite to a necessary activity for every individual in an organization doing any type of business. As you take up a career in any line of business, emails and its new avatars like tweets and blogs will doubtless become part of your identity. The tips given in this chapter will hopefully make that identity more effective.

33

Foreign Business Trips

"I dislike feeling at home when I am abroad."
–George Bernard Shaw

You are a young professional and you are sent on a foreign business trip by your organization—that is what dreams are made of. In spite of globalization, foreign trips are still glamorous. With the 'official' tag attached to it, it broadcasts to the whole world that you are now an important member of your organization and that they entrust you with their crucial assignments. With this importance comes certain euphoria—a feeling of elevation to the stratosphere and that you are in a different league now.

What we stress in this chapter are some basic etiquette that you need to follow before, during and after your foreign visit and not let the euphoria obscure what you have to do.

With foreign trips becoming an increasingly common part of regular work requirement and with such trips becoming very crucial to the success of the organization and your personal success, these tips on etiquette can help you to get higher mileage for your trip (no pun intended).

33.1 General Guidelines About Foreign Business Trips

Before we go into the specifics of what you should do before, during and after the trip, here are a few general guidelines.

When you are on a company business trip, your individual identity is overridden by your organization's identity and you will have to represent it throughout the trip. Not just this, but you will also be representing the face of modern Indian professionalism to the rest of the world. This means that you will have to exercise tremendous restraint and good judgement in case of any ordeals during your trip. You are not an anonymous tourist going on a pleasure trip. Some of the things to remember about this are:

- As an ambassador of your organization, ensure you don't let your organization down. Don't criticize or deride it under any circumstance, and especially in mixed company. Whatever grouses you may have within your organization, they shouldn't raise their ugly heads during a business trip.
- During the trip, if you have to make any business commitment to other parties on behalf of your organization, remember to make only those commitments that are within your level of authority.
- You are also representing your country—India. In your awe of seeing American expressways, do not bad mouth Indian roads and traffic to your American counterparts.
- Do not hesitate to keep up your religious and personal identity (e.g., religious symbols on your body) but don't let that divert the purpose of your visit—namely to transact business for your organization.
- If you have food habits that require special needs (e.g., vegetarianism), make sure you use the Internet and other resources to find out appropriate places nearby.
- Remember in the USA, travelling by car is the default option. When you ask someone for directions to a place, they will probably say 'take 101 North, turn right on Hillsdale East and take the third left and you are there . . .'. No one will tell you which bus takes you to the place. If you are not driving, you would have to put some serious thought on how to get to your destination. Cabs are prohibitively expensive. You may have to ask someone for a *ride* (not *lift*, as you say in India). Or you may have to extensive research on the modes of public transport in your destination and figure out the details.

33.2 Before You Leave on Your Trip

Like any form of activity, knowing your objectives and planning ahead is very essential.

33.2.1 Know Your Objectives

First and foremost, *know your mission.* Understand clearly why you are going on this trip. Learn also about the strategic plan behind the trip. If your trip is a part of a bigger plan, find out where your trip fits in the grand scheme. There should be a sense of purpose, an excitement in the air, about doing an important job for your organization and a 'now or never' kind of urgency to get the mission accomplished—like a batsman getting on to the crease.

Some possible missions that could be the cause for your trip are:

- A technical mission like installing a software product on your customer site.
- A knowledge transfer by which you are going to get trained by your foreign counterparts.
- A 'scoping out' trip to do due diligence.
- The final step in winning an off-shoring deal.

Other questions related to your trip could be:

- Who are accompanying you and how are you dividing your responsibilities with those travelling with you?
- Are there specific numerical targets or specific expectations? Is there a prized trophy you need to bring home on your return?

These may be the stated objectives of the trip that you have to achieve no matter what. But oftentimes, there are unstated objectives, which are even more important, that would have to be met. One such would be *rapport building*. It is likely that you and the people whom you meet in your trip are going to be interacting with each other frequently in future. This trip may well be the beginning of a new relationship. In that case, building a good rapport during the trip is of paramount importance. As we have seen several times in this book, there is nothing like a face-to-face meeting to get us to the same page. When you go on a trip, you have the time and opportunity to get to know your counterparts, and build (or cement) enduring relationships. You can use the entire arsenal that we have discussed in the book—small talk, body language, appropriate language, bridging cultural divides and the whole works. This rapport would take you and your organization to greater distances than just the tactical goals of your trip.

A second unstated objective of your trip would be *building networks*. In addition to meeting the people with whom you directly transact the stated business purpose, you would also be expected to build a network of contacts that would come in handy sooner or later. The network could be for potential future deals or just for getting help in certain areas where you know you or your organization need help.

33.2.2 Prepare Well

Remember that a lot may be riding on your trip. So, you have to prepare for it meticulously.

- Make sure you have assembled and organized all data required for your trip both in the hard copy and in the soft copy, as necessary. If hard copies are required, you are much better off taking them from your home turf rather than going hunting for printers and fax machines in a new place.

- Make sure you have written down the contact numbers of essential people and places in your organizer/cell phone as well as in your old-fashioned diary. There is no point arriving in London and discovering that you forgot to get the latest numbers or that all the numbers are on your cell phone and you are unable to charge your cell phone.
- Build redundancy and save your important material in two or three places. Make contingency plans for such possibilities as lost luggage and have someone in your home base who can feed you computer files, data and other things in a pinch.
- Make sure you desktop in your home base office is clean and properly organized. If you have to ask someone to send you things from your home base office, make sure the things are easily located on your desk—don't send him on a wild goose chase.
- Make sure you have all your travel documents in order. Also, look at the security notices and warnings that airlines and governments issue every now and then that places seemingly impossible restrictions on hand baggage.
- Make sure you carry power adapters for the several different power outlets of the parts of the world you are visiting. It is a good idea to have a universal adapter.
- If you are a part of a delegation, you will have to make sure that you have covered all the materials among all of you and that nothing has slipped through the cracks.
- Finally, make sure you bring with you plenty of your latest business cards and a diary or journal with a couple of good pens.

33.3 During Your Trip

Be aware of the local laws and practices: Be very careful about the local laws and about inadvertently violating them. For example, in several countries there are stringent laws about jaywalking or littering. Follow them diligently. If you take prescription medications, make sure you pack enough for the days you are traveling—otherwise it is next to impossible to get a new prescription in a foreign country and get it filled at the foreign pharmacies. Also, before you leave for your trip, find out the weather at your destination and dress appropriately. (Your company may also have a dress code for foreign trips. Consult it.) Remember that winters in the USA or Europe are far more severe than anything you have experienced in India and so, your winter clothing should be appropriate. In fact, you may want to buy them after landing up in the foreign country. Also, be aware of luggage rules and limits—they can differ for different countries and air carriers.

Respect privacy: Privacy is such an important concept that we have dedicated an entire chapter for it (Chapter 36). When you are abroad, respect for the privacy of your foreign counterparts is extremely essential. Do not expect them to chaperon you during the off-hours or go out of their way to help you with your travel or personal needs. (But most of them will tell you how to get around or what to do and give helpful pointers.)

Interface with your foreign team: Nowadays, most organizations have at least a sales office or other facilities in several foreign countries. Interface well with your permanent team in the foreign location. Get to know them and liaison with them. They will have a wealth of information about the organization you are going to visit, how to do business in that country and a host of valuable tips in general. Integrate your efforts with their efforts and put on a unified front.

Pay attention to networking: Understand that one of the main components of your trip is to build relationship and trust. A face-to-face meeting can help in building a strong relationship with your contacts in your host company and therefore, a cooperative environment between your two organizations. Even if it is only a scouting trip or even if you lose the deal eventually, such relationships are extremely valuable and you must practice on getting perfect at it. Right at the outset, get to know the names of the persons you meet (and also the name they want to go by). Some people would prefer to be called Robert, some others Bob and yet others Rob. (They may get offended if you referred to Rob as Bob). Project an exuberant, extroverted and confident personality. Remember that every person you meet in a foreign organization can be valuable in some way or the other and so, spend a lot of time talking and liaison with your hosts.

Help conduct perfect presentations and meetings: Pull off a perfect meeting with the hosts. We have already mentioned several pointers to achieve this in our earlier chapters. The only extra thing we want to say here is that often, you may have to present your colleague's presentation materials as well (your company cannot afford to send everyone in your group on this trip), in which case, make sure that you understand this presentation inside and out and can answer a lot of questions from your hosts. Likewise, your colleagues might ask you to obtain specific information for them from your hosts. Make sure you collect it for them. Work as a team with your contingent and make sure you are always connected with them. Don't drift away on your own private mission. Also, time management is very critical when you are abroad—given that you will be in a different time zone, your body clock can get seriously affected by jetlag and it will not have the time to adjust to the local time.

Be in constant touch with your home base and your boss in India: Be constantly in touch with your boss in India. Schedule a regular time slot for daily phone updates. More detailed reports should be sent to him via e-mail everyday and even more frequently, as necessary. Copy other relevant people. Before any major commitment or action, consult with the chief of your team and then clear it with your boss in India. Don't do anything major on your own—just because you think it is the right response—and hope that your boss will agree to it.

It is okay to talk in your native language amongst yourselves: If it helps you communicate better among yourselves—and also to have a semblance of privacy—you may want to switch from English to your native language in meetings in your host organization. However, desist from making any derogatory comments or nasty remarks about your hosts—in such an instance, often your body language will give it away and your hosts may figure it out. In fact, you have to be very careful about having private conversations with your team members or members from your permanent team in the host country. Just remember that even walls have ears and so, make triply sure that you are in a safe place to discuss such things.

A business trip is not a junket: Business trips cost a lot of money to your organization, on top of all kinds of man hours spent on getting your visas and other paperwork. So, it is important to treat it as a very serious business activity that should bring about favourable results in the end. Any personal sightseeing or visiting your relatives or shopping should be done only when there is free time available outside your meetings and office work. And don't be at all surprised if you are asked to go to London or New York City for just two days—and you actually spend the entire time holed up in an office building attending intense meetings and discussions.

Usually, you can schedule evenings and weekends for personal activities. Even then, make sure your group members know where you will be and how to get in touch with you. Sometimes your organization may allow you to stay back in the foreign country on a personal vacation, if your office schedule permits it—in which case, save your sightseeing and other tourist activities for then.

"Excuse me, but which way is it to the Buckingham Palace?...."

Fig. 33.1

Be frugal about spending money: Whether it is your money or the company's money, exercise restraint about spending it. Don't splurge. As such, it is an expensive proposition to send people abroad and so, do your part in being conscious about the costs. Find out your company's spending policy and adhere to it meticulously. If cities you visit have good public transportation systems, make use of them where you can. At the same time, you don't have to endure extra-ordinary tribulations to save a buck and walk five kilometres. Save all your receipts and file timely expense reports. A lot of things that are free in India and taken for granted, are not necessarily free in other countries. So understand what you are in for before requesting a service. Be very careful in using hotel phones, Internet facility or laundry services—understand the charges before indulging. In a country like the USA, labour is very expensive and so any labour-intensive service can be expensive. Get to know the tipping practices in various countries and what services need to be tipped. In Singapore, a tip is included in a restaurant bill, whereas in the USA, a tip on the order of fifteen percent of the bill is extra and is expected, whether or not the service is satisfactory.

The guiding principle should be to do things in moderation and to be always cost-conscious. While you should enjoy the many aspects of a foreign trip, don't overdo it or be that big-spending foreign tourist.

33.4 After the Trip

First, send a courteous 'Thank You' mail to your counterparts, thanking them for their hospitality and for the productive time you had. Then, sit down with your boss and brief him on the trip (if appropriate, you can do this in a group meeting with your entire team present). Write an appropriate trip report and circulate it among the relevant people. Next, follow through on the action items you promised and take them to completion. And of course, don't forget to file that expense report promptly with all your receipts, before you start your next trip on your globe trotting.

33.5 In Summary

Foreign visits are great opportunities to get exposure to excellent work ethics, diversity of cultures and it is an experience to see the different parts of our planet. In addition to achieving your business objectives—which are of course paramount—you should also try to get an appreciation of this diversity and ethics. That learning, together with the goal of building rapport and your network, would stand you in good stead as you move forward in your career.

Here is a quick summary of the points we discussed in this chapter.

- Make sure you understand the role you need to play in the trip.
- Plan well for your trip, get all data and documents organized before you leave.
- Carry everything you need for your work—business cards, relevant documents, etc.
- Have a backup in your office in India so that he can access your data, if needed.
- Respect the local laws and the privacy of your hosts.

- Build rapport and your networks in addition to accomplishing your specific tasks.
- Keep your home office informed.
- Be very cost conscious.
- Debrief the appropriate people after return and formally close out the issues with your foreign counterparts
- And don't forget to thank your foreign hosts for their hospitality.

34

Visits of Foreign Counterparts

"After one look at this planet, any visitor from outer space would say 'I want to see the manager.'"

–William S. Burroughs

Now that we have outlined the etiquette to be followed when you are on a foreign visit, it is time to look at the other side of the coin, namely the visits of your foreign counterparts and other foreign stakeholders to your location. Such visits demand that you be a perfect host, who not only exceeds the expectations of your foreign visitors had about their trip, but also set the stage for a sustained, strong and special business relationship with them.

Such visits will typically involve knowledge transfer, project kick-off, review meetings, planning meetings and so on. The profile of people travelling will vary from very senior-level people who would typically visit for business discussions, strategy planning and review meetings to operational-level people who would visit for knowledge transfer and operational work. This chapter deals with the etiquette to be followed when such a foreign visitor comes to India. This covers the preparations to be made, what to do on the days of the visit, how to conduct the meetings with the visitors (over and above the generic meeting management principles discussed earlier), coming to closure on the items discussed and the post-visit follow-up. We conclude the chapter with a brief coverage of some cultural issues.

34.1 Preparing for the Visit

Snapshot 34.1

Every once in a while your office might get into a high gear. New potted plants may suddenly appear along the otherwise drab hallways. The administrative assistant's 'cube' may get a makeover. And five star hotel rooms and luxury cabs will be reserved *en masse.* The boss would alternately cajole you into doing a few favours for him or yell at you for not doing something that was up to his expectation. It is announced folks, that the foreign client Mr Smith (whose project is one of the largest in your group's portfolio), is finally going to be in your campus for that much-anticipated business visit, accompanied by a six-member entourage. It would be emphasized that this client visit is 'most important' and that no stone should be left unturned to pull off a good meeting. (If your 'company' is an offshore unit of a MNC, then your foreign visitor could also be the top boss from your own headquarters. But, for the purposes of this chapter we will only talk about a foreign client visit).

There is always the danger of such visits as described in Snapshot 34.1 turning into poorly-managed, out-of-control, nightmare affairs, casting serious aspersions on your corporation's or location's abilities and status. However, a few simple, basic principles can turn these high-stress events into successful milestones that might not only strengthen your existing relationship with your client or your boss from HQ, but could also very well bring additional business to your location or company. The key to making the best out of such visits is to keep pressing on with the business agenda, while paying consummate attention to every detail of your guests' needs. While the agenda that you prepare would address the business needs of the visitor, it would be a good idea to check with the visitor whether he has any specific social or personal requests for which he may need help. For example, they may be interested in some weekend trips or may have some specific shopping to do. You might like to make provision for these, but don't impose yourself on the visitors.

34.1.1 Know Who the Visitors Are

The first step in planning how to handle a business visit is to find out who the visitors are. Even seasoned world-travellers may feel a bit odd at times in some foreign countries (and the visiting group might include some first timers to India) and may have special apprehensions and needs. Some of the things you may need to find out about them (without being nosy) to help you prepare for their stay are:

- Is this their first time in India?
- Did they get any not-so-pleasant experiences in India in their last visit?

- Do they have any special personal needs like medical, religious, food, mobility needs?
- Do they have any preferences for place of stay?
- Do they have time and do they like to take some weekend time off for sight seeing or shopping?
- Do any of your team members know anything more about any of the specific visitors? In particular, is there any tough nut among the visitors that you need to put special focus on?

Finding answers to these questions would put you in a better position to make the visitors more comfortable and put them in a better frame of mind for the actual business meeting that is indeed the purpose of their visit.

Many foreign business people visiting India are typically clients of Indian companies or line managers or senior managers from a parent organization abroad and therefore, are at the giving end of an unequal relationship. If this is the case, this will have to be factored in all of the preparations.

34.1.2 Preparing the Infrastructure for a Visit

Remember that first impressions are the best impressions. Also, in some quarters, there is a lot of negative baggage about India. It is important to not give opportunities for reaffirmation of such negative thoughts. Here are some tips to make sure your infrastructure preparations are going in the right direction:

- Make sure you have made appropriate arrangements for pick-up and drop-off, especially in case your visitors are coming to India for the first time and ensure that you have some English-speaking driver available to take them around.
- In case the visitors want to do any shopping or sightseeing, it would be great if the driver is an expert on the local shops and tourist spots. It is also okay for one of the local team members who knows the local conditions, to accompany them, should that be desired by the visitors and be acceptable to the team member.
- Make sure that you have back-up power supply to keep the meeting running uninterrupted and that all your audio and video equipment and other infrastructure are humming along fine.
- If the agenda calls for conference calls or video conference, then make sure that the right equipment is available. A conference room with video conference facility may need to be booked in advance.
- It is also a good idea to prepare for the availability of drinks like coffee and tea and not to assume that there is a one-size-fits-all coffee or tea. One must remember that some of them may drink coffee black and without sugar. Some people prefer 'regular' coffee and some may want decaffeinated coffee. So, don't pre-mix a concoction that you think of as 'coffee'. Have the basic components ready and give the visitors the flexibility to make their own drinks using what they want.

- What is called 'cool drinks' in India is often called 'soft drinks' in other places. Furthermore, some of the visitors are particular about 'diet' drinks and 'caffeine-free drinks'. Just make sure that the refrigerator is stacked with the various combinations.
- The visitors may want coffee or drinks 'on-demand', instead of the ceremonial, scheduled coffee breaks and therefore, have a pot brewing all the time and have easy access to the soft drinks. In business meetings in the USA, oftentimes you will be simply shown the coffeepot or the refrigerator and you are free to serve yourself at any time.
- Make sure that every one of your staff who is going to attend the meeting has his/her business card with their proper job titles, ready.
- Finally, (it might sound like a trivial exhortation) be sure your toilets are neatly maintained and easily accessible. In many countries, well-maintained workplace toilets are a given.

34.1.3 Preparations for the Business-side of the Visit

In parallel with the infrastructure arrangements, get started on preparing for the business end of the visit.

- Make an elaborate and all-encompassing agenda very much in advance. Get it okayed by your foreign counterparts. However, even if you get a formal okay, anticipate and plan for last minute changes. Flexibility is the name of the game.
- Gather the right personnel to cover the various items on your agenda. A visit by a foreign delegation is not a spectator sport to be witnessed by all your employees and so, be judicious about who needs to be present. Include only those people who are germane to the project or topic, but do have a few other support staff ready for contingencies.
- Find out if anybody else from your end or the visitors' side needs to join the meeting via telephone and make sure all arrangements are made for them.
- Assemble all the required data and make sure that the relevant team member has these on his fingertips. Think about various alternative scenarios, business proposals, negotiation points, negotiation postures and tactical re-orientation ideas and keep them handy in your back pocket.
- Your foreign visitors will be very interested in seeing things for themselves. So, make sure that you put on a show (a demo where needed) for them—your assembly lines, computer systems, communication lines and computer security systems—all should look and perform as advertised. The guest list, the agenda and the topics of discussion are all dynamic and could change right up to the last minute of planning. So be ready to accommodate a myriad requests and changes.

- Practise a couple of dry runs of mock meetings conjuring up all impossible scenarios and questions. If the visitors want to see data for the past three years, can that be arranged? If they want to meet that entry-level programmer who is working on their module (about whom they are very uncomfortable), can you take them to meet him?
- It helps to talk to your office-mates who may have dealt with some of the members of the client brigade previously.

34.2 The Actual Visit

Finally, after weeks of planning, the appointed day arrives. Your visitors have been received at the airport, have been ushered into their hotel and already the foreign delegation is sending out positive vibes—unless of course, they managed to lose their luggage (after a five-hour plane delay) and someone had to work some magic to mollify the agitated visitors.

The foreign delegation troops into your office and it is time to execute.

34.2.1 Start of the Meeting

Whether you are a main presenter at the meeting or a support staff, it is important to pay attention to your get-up. An unwritten rule is that clothing should be neutral to conservative. Make sure that the formal clothes that you had mothballed away in a closet fit you on the day of the meeting and that you know exactly how to do the double knot on your tie. For women, a saree makes a wonderfully elegant formal dress. Of course, a western-style dress slack or dress is equally appropriate.

In the western world a handshake—the mundane act of squeezing your palm into the other person's hand and pumping it two or three times—is considered an anchor on which a future relationship will be built. No wonder this practice has been much analysed, dissected and sterilized into a fine art. People in India generally don't pay much attention to the mechanics of a handshake, although they readily indulge in it, sometimes even gratuitously.

Remember to grab the other person's hand firmly, shake it vigorously two or three times and then let go immediately afterwards. Limp handshakes and extended handholdings are a no-no. Look into the eyes of the person introduced. However unfamiliar their name is, try to register it and remember it. If you don't get it the first time, ask for their name again. A simple, universal, 'Hi, I am Ajay' or something similar is okay. Avoid saying 'Myself, Ajay' or even worse 'What is your *good* name?'

The protocol used to be that men did not shake a woman's hand, unless the woman offered it in the first place. But nowadays, with the decrease in gender differences in the business world, any hand is shake-worthy, man's or woman's, as long as it is a hand that does business. So women should not be too bashful about a sudden, unsolicited handshake from a male.

"I am Bernie Smith, the CZO of the company. We are still trying to figure out what the Z means....."

Fig. 34.1

The next step is to hand over your *business* card to them and get theirs in return[1]. Although some cultures make a little ceremony out of this act—by holding the cards in both their hands and bowing slightly—a simple swap of cards in the most practical manner is okay in the Indo-US context. Make sure your business cards are not made of non-biodegradable plastic. If on the other hand, they are made of recyclable paper, you may win a few brownie points with your visitors for being environmentally friendly. Standard sized cards with standard job designation should suffice. If your card generically describes you as 'chief' or 'team leader', it does not convey much about your role in your company. Try to make sure that the job title indicates the role clearly.

Then at around the appointed hour, you seat yourselves—the more important persons in the pecking order taking the vantage positions—and usually the two delegations will sit across each other at the table. The support staff should sit at the back, away from the table.

You may not realize it, but your foreign visitor is scrutinizing every move of yours in the first ten minutes since you shook his hands. He is trying to ascribe meanings to your many, initial body movements, forming that all important first

[1] In India, business cards are called *visiting* cards and the use of this term leaves the foreign visitor flummoxed. Stick to the term business cards.

impression on which to hang his business dealings. A limp handshake might lead him conclude that you are quite a wimp and poor eye contact and nervousness might bolster his aggressiveness. In just the first ten or fifteen minutes, they may even have a fairly prejudiced opinion of who is good, who is not, who really matters and who is there just for the ride. Be aware that there are subtle undercurrents and that they always reference things back to the American or European sensibilities and then form opinions. Hence, put your best foot forward in the initial few minutes.

34.3 The Meetings Proper

The main meetings should proceed like clockwork. Time management is crucial and equally important is that complete ground is covered to the satisfaction of all parties, on all items on the agenda. If additional time is needed and cannot be provided right away, off-line meetings or extra presentations at the end of the meeting can be worked in. It is highly likely that you may have to depart from your carefully scripted presentation and may have to address some concerns of your visitor that you had not originally planned to discuss. Make sure you understand your visitor's questions and concerns and if you don't have a ready answer, either get it from someone who does have it or tell your guests that you need to research it further and will give it to them later and make sure you complete the loop later, as promised.

It is important to remember where you are horizontally and vertically in your organization and stick to the hierarchy and protocol during business meetings. Although you may be privy to a lot of information, if it is not your domain or function, it is extremely inappropriate for you to be talking about it. Don't steal other people's thunder and give other people's speeches. There will always be some information your boss might provide at his level (or the top management might discuss at their level) and here it is important that the tail does not wag the dog. Let the big boys and girls handle the mechanics of the meeting. (And if you are the big boy or girl, make sure you grab this ownership.) Your job must be to ensure that when you are called for your information or opinion, you give it clearly and to the point. If you don't understand your visitor's accent, ask him to repeat and likewise, if they don't understand your accent, repeat your utterance. If they still don't get it, try to form a different sentence to convey the same meaning. If a member of the delegation corrals you outside and demands some information—and you are not sure if this information can be passed on to him—guard your information and give it only after consulting with your boss. Don't do private favours to members of the visiting team. Likewise, don't give them the 'insider's view' about your company, however much you are prodded and made to talk.

Business meetings these days are reasonably informal. It is considered alright to go in and out of the meeting room, provided you don't disturb the proceedings with a splash entry. It is considered okay to carry your cell phones in your pockets (of course, in their silent or vibrate modes) so that you are still connected to the outside world. Make sure you don't have the phone ringing loudly especially with the fancy musical filmy ringtones. If you do get a call, step outside the conference room and answer it—only if it is absolutely essential to take the call interrupting your presence in the meeting. Giving undivided attention to your visitors is one way of telling them you care.

From time to time there will be 'side-bar' conversations between the presenters (or your boss) and the support staff that are waiting at the back of the room. This conversation is considered private and can take place even in a local Indian language, if that is a better way to communicate.

Coffee breaks are also the best time get to know your visitors a bit by indulging in some small talk. Usually about their flight, hotel room and if they got the latest e-mail you had sent about something—anything that is light, pleasant, ice-breaking and fits the definition of 'small talk' (see Chapter 35).

In the olden, glory days of business meetings, business lunches used to be the highlight of such gatherings, with a lavish spread and ceremonious proceedings. But these days, like many other aspects of business, the glamorous and elaborate luncheons have given way to simple, convenient, 'functional' meals. In fact, it is not uncommon for the meetings to go on while the food is being consumed.

Ceremonial or simple, here are a few pointers about food. Greasy, messy, spicy food and meats which probably require a sledge hammer to break are best avoided even though it may be tempting, given that somebody else is footing the bill. Food that can be conveniently eaten with a fork or held in hand (such as sandwiches) is ideal. It might take some practice, but you should learn to eat and talk (although not with your full mouth)—exactly the opposite of what your mother taught you. If you have a break in the proceedings for lunch, make simple, non-business, non-controversial, light and humorous conversation with your visitors. If your big bosses are at the table, let them do most of the talking. Butt in only as appropriate and that too, keep it short. If you are the prime host to your foreign guests, you will have the burden of keeping the conversation going.

During coffee breaks and lunch, one common pattern found is that all the Indian team hangs out together and chit-chatting (needless to say in the local language!), while the American visitors are haplessly looking over their shoulders and trying to make sense of what is happening. A golden rule is to let the social butterfly of your group lead the charge and draw the visitors in and help in the mingling process.

A frequent complaint is that there are too many people at the Indian site purporting to be on the project. ('Are they all billable?') Lunch is a good time to explain people's functionality and role in the project. It is also proper to allow a fifteen-minute 'settling time' after lunch, during which you can help your guests check their e-mail or make phone calls or generally relax.

From time to time, your clients might try to unleash their god-given (at least the management gods) right to client-ness and act difficult. They may find faults with anything you say, express utter disgust and dissatisfaction with all of your work and above all, might display fireworks just to get your upper management's attention. While such battles are best left to the senior management, there are a few things the foot soldiers can do. First, don't take it personally and become very sensitive. Treat it as a legitimate customer complaint and deal with it professionally. Gather all the resources necessary to resolve their problems. Remember that some of them would want the heaven and the earth and that too, for one third the price your business managers are charging them at present. Don't over promise or give away things which are not in the deal.

34.4 Getting to Conclusions and Agreements

With every successive hour the meeting goes on, fatigue and boredom might set in, giving way to sloppiness and wandering attention. It is important to stay alert and on top of the situation. Lack of stamina for a full day of meetings might make you particularly vulnerable to a bad deal in any negotiation. All kinds of psychological games may be played by both sides and through it all, a clear consensus should somehow emerge.

The last part of the meeting will usually be all negotiation, re-negotiation, status assessment, mid-course correction of the project and so on. Discussions, (sometimes heated) will give rise to new deliverables, new deadlines or new price tags. Negotiations on sensitive matters are best left with those who have the corporate power to make deals—usually the senior executives. Play a faithful employee by being present in the office and being around your boss, even during off-hours.

The *modus operandi* these days is that you don't sign the final deal right at the end of the client visit, but drag it on some more and dot the 'i's and cross the 't's afterwards, perhaps with your legal team poring over the clauses. Even as your guests leave, you may be left with the feeling that you could have done something better, pulled some other stops or been one day ahead to complete an important activity in your project.

34.5 Post-Meeting Review

Meticulous notes-taking is absolutely crucial. There should be a designated person to generate the minutes of the meeting, which should be promptly mailed out to all the necessary people in the project after the event (this has also been covered in Chapter 24). A clear-cut list of action items generated in the meeting must be ratified by both sides and be adhered to when moving forward.

It is also a good idea to walk up to your boss a few days after the meeting and ask him what he thought of your performance during the meeting.

The sweet smell of success comes when everyone in the office walks around with the triumphant after-glow of the meeting. This is when the upper management feels it has cut a nice deal with the foreign visitors and congratulates you on a job well-done. And then you feel even more congenial toward your teammates whose chemistry made it all possible. It is even more wonderful if Mr. Smith, on his plane-ride home, feels the same high about having signed a 'win-win' deal with you and vaguely contemplates giving some more business to you. And what would make it even sweeter is if he actually managed to sneak to Agra over the weekend with his wife and saw the Taj Mahal in all its glory.

34.6 Cultural Issues

People in India sometimes tend to mollycoddle the foreign business guests and even overwhelm them by going that extra mile or by being around them all the time. There is also the romantic view of the foreign business partners as simple, benevolent souls, who have a thirst for Indian culture and Indian history. It should be understood that their basic purpose of visit is to transact business and some of them may not take to India as some others. Don't be too surprised if a foreign guest declines your invitation to go to a Bharatnatyam performance, preferring instead to spend the evening alone in the hotel gymnasium or simply hangs around his or her hotel room reading a novel or staying in touch with their home office. The Westerners jealously guard their personal 'space' and privacy (see Chapter 36). So don't foist yourselves on them or have the urge to entertain them every waking minute of their stay.

Even when they are traveling, the foreign delegation always makes an effort to stay in touch with their home office.

Fig. 34.2

Avoid disturbing the visitors in their hotel. If you have to visit them at the hotel, call them first and when you visit the hotel, call them from the lobby. Don't just go ahead and knock on their door.

Finally, a word about gift-giving during business meetings. It is rarely encouraged in the American culture and if you must give mementos to your esteemed visitors, make sure the monetary value of the gifts is not very high. Personalized stationery, small handicrafts with personalized engravings would be sufficient, although not giving any gift to the visitors is perfectly okay. Also, go easy on all the ritualistic carrying-ons—like garlanding the visitors or applying a *bindi* on them. Simple courtesies are usually enough instead of elaborate ceremonies.

34.7 In Summary

We conclude this chapter with a quick recap of the do's and don'ts when a foreign visitor visits your office.

Do:

- Do enough homework. Collect all pertinent data, organize them and analyse data along various possibilities. Keep a copy for your record.
- Prepare a detailed agenda, but be prepared for the agenda to change on the fly during the visit.
- Know who the visitors are going to be and if needed get the agenda reviewed by them.
- Make sure the right people are available, if required for any specific information that the visitor may want.
- Keep all the infrastructure in perfect working order.
- Present your talk in a slow, neutral accent. If your accent confuses the visitors, repeat yourself, perhaps using another sentence structure. Ask them to repeat if you don't understand their accent.
- Know your place in the hierarchy and play accordingly.
- Dress and behave conservatively.
- Try to lighten up situations, make small talk and be humorous.
- Follow through on the action items from the visit.

Don't

- Steal other people's presentation material or speak out of turn.
- Suffocate your guests with your kindness.
- Discuss controversial topics like politics, personal life or religion.
- Talk about company politics—yours or theirs.
- And finally, don't openly ask them about employment in their country.

35

The Big Deal About Small Talk

"Don't knock the weather; nine-tenths of the people couldn't start a conversation if it didn't change once in a while."

–Kin Hubbard

Small talk is usually a prelude to a more serious business conversation later or it supplements the main activity or conversation you are pursuing. It is that shallow, informal and somewhat impersonal conversation which can last anywhere from a few minutes to a very long time. It is a part of the ice-breaking process, setting up the environment to be more conducive to serious business conversation.

Small talk is all around us, like oxygen in the atmosphere (see Snapshot 35.1 for some examples of small talk). Like oxygen, we feed on it and keep going through good days and bad days. Annoying at times, exhilarating and gratifying at other times, we alternately tolerate it and seek it. What is interesting is how it has crept into the world of business over the years and now holds an important place as a catalyst of business communication. A culture of healthy small talk is now being nurtured in

Snapshot 35.1

SMALL TALK IN THE OFFICE

1. You are on the phone with your client in the USA. Before all the serious conversation about migrating a database to another data centre, you ask him about

the weather in Colorado and tell him about how you saw footage of their snow, on TV in India. This gives a nice personal touch to the relationship.

2. You have a room full of visiting partners from Singapore. It is the first visit to India for many of them. The meeting is about to start in ten minutes. You have just finished exchanging business cards. You treat the cards with great care and use them as a cue to start small talk about where they are located in Singapore and how they get to work every day and so forth. You try to draw in everyone from their delegation into the conversation, just so that they all feel included and comfortable.
3. You are in your manager's office to discuss some important things about the project. Your gaze falls on his bookshelf and you see a book on statistics. That paves way for you to start small talk on how your uncle was a professor of statistics—setting a pleasant tone for a more serious and 'dry' discussion on schedules and activities.
4. You are at an office party. You know half the people very well. But there are many you don't know that well. You walk up to a small circle of people and join in. The conversation moves from topic to topic (and occasionally even to 'shop-talk') and you participate in it without being shy or awkward about it. In another corner, you see the CEO himself chit-chatting with a bunch of people and you walk up to him and manage to get a few words with him.

business communities the world over. This is also a part of the image make-over of the world of business, from being utterly serious, quiet places to being fun, expressive and animated environments.

And you can add even more circumstances where you indulge in small talk—a luncheon at a technical symposium where you hobnob with all the technical experts, a chance encounter on the street with a business partner, a 'pit-stop' at the administrative assistant's desk and so on. Almost no place is immune to small talk.

The ability to make small talk is no longer considered just social grace, but is seen to be an important business soft skill. While Indians are by no means bashful when it comes to speaking, the finesse and perfection of the art of small talk that is seen in the USA and the divide we see in this area between Indians and Americans, have convinced the authors to have a separate chapter to discuss what small talk is in context of today's business world and to look at its various attributes and scope.

Most of us only have a vague idea of what small talk is, or how it is different from other kinds of talk, how it can be used effectively and how we can be good at it. We don't even realize that small talk is no longer the simple-minded, impulsive act that it used to be, but has evolved into a highly engineered, painstakingly cultivated and skillfully delivered product. The purpose of this chapter is to highlight the importance of small talk as an important element of business etiquette to develop in your soft skills armory, characterize what is and what is not small talk, give you some tips on how to use small talk effectively and suggest some typical small talk topics for the Indian/American work cultures.

It should be remembered, however, that small talk should not hijack your primary effort or draw attention away from your real activity. No action item comes out of small talk, unlike your main business conversation.

35.1 Why Small Talk?

Here are some reasons why we need small talk in our offices.

- Small talk is a nice lead-in for a more serious business conversation.
- It helps the participants to settle down.
- Right at the outset, small talk conveys the message, 'I am a nice and friendly person. You will be happy to deal with me' and therefore, helps the rest of the transaction to go smoothly even if there are technical or business problems encountered along the way. Thus, it is a nice preamble for later technical sessions or business negotiations.
- You create a friendly, fun atmosphere to work in and transact business. You obviously don't want to work in an ambience that is grim and graveyard-like, where everyone is tense and tongue-tied.
- You can 'scope out' people and identify the friendly ones.
- You can network with people and strangers and build relationships.
- It helps you mingle socially. It breaks the ice with strangers.
- It makes it easy to navigate through rough spots, lightens up tense situations and can ease the 'customer-vendor' gap.
- Is a measure of hospitality displayed by the hosts

35.2 Some Characteristics of Small Talk

The first and most important characteristic of small talk is that it is highly culture-dependent and its style and content can vary from country to country. In countries like the USA, small talk is practised almost to perfection. It is not uncommon there to see an end-customer carrying on a two-minute chit-chat with the checkout counter clerk in a store, while transacting business. Or for an air passenger to have a parallel small talk session with the airline employee about his mother-in-law in Chicago while checking in his luggage. Some other countries are more formal and less talkative—especially with strangers. But all cultures are now beginning to see the value of small talk and are actively encouraging it among their employees.

Small talk should be bright, fun, positive and light. And when a huge group indulges in it, it should bring out a variety of views, quips and points. Everyone participating in it should feel elated and good. Small talk can be about a variety of

Fig. 35.1

topics—as long as they are non-intrusive and neutral—we have listed some of them towards the end of the chapter. In our chapter on 'privacy' (Chapter 36) we have provided a list of topics that are absolutely inappropriate for small talk (from the privacy standpoint). In essence, small talk should lighten up the atmosphere around, so that it facilitates actual business discussions.

Small talk should be an exercise in building chemistry among the participants. For example, if your colleague says, 'I am going to Delhi tomorrow to see my brother', you may ask, 'What does your brother do in Delhi?' and carry forward the conversation. Your response is more out of courtesy than out of a desire to get to know your colleague, or his brother, for that matter. (If on the other hand your colleague says 'I am going to Delhi on a personal visit', it is definitely inappropriate to ask 'What are you going to Delhi for?') Small talk is usually fuelled by a desire to build rapport, rather than by a desire to get to know the personal details of the other person. It is very unobtrusive and the other participants do not expect to field any personal questions. And therefore, it creates a relaxed and friendly atmosphere for everyone.

During small talk, you can move from topic to topic and the number of people participating in it can vary (often people go in and out of a group). This is typically the case during the waiting time before the start of a meeting (when some people come late).

Small talk has a staccato-like structure, with people adding their own comments, anecdotes and points to the conversation in a piece-meal fashion, punctuated with a lot of jokes and mild digs. Since people you don't know at all may be participating in it, the conversation should provide enough openings and comfort level for them. And also because the conversation is fragmented, it can end any time without anything going amiss.

The content of small talk should be genuine—you don't lie that your mother-in-law is in Chicago and nor do you spread cooked-up stories to keep the conversation going.

35.3 What Is Not Small Talk?

Small talk is not the same as technical talk. If anything, they are opposites. Occasionally in the middle of small talk, you may migrate to some technical conversation and shop-talk, as appropriate. But keep the two separate. Small talk or tech talk, you should be an expert in both and be able to don both the hats effortlessly.

It is not the big talk or the 'regular' conversation you have with your trusted friends and colleagues in your office. When you have personal conversations with your friends, you are not on your guard. Whereas, in office small talk (like in office technical talks), you are careful about what you say and measure your comments.

It is not personal conversation, no matter how many times the other person talks about his mother-in-law in Chicago. Don't for a moment assume that you have become great personal friends with the other person, based only on the history of small talk you had with him, unless the other parameters check out.

Small talk is not a sales talk. Sales talk has an agenda and an underlying motive. Small talk has no such driving force or pressure. It is not cooked up and dished out only to persuade the other person through a business transaction that would otherwise fall through and after which you go back to your old ways after the transaction. The personality you display while engaging in small talk is your real personality.

And lastly, small talk has a place and a purpose in corporate life. If done appropriately, it is neither unnecessary, nor a waste of time.

35.4 Some Small Talk Considerations

When to Engage in Small Talk

Practically any time is a good time for small talk. Just before meetings or just after meetings are ideal times to unleash your small-talk talents. Company events like picnics, visits, canteen sessions, running into someone in the hallway, conferences and so on are convenient situations for small talk. It is somewhat expected in non-emergency phone calls. A one line 'small-talk' comment or question in an e-mail is also appropriate.

Of course, before starting a bout of small talk, determine if the other person is in a mood for it. It is most inappropriate to make small talk when no one is in a mood for it or when you are in the middle of a serious discussion.

How Small Should It Be?

As the name implies, it better be shallow and general. The topic should generate comments that are innocuous and inoffensive. Be sure nothing you say is controversial or is a transgression. Also make sure that you are not boring or irritating. Watch out for others' reaction towards you—they will switch you off if your small talk doesn't cut it. If an untenable situation arises, just make some excuses and end the session.

You can enter into small talk anytime and can also exit any time. But if a talk is already in progress, make sure you don't throw its flow off by your untimely remarks.

Since small talk is ephemeral, you have to make sure that your comments follow the flow and are in synch with the rest of the conversation. Be alert to how quickly the topic changes and takes different flavours.

You can occasionally stick in a short serious question in a small talk situation. If you see that your boss has sufficiently loosened up after a nice dinner and is engaged in a session of small talk, you might ask him a serious question in the middle of it. ('I wonder what it will take for me to be on the Citibank project.') But don't embarrass the other person by dwelling on it.

Who Do You Have Small Talk With?

You can have small talk with anyone—your colleagues, your managers, your business partners, your canteen workers and even with total strangers. You will have to acquire a slightly extroverted personality and a smiling face and somewhat of an aggressive demeanour.

In a large gathering, such as in your office party, make sure you take on the avatar of a social butterfly and flutter from group to group. This is a golden opportunity to snare your otherwise elusive office bigwigs. Making small talk with the introverted and the language-challenged can be frustrating, but is important and necessary. Draw them into the conversation somehow. Don't just stick to the talkative. One of the objectives of small talk is to mingle and get to rapport with the other person—all of them.

Small talk is also extremely socialistic—in the sense that all are equal, in spite of rank and seniority. It integrates everyone, whether someone is your customer or vendor, whether the other person is in your organization or elsewhere.

35.5 How to Be Effective in Small Talk?

Like we have mentioned earlier, you should acquire an extroverted personality and get rid of any shyness that you may have. This comes only with practice. Remember that through your small-talk skills, you are projecting a certain poise, confidence and smartness. Remember too that all your communication skills like body language, listening skills and so on, apply here too.

Since the effectiveness of small talk depends on the interest levels of the topic of small talk, you better choose topics that are current and engrossing to people around you. This calls for a very informal audience analysis and knowing their pulse as to what excites them. This also requires that you be aware of the most topical issues to engage in small talk. This may require you to be an avid follower of current events or at least to glance at the newspaper to know the major happenings around you.

Until you become somewhat of an expert in the matter, stick to some standard topics. Also, in the beginning stages of your small talk career, stick to smaller groups where you can be more comfortable, instead of trying to nucleate a new group. If you cannot come up with a good topic, 'you' be the topic and narrate one of your anecdotes. Try to come across as genuine, amusing people with tales of your own mistakes and mis-steps.

Take the initiative. It is not out of character to walk up to a strange person in a business setting and start a conversation. There are standard ice-breaking topics—your company, the weather, the state of your favourite cricket (or football) team. As mentioned earlier, business-card exchange itself can be a nice setting for a lot of initial small talk, not to mention the flood of topics that are available if the other person is from a different country. Don't abruptly leave a person or a group to go elsewhere—be courteous enough to smile and say a 'please excuse me' before you split from the group.

At no time should you come across as a slick salesman or investigator who is plumbing for information. Avoid probing questions. Instead prompt the other person to talk. If one topic gets stalled, try to launch another topic.

If you are already a good small talker, be inclusive of everyone. Make sure that it is an open forum and does not degenerate into a clubby, exclusive group chatter. Ask others questions and drag them into the conversation. Try to steer the talk and close gaps in conversation. Likewise, watch out for any potential controversies or embarrassments or potential conflicts and nip them in the bud or make a joke out of them.

Remember that as an effective small talker, you just have to conduct the conversation and engage the participants. You don't have to be the main speaker and overwhelm the other person (unless you are a superior or a boss—in which case, your underlings will naturally show deference to you and let you do most of the talking. As a corollary—the more you go up in your career ladder, the more you should be prepared to engage in small talk).

Also, remember that people expect you to be good in both small talk and serious technical discussions. So, you should be ready to switch back and forth between these two modes of talk. Make points and comments that others will find interesting. Long after the conversation, people should remember you for your views and comments.

Remember that even if you are not a great talker, you can participate in small talk very effectively by being a good and active listener. Just know when to laugh, respond, comment and interject.

35.6 What Are Good Topics for Small Talk?

Often 'you' will be the subject of your small talk and you will find yourself coming with your anecdotes or your viewpoints. In which case, bring something to the table—either an exciting hobby or stories of some places you have travelled to or some interesting things that happened to you. But don't make this an incredibly boring autobiographical note of your childhood or your heroic efforts in solving a serious problem in your previous job. Small talk is not the time to brag about yourself, nor is it a forum to moan about the not-so-good things in life.

Apart from these, here is a short list of topics to have small talk on:

- Matters of taste, preference (e.g., restaurants)
- Traffic, cars
- Weekend activities

- Activities around the house (gardening, kitchen re-modelling)
- Vacation stories
- Books you have read, movies, TV shows
- Sports events (but remember that most American don't know or care for cricket)
- Relatives (but don't dwell on this too much as the other party is sure to become disinterested very soon)
- Shopping activities and experience
- Children, school (be sure that others around also show interest)
- Doctor/dentist visits—just the non-medical part
- World events (avoid controversial and sensitive topics, especially things like the state of Indo-US relations, nuclear deals and so on)
- New purchases, gadgets
- Hometown, childhood anecdotes
- On-the-job experiences and how life used to be in the organization
- Non-malicious stories about other people present and past(but no company politics)
- Pets (definitely a common small talk topic in the USA, but very uncommon in a typical Indian middle-class household)
- Weddings, parties.

As you can see, there is a significant cultural and personal component in these topics. For example, sports can be a neutral and fun topic for small talk. But there is hardly any common ground between Indians and Americans in sports. Typical American sports like professional basketball, baseball and American football have virtually no following in India and similarly, there is no following of world cricket or even tennis and the USA.

The challenge then is to choose topics with which you are familiar (at least superficially) and that are likely to be of common interest. As mentioned earlier, this will come only with practice and by keeping current with various events and goings on. Now is as good a time as any to start this practice and hone your small talk etiquette.

35.7 In Summary

It is somewhat interesting that something as remote to business as small talk is now actually considered a strong business soft skill and held in high value. Like all other soft skills, you have to groom yourself in this as well. More than business degrees and experiences, the amount of networking and connections you make via small talk can contribute to your successful career. However, remember that the ability to make small talk should be in addition to all your other competencies—small talk by itself will not make you successful. Like any other soft skills, it is not a replacement for hard skills in your job. It is just the veneer.

36

Respecting Privacy

"Privacy is not something that I am merely entitled to; it is an absolute pre-requisite."

–Marilyn Monroe

Privacy refers to how much physical and mental space we desire from others and how much of the same they desire from us. While it is good to have a professional bonding for a team to gel together, it is also equally important to maintain a reasonable distance with our colleagues in a work environment. What is 'reasonable' is debatable and is the subject of discussion for this chapter.

There are two dimensions of personal privacy—*personal space* and *informational privacy*. Personal space refers to the physical distance you should maintain with a colleague, in terms of where you sit or stand, your gestures and what you can and cannot do. Informational privacy on the other hand is about what you can and cannot say (or if looked another way, what information you need to or need not to give about yourself). In addition to personal privacy, there is also organizational privacy which is about safeguarding the relevant company information.

36.1 Why Are Privacy Issues Important?

A few things have happened in the recent decades which have pushed privacy issues to center-stage. First, the Western style professionalism is now being embraced by most corporate houses in India and central to such a professional life is a clear separation of one's private life by keeping it away from the office. It also calls for keeping a clear physical distance from your colleagues. Next, with rampant globalization comes a huge exposure to prevailing sensibilities and norms regarding privacy in other cultures. You have no choice but to learn, respect and be sensitive to them if you want to do business with those cultures. Thirdly, now there are definite legal implications for non-compliance of privacy laws and therefore, you should stay current on any legal developments in your client countries. Such legal aspects of privacy have come into even greater focus with the maturation of e-business and after the telecom revolution.

Legal or ethical, it makes good business sense to follow the international etiquette on privacy issues with our global partners. Given how difficult it is to pull off international business deals, the last thing we want is a silly thing like our partner's privacy worries to come in the way of business. That's why we would like to elevate 'respecting privacy' to a soft skill. By 'respecting' we mean not only the general awareness of international norms and practices, but also specific sensitivity to the person standing in front. Such a skilled employee will be able to offer a comfort zone to the other person to communicate in and an office-full of such professionals will create a non-threatening atmosphere for business transactions. Such persons will also be very careful with their own personal data and make sure they are well-guarded. They will be aware of security threats and data integrity issues. Not just that, they will also be very careful about their organization's private and proprietary information.

In this chapter we will walk you through the various steps of gaining such respect toward others' privacy and towards your organization's privileged information. We will look at privacy of physical space first and then follow it up with informational privacy issues. Even if you already have an intuitive feel for appropriate behaviour when it comes to privacy, you may still pick up a point or two from these pages which talk about how you succeed in this privacy based workplace, which leads us to organizational privacy (as distinguished from personal privacy). The perception of what constitutes each of these dimensions and what is right and what is wrong as far as privacy is concerned is highly culture-dependent. In particular, there is a significant gap between the Indian and US cultures in this aspect. In this chapter, we will highlight some of these differences and recommend that you err on the side of conservatism.

36.2 Physical Space

In general, there is a greater sensitivity to physical space in the USA than in India. Here are some examples:

- Americans, by and large, stand farther from you when they talk to you (may be because geographically their country is large and they are used to a lot of space.)
- A lot of Europeans shake hands with their colleagues almost every day, whereas with Americans it is a remote 'hello' or 'hi'—the handshake is reserved only when you first meet someone or when you meet them after a long gap or when congratulations are in order.

- In restaurants Americans tend to sit far from other guests and almost never share a table with strangers. In India, it is not uncommon to find people sharing restaurant tables (may be because there are not enough tables in many restaurants).
- Even in crowded places, Americans tend to protect their private space (and respect others' personal space).
- While it is common in India to find four people sharing three seats or six people squeezing into a compact car (by 'adjusting', to use a common Indian term), you will never find this in America.
- When Americans go to a restaurant, they usually 'go Dutch', in the sense that each person pays for himself. In India, it is very common that 'someone takes you for a treat'.
- An Indian does not mind an occasional back slap or doesn't think too much of putting his hand over his colleague's shoulder, but people from some other cultures, like the Americans, may not appreciate such a gesture.
- Even while driving, Americans maintain a 'space' around their car.

In short, the Americans are highly protective of their privacy and *personal space*—much more so than many other cultures in the world. Here are some of the common ways people err and violate this personal space and our suggestions on how to avoid such mistakes.

Maintaining physical distance: In India, it is common to find people walking very close to each other and putting their hands over another's shoulder. This is not done in the USA. You have to literally maintain at least a distance of an arm's length with your colleagues. Avoid unnecessary physical contact. No literal pat on the back (only figurative ones); no hands over shoulders.

Respecting your colleague's office space: If your colleague has an office (not a cubicle), then the space behind the desk, where he is sitting is part of his personal space. Never cross over to that side of the table. In Indian terms, the table is 'the *Lakshman Rekha*' that marks your boundary of how far you can go. Also, if your colleague is not there, do not take the liberty of entering into his office and sitting and waiting for him to come back.

Not borrowing or requesting to share your colleague's personal belongings: In India, it is quite common for someone to borrow his colleague's car or a motor cycle for short (or even long) rides. This is usually not done in the USA. Americans guard their personal belongings as a part of their physical space. As an extension of this, never use the phone on your colleague's desk without seeking his permission first.

Not using his computer: As a corollary to the above two points, never fiddle around with your colleague's computer or mobile phone for that matter. Resist the temptation to peek through his open e-mail or whatever is on his screen or the text messages on the phone—especially if your colleague is not around. Nowadays, computers are truly *personal* and no one would like someone else to peep through them.

"Our CEO Mr. Srivastav is very particular about his privacy….."

Fig. 36.1

Not visiting his home, unless invited specifically: In India, it is common to cold call on your colleague's home on a Sunday evening with your family. This is considered 'a pleasant surprise' and is not frowned at. This is simply a no-no in the US culture. Never knock on anybody's door without notice.

36.3 Informational Privacy

With a large amount of personal data circulating in the cyberspace and open to attacks from lurking predators, you now need to know enough about cyber-security and how to protect everyone's confidential data from such attacks.

Just what personal information is considered private and needs to be kept under wraps? We give a list of such items below and we would like to emphasize that this list is by no means complete. Also, just like personal space, the limits of this are very culture-dependent. You may be surprised at some of the items that have made the list and are therefore, considered highly personal topics. So the next time you have a conversation with your colleague (or even a candidate for a job interview) and it touches on his or her personal life, make sure the topic is not off-limits due to privacy considerations. Be especially careful when discussing such matters with your foreign counterparts. Don't put others in an awkward situation. Some topics not to be touched upon:

- **Date of birth, age:** These are big taboo topics and any discussion of these in the office should be avoided. In fact, it is illegal to ask about these things in interviews you conduct for US companies. A typical resumé (and job interview) in

India dwells upon age and date of birth but in much of the world (especially in the USA), this is a no-no. And contrary to the popular belief that only women like to keep their age secret, even men do not want to advertise their age (and leave themselves vulnerable to age bias and other possibilities). Don't even ask indirect questions about their age ('who was the prime minister when you were in college?'), because nobody wants to 'date' themselves and give clues about their history that you can use to back-calculate their age.

- **Marital status, romantic life, children and family, sexual orientation:** You do not ask about the marital status of someone or how many children someone has or their living arrangements (whether they are living with their parents or children, etc.). In India, we don't think twice about asking if someone is married. But if you asked a foreign colleague, they may surprise you by saying that they don't want to answer the question. So, don't stick your foot in your mouth by asking such questions—especially, soon after being introduced to them. Likewise, unless you have a close personal rapport with your colleagues, do not probe into what their children (or brothers and sisters, boyfriend/girlfriend) are doing. If your colleague keeps mentioning their family or spouse or siblings/children in the course of the conversation, it may not be out of place to ask natural questions about them in a 'small talk' type of manner. (See the Chapter 35 on small talk.) But you certainly do not want to come across as being overly inquisitive.
- **Salary, property, jewellery, financial transactions and stock market activities:** Your salary details are confidential. So if your colleague at the neighboring desk asks you 'what is your take-home pay this year?' you really don't have to answer. Similarly, information about your incentive bonus, raises, travel allowances and so forth are personal data. So are data about your financial life—cost of your apartment, stock market profits, insurance details and so on. On the flip side, do not attempt to find out such details about your colleagues. Again, in India, the day after an annual performance review is over, everyone knows the other persons' raise and bonus and that is the topic for 'big talk' (if we can coin a term as an opposite of small talk!). Annual performance reviews and other personal meetings with your managers are also confidential events and you don't have to –and should not—share the details with each other.
- **Phone numbers and addresses:** We already mentioned that you should not ask your foreign partners for their personal mobile or home phone numbers. Neither should you ask them for their home addresses. If you are abroad in their city and they invite you to their home, then get to know their address. But otherwise, the only window to them is through the office.
- **Health parameters:** How much they weigh, waist size, sugar level, blood pressure numbers, whether they have any physical challenges and so on are confidential information too. Even if you know that your colleague has high blood pressure, you don't make him uncomfortable by asking him how high it is and try to extract a number out of him.

- **Health conditions of family members:** When your colleague or his relatives are in the hospital or have a health condition, don't go 'What is the matter with your mother in law? What is she suffering from?' The state of health and the nature of any illness someone is suffering from are also private topics and you do not ask pointed questions about them to someone.
- **Religious orientation:** Your colleague's religious practices, religious rites, personal habits (like eating habits based on religion) are also in the private realm. Don't try to find out such details and worse still, pass judgement about it.
- **Educational qualification, resumés:** Although it may be common knowledge, don't discuss such things with your colleagues ('How did you do in your first year college mathematics course?').
- **Marks, grades, annual performance review details:** Test grades and exam results are considered very, very private data in the USA and most other countries and you don't ask each other for your marks. Interestingly, there are cultural differences between India and other countries in this regard too. Here in India, university exam results are announced over public websites and all you need is a university 'roll number'. Not only can you find out the marks and grades that you have obtained but of your entire class, because the roll numbers of students in a class are assigned sequentially.
- **Reasons for their absence from work yesterday:** 'So, what happened to you yesterday? You didn't come to work?' is an innocuous enough question. But your colleague doesn't have to answer it (or he could say 'something suddenly cropped up' and leave it at that).
- **Itinerary, plans and schedules:** Don't embarrass your colleagues by asking them to outline any of their plans—even vacation plans. They don't have to share their innermost ideas with you or consult you on their plans. In India, it is quite common to share vacation plans with your colleagues—even if they are not very close to you.
- **Political orientation and views:** Your colleague's political views, affiliations and voting choices are his own and he need not reveal them to you. Neither does he have to be drawn into a political discussion with you and others, if he is disinclined. This contrasts with the Indian ethos where politics is one of the main topics of discussion and talk at any time.
- **Don't volunteer unsolicited help:** Volunteering to help someone is generally a good idea, but don't impose your help on people, unsolicited. Let the person in need actually request help. Some people who are really in need of help may prefer to struggle and get over the hump by themselves, without any external assistance. It may offend them and embarrass them if you offered unsolicited help. If you can't wait to help, ask them 'May I help you?' and only if they say 'yes', extend your helping hand.

The above discussion is moot if your colleague thinks he is a good personal friend of yours and does not mind confiding in you or sharing details about his personal life. In which case, nothing prevents you from discussing any topic in depth and you can go as far as he is comfortable. But the default behaviour is not to broach any of the above topics with your colleagues, especially with people whom you are barely getting to know and even more particularly, with people from other cultures. Let them keep their firewall, just like how you should keep yours.

Sometimes, others' private and confidential information may come your way unsolicited, through leaks and the grapevine. In such cases, go on with life as if you didn't hear anything. Don't be instrumental in spreading it even more. And finally, discussing technical and work-related matters with colleagues—even foreign ones—is a safe bet and does not typically violate any privacy norm and so, stick with it when in doubt!.

36.4 How to Live in a Privacy-based Workplace

Get over the misconception that there is nothing wrong about getting other people's personal information: The biggest challenge to respecting privacy comes from ignorance about privacy and its legal aspects. One simply needs a quick lesson on the matter—about what is considered to be the public domain and what is private, what information about your colleagues is protected and off-limits, and how you can be sensitive to the personal space of the other person. You may think it is a part of good friendship to share information about each other's bonuses or health conditions, But that is not how relationships work at the workplace. Don't be offended if your colleague does not share his personal space with you. Don't try to find out his private details one way or the other—especially by mining office records or trawling personal information. By doing such things you are not only being disrespectful of others' privacy, but may actually be violating some laws.

Use the correct way of building profiles on people at work: This is a corollary of the above point. Some people tend to take the wrong approach to building a mental 'profile' of their colleagues. They start with numerical and parametric details first—age, educational qualification, salary level, family background, etc. and then go on to add other things. Instead, in a modern work environment, you should start with the professional description and attributes of the other person and build around it. Instead of saying Rakesh Lal is a thirty two year old, second year test engineer with a mechanical engineering degree pulling in six *lakhs* a year, you should think of him as a test engineer first, who is good at reliability testing and designing elaborate quality metrics and then add to this profile as necessary. It really should not matter to you how old he is or what his cholesterol numbers are.

Give evasive or curt answers to curious cats: This is still another corollary of our first point. Some people at work can be overly curious about others' affairs, to the point that they become annoying. In which case, if you want to protect your privacy, it is okay to give evasive answers or simple, curt responses. 'If you don't mind, I don't want to talk about it' is an appropriate response. Be very careful about the persons who might keep pestering you over and over. Don't relent or be intimidated into giving personal information.

Let the topics evolve naturally, don't force them: In the initial stages of your relationship-building with your colleague, you should stick to just non-sensitive topics ('What did you do over the weekend?') and confine your conversation to technical/office matters or small talk. Once the relationship becomes stronger, personal details may also figure in the conversation. If it does, let that happen naturally, on its own. Don't force it.

Let the other person open up as much as he or she feels comfortable with. Lob a gentle question 'Heard your mother-in-law is in the hospital. Hope it isn't anything to worry about?' If the response is lukewarm, ('Yes, she is doing much better. Should be discharged today.') drop the matter. If he is forthcoming, hear him out, but don't probe him with question after question. When you do ask questions try to ask them in a neutral, non-judgemental, matter-of-fact way, rather than looking nosy.

Leave the other person(s) alone if that is their wish: You will meet all kinds of people at work. Some of them will be habitual introverts with a virtual 'do not disturb' sign on them. You should leave them alone, except for the occasional courtesies. Some others would like to get into their shells from time to time to concentrate on their work, for personal reasons and so on. And yet others may want to be left alone with another colleague or a small group of co-workers. In which case, don't invite yourself in.

Never assault other people's sound space: Some people talk very loudly in public by habit and some others just to attract attention. The office is a public place, so speak softly, especially in today's open office environment. Likewise, tone down your phone ringtones, desist from playing music loudly (use ear phones) and keep your phone voice to a manageable decibel level. In a quiet office environment, never talk on your cell phone loudly. If you get a call that you have to answer, excuse yourself from the office, go to the corridor and take the call.

Be careful about your personal information: Organize and secure your personal data, especially your identity-defining data like your passport or PAN or social security number details, driving license information, employment-related details and so on. Next, keep your financial details in order. Make up appropriate usernames and passwords to protect your transactions and keep changing them often for safety. Keep phone numbers of your banks and other agencies handy so that you can contact them in case your confidential data is compromised.

Be alert and be paranoid about your personal data falling into the wrong hands in cyberspace. Be on top of scams and unauthorized attempts to penetrate your cyber firewall. As much as possible, keep your professional and private lives distinct. Be very careful about logging into office accounts from public computers and likewise, reaching a public domain website or e-mail site through the office computer.

36.5 Organizational Privacy and Proprietary Information

Not just people, even organizations have their privacy and proprietary information. Just because you are privy to some of it, don't assume that everyone knows it. And don't ever be tempted to pass it around, even among your own colleagues, because such information may be privileged and perhaps given only to people on a 'need-to-know' basis. You must remember that there are active parties interested in getting your organization's business secrets and you will have to be doubly vigilant to safeguard those secrets.

Don't discuss business details with family members: Since you spend so many hours in the office, it is often tempting to come up with a war story for the benefit of your folks at home and talk about what happened at work. This is fine, as long as you don't inadvertently talk about how your organization missed a deal or how much money they are losing in another project. Proprietary information coming out of your office should be off-limits even to your personal friends outside work.

Don't spread information about company decisions, project status, etc.: These are very sensitive information. You don't know how many people are interested in such details like the names of your suppliers, whether you are half-way or three-quarters through your project, your company's latest product portfolio and when they are going to be released. A certain amount of leak may occur anyway, given how interconnected organizations are these days. But do your part in being tight-lipped about such information. Be wary of vendors and outsiders trying to get information about each other and trying to find where they are with respect to you.

Don't discuss company's future plans: Only some parts of your organization's strategy and tactical response are in the public domain. Your organization's comprehensive strategic plans and their specifics are again, privileged information that may only be known to selected employees. Be protective of such information as well, if you are privy to it.

View customer data as sacred: If you interact with end customers, you may be handling a lot of their private data, in which case, handle them with extreme care. You must remember that most customers have a solid trust in your organization and that is why they are handing over any of their personal data to a third party like you—their credit card numbers, addresses, phone numbers, etc. You have to put them at ease and make sure they don't have even a shred of doubt about their data falling into the wrong hands.

Protect your company's intellectual properties: Be cognizant of any patents, copyrights or technical secrets that you may come across in your organization during the course of your work. Such intellectual properties are major assets for any organization. Do not reveal any of it to anyone—don't even give hints about it. What chemicals go into your insulating layer in circuit fabrication or how exactly you deposit it and so on may be company secrets and should stay within the company, that too only with people who do such fabrication day in and day out.

Guard privileged information: You may be an engineer in R and D. But you might still be privy to some information about another function in your organization, such as sales. For example, you may know that the sales department is planning to have a big promotion in the Mumbai region next month. But you must remember that it is the duty (and the protocol) of the sales people to publicize it. You are not supposed to talk about it under any circumstances just because you know about it. Don't wear the wrong hat and talk out of turn—even if you are the only one who knows that information in a crowd. Similarly, production figures, product yields, quality issues, profit margins and so on are also confidential information and should be under gag.

36.6 In Summary

In today's global workplace, you have to be privacy-savvy at many levels. To begin with, you should display simple courtesies about respecting the other person's privacy and be aware of their personal firewall and need for personal space. This is especially important if the other person is from a different culture with a slightly different notion of privacy. It is absolutely important to create a pleasant and relaxed business climate where the other party's privacy concerns are put to rest and you gain their confidence and trust.

Equally important is to care for and safeguard your customer's personal data and your organization's business secrets and intellectual properties. And finally, if you can extend your skill to cover cyber-security and protection of everyone's data in the cyber-space, that will give you an even greater edge at the workplace.

You should not have the notion that you can earn the goodwill of someone by sharing a secret or intruding into his privacy. The hints given in this chapter serve as guidelines on the optimum distance (both literally and figuratively) to maintain with your colleagues and to strike the right balance between being cordial and not sounding impersonal.

37

Learning to Say 'No'

"You have to decide what your highest priorities are and have the courage—pleasantly, smilingly, non-apologetically—to say 'no'..."
–Stephen Covey

Snapshot 37.1

RAJIV SHARMA, THE 'YES' MAN

Mr Rajiv Sharma is not just your average business analyst. He is a business analyst plus a superman. He is ten employees rolled into one. He is the official trouble shooter and the unofficial 'go-to' guy when things get a bit rough around his cubicle. He has a heart of gold and never says no to anyone.

Take last Monday evening, for example. It was 5.00 p.m. Sharma was just putting the finishing touches to his feasibility report when his next-cube neighbour came rushing in for some help with inserting a graph into an Excel file. 'That should be easy' Sharma declared, as he volunteered to help—but it was only after delving into the problem did he find out that it was not that simple. Quite challenged, he sat up the next hour trying to help his friend. In the middle of it, someone walked by his desk to remind him of the 6.00 p.m. conference call with Ireland. Somebody else pulled him into a conference room for five minutes because the overhead projector was acting up. While he was out doing it, Mr Banerjee walked into Sharma's cube with a business proposal he had written that he wanted Sharma to look over and give feedback on. Just when Sharma got back to his desk, his boss dashed in and dragged him over to his office because his Japanese client was on the phone about something that only Sharma knew. In the middle of all this, his wife rang him up to remind him that he was supposed to pick her up from her office and drive over to her grand-aunt's ninety-third birthday party. Didn't Joshi borrow his motorcycle for the afternoon?

Life is no doubt hectic for Sharma. But he would rather extend his helping hand and be popular than quietly do his job in a corner, unperturbed. He is so glad that so many people count on him and that he is an important hub of his organization. He knew that there could not be a conference call within two miles of his desk without him taking part in it. He is proud of donning so many roles—business analyst, the great communicator, Excel expert and a caring relative who takes the time to look up an old lady. He often reaped rewards and recognition for his selfless attitude—not to mention the eternal gratitude of the many people he helped. No wonder he is considered an elite employee who was always the first one to be summoned at the slightest hint of trouble.

But of late, Sharma has been re-thinking his Mr Nice Guy policy. He was finally starting to get tired of saying 'yes' to everyone who needed help. He began to notice that he was overdoing it to the point where he had no time for the most important person in his life, namely himself. He was stretching himself thin and was beginning to wear down. His efficiency was dropping, interruptions were becoming more annoying and he found his days shrinking. More importantly, his effectiveness was dropping and he was not completing what he was supposed to deliver. Most times, he had trouble finishing his own work. Enough was enough! He was going to add a new word to his vocabulary called 'no'.

Snapshot 37.2

SRINI VARADRAJAN, THE EVER SOFT-SPOKEN PROJECT MANAGER

Mr Srini Varadarajan is the quintessential customer-facing project manager, doing high-pressure software projects for his US client. His client asks him in a conference call, 'By the way Srini, I forgot to tell you . . . my management wants to add in the new costing feature to our billing system that does . . .'. Srini makes a quick calculation in his head and reckons this new feature will take an additional ten person months that will throw a spanner in the project cost. But instead of coming out and saying 'If we add this feature now, it will cost an additional half a million dollars and push the release schedules off by another three months' or something to that effect, he in his typical 'soft-spoken' nature says, 'Hmm . . . that will take quite a bit of time . . .' The foreign counterpart bulldozes by saying 'C'mon, you can do it man . . .'. Srini replies 'Let me see what I can do . . .'

This 'let me see what I can do' is taken as a 'yes' by the US counterpart. (And Srini would never be firm even in his e-mail about the specific extent of damage of this seemingly innocuous request for change.) What should have been categorically and professionally stated has now been beaten around the bush.

Clearly, Srini neither has the confidence nor the intention to meet the new demands that his foreign counterpart made and was meaning to say 'no'. But he is soft-spoken enough to not to say a loud 'no' (and in the back of his mind, he does want to explore the possibilities of accommodating his business partner's requests). Meanwhile, his more aggressive and forceful US counterpart has presumed that he has arm-twisted Srini into saying 'yes'. Although the US partner is wrong in interpreting Srini's actions, the onus is on Srini to be more clear-cut and less ambiguous on such a binary decision as saying yes or no. We would say that such instances of wishy-washy communication and sending mixed or wrong messages can cause more trouble and heartaches than the previous case of Rajiv Sharma.

37.1 The Two Types of Wrong Yes-s

There is a bit of Rajiv and a bit of Srini in all of us (see Snapshots 37.1 and 37.2). You must have sometimes said 'yes' to things that you should have really said 'no' to and later lived to regret it. Without thinking, sometimes you tend to be very generous with your time or things to the point of placing somebody else's needs ahead of your own or your project's welfare. True, these generosities can earn you a lot of goodwill, but how much sacrifice should you make without jeopardizing your self-interest or the interest of the project that your organization has entrusted you with? Where should you draw the line about saying 'yes' to people and taking on added responsibilities? How do you strike the right balance between saying 'no' to some people and saying 'yes' to some others? Why do you say 'yes' when you actually meant to say 'no'? Is it your ego? How do you say 'no' without sounding rude?

We will try to answer all these questions in this chapter. This chapter will help you recognize the situations where you will have to decide between saying 'yes' and saying 'no'. We will first look at two different scenarios that have the same effect—of making you say 'yes' when you mean 'no'. Then we will see how to say this 'no' in a courteous, acceptable way. Finally, once you decide to say 'no', we will see how not to be pressured into saying 'yes'.

Rajiv and Srini present two scenarios by which a wrong yes is given (when a no is what should have been said). Rajiv is the one who is always helpful, who does not mind working long hours with the clear intent of helping others. His problem is that he over commits himself and even forgets his priorities. If Banerjee or Joshi feel that they will get all the help they want from Rajiv, this is exactly the impression that Rajiv intended to convey.

But Srini's case is even worse. He did not *intend* to complete the project enhancement. But he has given the wrong impression to his US counterpart that he will complete it. He has simply been a nice guy on the phone and been an escapist, not willing to put his foot down and articulate a professional 'no'. He is just sitting on a time bomb ticking off and when the US counterpart does realize that what was meant was a 'no', it is going to be too late and too expensive.

There are a couple of reasons why this 'saying yes when you mean no' is so important an issue that it deserves a separate chapter. First, there is an innate belief (more so in India than in the US and in a number of other places that we have seen) that saying no would lead to a bad feeling in the mouth of the other party and will jeopardize the relations in the long run (true of both Rajiv and Srini). Second, there is a tendency to postpone saying no. By postponing, it is hoped that the situation will take care of itself and that the 'no' will no be longer required (the Srini syndrome). Third—and this is something that is complained of often about Indians—they don't say no explicitly. In case of people with the Srini syndrome as seen in Snapshot 37.2, the 'no' is camouflaged as a 'yes'.

The problem arises because you don't have the heart to say 'no' to a helpless colleague or are afraid to be 'disrespectful' of the client by saying 'no'. This attitude stems from the values you learnt as a child—to be unselfish, to help out people who need help and to make sacrifices for the greater good. Now it is time to re-educate yourself into thinking that a well-reasoned 'no' from you is appropriate in several situations and is not the end of the world. It is not even the end of the project, because a good project manager will re-assess the situation and make sure that somehow the right resources are deployed, even if you cannot help out. If you have good reasons for saying 'no', your response will not be considered as negative behaviour and neither will you be thought of as being unreasonable and uncooperative. It will not affect your popularity at work. You don't always have to be a part of the solution to everyone's problems. So get used to the idea that you can indeed say 'no' on occasion and live with that decision. In fact, it is far better than the alternative—saying 'yes' when you had actually meant to say 'no'.

37.2 Why You Say 'Yes' When You Mean 'No'—The Process Explained

Let us walk through the various stages of this process—right from the time when someone needs help and how you get trapped into saying 'yes' to how you get psychologically affected by this wrong response on your part.

Stage 1—People in need of help have you in their cross-hairs: It starts innocuously enough with a boss running into your cube or a colleague phoning in his request. Often the requests are so subtle that you don't even realize that an action item is being solicited. So the first thing to develop is an automatic warning system that a new demand is going to be made on your time and resources. Be alert when someone walks in, be careful about analysing their requests and above all, don't fall head over heels over them. ('*The VP of finance is himself coming to me for help. This must be my chance to glory.*')

Fig. 37.1

And why would *they* come to you when they are in need of help? Here are some reasons.

- They need to get the job done somehow. *Any* help is okay. They just happened to stumble on you.
- You are an expert in the field (or at least you know more than them).
- You have a reputation of being patient and generous.
- You are a pushover.
- You have the reputation of overloading yourself or you are the 'go-to' person.
- You are perceived to be relatively 'free' and available for such spontaneous exercises.
- You can be flattered or ego-fed into doing it.
- They can use their authority to push you.
- They need to use that gizmo, gadget, software and so on that you have (umbrella, comb, pen, motorcycle, employee handbook *ad nauseum*).

Stage 2—Why you might want to say 'no': There can be many, many reasons for you to say 'no' to someone, not merely because your plate is full. Sometimes even when you have plenty of time and flexibility in your schedule, you may still want to say 'no' because you may find the proposal to be uninteresting, unnecessary for your career advancement, unpleasant or unrewarding—like the time your boss asked you to be on the 'canteen committee'. Sharma (in Snapshot 37.1) could have said 'no' to helping out with the overhead projector for a variety of reasons—being too busy, not having enough expertise in the matter and also because the audio-video service technicians are just a phone call away and could be summoned right away. He could have said 'no' to his colleague who wanted to borrow his motorcycle because Sharma needed to leave the office on time. He could have said 'no' also because the colleague was known to be a rash rider—although Sharma would not have explicitly stated that.

Here are some of your reasons for wanting to say 'no' and ways of saying no.

- You have no bandwidth. You are in the middle of something critical and important for your project.
- You have other plans and commitments.
- You don't want to work with the others in this activity (although you may want to state this diplomatically).
- It is too much of a risk—not an easy request that you feel you can do justice to. ('You certainly need someone with more experience to handle this.')
- You don't know how to do it. You know you don't have the expertise, even if they think that you do. You know your limitations and don't want to enter into an area that you are not comfortable in. ('I appreciate your confidence in me, but I know my limitations.')
- You have more fun things to do. You would rather be sleeping (again, be careful as to how you phrase this).
- It doesn't appeal to you. You just don't want to do it. (There is no reason why you cannot say this directly but politely 'Oh, this is not my cup of tea.')
- You don't want to lend your things to them because they will not handle them as well as you want them to. ('You know, as a matter of principle, I don't lend this to anyone, even to my wife or brother.')

Stage 3—Why you end up saying 'yes' when you meant to say 'no': Just imagine you are sitting across the table from a foreign contingent. Everyone (except you) is at least a director or higher up. Even the language they use seems superior to anything you have ever heard. You are feeling so intimidated and out of place that you can feel butterflies in your stomach. You somehow want to belong. You want to announce, 'Hey, look. I am capable. Give me some task to do.' And then your boss (who also wants to look good) tells you in front of all of them 'Rajiv, why don't you take care of that activity and do it?' It suddenly feels like the entire project's success, your organization's fortunes and perhaps even the advancement of the human race is in your hands. You scream a loud 'yes' (but it comes out as a feeble whisper of a 'yes'). Scarcely ten seconds later, upon reconsidering your boss's request and mulling over all your other commitments you have pending, you realize that saying 'yes' was a bad idea. You should have actually said 'no' or at least a 'let me see'. Why did you thoughtlessly get into the trap when you were actually way too busy with other projects? You also realize that you don't have a lot of competence in the field he wants you to work in. Now you cannot back down without looking bad. As a professional, you have to execute. You think you have learnt a lesson and will never do it again. But come next week, you have done it one more time in another context. Why is this happening and what is wrong?

Fig. 37.2

Here are some psychological factors which force you to say 'yes' when you would rather say 'no'.

- You want to prove yourself and project yourself as powerful, important, Mr or Miss Reliable.
- Your desire to perform on the international stage.
- You want to make a positive impression on the client and the boss.
- You expect monetary and other rewards.
- It is a cultural thing. You want to prove that you are as good as any in the world.
- It is a cool thing.
- You are worried about all kinds of negative consequences if you don't say 'yes'.
- You don't want to look selfish and self-centred.
- You are worried that you will miss an opportunity.
- You are worried about what they will think.
- You don't want to hurt the other person's feelings.
- You don't want to seem uncooperative and as not stepping up.
- You are intimidated into it.
- Your boss was very persuasive.
- You feel obligated or are afraid looking bad.
- In your own mind you are ambivalent and would feel guilty if you had said 'no'.

You say a big fat 'yes', kick yourself and feel miserable.

Stage 4—You live with your decision: When you say 'yes' and take on more assignments—even though you had meant to say 'no'—you are on the hook. As a professional, you are now committed to completing the task in hand (unlike your personal life where you can sometimes say 'yes' and later make excuses for not doing it). Your professional ethics dictate that you assume ownership of that activity and go through the whole nine yards. You cannot abandon it or give it a half-hearted attempt just because your mind is not in it.

This can be very agonizing because often, only in hindsight will you realize that you never wanted to do that activity in the first place. This agony itself is a very negative feeling to have. The feeling that somebody has hand-wrung you into doing it and you were not too careful can haunt you for a long time. Also, you will get the feeling that you could rather be doing something else that is more interesting and more rewarding, instead of fixing your colleague's Excel mistakes.

Here is a short list of what happens to you when you are pressured into doing something because you didn't know how to say 'no'.

- You have no time to do everything properly, given how much there is on your plate and all the deadlines you face.
- You feel betrayed.
- You feel like you are sacrificing too much and neglecting your own welfare.
- You have to work with people you don't enjoy working with.
- You get into a wrong project or activity in which you have no competence.
- It is an activity with no visibility where you will be unappreciated.
- You feel you will not get the right reinforcements or help.
- You are psychologically not motivated to perform at your highest level.

37.3 How Can You Say 'No' and Still Come Out Ahead

An honest evaluation of what is on your plate and what the organization (or a colleague) needs is the key to saying 'yes' or 'no' to new commitments that come your way. If at the end of your situation analysis you decide that 'no' is the appropriate response, how will you convey that response to the other party (and to yourself) in a polite, acceptable way? Here are some suggestions.

Say a firm, unequivocal 'no': 'No' is perhaps one of the simplest, yet very clearly-understood words in English. So if your answer is no, give it to them straight. Tell them you are sorry, but there is no way you can help them. The abruptness of this response might unnerve you at first. But this takes out any ambiguity in your response. The trouble starts only when you try to give the impression that in spite of your 'no', perhaps there is a possibility that you can help them. ('There is a chance that my boss will not ask me to do this testing, in which case, I may be able to help you'—the Srini syndrome, that we saw in Snapshot 37.2).

Keep smiling and look genuine when you say no. Convey this message through your body language as well. Don't say anything ambiguous or confusing. They should get the impression that yours is a firm 'no', but if you had the time and resources, you would have definitely helped out.

Substantiate with hard data, don't make it look personal: When you say no, tell why. 'After sizing the project, I realize that it will take another ten person months and it will go way beyond the budget we committed to each other. We should defer it to the next release.' By this method, you are not only saying a firm no, but also substantiating it with clear numbers and even offering a solution.

Point out that something else might suffer: If it is your boss or someone high up that is trying to twist your arm into doing something and you cannot look in their eyes and say the word 'no', just point out to the things you are already doing and are committed to. Tell them in no uncertain terms that those things might suffer if you took up extra load. If they still insist on your doing the new activity, ask them to reprioritize your tasks and set their expectation level lower on some of your assignments.

Don't dwell on it and feel anguished about having said no: The guilt feeling can overwhelm you if you said 'no'. The image of a poor, helpless colleague struggling with Excel software, unable to get the graph right, can wrench your heart. What if this happened to you? But let it pass. It is his problem and he will certainly find someone else to help him. Even if he doesn't, you are not the owner of this problem. Don't be emotional about it and agonize over it.

In some other cases, buy time ('let me think about it'): Instead of immediately committing to the request one way or the other, ask for some time to think about the proposal—think offline about it and come up with a response in a reasonable time. This way, your response will be honest and well thought out. Of course, this won't work if someone needs your help right away.

Take on a partial commitment and find a halfway solution or ask for help: It may be possible for you to take on a part of the request instead of the entire thing. Or perhaps you can take on the entire request if you got some help yourself. In that case, suggest this to the requester and they may be amenable to such a suggestion. However, in some cases, they may want the entire activity to be done by one person and your idea may not be feasible.

Don't be defensive: One of the worst things you can do is to keep on apologizing after having said a 'no'. 'I would have helped if my I didn't have this vendor meeting' or 'Just last Thursday I helped someone with a similar request' will only end up making you feel awkward about having said 'no'. Remember that most help-seekers are not very interested in what exactly your circumstances are that made you turn their request down. If you can't do it, you can bet that they will scour the entire office for someone else who can.

How to deal with the boss and other very pushy people: First of all, remember that there will be commitments put forth by your boss that you simply cannot refuse and don't have a choice of saying 'no' to. However, under some circumstances you can stand up to your boss, if you have a case for it. Of course, it will be very difficult to say 'no' to your own boss, because he is all-in-all for you at work and also because somehow, he seems to have a way of coercing you into things.

The strategy here is to not say 'yes' or 'no' explicitly, but discuss the matter completely. Even after you put forth that 'something else might suffer' defence, if he still insists on your doing it, have a bigger and more comprehensive discussion on your role in the organization. Come up with reasons why your entire group might benefit by your not committing to this activity. Have some other neutral observers (such as the project leads) in the discussion to help steer it to a decision.

Stick to your 'no'. Don't let the other person brainwash you: Some people can be persistent. They will walk up to your desk ten times hoping to change your mind just by putting pressure on you. Some others may try to sweet-talk you into it. These are the people who don't easily take 'no' for an answer. The way to deal with them is to be equally hard-lined about your stance and flash the biggest smile you have and splash an even bigger 'no' that you can come up with.

Suggest somebody else or alternative solutions: This is the age-old response in lieu of saying 'no'. But beware. Some people may find it insulting that you are advising them when all they are after was some solid help. And don't use it on your boss—he knows the big picture better than you.

Sometimes you can change your mind and say 'no': Even if you had thoughtlessly said 'yes' to someone, some commitments are reversible and you can later turn around and say 'no' after deliberating the matter for sometime. But do it very, very soon, before the ripple effects start to take shape.

37.4 How to Take 'No' for an Answer

The flip side of saying 'no' to someone is that when you request help from your colleague and have to take 'no' for an answer. You may have feelings of rejection or desertion by your colleague and experience anger at being unable to solve your problem. Let us for a moment look at how to take 'no' for an answer, without all that hurt.

Remember they don't have to say 'yes': It is not your birthright to get help when you need it. *They* are simply doing you a favour—and they don't always have to. You should not feel insulted or let down. It is not personal.

Don't keep bugging them. Leave them alone: Take 'no' for an answer. Don't haunt the other person over and over, hoping they would relent on your fifth attempt. In some countries, repeatedly hounding the other person to service your request can be construed as harassment and can lead to legal situations. So draw a line after one or two attempts at persuasion.

Don't let that hurt your pride. Keep asking others. Don't give up: The bottom line is that you will have to solve your problems and it doesn't matter if Sharma is not able to help you. Seek other people or be resourceful in other ways about solving the problem. Think laterally about what else you can do.

Be better prepared the next time: Learn a lesson every time and be better-prepared the next time. Maybe it is time to read up on Excel software so that you get better at it and then you will not have to rely on Sharma to bail you out.

37.5 In Summary

Learn to say 'no' to some requests that can potentially hurt you somehow or that are not humanly possible for you to pull off. And definitely don't say 'yes' when you meant to say 'no' (see Snapshot 37.3). If you are wont to doing it, you might as well move to some parts of Ethiopia where 'aye' actually means 'no'.

Snapshot 37.3

Rajiv Sharma, the 'no' man!

Now Sharma is a changed man. Ever since he learnt to say 'no' he has been able to free up time for himself and for projects closer to his heart. Nowadays, he doesn't get caught up in a cesspool of other people's problems.

Some people who took him and his helping heart for granted are certainly disappointed at his about turn. They think that some evil, jealous persons drove Sharma to be mean and cruel. But even they accept his new personality. Even now he does step in and help people, but only when he has the bandwidth for it. He never gets mixed up between saying 'yes' and 'no'. He is very polite and apologetic about saying 'no', but doesn't dwell on it much or feel defensive about it. It was very tough for him to turn down his own boss at times. But now everyone's view towards Sharma's helping tendencies has changed and no one expects him to be readily available whenever there is trouble around the corner. Sharma is at peace with himself and feels more in control. Also, his popularity has not diminished any because of his change of personality. And oh, by the way, even now the administrative assistant approaches Sharma first when there is a paper jam in the office Xerox machine, before calling the service people. When it comes to fixing paper jams, Sharma is still faster than a speeding bullet.

We also want to dispel any misunderstanding that we are going tangential to our basic philosophy espoused in this book. Throughout this book, we have been asking you to put your organization's interests ahead of your own and be a team player and step up to the plate in crunch time. Now it might seem as if we are giving you the opposite message of being self-centred and looking after your personal welfare.

But actually we are not. We still maintain that when a project is in its critical stages, you must step in, in whatever capacity and help out the team—this includes pulling for colleagues in their activities and taking on additional responsibilities wherever you can. We obviously don't want you to be your own show-stopper. We want to bring your attention to the extreme situation when you over-commit yourself and over-schedule your time and make your life miserable—just because you don't know how to turn down people's requests for help. Your psychological well-being is absolutely important and we don't want you to have a burn-out or get the angst of being a simpleton that everyone takes advantage of.

Once you learn to say no to a few things, you will find that you have more time to do the right things—and to do them more efficiently and effectively. You will find that you are more in control. This will definitely make you integrate better into your environment.

Fig. 37.3

38

The Role of Humour in the Workplace

"Through humor, you can soften some of the worst blows that life delivers; And once you find laughter, no matter how painful the situation might be, you can survive it."

– Bill Cosby

Humour is such a primitive mental faculty that we are practically born with it. As we grow up, our sense of humour also evolves and becomes a significant part of our identity. Irrespective of our personality type, we all believe that we have a fine taste for humour and that we can spot a good joke from miles away. We all fall for good humour and let it entertain and charm us. Not only do we recognize and respond to humour, we also generate it in various forms—right from a funny, off-the-cuff remark to playfulness to elaborate gags. In fact, some of us are such good humorists that it endears us to others around us and earns us special attention and popularity. It even gives some others the impression that we, the witty ones, are also generally smart and intelligent. However we dissect it, humour is the very tonic of life and most of us have a natural pre-disposition toward leading cheerful lives, with gentle, enjoyable humour running in the background.

In this chapter, we will see how humour helps in the workplace, and why it is an important and useful soft skill to develop. We will also discuss what the etiquette issues are in using it in our work lives. We will give some useful tips on how to use humour and say a few words about where humour can be ineffective or inappropriate.

38.1 How Humour Helps in the Workplace

So, what does a basic instinct like humour have anything to do with a seemingly stuffy, grumpy entity called the workplace?

For a start, here are some connections.

Humour is a stress-buster: Modern workplaces can produce a lot of tension given the heavy global competition and inter-connected world economies. To survive and succeed in this environment, you need every defence you can muster. As in other spheres of life, even at work, humour can dissolve tension and instil a 'nothing can bring me down' kind of positive attitude and optimism. It can relax you and re-charge your drained batteries. Humour makes you cool and level-headed and fit to meet the many challenges of the workplace. A cheerful ambience and a bunch of high-spirited colleagues around you can certainly make work a lot of fun.

Besides being a motivator and therapeutic at a personal level, humour can also diffuse some tense and unpleasant situations at work. For example, high drama in an office meeting may be brought to an amicable end with a bit of humour and back-slapping. Has your organization announced yet another round of huge losses? Nothing like a dose of dark humour to help absorb the blow.

Humour relieves boredom: Work days can be long and our work can drag on. Humour can provide us with that much-needed comic relief. A session of mild-mannered ribbing with a colleague can be a great antidote to an insufferable five hours spent in testing a difficult piece of code. Breaks are usually scheduled into monotonous and repetitive jobs and workers typically tend to indulge in light-hearted and boisterous activities during such breaks.

A drab presentation or a report can always be livened up by lacing it with humour. Long drawn out office functions with elaborate protocols, can turn into memorable events with a touch of humour and informality.

Humour improves inter-personal relationships: Humour is a major catalyst in inter-personal relationships. It breaks the ice in the initial stages and later, bonds the parties strongly. Even the surliest person responds to humour and so, it opens a lot of doors for new office friendships.

If you are perceived as a lively, humorous person, people at work will be naturally drawn toward you. You will be perceived as a well-liked, congenial person with a cool temperament. This can directly translate into goodwill and help in hours of need.

Humour is often a shared experience. We frequently sit down as a group and share jokes with the other members and this has the effect of improving group cohesiveness. A well-adjusted group is absolutely essential in today's short-duration group projects.

Humour helps build international teams: Humour is probably the best weapon we have in building formidable international teams. With potential language problems, humour becomes the *de facto* force in bringing people from different cultures together. If you can bond with your international partner over humour, you can move through the rest of the business quite effortlessly.

With a dash of humor Mr. Mehta, the CEO, is able to turn his annual budget meetings into fun events.

Fig. 38.1

Humour helps communication: Humour is a powerful communication tool in business. Besides amusing us, it can help drive home several points and complement and reinforce certain others. People will remember a humorous punch-line for months and therefore, any message associated with it. This is especially true in presentations and reports where you communicate with several people at the receiving end. A dab of humour is all it takes to earn the reputation of a 'good communicator' around the office.

So humour is a great trait to have at the workplace—not merely to tide over the ups and downs at work, but also to signal to our organization that we are well-adjusted employees with a great attitude. The ability to generate and respond to humour are no longer treated as in-born qualities that only the gifted have, but they are now looked upon as habits that can be cultivated with effort. You may not put it down on your resumé, but your sense of humour is the vibe you send out to the other person, right after the first hand-shake.

There is no clear indication that humour leads to increased productivity at the workplace. The implication is that it does not. (Otherwise, many business schools in the world will offer a course on business humour!) It is also not clear if big companies are more stuck-up and humourless, while the small ones are the jolly good fellows. Whatever may be the case, business and humour are now much married and we ought to master the art of workplace humour (Box 38.1).

Box 38.1

Where does humour figure in the workplace?

- In informal, one-on-one interaction with co-workers
- In formal and informal interaction within a group
- In one-to-many verbal communications, like meetings and presentations
- In most written communications like e-mail, user documentation and so on
- In off-line verbal communications like phone calls, chat, etc.
- In executive communication.

38.2 Some Pointers to Effective Workplace Humour

We cannot coach you on how to be humorous. But we are going to give you some suggestions on when and how to use humour effectively at work and what types of humour are usually received well in the office.

Size up your environment, audience and the mood: Humour is always situational and it is more so at workplace. You have to be keenly aware of what's going on around you and the people at whom you are going to direct your humour. The unfortunate people sitting in on your seminar—have they been sitting there for four hours without air-conditioning and can't wait to leave or do they want to be enthralled by you? How appropriate is humour to what you want to say—is it going to reinforce your points or will it be a distraction? What is the composition of your audience and will your jokes be okay for all of them, including your super-serious, no-fun general manager sitting just three feet in front of you? The moral of the story is that the audience should be receptive to your humour in order for the humour to be effective. Stated another way, you don't joke around with people who are not in a mood for it or interested in it.

You have to be extra-careful in meetings with guests, especially from other countries. A little bit of humorous small talk is always a good idea. But size up the temperature of the room and unleash only the appropriate humour. Shy people and the language-challenged may need extra time and extra attempts to warm up to your humour. Remember the cultural variations in humour. What your German visitors may find funny, your American visitors may not relate to.

You don't have to be uproariously funny. A subtle hint of humour is enough: You don't have to be a stand-up comedian or a circus clown. Neither are your reports required to be Dilbert-funny to earn you top marks. You just have to reveal that you have a reasonably good sense of humour and that you can generate it in a gentle, non-offensive manner.

The workplace is not a street-corner tryst with your friends. So don't overdo humour. Being frivolous and ludicrous is exactly the wrong thing to do at work. How much they laugh at your jokes is not important. How often they are gently amused and smile is what counts.

You should be able to alternate between seriousness and humour: At work, humour is treated as the gravy. The serious business details are obviously much more important and need to come through effectively. So often, presentations tend to be one long serious speech, with jokes as occasional punctuations. The speaker should fluidly move from the serious to the funny to the serious again. (Besides, if your joke falls flat, you can always use the serious part of your presentation as an escape route and bail yourself out) Dwelling on the funnies or getting side-tracked will not be taken too kindly. Remember you are not running the local chapter of the humour club.

A standard situation with an unexpected twist can result in good humour: Humour has to be familiar yet different. One of the standard tricks, especially in the realm of business, is to take an existing story or situation as a base, build a narration on it and then contort it at the end to come up with a funny and powerful punch-line.

For example, you can take the 'hare and the tortoise' story, but put a twist on it and talk about a rematch of their famous running race (see Snapshot 38.1). Similarly, when talking about a clumsy engineer, you can describe him as a person with a 'reverse Midas touch', a twist on the familiar Midas story.

Fig. 38.2

Snapshot 38.1

The Hare and the Tortoise—the re-match

Mr Hare, the CEO of Hare and Co. and Mr Tortoise, the CEO of the Tortoise Pvt. Ltd, decided to have a re-match of their historic race. Hare figured that he lost the race mainly because of poor management and because he had been too complacent. (Since then he has fired his old management team.) He knew he could not afford to make the same mistakes in the modern, competitive world. Tortoise, for his part, realized that the strategy he used the last time may not work this time and he would have to come up with a new weapon and new strategy to beat out his more agile rival.

His management team—some of whom had over a hundred years of experience—has been working overtime on this.

They both practised hard for the race. Tortoise tried to get into some kind of a shape and the Hare consulted experts. On the appointed day, they exchanged their pinstripe suits for running shorts and quickly shot out of the chute at the sound of the gun.

Tortoise decided to get into a rhythm and keep pushing constantly and methodically, whereas the hare would run at top speed and had to rest—and even sleep—for some time. But unlike last time, Hare had nice alarms and alerts to warn him if the Tortoise passed him. Tortoise's team collected good 'intelligence' on what Hare was doing, whereas Hare had a group of good VPs who could make on-the-fly tactical adjustments.

It was a gruelling race. Along the way there was a river. Tortoise realized that he had a special skill called 'swimming'. He turned it on and crossed the river. Hare, on the other hand, had to go on a long detour to find a bridge and had to run really fast to catch up with Tortoise. At some other places, the hare had the advantage because it could jump over obstacles and run away. At another point, they were confronted by a ferocious animal (its name sounded like 'recession') and while Tortoise discovered that it had a solid defence and could retreat into its shell and wait it out till the danger passed, the animal chased Hare backwards down the race route for a huge loss.

Hare and Tortoise both had their admirers. There were fans who favoured the steady, 'stay the course' approach of Tortoise (although they loathed the 'slow' part of it) and then there were those who liked Hare's agile, aggressive approach coupled with the strategy of taking adequate rest as often as needed.

Who is the winner of this re-match? We may never know, because this is a race that is unlikely to end anytime soon. And the moral of this story? Keep watching and analysing this race, because it offers a goldmine of management lessons for everyone.

Build-up, style and timing are important to humour: When verbalizing humour—whether you are addressing a gathering or simply chit-chatting with your cube-mate—your style and delivery matter. The build-up leading up to the punch-line is as important as the punch-line itself. Glib talkers have a solid advantage in this department. A standard topic or a familiar person will make for a great build-up. The punch-line should be delivered at the most appropriate point in the narration with the right intonation and emotion.

Also, make sure you don't drag out the build-up for too long. The audience may get restless—especially if they can already figure out the punch-line. Equally importantly, don't harp on the punch-line and try to milk it for several laughs. Move on.

I, me and my self-deprecating humour: Jokes about oneself and one's groups are always the easiest to make. This is also by far, the most used genre of humour in the office. Something like 'I always forget where I keep my things' or 'We engineers are a nerdy lot. We will be lost without our calculators' or 'We Indians speak gooder

English than most others in the world'. Not only is self-mocking funny in itself, it also announces to the other party that you are a simple person with humility and practically no ego problem to speak of. It also shows that you readily recognize and accept your many faults. Of course, make sure your audience knows that you are doing it just for laughs and that you don't have any serious problems with basic pride about yourself.

Laughing at oneself or one's group is also safe and risk-free—the group won't be too offended if one of their own pokes fun at them. So if you are an engineer, make fun of the engineers but leave the lawyers alone!!

Funny stories are also often true and reality based: Many humorous narrations and punch-lines often ring true. So, use humour to drive home the gravity of a situation. 'My computer broke down yesterday. I called for the service person. This five-year-old came and repaired it in ten minutes. Of course, he also got ten phone calls on his cell phone while he was doing it.' This is, of course, an exaggeration of reality, but has a grain of truth in it.

Dark humour and cynicism are okay with some audience. Saying 'of course, these days, even five-year-olds have cell phones,' can endear you to some people. But a repeated volley of cynical comments can make you look like a whiner.

Repartee and retort: Repartee, retorts, quips and digs are examples of quick-wit and on-the-feet kind of humour. This is the most effective form of office humour, if you can pull it off. It clearly tells the other person that you are not only humorous, but also quick-thinking and smart in other respects as well. When you indulge in such shot-gun humour, make sure you don't get out of control or insult and demean the other person.

Language jokes, word-play, puns, double-entendres can produce some quick, high-voltage laughter. ('Where is the assistant damager' she asked the administrative assistant.) However, such jokes call for the audience to be 'in tune' and knowledgeable about the language. And if overdone, they run the risk of being boring and predictable.

Also, it is best to quietly slip in your joke or deadpan it, rather than hammer it five times so that they all know that you just made a joke. Sure, some jokes may be lost in the shuffle, but once people catch on to your brand of humour and your non-intrusive way of making jokes, you may have quite a reputation around your desk. A corollary of the above rule is that you should not waste much effort or time in 'explaining' your jokes.

Some things are always safe bets: Some topics and themes easily lend themselves to office humour. Your CEO in the garb of Spiderman always evokes a few laughs, even after being used the hundredth time. So does a gratuitous Mickey Mouse or a cartoon character in a report. Keeping the title of a current hit movie for your seminar/presentation is an age-old trick that never fails to amuse the crowd. In hallway conversations, kids, pets, in-laws, week-end dentist visits, etc. offer a reservoir of humour.

Current topics and topical humour is always a safe genre. Current political happenings, sports events, TV commercials, off-beat news items are all fair game. But make sure the person at the receiving end is up to speed on the current events and follows the joke.

Coming up with appropriate metaphors, sayings, jargons, analogies, etc. are usually guaranteed to tickle the other person's funny bone. A caustic remark like 'I think he just bowled a googly' or making up a new saying like 'that's like putting perfume on a pig' can always be banked on for a laugh or two. Just a word of caution: some of these humorous metaphors can be culture dependent and the other person may not catch them easily. For example, the 'googly' used above may not be understood by an American who does not follow cricket.

Be careful about 'transferred' jokes: Transferred jokes are second-hand jokes. The biggest danger in using them is that others may have already heard them. Even if you are about to utter a gem that you are sure nobody would have heard of, make sure the context is appropriate. Thoreau may have said that 'men suffer in quiet desperation'. But do the men surrounding you in an office lunch want to hear that? Be very careful about jokes from other cultures and other languages because you may lose something in the translation.

Learn from humourous people. Be around them: Humour is a contagion. You can catch it easily. You can learn what is funny, how to be funny and when to be funny. The easiest way to pick up such things is to be around those whom you consider to be humorous. Ask yourself why they are humorous or what marks their sense of humour. Is it their style, language skills, inborn humorous instincts or timing? Can you imitate them in another crowd? Why is it that when they say 'I am on a sea food diet—when I see food, I eat' everyone laughs, but when you say it, the joke falls flat and there are only embarrassed smirks everywhere?

If you don't have ready witty company, humorous movies, books, TV shows, etc. form the second best source to learn from. Especially, read business-related books with a touch of humour to get a feel for business humour.

Learn to take a joke: You have to learn to lighten up and develop somewhat of a thick skin while at work. Remember that you are going to spend a good part of your waking hours with your colleagues at work and occasionally you may be the butt of some jokes. Take it sportingly, but clearly define your limits of tolerance. By and large, only mild-natured jostling around takes place in the office and by being 'cool', you are simply telling others at work that you have a fine sense of humour and appreciate a good joke, even if it is on yourself.

Be aware if your jokes fall flat or are unappreciated: Nothing is more embarrassing than your joke falling flat—especially when you are speaking to a large audience—and especially when you had laboured over your speech and the humorous lines for hours the previous night. The only thing to do when this happens is to pick up the pieces and go on with the rest of your talk. Don't start giving explanations. Remember, such things happen to even seasoned humorists on occasion.

Fig. 38.3

Long build-up, un-funny content, poor delivery, extending the joke beyond a limit, etc.—any of these might have contributed to your joke going awry. Also, a poor reading of the audience can be a cause. Learn the appropriate lessons and try a different trick the next time.

Box 38.2

Genres of humour that go well at the workplace

- Cartoons
- Absurd humour
- Puns, wordplay
- Topical jokes/Current events
- Anecdotes/story telling
- Irony/Truth wrapped in humour
- Self mocking/Self-deprecatory humour
- Deadpan give-aways, repartee
- Using interesting metaphors/analogies, etc.

Genres of humour to be handled with care at the workplace

- Jokes targeted against specific groups, like lawyers, engineers, etc.
- Jokes from other cultures/contexts/transferred jokes

- Satire/Political jokes/ sarcasm
- Lampooning someone
- Dark humour/Cynical humour.

Genres of humour best avoided at the workplace

- Parody/Mimicking accents/Farce
- Elaborate gags
- Slapstick/Juvenile content
- Ethnic jokes/Offensive jokes
- Jokes with sexual content or gender bias.

38.3 Some Absolute No-No-s About Workplace Humour

Humour and political correctness: Not too long ago, jokes and humour didn't have to be politically correct. Very cruel and tasteless jokes used to circulate in the workplace. Now, with tremendous attention paid to political correctness, a lot of topics are completely off limit to workplace humour—and rightfully so. Now you have to run your jokes through a 'p. c.' ('politically correct') filter before you can let them out for public consumption.

On top of this list of banished jokes are ethnic jokes (see Box 38.2). The world has come a long way since the days of picking on specific ethnic communities. Likewise, sexist jokes and 'humour' demeaning women are highly offensive and are not funny. Jokes about a particular religion or religious practices are also to be avoided. Politics can touch a raw nerve in many people and is best left alone as a subject for humour. Never make fun of a visiting culture—not even gentle kidding. Tasteless jokes about physical difficulties or special needs, looks—or just about anything that the other person cannot help—have no place anywhere in the world, much less in the office. If your jokes are unfunny, that is okay. But if they are politically incorrect, it is not okay. Whatever you do, don't put your foot in your mouth.

No locker room jokes: Jokes with explicit sexual content or otherwise crude and indecent are absolute no-no. Be extra careful about inadvertently forwarding such jokes via SMS or e-mail to your co-workers.

Humour on taboo topics is not okay. However, you may be able to get away with jokes on transgressions if you do it tastefully and if everyone around knows that it is just a joke.

Slapstick humour and clowning around—if used at all—should not last for more than a few milliseconds. Don't behave like Mr Bean in the office.

Know your limits when pulling someone's leg: Gentle kidding around has always been a part of office camaraderie. But some people may have a low threshold for taking a joke. Remember that one man's joke can be another man's insult. Leave such sensitive persons alone—especially if they explicitly ask you to stop. Apologize profusely and desist from such activities. Do not argue with them that you were only joking or that they are being unnecessarily high-strung. Some people would like to be very formal in the office and do not drag such persons into situations. Also, don't boycott them or discriminate against them in the future, just because they happen to be this way. Respect their right to be introverted and distant.

Also, be very careful about making deeply personal jokes in mixed company or spilling inside jokes to a general audience.

Humourous people can get away with a lot that you and I may not always be able to: Know where you are in the pantheon of humorists in your organization because the persons who are branded as the 'funny guys' can get away with a lot more than you and I. They can make borderline politically incorrect jokes or couch their real jokes with layers of political correctness or somehow improvise an old half-way offensive joke and give it a palatable form. Don't try to copy them just because it worked for them.

Mean-spirited humour can be okay under some circumstances: Mean-spirited humour is sometimes considered okay when the audience is on your side and you are taking on a common 'enemy target'—the bad economy, politics, rival companies, the market, etc.

But mean-spirited humour directed at specific individuals and groups within your workplace will not be tolerated. There are strict laws against hazing, ragging and the so-called initiation ceremonies in most places. Even sarcasm and insults are strongly discouraged these days. Organizations don't usually have an official policy on humour, but they all have clear policies on harassment, taunting and discrimination at work. Nowadays, any rude or indecent workplace behaviour in the name of humour is heavily censured and punished.

38.4 In Summary

There is no question that humour brightens up our office environment and is highly desirable. But it has to be used with imagination and sagacity. Workplace humour is indeed very restricted in scope and very limited in choice and with all the decorum and political correctness to worry about, it may seem like there are only five jokes that are fit enough to be told inside an office. (And after all this, your audience may turn out to be indifferent.) But to joke is human and even the grungy, foam-insulated walls of an office cubicle can inspire humour in the skilled and the witty and we will always find new things to amuse ourselves (see Snapshot 38.2).

Snapshot 38.2

CEO-speak

Mr Mehta, the CEO of White Lily Corp., a leading manufacturer of personal health and beauty products is a funny man. In the spectrum of 'should a boss be loved or feared' he has chosen to be 'loved', which basically means that he would run his once-a-quarter all-employee meetings like he is one of the guys.

He starts his talk with a personal travel anecdote. (It always works.) When he tells them about how he was looking for a place to eat in Bangkok at 3.00 a.m., the audience finds it hilarious. *(His build-up and style helped, but people laugh at their boss's jokes anyway, even if they are unfunny. Some others found it funny that such indignities happened even to a powerful person like a CEO).*

Then he shows them the latest advertisement video his marketing department shot—it's about a shy and insecure man who one day starts using White Lily's soap, which pumps so much confidence in him that he wins a marathon race. *(The audience goes wild at this use of absurd humour, although it is unclear if this humour will help in White Lily's sales and bottomline.)*

He then turns the heat on White Lily's nearest competitor in the market. He keeps calling them 'the bleach guys' and the 'one-sigma company' and refers their soap as a 'brick in a soap dish'. He derides them about being nothing but 'bubbles'. 'We will burst their bubbles,' he reaches a crescendo 'and we will win the market share from them.' *(The CEO draws a huge cheer for his mean-spirited humour and the audience is in raptures.)*

As someone said, humour is no joke.

DO

- Bring humour to your office.
- Use your humour and punch-lines to make a point or to add clarity to your message.
- Sprinkle your reports, e-mails, presentations, etc. with humour.
- Use humour to diffuse tense situations.
- Make jokes on yourself or your group but without compromising your and your group's pride—it is more of self-effacing humour.
- Pay attention to your audience, their mood and the situation.
- Use humour to break ice and forge strong international teams.

DON'T

- Taunt or otherwise pester a person if he or she wants you to stop.
- Make ethnic, sexist or any politically incorrect jokes.
- Use crude, vulgar and sexual content in office humour.
- Dwell on a joke for too long.
- Forget that delivery and timing can make or break a joke.
- Attempt to be a circus clown or a stand-up comedian.

39

English-language Skills

"I am so clever that sometimes I don't understand a single word of what I am saying."

–Oscar Wilde

Often equated to communication skills (and sometimes even to soft skills in general), English-language skills occupy a vaunted position in the skills list of any modern day Indian professional. In fact, in many of the so-called 'soft skills training institutes' that have mushroomed across India, 'soft skills' is taken to simply mean 'spoken English' and nothing more. Some of them also go at length into basic English grammar elements like articles, propositions, pronouns and so on. We have stressed throughout the book that while English-language skills are indeed essential in today's globalized business world, they are not stand-alone skills to be acquired in isolation. Rather, they should nicely complement the other skills in your portfolio. They should offer a window into your personality and reveal how well you articulate and verbalize your relationship with your environment.

Keeping all of the above in mind, this chapter looks at some of the simple pointers on how to improve your proficiency in English. It also takes a close look at some of the main distinguishing features of American English and how some of them are tightly coupled with American cultural/business norms. This is why we have included this chapter in the etiquette section of the book and fittingly, kept it as the last element before the concluding chapter. We expect it to serve it as a garnish to the rest of the array of soft skills. We don't intend this chapter to be a training manual on English-language skills. Nor do we want to dwell on things from a pedagogic point of view. We also want to reiterate that as important as *language* skills are, it is much more important to have good *communication* skills first, and the foundation for that is a solid attitude. There are many, many cultures in the world which lack in English-language skills but do a great job in business communication.

39.1 'Our' English and 'Their' English

The good news is that we in India don't have to start from scratch. We have a long history of English in Indian schools. Even the ones in remote villages teach some amount of English. And there are several elite high schools which impart very specialized and high level of English education to its students. A large number of people are familiar with rudiments of grammar and have a basic vocabulary of several hundred words. India generates a lot of material and content in English, like newspapers and TV channels. One gets many opportunities to practice spoken English and there are many avenues available if one wants to improve one's language skills. When comparing the strengths of India *vis-à-vis* other nations like China, English-language competency is projected as a competitive advantage for India. Not merely in communicating with our international business partners, good English skills can also help us to communicate better among Indian colleagues from various regions of India. In fact, in many cases, English is the only common language that people from different regions of India can use to communicate with one another. So in principle, most of us should be able to sit down in business meetings with, say, the Americans and communicate effectively.

But the bad news is that despite all this emphasis on English education, exposure to and knowledge of English in various media, there is still a significant gap in the English-language *skills* of most professionals. Our frequent boast that we have a large pool of English-savvy professionals isn't entirely accurate. The raw English-language skills that most Indians have at the end of college are by and large inadequate to effectively communicate with our global business partners. Our basic language skills and our knowledge of modern business communication are woefully lacking and need to improve vastly. It is no wonder then that new recruits in several call centres and multinational firms are coached not only in the business processes, but also in language skills for several months before they are let loose on the phones or before they are allowed to communicate with their foreign stakeholders.

Why is this apparent contradiction there?

- English education in India is very archaic and even somewhat irrelevant to modern-day business communication. Indian English is plagued with hackneyed usage and a very formal style. Vestiges from the British Raj-era are still being used in modern-day conversations. The highly colonial 'Respected Sir' type English that is taught in schools, seldom cuts ice with the modern informal American way of doing business.
- Indian English has evolved on its own over time and quite often uses its own syntax, vocabulary and slangs instead of what is used in English-speaking

countries. For example, when an Indian says 'Where you are going, *yaar*?' a non-Indian might blink, but this sentence will be understood perfectly by other Indians around him. Good communication, this maybe. But it is bad English.

- In addition to the Indian English lingo, there is a strong regional influence in the way we speak English and consequently, we have Hignlish, Tanglish, Benglish and many other flavours of Indian English which come in the way of learning proper English.
- There is not sufficient emphasis on *spoken* communication at the school or college level. There are inadequate numbers of audio language laboratories to train listening and spoken skills.
- Finally, the kind of skills that are taught about English do not cover important issues like writing good e-mails. Rather they address arcane issues like writing leave letters and permission letters.

Also, over the past few decades, American English has emerged as the *de facto lingua franca* of the business community the world over and English-language skills have now largely come to mean English, the American way. (And we are saying this despite this book itself being in British English!). While the purist English connoisseur like Professor Higgins of *My Fair Lady* will not take a favourable view of 'American English', a premium is now placed on being able to speak it, write it and understand it perfectly. We may never be able to convert our Indian English accent to an American accent, but a lot of us certainly hope to acquire a degree of mastery over American English—right from the prevailing business jargon, down to the latest slangs. It is the dream of many young Indian professionals to be able to sit across the table from an American delegation and transact business with them on an equal footing—in chaste English. The net result is that now there is not only a clamour for acquiring generic English-language skills, but also to orient those efforts toward American English and put it to good use, whether it is in a call centre or in a board room. But unfortunately, there is a serious shortage of American English teachers in India.

39.2 How Can You Try to Improve?

Here are some tips on how you can get better in English. Some of it calls for a behavioural change and some other tips are simply good practice and craftsmanship.

Simple things first: The first thing you should concentrate on is to get rid of your 'heavy' regional Indian accent (if you have one) and acquire what is called a 'neutral accent'. This may be easier said than done because some language habits can be very difficult to unlearn or get rid of. Next, try to speak a bit slower and with intonation—trying to put stress at the appropriate places. Similarly, try to be more 'fluent' or talk in a 'running' manner, minimizing the pauses and the gaps. All this comes with practice. So whether you make mistakes or not, stick to practising your diction. If you have a serious problem with your accent, and if you can afford it, consider having a language coach and remedy the problem. Lastly, don't try to acquire an American accent overnight. It might take a very long time—and in some cases even years of immersion in American culture may not help. The idea is not to necessarily speak like an American, but to speak like a generic native speaker.

Be actively interested in improving your English. Catch on to your mistakes as well as others' mistakes and see what the right usage is. See if there is a pattern to your mistakes. Pay attention to grammar and learn a new grammatical point every week. Learn to think in English and avoid translating idioms and phrases from your native language.

Build your vocabulary by reading newspapers, magazines and blogs. Don't just include words—also include phrases and metaphors. Try to find out the subtle differences between words with similar meanings. Search the Internet for English resources. Read up business speeches in newspapers or websites and see if you can glean the business/technical parlance.

Change from being vague, general and abrupt to being specific and effective: One of the complaints about Indian spoken English is that speakers often tend to be vague and general. Just imagine if someone walked into your office and said 'That is done sir.' Unless you are familiar with the context, you will never guess what 'that' means. One has to learn to express things more clearly and elaborately on potentially confusing things.

Don't be abrupt when you start to talk. Give the context first and build a prelude. Likewise, don't think a matter is closed just because you have understood it. Bring it to a logical and complete conclusion. This is in line with the 'tell them what you are going to tell them, tell them and tell them what you told them' concept we discussed in Chapter 21.

Give yourself exercises on how to be precise in your expression. If you are happy, can you explain 'exactly' how happy you are? On a scale of one to ten, if your happiness ranks a five, how can you describe it? How is a rank four different from rank five? Can you describe the difference clearly and without ambiguity? Since it takes two people to communicate, can you be more sensitive to your listener and be listener-centric instead of being 'you-centric'?

And finally, in business meetings if there is anything that is half-way confusing, it is best to write it down and send an e-mail about it to the person who said it, just to make sure that you and the other person are on the same page of the book. (And by the way, what does one mean by being on the 'same page of the book'?)

Don't sink into a 'defensive' or 'minimal' mode: Sometimes, when you are overwhelmed by the person(s) in front of you, your may feel that your jaw is locked and you may find yourself only able to utter simple sentences and phrases. By behaving thus, you are telling the people in front that you are being submissive and acknowledging defeat. You also convey the message that they should end the conversation and leave you alone. But even if you feel like you have marbles in your mouth, just try hard and keep the conversation going. Struggle out of this gridlock situation and recover. The last thing you want is to stop cold in the middle of a communication and let the other person think poorly of you.

Integrate all the communication skills: Move to the next level in your language skills—from being a simple user of a language to being a proficient, articulate communicator. Try to talk like a native. This means that you will have to know how the native speaker uses certain words, combination of words and metaphors. For example, he might say 'I beg to differ'. This usage has been around for years and to a non-native, this might sound like a strange use of the word 'beg'.

Remember that communication is holistic. Make your pitch colourful. Use a lot of humour. Making jokes in a new language can be quite challenging and you might have to practice it extensively to be good at it in front of your American business partners. Get into the habit of conducting small talk in English.

And finally, incorporate effective non-verbal communication as a part of your English training. Get to know the non-verbal sounds, body language, laughs, grunts, smirks, etc. and use them in conjunction with spoken English.

39.3 Some Sources to Improve Your English

- Reading magazines, newspaper and Internet blogs: Nothing improves English like reading. Magazines, especially those with modern and informally written articles, are ideal. Equally good are some of the blogs and websites. But beware of sources that are either very high-brow or use a lot of slang.
- Watching TV shows, movies, etc.: These are ideal sources for listening comprehension. Although you may not learn much from popular shows in terms of business communication, you may still find them useful in building your accent and pronunciation
- Listening to people: Listening and talking to other people, especially at work, is a nice way to improve your English. Choose people either at your level or slightly higher.
- Getting feedback from friends and colleagues.
- Getting a language coach: There are professional services which will tutor you on your English problems and try to remedy them. They are perfect for neutralizing your accent, effective small talk and so on.
- Attending Toastmasters meetings regularly to improve communication and leadership skills.
- And finally, immersion: The most effective way to learn American English (or for that matter, any language) is to actually be in the USA for some time and interact with the native speakers.

39.4 What Is So Different About American English?

There is a lack of awareness in India that the American English language is indeed a distinctly different entity, with its own rich history, heritage, literature–and of course, quirks. Learning this brand of English involves not merely rolling your 'r's or emulating that nasal twang, but also involves grasping a bit of the American cultural and business etiquette.

American English has several distinct characteristics. If you want to master it, you should pay particular attention these points—and this will be in addition to your efforts to improve your general language skills like fluency, vocabulary and idiomatic usage.

Accent, stress, pronunciation, spelling, etc.: Accent, pronunciation and related elements are perhaps the most distinguishing features of American English. When Americans say words like 'car' or 'pay', they aspirate the first syllable (and let a bit of air come out) and pronounce them as 'khar' and 'phay' (note: not just Americans, but several other native English speakers also aspirate their first syllables). American pronunciation can also be unique—like the word 'schedule' is pronounced 'skejool' and so on.

When Americans speak, they lay stress on different syllables of the sentence as appropriate. For example, they might say 'WHERE are you going?' to find out which place you are going to. Or they may emphasize 'He has gone to school. Now, where are YOU going?' This kind of stressing gives a special cadence to their speech and the sing-song feel (we discussed some of these in Chapter 19 on vocal variety). Such intonation is usually very similar among all native English speakers, whether they are British or American. Indian English, on the other hand, tends to roll out the syllables at a constant rate, instead of stressing particular syllables.

Syntax and grammar can be different, but are mostly the same: Grammar and syntax are reasonably similar across the various native English speakers of the world, although American English does have its quota of peculiarities. For example, they often use double prepositions like 'I live *across from* Ram' or '*Up until* now . . .'. (By the way, prepositions are also the weak points of many Indians and we often get confused whether it is 'Shyam met Ram in London' or 'Shyam met Ram at London'. The good thing is that prepositions have less weightage in a sentence and even if one gets it wrong, the meaning is pretty much conveyed to the listener.)

Non-natives of English—like the people in India—can sometimes subconsciously use regional language syntax in English. For example, we may say, 'Look! In that cage, a tiger is there' (instead of 'Look! There is a tiger in that cage'). So take the time to learn the American syntax—even if they adjectivize their adverbs on occasion! ('His suitcase is fully loaded' is an example of an adverb 'fully' being used like an adjective)

American usage of words can be different: As is well-known, American spelling, usage of words and so on, have their own oddities. Some words may mean diametrically opposite things in India and in the USA. Make sure you are aware of such differences, lest there be confusion or misinterpretation (see Box 39.1 for some examples).

Box 39.1

Some differences in American usage of words

Oversight: Oversight in American English refers to overseeing or monitoring. A typical usage is 'We will do periodic project oversight' (meaning we will periodically monitor the project). The same word, 'oversight' has an almost opposite meaning in Indian English and refers to 'mistake' or carelessness!

Momentarily: In American airports, it is common to hear an announcement 'the flight will leave momentarily'. This means the flight will leave shortly or in a moment. The same phrase in India will mean 'the plane will leave just for a moment'!

'I don't care': When presented with more than one option on which he does not have any specific preference, an American may say 'I don't care which one is there', which means 'I don't mind anything'. The phrase 'don't care' can be construed as offensive by an Indian who does not understand the nuances of American English.

Soda: What is called 'soft drinks' (or even 'cool drinks') in India is also called soda in the USA. In India, 'soda' refers to a particular type of aerated drink that goes by the name 'club soda' in the USA.

Moving to informalism and colloquialism: Americans generally tend to be very informal and use straight-talk and direct questions to communicate. They even address the other persons by their first names (or their nicknames, if that is okay with the other persons). This inevitably results in informalism and colloquialism even in business settings and a liberal use of prevailing slangs. Americans are wont to use such colloquial phrases like 'give me a holler' (meaning, 'give me a call') or 'that is a no-brainer' (meaning 'that is simple'). If you are in a meeting with Americans, observe and register such informal and slang terms and ask them for their meanings if you don't understand what they mean.

In comparison, Indian business English tends to be much more formal and devoid of familiarity. For example, starting a letter with 'Respected Sir' and concluding it with 'Yours obediently'(or even, 'I remain, yours obediently') is not something that an American would use. In American context, these are usually replaced by 'Dear Sir' and 'Sincerely/Cordially'). Also, 'I kindly request you to send me the document'[1] is arcane. It is more common to use the phrase 'I would appreciate it if you could send the document.' The idea behind any effective business correspondence is to quickly come to the point and not get stuck in the structure of the niceties. Refer to Chapter 32 on e-mail etiquette on pointers on e-mail greetings.

[1] By the way, 'I kindly request you to send me the document' by itself is wrong. It should be 'I request you to kindly send the document'.

The mood—the use of modal (auxiliary) verbs, conditionals and expressions of doubt: Spoken American English is peppered with the clever use of verbs that accurately express subtle shades in the speaker's moods and his assessment of the situation. This is achieved through the use of what are called modal or auxiliary verbs that go with other verbs to alter their meanings as appropriate. For example, an American may say, 'I ought to write that report' or 'I might write that report' implying different moods—necessity in the first instance and hesitation in the second case. In Box 39.2, we give some more examples.

Box 39.2

- I can write that report if he cannot. (expressing possibility)
- I have to write that report tonight. (expressing certainty)
- I should be writing that report. (expressing the protocol of events)

On the opposite side of the spectrum, Americans use a whole slew of words expressing doubt, uncertainty and hope. They may say 'I guess Shyam will be the one to write the report'. Or they may make a qualified statement like 'I may be wrong, but I think Shyam will write the report.' If you carefully look at the last sentence, you will find that it is actually a loaded statement. At one level it implies that the report will be done by Shyam, no problems. But at another level it implies a measure of doubt and Shyam writing the report is only the speaker's interpretation of things. Basically, the speaker is safe-guarding himself while passing on information, just in case trouble occurs over the report tomorrow.

Similarly, Americans frequently use what are called conditionals that express desires, wishes, hopes and in the extreme case, the so-called subjunctive mood. For example, 'I would write that report if I had time' or 'I can write that report if my boss wants, although I doubt if he would want me to.' Things are basically couched in a lot of iffy possibilities, resulting in several subtly differing scenarios. Such usage gives Americans latitude and a huge space to operate out of when expressing their observations or viewpoints. In India we are not very well versed in using auxiliary verbs and often end up talking in yes or no kind of definitives, not conveying the shades of meanings in between.

In addition, Americans tend to be very precise about using the right words to bring out what exactly is on their mind—especially if there are several closely-related words. This is a natural advantage of being a native speaker, but it is more due to an emphasis on vocabulary building. For example, an elderly American might say 'I listen very well, but I don't hear too well.' Articulation and accuracy are important to Americans in speaking and that is why they get confused when an Indian gets mixed up between weather and climate or doesn't understand the difference between tactical and strategic. If you want to really speak like an American, start with a bagful of auxiliary verbs and figure out how to express yourself effectively with them.

The business/Technical lexicon: Americans seem to have a special vocabulary for business and technical communication (see Box 39.3). Not only do they have specific buzzwords, they also seem to use a specific subset of English words to describe business happenings. Because of the proliferation of American business language and style around the world, much of this lingo has entered the business lexicon everywhere and is beginning to penetrate even the general population. Here are some examples.

Box 39.3

Examples of American business jargon

Example 1: A CEO presenting a quarterly earnings report to his shareholders might say something like 'We are pleased that we continue to execute on our plans even in a challenging business environment. . . .' Here the use of a stock phrase like 'challenging business environment' not only sanitizes his speech and makes it formal, but also presents his audience with a clear and vivid picture of the difficult 'environment'.

Example 2: The same CEO may announce the merger of his company with another company and state '. . . the synergy of this merger will facilitate our Asian market penetration and will enable productizing some of the key technologies in our joint portfolio . . .'Again, once you digest this sentence and re-cast it into its non-technical version, you will appreciate how much meaning is conveyed in just a few words, with each word like 'enable' or 'productize' and so on standing for complex and convoluted activities.

Example 3: The CFO of the company might also say '. . . the headcount rationalization in Europe will bring it in line with our Asian operations . . .', obliquely referring to job cuts.

Similarly, document writers and technical people also converse in a different space, fraught with buzzwords and extremely well-defined jargon. One has to develop a complete vocabulary of such business and technical terminology to be able to talk to the Americans effectively. The use of jargon and technical terms ensures that the meanings and scenarios are understood very clearly. American tech-talk is definitely not ornamental, but is very expressive, informative and specific.

The use of metaphors: American speakers also use a lot of metaphors to supplement their standard words and phrases (Box 39.4). It might seem like almost each of their sentences is loaded with such metaphors. The purpose of using metaphors is to nail a point and to clearly bring out the context in a nutshell. For example, the speaker might say, 'This is where the rubber meets the road' (meaning, this is the real test of the concept). To the uninitiated, this metaphor may not mean much and he might take it at its face value. But if you think about it, in one concise metaphor the entire context and situation are brought out. Besides, metaphors also make one's speech very colourful. In American business usage, a lot of metaphors tend to be sports-related and many of this may be lost on the Indian professionals who don't have much exposure to the American sports scene. We strongly suggest that you read up on American metaphors and become familiar with the ones used in business circles.

Box 39.4

Examples of American metaphors

'We are in our home stretch': This is taken from athletics and means that we are in the last lap of the race. It means to be in the last phase of an activity or a project in hand.

'This is a ball park figure': The origin of this metaphor is not clearly known and perhaps it originally used to refer to 'estimates' of baseball stadium ('ballpark') attendance figure. Now it means 'an approximate figure' or a 'guesstimate'. Sometimes, Americans also use the phrase 'back of the envelope calculation' to indicate that their computations are only approximate.

'Let us not follow a shot-gun approach': Shot-gun approach refers to hasty use of wide-ranging methods in a haphazard manner instead of a narrowly focused, methodical plans–the latter is sometimes called the 'rifle approach'.

The unsaid and the unspoken: Non-verbal sounds and body language are big parts of American English. Interruptive sounds like 'ammm' (or 'excuse me' or 'may I?') or pauses or fillers are used effectively by the Americans in communicating. In any meeting with them, there is always a lot that is unsaid and unspoken, but occurs on the side (see Chapter 19 on vocal variety and the use of pauses and silences). There is a sub-text to the meeting and we need to watch out for any indications of tension, disagreement, dislike and so on. The eye contact (or lack thereof), the way they sit in the chair or the grimace on their faces can all be indicative of bigger things at play. Likewise, they are experts in observing our body language or any other clues we might transmit (see Chapter 18 on body language). Note that even body language can be culture-dependent. Don't interpret an American gesture using Indian sensibilities and likewise, try to educate your American counterparts about some standard Indian body language components that may otherwise lead to wrong conclusions.

39.5 In Summary

English-language skills—on top of all the other soft skills that we have described in this book—can be a powerful asset in your grab bag of soft skills. In a number of job interviews, a command of English can tilt the process in your favour. An ability to talk in English without a heavy accent is still considered a measure of your smartness in many circles. Whatever may be the conventional wisdom on English-language skills, it is definitely to your advantage to sport a good command of English if you want to thrive in today's business world. So start today!

Fig. 39.1

40

Reach for the Moon

"Tell me and I forget; Teach me I and I remember; Involve me and I learn."

–Benjamin Franklin

Congratulations on making it through! We are sure your head is swimming in time management, e-mail etiquette and so on, while your mind is debating whether it is resilience that you need to spruce up or your vision. Now it is time to sink into your chair, take a deep breath and mull over the key take-aways—and then convert your understanding of this book into an action plan to improve your soft skills. Let us first look back in the rear view mirror and see how far we have come.

40.1 The Journey So Far

The first aim of this book was to present you with a grandstand view of today's corporate world and broadly educate you on how it operates. We wanted you to realize that modern corporations offer an exciting work environment that rewards merit and hard work over bureaucracy and job titles. Soft skills are a big part of this 'merit' and can indeed be a major differentiator between successful and not-so-successful employees in an organization. By now you should be completely convinced of the importance of soft skills as necessary factors in your career growth. We not only took a bird's eye view of the ACE dimensions of soft skills, but also swooped down to take a close look at each of these skills at the ground level.

Next, we wanted you to be aware that there is a long and exhaustive list of such soft skills, making it difficult to cultivate them in a hurry or to do it in an organic fashion. Rather, you have to take the trouble to master these skills in a methodical manner, with a lot of grit and effort. Despite the complexity of the process, workplaces expect their star employees to possess and deploy a wide array of soft skills.

We want you to understand that each soft skill has a role to play at work and even if two soft skills seem similar, there are subtle differences between them. Your success in developing soft skills is dictated by how well you can combine these different soft skills to suit your personal style, your environment and each specific situation you face. By cataloging and discussing a long list of soft skills in one place, this book should help you put your finger on these things, organize your own thoughts on the matter and combine them in a way that is most appropriate for you—much like how you choose what you want to eat from a well organized buffet. Although we discussed a lot of different soft skills in this book, we had to leave out skills like negotiation skills and so on, for brevity's sake and we only managed to skim over topics like cultural-issues and English-language skills.

Finally, we wanted to instill in you that burning desire to improve your soft skills and motivate you to go beyond a superficial window dressing. We believe this is the single most important ingredient we bring to the table—enabling you to change your attitude, improve your communication and fine tune your etiquette, especially for the Indian-American business environment. We want you to stir yourself from within and create in yourself a paradigm shift in the way you think, act and talk. We then want you to take the next step and actually embark on a personal mission to improve the level of your own soft skills—convert your understanding of the book into an action plan.

How do you motivate yourself to go after a skill? How do you motivate yourself to get rid of bad habits and practices? By consciously telling yourself '*Yes, I can do it*'. It is like remembering the pot of gold at the end of the rainbow. It is the obsession you should have for success and self actualization. It is by looking at all the role models you have in front of you. It can be achieved through listening to mentors and self-improvement experts enunciate the need for attitude adjustment. It is made possible by deep introspection and convincing yourself that the change in attitude is necessary and for the better.

Obviously you will have a question looming large in front of you, 'How do I move forward?' Let us tackle this question next.

40.2 The Journey Ahead

Let us now look at some steps that would hopefully give you a track to follow and will make your soft skills self-improvement plan more systematic and practical.

Take stock: A journey always starts with knowing where you are. And believe us, you already have something of each of these soft skills in you, waiting to be tapped, nurtured and developed. Rather than looking at the glass as half-full and grouch about the soft skills that (you think) you don't have, focus on those soft skills that you do possess and which are your strengths. Then you know where to start from. At the same time, don't be oblivious about your weaknesses. Not having a particular strength may not be as bad as not knowing your weaknesses! As far as soft skills are concerned, ignorance is *not* bliss. But *how do you know where you are today on any of your skills? How do you take stock?* This is indeed a difficult question. You have to examine yourself extremely objectively or get feedback from your well-wishers, mentors, managers and others to arrive at a baseline score for where you are on specific soft skills.

Build on your strengths: When you set out to build on your strengths you will find that there are certain sets of soft skills that are somewhat related to each other. For example, the communication vehicles are all related. Similarly, teamwork and diversity are related[1]. For instance, if you are already working well with your Indian teammates but are not so effective in English language, you can attempt to work with an international team with members from other cultures. This way, while contributing to the multi-cultural team with your team intelligence, you can also benefit from it by improving your English-language skills.

Prioritize what you want you to improve: As we have said before in this book, if everything is important, nothing is important. You simply must not dilute your priorities and stretch yourself too thin. Focus on a few (may be two or three) soft skills at a time and put a plan in place to improve those skills. You can also pluck a few low hanging fruits by honing the less-abstract skills like e-mail etiquette and phone etiquette, while working on the more abstract ones like the vision for the long term. Improving some skills may be as simple as getting rid of some annoying bad habits (like being habitually late to appointments). Again, prioritize and strategize how you plan to go about improving your soft-skills set. Don't keep scores on how many soft skills you have conquered or how many more are left to go. Just do it!

Grab opportunities that come by: Soft skills cannot be improved by sitting at home and just brooding over improvement. Like cycling, it improves by practice. Use any formal learning resource, where available (short courses, books, lectures, etc.), to learn the soft skills effectively. Assiduously practise what you learnt. In a business environment, there are ample opportunities that come by your way. It is up to you to grab such opportunities with both hands and try to polish your skills. Better still, be on the look out for opportunities, openings and special circumstances where you can step in and display your new personality. Developing a reputation takes time, but persistence pays off. You will not only get noticed (like we discussed in Chapter 10 on stepping up to the plate), but will also find an opportunity to test your newly-honed

---

[1] In this book, we have grouped the soft skills most related to each other together in contiguous chapters.

skills. This initiative will set up an ever accelerating process of increasing your confidence and attitude. You have an entire highway on which to practise riding. Go for it!

Don't be afraid to make mistakes: As we discussed in Chapter 7 on lifelong learning, mistakes are part of a learning experience. As someone said, 'A ship is safest in the harbour, but that is not what it was designed for.' So don't let the fear of failure come in the way of executing your self-improvement plan.

Set yourself targets: Just telling yourself 'I will improve my soft skills' is not sufficient. You need to set yourself SMAART targets (that we discussed in Chapter 28). For example, if you are concentrating on your presentation skills, try to have numerical goals where possible—such as trying to improve your instructor rating from your current rating of, say, seven out of ten to nine out of ten, by next year. Or you can have other measurable targets like trying to do 30 per cent more presentations this year than last year.

Don't try too many things at one time: Seeing the long list of soft skills can make you feel intimidated. It is possible that you may tell yourself 'Wow, I know I lack in time management and meeting management and I don't have a clear vision and I know I am considered a bore and I need to improve my use of humour. Let me embark on all these things from today.' Trying too many things at the same time will lead you nowhere. They may simply pull you in different directions and would in fact, be detrimental to your soft skills. As we said in the preceding paragraphs, do start from your positions of strength and build on those areas.

Don't be a perfectionist and try to get '100 per cent' in any one soft skill before going to the next: Soft skills are not like theorem-proving in geometry, where every step depends on the completion of the previous step. If you try to be a perfectionist in honing one skill to 'perfection' before going on to the next, you will get nowhere. You may never have the time to be perfect in every single soft skill outlined here—but you can do the next best thing. You can be reasonably perfect in several of them, very good in many others and competent in the rest of them—enough to stand out, overall.

Constantly review, revise and refine your strategy: Improving soft skills is a moving target. What is 'good soft skills' today may be completely inappropriate tomorrow; what is appropriate in one culture may be completely unacceptable in another culture. Hence, it is important to have your antennae up all the time.

There are no short cuts: Our approach in this book has been *values-based.* We do not recommend any short cuts or unethical or uncouth methods to acquire soft skills or to be used in place of soft skills. We have left out shrewdness, cunning, Shylock-style vengefulness, avarice and so on from our discussions, even if some people may profit from such things in a business environment. A values-based approach should never be compromised on.

Be patient! And finally, we want you to realize that changing one's habits, acquiring a soft skill or exercising a high level of control over one's work life can be quite an arduous process, consuming a lot of time and effort. This is not one of those processes that offer instant gratification. You should be aware that success comes slowly over time and one has to be absolutely patient and persistent to reap the benefits. Soft skills should be a way of life—and should not be looked upon as a 'use and throw' mechanism to achieve some desired short-term goal to be dumped later.

40.3 Reach for the Moon

Most of what this book says is just common sense. Basically, you just need to fine tune your attitude, tweak your communications skills and pay attention to some standard etiquette principles.

At the end of the day, *you* have to have the necessary determination to change your life and take the necessary efforts—however hard it may be on your system. You must develop the right attitude to enjoy learning things in spite of their difficulty. We would like you to recall how President Kennedy justified his quest for the moon (see Box 40.1).

Box 40.1

'*We choose to **go to the moon.** We choose to go to the moon in **this decade** and do the other things, not because they are easy, **but because they are hard,** because that goal will serve to organize and measure the best of our energies and skills, because that challenge is one that we are willing to accept, **one we are unwilling to postpone,** and one which we intend to win, and the others, too . . .* (Emphasis added by the authors)

After all, if man could land on the moon when technology was not as advanced as it is today, what can stop you from improving your soft skills?

Let us attempt the challenging. And let us remember that what we have got inside us, doesn't have to be what we were born with—we can always reboot ourselves with new tools and techniques. We can turn our good habits into skills. These skills can blossom into competencies. And these competencies in turn can bring about our ultimate career success. Go for it!

Index